T0159414

THE GÜLEN MOVEMENT
CIVIC SERVICE WITHOUT BORDERS

Muhammed Çetin

BLUE DOME

Copyright © 2010 by Blue Dome Press

13 12 11 10   1 2 3 4

All rights reserved. No part of this book may be reproduced or transmitted in any form or by any means, electronic or mechanical, including photocopying, recording or by any information storage and retrieval system without permission in writing from the Publisher.

Published by Blue Dome Press
244 Fifth Avenue #2HS
New York, NY 10001

www.bluedomepress.com

Library of Congress Cataloging-in-Publication Data Available

ISBN: 978-1-935295-01-3 (Paperback)
ISBN: 978-1-935295-08-2 (Hardcover)

Printed by
Çağlayan A.Ş., Izmir - Turkey

CONTENTS

ACKNOWLEDGEMENT

Scholarly writing is never a solitary process. I was certainly blessed with the company of wonderful individuals during the research for my PhD dissertation and of this book which grew out of it. I express my most sincere thanks to Dr. Paul G. Weller, my Director of Studies at the University of Derby, UK, a wonderful person whom I came to admire in many ways. My thanks also to the other supervisors of my dissertation, Dr. Ian Williams and Dr. Simon Speck, for their help and encouragement. I was fortunate indeed to have a considerate and understanding colleague in Dr. Lynn E. Mitchell, at the A.D. Bruce Religion Centre at the University of Houston, who urged me to finish work on my dissertation while I was working at the University of Houston.

My research would not have been possible without the co-operativeness of the many volunteers and participants in the Gülen Movement who answered the questionnaires. My thanks to them all, and in particular to Abdullah Aymaz, Ergun Çapan, Enes Ergene, Bahaddin Eker and Cahit Tuzcu for their time and contribution to my work.

I am most grateful also to Dr. Jamil Qureshi, a friend and colleague of many years who, as ever, was most helpful in suggesting improvements to the language and other presentational aspects of this book.

Finally, I wish to record my gratitude to my parents and my dear wife for their steadfast support over the many years that I was intermittently engaged in the research and writing up of this book.

FOREWORD

O
ne of the greatest challenges that faces anyone wanting to promote dialogue and understanding is the relationship between the West and Islam. A recent Pew survey* found that the gap between the West and the Muslim world, far from decreasing, has increased. Many in the West saw Muslims as violent, fanatical extremists. Muslims in turn saw Westerners as violent, fanatical extremists, but also immoral and greedy. In this negative environment it is crucial that we go on striving to understand each other and help to build bridges between these two world civilizations.

This important book, a study of the world-wide Sufi-oriented movement of Fethullah Gülen, provides a way of doing this. Its author, Muhammed Çetin, a well-known Muslim scholar from Turkey, gives us for the first time an insider's view of the movement. His approach, combining on-the-ground knowledge of a senior participant in the Gülen movement with the erudition and expertise of a professional social scientist, places the movement in the context of Islamic history and culture as well as contemporary Western social movements theory.

Gülen is considered one of the most influential Turkish Islamic scholars of his generation. I was not surprised to see Fethullah Gülen take first place in the *Foreign Policy/Prospect* poll of the World's Top Public Intellectuals in 2008. The movement he initiated in the late 1970s now has millions of participants. It has founded and runs hundreds of modern educational institutions, as well as print and broadcast media outlets and dialogue societies. The author of more than fifty books, Gülen has dedicated a lifetime to promoting peaceful interrelationship within and between different communities, societies, cultures and religious traditions.

---

* "The Great Divide: How Westerners and Muslims View Each Other." Prepared by Pew Research Center, this report was released on June 22, 2006. Accessible at www.pewglobal.org.

Muhammed Çetin's thoroughly referenced study provides an excellent introduction to the movement by someone who knows it inside and out. The Introduction presents an overview of developments in social movements theory, which helps to locate this study precisely in its disciplinary context. The second chapter provides a valuable overview of key figures and events in recent Turkish socio-political history and explains the rise of the Gülen movement against that background. In chapters 3 and 4, Çetin applies the various theoretical paradigms he discussed in the first chapter to the Gülen movement, situating it in the necessary social, political, cultural, and theoretical context. He also analyzes and explains the motives, methods and rationale of the opposition to the movement. This approach will be helpful for Western readers who may be coming from a tradition of activist, or "protest" movements, from which Gülen's spiritual movement is quite different. Çetin subtly and persuasively draws out the important comparisons and contrasts, without which we cannot understand the extraordinary success of the Gülen movement. The fifth chapter presents the results of questionnaires and interviews with members of the movement. This view from within and Çetin's analysis of it open for us an unprecedented window onto this worldwide Islamic movement and help us appreciate the depth and firmness of its commitment to peaceful action, pluralism and democratic processes.

I have long been an admirer of Fethullah Gülen not only because he speaks of and promotes a compassionate version of Islam, but also because the movement he has inspired enables that vision by establishing educational institutions that practise and embody what they teach. My recent travels in the Muslim world have shown me just how influential the movement has become. While conducting a research project, which culminated in my book *Journey into Islam: The Crisis of Globalization* (2007), I traveled to nine Muslim countries with a group of young Americans in order to understand the contemporary Muslim world better. Often we found anger and alienation as Muslims feel under attack and seek to defend their religion and culture. Some Muslims seem to feel, as do some Westerners, that there already is a clash of civilizations taking place. For all the connective power of globalization, people across the world may in reality be growing further apart. Yet, notwithstanding the anger that is out there, the figure of Fethullah Gülen, with his Sufi-oriented message of love and compassion, was the number one contemporary role model in Turkey, as also in much of the rest of the Muslim world. I believe this speaks to the readiness of Muslims to answer the challenges that face them with forbearance, patient self-examination and self-reform – an authentically Islamic response that Gülen has revived and nurtured, and all of us need to support.

There is a need for a study like this, for both Muslims and non-Muslims. Americans, for example, may be surprised to discover that the leader of one of the world's great social movements resides in Pennsylvania. The influence of the Gülen movement has grown exponentially over the past thirty years. Its educational institutions, media outlets and other organizations now have a substantial presence in all continents, not just in Turkey and Central Asia. The movement has grown not as a political movement but as a social and spiritual one. A unique social reformer, Gülen has introduced a new style of education that begins to integrate scientific knowledge and spiritual values. This vision of Islam which celebrates compassion as well as *'ilm* or the search for knowledge is needed now more than ever. It is well to remind ourselves that *'ilm* is the second most used word in the Qur'an after God. I often quote one of my favorite sayings from the holy Prophet (peace be upon him): "The ink of the scholar is more sacred than the blood of the martyr."

Muslims need to rediscover the importance of compassion and *'ilm* in Islam for themselves, while Westerners – who are used to seeing on their television screens only angry violence coming from the Muslim world – need to appreciate these central features of Islam. The teachings of Gülen represent a strong, compassionate form of Islam that, in the face of adversity and controversy, remains resilient and peaceful.

I spoke to Muhammed Çetin at a conference in Gülen's honor at the University of Oklahoma in November 2006. I asked him for his favorite Gülen quotation; it was: "Be so tolerant that your bosom becomes wide as the ocean. Be inspired with faith and love of human beings. Let there be no troubled souls to whom you do not offer a hand, and about whom you remain unconcerned." Gülen's message is to embody Islam in service of others, not just to speak it, and the way to do this is through the discovery of love: "A soul without love cannot be elevated to the horizon of human perfection…Those who are deprived of love, entangled in the nets of selfishness, are unable to love anybody else and die unaware of the love deeply implanted in the very being of existence."

At the same meeting, Professor Barbara Boyd, the director of Interfaith Religious Studies at Oklahoma University, felt that Gülen was "like Jesus." When I asked why she compared a Muslim to Jesus, she said, "He radiated love." These were significant words not only because they were coming from a Christian but also because we were in the heart of the American Bible Belt. For me, here was evidence of successful interfaith dialogue and understanding.

I have seen the extraordinary response many Americans have given Gülen, which has led to a greater understanding of Islam as a whole, so vital in our post–9/11 world. In this world of religious and ethnic turmoil, the millions participating in the Gülen movement continue to provide us with both spiritual and practical guidance on how to build peace and tolerance. The spirit of love and compassion that Gülen preaches is more necessary now than ever, and one could ask for no better guide to the worldwide phenomenon of the Gülen movement than this book. It is essential reading for anyone wishing to understand contemporary Islam and we should be grateful to Muhammed Çetin for writing it.

Professor Akbar S. Ahmed
Ibn Khaldun Chair of Islamic Studies
American University
Washington, DC

INTRODUCTION

0.1 PARTICULAR AND GENERAL AIMS OF THIS STUDY

This book is about a contemporary social phenomenon, generally referred to as 'the Gülen Movement', and about the need to develop an appropriate discourse for studying it and phenomena like it. The Movement* originated in 1970s Turkey as a faith-inspired initiative to improve educational opportunities for a local community; over the three and half decades since then, it has grown into a transnational educational, inter-cultural and interfaith movement, with participants numbering in the millions, as well as securely established, respected institutions (of different kinds, but mostly schools) on every continent. It has, naturally, begun to attract a great deal of scholarly attention, but studies so far do not describe the Movement fully and accurately or explain adequately the effectiveness of its mobilization and its durability as a collective actor.

A part of the reason is that those studies have focused on individual projects or aspects of the Movement's work in isolation from the whole. Also, they were done by outsiders who, perhaps because they were not specialists in collective action and social movements, were unaware of the reductionist perspectives they brought to their study, and could not see the benefit of referring to the Movement participants' own discourse about and interpretations of their work. The principal reason, however, is that the various theories and approaches within contemporary discourse on social movements are not, separately, equipped with the conceptual tools needed to give an adequate account of phenomena like the Gülen Movement. In the first chapter, through an historical overview of recent and current theories and approaches, I set out my arguments for that judgment in some detail. Here, I will say briefly that the established discourse concerns itself with social movements as 'protest', as 'challenge' to the System, as contentious actors looking to alter or even over-

---

* 'Movement' with initial capital will hereafter mean 'the Gülen Movement'.

turn existing structures and/or policies in some field, usually political or economic. But the Gülen Movement is, as it has always been, non-contentious; it is not a marginalized actor working on the System from the outside. On the contrary, it has always worked within the System – within the boundaries of the laws and public norms that obtain in the different local and national settings where it has set up institutions.

An important feature of the complexities of life in modern industrialized societies, especially but not only in urban settings, has been a contraction in the space available for collective (and to some extent also individual) expression of moral and cultural values. The Gülen Movement and others like it can be considered a response to that contraction – to put it in very simple terms, they offer an opportunity for individuals to construct meaning for themselves by unselfishly doing some good in their lifeworld, without contention or violence, without seeking to disadvantage any person or institution or diminish their power or question the legitimacy of their authority to exercise that power. I shall argue, and in subsequent chapters, hope to demonstrate, that to study mobilizations of this kind requires a synthetic theoretical discourse, one able to deploy conceptual tools taken from different theories, and able also to juxtapose insider and outsider perspectives and interpretations of what the movement is doing or trying to do. The alternative is socio-political reductionism, a potentially harmful misreading of what this Movement and other faith-inspired cultural initiatives are trying to achieve – a misreading that may lead on to disastrously inappropriate responses.

Even as I write these words (April 2008), a legal action is in train in Turkey accusing the civilian government (elected by a substantial majority of the country's population) of seeking to subvert the state by giving public visibility to symbols of Islam, whereas such visibility is not forbidden by the constitution. As Chapter 2, the historical background, will show, this legal action is quite predictable in that it follows a pattern of action and reaction embedded in the socio-political life of the country since at least the 1930s: the danger of yet another military or bureaucratic coup in Turkey is quite real. It does not follow from an action's being strictly *cultural* that the response to it will not be crudely *political*. From the research-scholar's point of view a particular attraction of studying the Gülen Movement is its potential to show the capacity of an Islam-inspired movement to mobilize huge numbers of religiously-minded and observant individuals not only to accept but to *cherish* a secular, pluralist, democratic social and political order. The Movement is not a marginalized, alienated, anachronistic entity; it is actively engaged, in Turkey and world-wide, in establishing collaborative relationships through dialog and joint projects with like-minded individuals and institutions of different religious and cultural background. It is, in this sense, a thoroughly forward-looking movement, concerned to contribute constructively to the mainstream. Therefore, the issues raised in this study are relevant to current problems and trends in Turkey and the international scene generally, and I hope that it may contain or enable insights that have a broad applicability.

Civil society movements have been explained by social movement theorists using a variety of theoretical insights. In this study I evaluate these insights in relation to the actual practice of the Gülen Movement. The effort to say what kind of movement it is carries academic implications for collective action and social movements theory, and, beyond that, socio-political implications for Turkey, the region and the world.

I hope that this book will contribute something to the development of a new method of approaching non-contentious collective action and actors. I hope also that advancing our knowledge of the Gülen Movement will improve our understanding of contemporary social movements, our ability to analyze future events and to resolve contradictory socio-political analyses of Turkey and the region. More generally, I hope that a clear understanding of this particular Movement will help other cultural actors and peaceful movements to expand their repertoires of action for societal peace and inter-civilizational co-operation. Finally, at a personal level, my aim is to contribute to the vitality of civil society, and to diminish polarization and fragmentation in Turkey and similar societies. In short, the concerns and issues raised here have a scope that is well illustrated by, but not limited to, the Gülen Movement as collective actor or its participants.

0.2 METHODOLOGICAL QUESTIONS

I describe the collective action of the Gülen Movement, within the period from the 1970s to 2006, in the light of mainly three contemporary approaches, namely 'political opportunity structures', 'resource mobilization' and 'frame theory'. The reason for using these approaches was to have more and better tools to analyze a complex social phenomenon in the light of contemporary realities, rather than apply geographically-, politically- and culturally-oriented (and therefore restrictive) theoretical interpretations. In this way I endeavor to avoid reducing the complex reality of what is being studied to any one of its component levels.

In addition, I bring in to the analysis dimensions of the collective action that are not immediately visible to an outside observer. I directly address the question of how the Movement's action is understood and constructed by its participants. To this end, I used questionnaires and interviews. The interviews were conducted in Istanbul in 2005 and 2006. The questionnaires, altogether 1200, were sent out in 2006 to educational institutions set up by Movement participants in Turkey, Turkmenistan, Kazakhstan, Azerbaijan, Germany, Holland, Belgium, the USA and Australia. (They are presented in their entirety in Appendices 3 and 4.) Through these questionnaires I was able to evaluate the perceptions and attitudes of administrators, employees and volunteers through the insiders' perspectives, and the disparity between their representation of the collective action and that of outside observers or opponents. Without understanding the internal factors and dynamics of its SMOs (Social Movement Organizations) it is not possible to understand how a social movement succeeds or fails in becoming a collective actor or producing outcomes.

I have attempted to overcome potential limitations by working within multiple and explicitly defined theoretical frameworks and by testing my hypotheses both theoretically and empirically. I discuss several aspects and ideational categorizations in the light of the production and outcome of the Gülen Movement in discourse and action. In other words, I evaluate what is theorized about the Movement by comparing it with its social production. In this respect, I present the perspective and the work of the Movement as actor and the perspectives which oppose its ideas, in order to clarify the location, social space, problems and solutions of both.

This work argues that, for faith-inspired movements, especially Islamic ones, a focus shift is necessary for social movement researchers accustomed to work on the protest movements and political understanding of Europe or North America. As to the functioning, strategizing and mobilizing of collective action and SMOs, much of what this book deals with constitutes problem areas in social movement theories.

As I have said, categorizations derived from the major contemporary movement theories are tested against the Gülen Movement – these include macro–micro relations; macro-, meso-, micro-structures; form, end, means, and environment; structure and agent; identity and culture; and mobilization and counter-mobilization. I show that these categorizations are not always mutually exclusive; rather, in many respects, they are overlapping and interrelated, or similar but formulated discursively or politically in different ways. I show also that none of the theories is adequate on its own to analyze the Gülen Movement. That said, I should clarify that my arguments and findings do not invalidate contemporary social movement theories within the western European and North American contexts. However, I emphasize that an evaluation of the Gülen Movement requires a very different *mode* of analysis and suggest that the use here of a syncretic framework may have implications for all other faith-inspired and civil society movements, but particularly for movements originating in non-European and non-North American contexts.

0.2.1 Insider/Outsider Research and Perspective

A feature of the methodology used in this work is the insider's perspective that I bring to it. It is of some importance that being an insider in the Gülen Movement is not an exclusivist belonging: as will be detailed in the proper place[1], solidarity and identity are not pursued as goals in this Movement; it does not have membership as such, let alone a closed membership; it encourages openness to the world, multiple belonging in many, diverse networks, and social and intellectual mobility; it urges continual access to sources of information, ideas and arguments outside itself, and co-operation with others on the basis of universal values.

An advantage of the insider role has been its enabling me to obtain the collective actor's perspectives without causing any apprehension about the possible repercussions to individuals as a result of their answering my questions,[*]

---

[*] Movement participants are aware that the outsider-researchers' interpretations of their discourse and action may, when reported, harm a SMO because of the sensitivities of the Turkish state and political system (in which the balance of power can shift abruptly and unpredictably) and the current world situation related to Muslims or Islam-inspired movements. This leads people to a prudent cautiousness about expressing ideas which, if recorded in any way, may later bring unwanted consequences.

or of distorting or dismissing their understanding of what they are doing. Being an insider-researcher can be seen as a positive feature, in the sense that it is illuminating: it reveals important aspects of phenomena, such as the movement's self-reflexive internal critique and culture, which outsider-researchers (especially if they have little experience of, or little sympathy with, faith-inspired collective action) may have difficulty in seeing or understanding.

If we consider the relation between outsider-researcher and actor, the assumptions and interests of the two are not identical or located in the same position in the social field. They articulate their mutual differences, together with their common (and often provisional) goals in collecting and sharing information. The relationship between the observer and the observed must also therefore be incorporated into the research framework. An outsider-researcher tends to interpret action in relation to the observer because he or she may not have access to the actor. By contrast, the insider-researcher has that access because of the necessary rootedness, familiarity and mutual trust, refinement and sensitivity to nuances, in a particular location in the field of social relationships and discourses; this allows him or her to dig out the less apparent side of the issues. The Gülen Movement has already demonstrated its capacity to define effectively the meaning of its own action, and the possibilities and constraints of the social field. Being able to locate myself temporarily at a level outside the relational but in a discursive field, I could observe 'natural' action. My work derives from the action itself, not only from the observation of collective processes and effects – as is seen in the work of outsiders. The latter represent the social actor of the Gülen Movement as never being entirely in control of its own action. (The distinction between objective reality and its social construction will be explored in §5.2.5.)

The questions I put are drawn from the relevant social movement theory literature and from the work of third parties who write on the Gülen Movement, whether they are hostile to it or not. I also present the historical background and the Movement's response to emergent realities through the words and arguments of third parties.

0.2.2 Methodological Consequences of the Research

A social movement should not be the object of knowledge as constructed by a few scholars – such construction does not reflect the empirical complexity of the action and its meanings and consequences. It is necessary to challenge simplistic conceptualizations of the Gülen Movement, whether positive or negative in tone. Social change needs to be discussed in analytical terms and with systemic points of reference rather than in relation to ideological grievances and ambitions.

In this sociological analysis, I try to avoid reducing the collective action of the Gülen Movement to just one of its levels. My intention is not to provide some sort of 'official' definition of the Movement. I have never consciously diminished the complex articulation of meanings that the Movement carries in itself. Rather, this research reveals some of those meanings of the collective action that may not be easily visible to an outsider. This should help in understanding how a social movement can succeed in becoming a collective actor or producing collective action.

As well as participants, third-party observers (whether sympathizers or opponents) are utilized to deconstruct the apparent reality and to let the plurality of relations and meanings appear. The methodological consequences of this theoretical stance require study of the Gülen Movement in its discourse, action, production and in the perception of its actors and others. This allows an adequate account of the multiple processes that constitute the empirical field of the Movement. Because these processes overlap and intertwine, they require a wide array of conceptual tools.

Drawing upon the literature for pertinent conceptual tools, interviews and questionnaires for insiders' perspectives, using my insider-researcher role, and adopting a syncretic framework, the approach I bring to the subject may rightly be called *multi-polar*. It has allowed me to analyze beyond the confines of the discourse or logic of only one of the observers, actors or systemic dimensions. The reciprocal influence of the many elements is investigated: in this research I have mapped out in particular those dimensions that resist reduction to political exchange.

If inquiry and analysis are restricted to the political dimensions of the observed phenomena (for example, a clash with authority), it leads inevitably to socio-political reduction of the field of action. It ignores specifically social dimensions of collective action and focuses exclusively on those more readily measurable features which, because of their high visibility, attract attention. Also, historical narrative does not adequately reveal the meaning or the interactive nature of an action but easily ends up identifying action with the ideology of the researcher.

Therefore, I have applied analytical tools to the Gülen Movement rather than a historical narrative, or historical-descriptive account, or historical–comparative approach based on subjective observation. My approach considers the processes of collective action as resulting from the interaction of diverse analytical components. I therefore identify theoretical components and explain how they come together in a specific conjuncture in Turkish society. If the diverse elements are kept analytically separate, and if distinct and appropriate conceptual schemata are not applied to the Gülen Movement, discussion of socio-cultural phenomena inevitably lapses into stereotyping and fruitless debate about the nature and outcome of the Movement.

0.2.3 Data Collection and Presentation

I had intended to interview ten or twelve people for this study. Two businessmen, Mr. Cahit Tuzcu and Mr. Bahaddin Eker, who are active sponsors of and participants in the service-projects of the Movement were interviewed for half an hour each in Istanbul in January 2005. These two interviews are mainly used in the fourth chapter. Later, three more individuals were interviewed: Mr. Abdullah Aymaz, a teacher, journalist and writer; Dr. Ergün Çapan, an academic and writer; and Mr. Enes Ergene, a sociologist and writer. They were interviewed in person in Istanbul, in three sessions each, in December 2005, and then again in April 2006. There was no time limit for the interviews. The spoken answers were recorded during the interviews and later transcribed. In addition, as the need arose, they were asked questions by e-mail and occasionally also by telephone.

There are some people who do not look favorably on the Gülen Movement. One such organization, Çağdaş Yaşamı Destekleme Derneği (The Association in Support of Contemporary Living), were asked repeatedly to take part in the Questionnaires and interviews but did not respond in any way to my requests. However, I was not alone in encountering this lack of cooperation. Social scientist Berna Turam, who as an outsider-researcher claiming neutrality might have expected cooperation from this group, had quite bruising encounters with them and those in sympathy with them.[2] (Another factor in their lack of response may have been that the request to participate went out in 2006 just as a significant court case against Gülen, which they had been supporting, was dropped.[3] This may have made these opponents of the Movement hesitant to restate arguments on record.)

For this reason, finally only five people were interviewed and they were all insiders to the Movement.

On the questionnaires there was a very high rate of return. This can be accounted for by a number of factors. Across the Gülen Movement the rate of computer literacy and access to computers is very high. While my insider status may helped me to obtain cooperation from respondents, Berna Turam, an outsider-researcher, has also reported how open she found Movement participants to her ethnographic research.[4]

Those who are not in favor of the Gülen Movement did not contribute to or co-operate with my research for the reasons alluded to above. However, their perspectives, though (regrettably, and not for any want of effort on my part) not present as a direct, original input to the research, are nevertheless represented in this study in the form of citations from their published statements in the media and press. I paid particular attention to avoid integrating their arguments into a coherent whole, and to avoid reducing the content of those arguments to one particular level of analysis or another. As far as possible, I have also represented the views of neutral and third-party observers through the literature review. I made every attempt to get the views of Movement participants on the criticisms of opponents and neutral outsiders by presenting those criticisms to them unmodified and 'unsanitized'.

Questionnaires A and B were distributed not among the general public but among people active in the social production of the Gülen Movement, in particular as teachers and administrators at Gülen-inspired educational institutions. The questionnaires were designed to determine internal factors within Gülen-inspired SMOs as seen through the eyes and the words of only the participants. The ages of the participants are between 25 and 40. The ratio of female to male respondents varied from country to country, but was relatively high in Germany and highest of all in the USA. In Central Asia, the overwhelming majority of respondents were male and relatively young (between 23 and 37).

The results of Questionnaires A and B show the respondents to be very aware of what they are thinking and doing, fully integrated and dedicated to their jobs, and willing to sacrifice much in their personal lives for the service, including leaving home to work abroad. It is this quality of dedication of the Movement participants at the SMOs that best explains the consistency of the results.

0.3 PRESENT AND FUTURE RELEVANCE

The present study is innovative in that it brings insiders' interpretations into focus through its multi-polar approach. In this respect, it should encourage future work on the same and larger topics. Current and future research on related interdisciplinary topics – social change, political studies, sociology and sociology of religion – should find the resources, ideas, analyses and discussions in this book of relevance. My findings and their implications could helpfully inform a variety of theoretical and analytical perspectives, and sensitivities about and discussions of social and religious forces related to Islam and peaceful Muslim social or cultural movements. This books also sheds light on circumstances and issues in the recent history of Turkey and the Gülen Movement. While examining whether or not the Movement can properly be classified as contentious, it becomes necessary to question why some social actors have constructed the reality they have. This is not done in order to challenge their authority but to establish clearly and accurately the nature and outcomes of the Movement. By questioning some of the simple assumptions often made about the Gülen Movement, this book will I hope motivate and open up fertile avenues for future research.

0.4 ORGANIZATION OF THE BOOK

The book begins with the theoretical and historical background (chapters 1 and 2), then shows how the collective action of the Gülen Movement and the opposition to its action are mobilized and framed in practice (chapter 3), and how these are combined and interpreted in the light of conjunctural factors (chapter 4); it examines how the internal (organizational and operational) factors are seen and interpreted by participants in the Movement and by those outside it or opposed to it. Finally, in chapter 6, there is a detailed summary of the arguments and their implications.

0.5 THE ARGUMENT IN BRIEF

I hold that understanding collective action requires the analysis of all social, cultural and spiritual factors, i.e. material *and* immaterial resources, and that transformation can be willed, intended, planned and achieved by any collective actor *without confrontation*. These and other points are developed in the course of the following chapters. I should mention in passing that it is rare to encounter any research on matters and issues related to Muslims or to countries where Muslims are the majority population, that is not, to some degree, motivated (and accordingly limited) by political, ideological and even religious preferences.

There have been circumstances specific to Turkey over the last thirty years which explain why the Gülen Movement does not map neatly onto current general theoretical paradigms. Very many determinants are at work for a movement to rise and develop, and movements cannot be reduced to one determinant like historical context, grievances, economy, norms, class, beliefs, resources, networks, strategies, ideology, organizations, leadership, adversary, etc. There are unique combinations of different factors. I identify such factors in the case study here and weigh their relative significance. I then extract some 'core' propositions, not necessarily found in every approach, which relate to key aspects of social movements, namely contextual and historical background, mobilization–counter-mobilization, conjunctural factors, and internal factors and components.

I hold that social movements theory needs to give equal weight to the insiders' viewpoint, rather than ignore a movement's framing and internal factors. In the case of the Gülen Movement, because it originated as a faith-inspired civil society movement, motivations for participation include spiritual resources and moral values drawn from the Islamic tradition, like altruism and other non-material incentives. Faith is indeed a motivating force and helps to constitute social capital for peaceful civil society movements – not only conflictual ones – and it cannot always be discounted or analyzed in terms of something other than itself. Faith and empowerment by it are not a dependent variable, determined and structured by the social, economic, and political conditions; religious experience cannot be dismissed as a proxy or substitute for something else like, for instance, direct or contentious political action.

Current social movement theories are unable to describe the Gülen Movement adequately because of their political and social reductionism in dealing with faith-inspired movements generally and Islamic movements in particular. Evaluation of the Gülen Movement requires a very different mode of analysis from the kind of theoretical perspectives developed to account contentious social movements in the European and American experience. That is why I have suggest the use of a *multi-polar* approach with a syncretic framework for analyzing faith-inspired civil society movements comparable to the Gülen Movement.

0.6 THE MULTI-POLAR APPROACH

The multi-polar approach can avoid reductionism because of the three elements it comprises: a) the insider perspective and insider-researcher role; b) the empowerment believers gain from their faith; and c) a syncretic framework.

The insider perspective highlights the need to evaluate perceptions, attitudes and actions through the insiders' perspectives, and the disparity between their representation of the collective action and its perception by others – by the insider-researcher and by external observers, whether neutral or sympathetic or hostile. This approach improves on existing ones insofar as it returns the collective actor to the center of the analysis, treating it as 'subject' rather than 'object' of collective action or mobilization.

Including faith and empowerment by it as a factor in the analysis underlines the importance of specifically religious differences for the development of collective action and society. Faith and empowerment by it form a substantial part of civic society and democracy. They contribute significantly to the preservation and development of volunteerism, dialog and relationships to achieve shared goals, competitiveness and non-materialistic and non-contentious services. Religious experience involves meanings, values and experience other than those entertained in protest theories or conflictual political actions. The real social significance of these factors needs to be acknowledged as a causal power affecting people's views, choices and actions. Religious experience or its influences are located at the heart of all societies and they are not just private, epiphenomenal, sub-systems for the status quo, conflict-evading pacifism, etc.

Any social, political, economic or methodological reductionism offers at best a partial explanation of collective action. It is unsatisfactory because it does not take account of or distorts key aspects of a movement and its history – for example, it may treat philanthropic services and culturally innovative potential as politically subversive, when it is not.

The syncretic framework draws upon a) contextual and historical background, b) worldview or belief system, c) mobilization and counter-mobilization, d) conjunctural factors, and e) internal factors and components of a collective identity and action. Adopting core propositions from key aspects of social movements and from theories about them, this framework allows the researcher to look and explain beyond the confines of the discourse or logic of only one of the observers, actors or systemic dimensions. The reciprocal influence of all the different elements needs to be investigated as well, so that the complexity of reality and interrelations of its different dimensions and levels are not reduced to what is easiest to see or easiest to discuss – most typically the level of political exchange between contending actors.

1

Theoretical Background: Collective Action and Social Movements Theory

1.1 INTRODUCTION

Theories about social movements and collective action are useful and necessary. They enable us to describe and explain such movements – how they form and mobilize, what they try to achieve, how they are mobilized against, why and how far mobilization or counter-mobilization succeeds or fails – and, to some degree, evaluate policies and strategies in the light of particular outcomes. Self-evidently, the terms and concepts, the discourse, that we bring to bear must be appropriate and effective for the particular social movement we are studying. Theories neither arise nor operate in a vacuum; they have a history, they change in response to the realities of the subject-matter. In this chapter, I survey the three main contemporary theories that make up the general framework within which I have approached the task of describing and explaining the Gülen Movement. The survey is critical – that is, I try to explain how these theoretical approaches arose and in what particular respects the intellectual tools that they provide are unsuited to the job of explaining social movements like the one we are studying. I also suggest that a syncretic approach, combining particular features from the different discourses, should and – as I hope to demonstrate in later chapters – does yield better results, namely more accurate and complete description and greater explanatory efficacy.

1.2 HISTORICAL OVERVIEW OF COLLECTIVE ACTION AND SOCIAL MOVEMENTS THEORY

Theories about social movements have changed markedly since the 1940s, and especially over the last couple of decades.[1] Buechler has suggested that the changes reflect 'changes in socio-historical contexts' and in 'the experiences' that led theorists to re-think 'the definition of their subject-matter'.[2] That different types of movements emerge in different social conditions,[3] and the variations in how they are identified,[4] will be discussed more fully in later chapters. Here, we shall focus from a historical perspective on the three leading contemporary approaches in social movement theory – Resource Mobilization Theory, Political Opportunity Structure Theory and Frame Theory.

The main point of theorizing about a social movement is to 'account for the specificity and autonomy of social action', to 'give a foundation to its collective character as something different from the sum total of aggregate individual behaviours'.[5] The roots of contemporary approaches lie in six classical traditions: class struggle (Marx), collective conscience (Durkheim), a sum of individual cost–benefit calculations (Mill), charisma and bureaucracy (Weber), interaction of individuals (Simmel), and crowds (Le Bon).[6] The enduring influence of the classical approaches has been in creating the different worldviews of the research traditions to which they gave rise. Both Durkheim and Weber highlighted the significance of religion, but in social movements studies proper there is little emphasis on the study of religious movements: that emphasis has to be looked for in the quite distinct research traditions of theology and anthropology.[7]

1.2.1 The 'classical' approaches

Up to the 1960s, the major sources for sociological understanding of social movements were: Marxist theory, Psychological theory, and the Collective Behavior tradition. The Marxist intellectual tradition is one of the most persistent and still leaves its mark on the study of collective phenomena. This may be due to the fact that many leading social theorists come from a Marxist background and to the (Marxist) student movements of the 1960s and 1970s.[8]

The psychological theories placed particular emphasis on studying anti-Semitism, paranoid conspiracy theories, and authoritarian personality structures and exaggerated deference toward them in the movement adherents. It is important to note that psychological theories and those of the collective behavior tradition developed almost during the same periods, are not mutually exclusive, use similar explanatory instruments, and have important features (and advocates) in common.

The empirical content of movement actions was viewed as a manifestation of deeper conflicts, structural strains experienced, dissatisfaction and breakdown. Thus, social movements were seen as secondary, potentially dangerous, irrational in their ideas, a temporary aberration in the otherwise smooth-flowing social system.[9] Therefore, collective behavior theory failed to develop an effective alternative to the psychological theories, one capable of explaining how mobilization happened, and producing a theory of social change.[10] The theory was attacked in the 1960s when it was found not to fit the student movement; a paradigm shift followed to the Resource Mobilization approach in the mid-1970s to mid-1980s. 'Like all such shifts, this one raised new questions and marginalized old ones; in the process, the roles of strain and breakdown theories were effectively driven underground.'[11]

1.2.2 The contemporary approaches

The 1950s and 1960s saw collective action that mostly ignored the conventional avenues for political participation, and advocated causes/ideas, like civil rights, freedom, and peace, that were not self-centered. Participants included those who were educated middle-class; religious communities; and, in both America and Europe, academics. Also noteworthy were the role of voluntarist and Church organizations, and the new significance attached to 'knowledge' (as opposed to ownership of the industrialized means of production). Most social scientists, rejecting the labeling of such participants, under collective behavior theory, as politically and socially 'underclass' or 'irrational', were persuaded that a new approach was needed. Attention turned from the psychology of the individual and societal stresses – respectively, the 'micro' and 'macro' levels – to the organizations around which movements cluster – the intermediate or '*meso*' level. The new generation of sociologists who came to the field during this period were deeply affected by the student movements of the time, and this affected their conceptualization of social movements.[12]

Contemporary treatments of collective action and identity build upon classical and social-psychological foundations. Classical approaches, such as Marxist theory, Psychological theories and the Collective Behavior tradition, are macro-oriented. They underline the importance of the emerging large structures, the resulting strains, and the reactions to them in the formation of organized movements. There are differences and divisions within such perspectives, especially between European and North American social psychology, but both suggest that collective behaviors and identities are produced by interaction and socio-cultural stresses. The inter-war and post-war periods gave rise to some politically motivated scholars, theories and publications, especially in the Collective Behavior tradition, which sees collective actions as (potentially dangerous) temporary aberrations in the otherwise smoothly-flowing social system.

Disillusioned by the class-based ideology, lack of revolutionary consciousness, and undemocratic tendencies and practices in socialist movements or states, activists and scholars in post-industrial societies started to focus on non-class-based action and movements for change. Among contemporary approaches, Resource Mobilization theory – while largely ignoring ideology, origins, structure, and political style – sees the emergence and development of movements as arising from the availability and use of resources. It looks primarily at how networks of people, professionals, leadership, permanent organizations, incentives, and cost–benefit calculations come together to generate direct, measurable impacts on political issues. This emphasis is generally accepted as reflecting the American federal system and the opportunities it provides to organizations and supporters. It draws attention to the institutional locations of mobilization (SMOs) but ignores cultural variables.

Political Opportunity Structure theory studies the impact of structure on collective action, or vice versa. It highlights the role of the political system, the larger social environment and culture, in the emergence, dynamics, and outcomes of social movements. It argues that social movements must be studied within their particular, societal, political and cultural contexts, and it is able to show how 'open' or 'closed' political systems affect the nature and tactics of collective actors, how they create new possibilities, or provoke or radicalize forms of collective action.

Frame Theory studies the role of the shared assumptions and meanings held by actors in interpreting events and redressing problems. It seeks to explain collective action in terms of the motives, beliefs and discourses manifested by actors. It focuses on how frames are produced and utilized during different phases of a movement, and on how ideas, sentiments and culture affect the repertoires of action and contention. It points to the functions of ideology, its ambivalence and implications for supporters, counter-movements and authorities. It argues the pertinent role of language, leadership, social movement organizations and the media in framing processes.

1.3 CONCLUSION

A number of intellectual disciplines, traditions and theories focus on the emergence and success or failure of specific movements, explaining them in terms of structural stresses, resource mobilization, political opportunity structures and framing processes. Different societal, political, cultural and conjunctural events, trends and factors influence the possibilities for collective action. These are in constant interaction and have also caused shifts in perspectives and paradigms in social movement studies. Therefore, it is important to be flexible and sensitive in characterizing social movements, especially in the case of multi-purpose or general movements which are not class-based, not adversarial, and not oriented to particular material objectives.

It is hard to classify any collective action into only one category, as classifications depend on different phenomena: situation, opportunities, organizations, worldviews, and human factors, including supporters, adversaries, and authorities. Some aspects are no longer local and national but, instead, international or even global. Aims and claims for change are more measured in style and may have culturally, rather than politically, radical dimensions. Through their participation in collective action, people are expressing something that cannot be expressed within the confines of conventional politics. The networks and organizations are more decentralized, professionalized, and less formal and less hierarchical. The tactics employed are both conventional and unconventional but less risky for participants, though unconventional tactics and direct action may still be held in reserve as part of an action repertoire. Collective action provides and revolves around cohesion and normative frameworks based upon collective conscience. This enables a mutuality in relationships within society and enables individuals and groups to relate in terms of shared values, morals and goals.

The theories we have discussed focus mainly on First World and national contexts. Third World settings and scholars are severely underrepresented in the discipline. If Talcott Parsons' stress on cultural backgrounds were taken seriously, it would mean that the theories do not necessarily fit well to a context outside Judeo-Christian culture. Nevertheless, a theory developed in one context could have at least some validity for another. The question should be how far such theories are adequate to other contexts. For an answer to that question, empirical testing is important. To date quite a few studies have tried to take into account the global perspective, but these are concerned only with gender, sexuality or environmentalist movements. There has been little research into peaceful, faith-inspired social movements arising from Islamic backgrounds.

Thus, the theories have quite narrow historical perspectives and indeed are heavily oriented to the explanation of short-term, spontaneous actions or 'protests'. The root metaphors of collective action have changed with advances in communications. Transnational or worldwide movements can be in different stages in different countries, highly institutionalized in one country and, at the same time, still in a formative stage in others. People understand and interpret the world, its affairs and issues, no longer in a single fixed way, but in competing and shifting types of explanations – a change no doubt facilitated by the diffusion of internet services. It is obvious that the old conceptualizations and paradigms cannot encompass and deal with some aspects of the emergent realities. Confronting cases and competing perspectives drawn from a number of different national contexts require scholars to adopt more comparative, eclectic and synthetic approaches and to deploy a profusion of useful analytic tools.

Definitions or categorizations of social movements are shaped by any combination of contextual influences, including the historical setting, political and cultural understanding, the social and intellectual milieu, the cognitive praxis, of the individuals doing the defining and categorizing. Among scholars it is agreed that there is no agreed definition of collective action and social movements that would satisfy the different approaches dominant in any epoch or fit well the different realities being studied. Contemporary accounts of what a social movement is are likewise subject to contextual influences. They focus on selected concrete features of a movement; they vary with the frame of reference, the relative weight of the levels of analysis, and their various relations, combinations and overlaps. The following list will give some sense of the range of conceptualizations of social movements suggested in recent years:

> a social movement is *a purposive and collective attempt of a number of people to change individuals or societal institutions and structures* (Zald & Ash, 1966);[13]

a social movement is *a set of opinions and beliefs in a population which represents preferences for changing some elements of the social structure and/or reward distribution of a society* (McCarthy & Zald, 1977);[14]

social movements are *1) informal networks, based (2) on shared beliefs and solidarity, which mobilize about (3) conflictual issues, through (4) the frequent use of various forms of protest* (Della Porta & Diani, 1999);[15]

social movements are conceptualized on *three or more of the following axes: collective or joint action; change-oriented goals or claims; some extra- or non-institutional collective action; some degree of organization; and some degree of temporal continuity* (Snow et al., 2004);[16]

the concept of a social movement comprises *three analytical dimensions: the mobilization of a collective actor (i) defined by specific solidarity, (ii) engaged in a conflict with an adversary for the appropriation and control of resources valued by both of them, (iii) and whose action entails a breach of the limits of compatibility of the system within which the action itself takes place* (Melucci, 1999);[17]

new social movements are *a self-understanding that abandons revolutionary dreams in favor of the idea of structural reform, along with a defense of civil society that does not seek to abandon the autonomous functioning of political and economic systems – in a phrase, self-limiting radicalism* (Cohen, 1985);[18]

social movements in the 1960s were structured as *segmented, polycentric, and ideologically integrated networks* (Gerlach & Hine, 1970);[19]

a social movement is a *sustained and self-conscious challenge to authorities or cultural codes by a field of actors – organizations and advocacy networks – some of which employ extra-institutional means of influence* (Gamson & Wolfsfeld, 1993);[20]

social movements are *sustained challenges to power-holders in the name of a disadvantaged population living under the jurisdiction or influence of those power-holders* (Tarrow, 1996);[21]

social movements are *more or less organized attempts by relatively powerless groups to change politics or society* (Vanneman, 2005).

In the definitions just listed, the common themes – such as challenging or protesting against power-holders, seeking structural reform, using extra-institutional means (transgressing legal or other accepted boundaries) – derive from a very specific wave of collective actions in western Europe and North America in the late 1960s and their aftermath. These conceptualizations are very much still in use. However, I contend that they have a number of major drawbacks or weaknesses:

(1) They are too narrow to include all or most social movements, and too broad to distinguish between different types of movements.[22] (2) They do not adequately describe the continuity between the structural location of the actor and the cultural and intellectual world by which it is identified and mobilized. The sociology of collective actors is now dealing increasingly with movements that cannot be referred only to one specific social condition.[23] (3) They differ among themselves in terms of what is emphasized or accentuated.[24] (4) 'Much of the social movement literature either searches for generalizations across movements at different times and places, or focuses on single movements at one particular time and place.'[25] (5) The conceptualizations draw far too much upon contexts in which *oppositional* or protest movements are rooted (an indication of the explicit bias of the majority of the students of collective phenomena bring raised in the late 1960s and 1970s). (6) Because, in discussing the variables for social movements and SMOs, researchers 'prefer to think of causes in terms of competing "schools", "perspectives", or theories that are pitted against one another in pseudocontests over correctness',[26] they tend to mask some of the features of the very phenomena they are seeking to clarify. (7) They overlook the presence of non-political elements in emergent movements, and totally ignore[27] themes such as philanthropy, altruism and voluntarism, which help explain the dynamics of participation in activities that do not directly benefit those taking part.[28] (8) Finally, the conceptualizations fail to address the reasons why (and how) faith – Islam in our case – meets the need for cultural or political empowerment.

There are contemporary movements throughout the world which concern themselves with forms of action, content and meanings that are qualitatively different from the tradition of struggle frequently seen in European societies. They do not fit into the conventional categories of the workers' movement of industrial capitalism and modern leftist movements. There is a sharp discontinuity between contemporary issues and events and those of the past.[29] Along with inequalities or changes that are economic and political, there are changes and meanings that arise and gain prominence from diverse contractions of the fields in which cultural and moral values can be expressed. There are movements emphasizing or motivated by a different array of factors, including values, such as equality, freedom, dignity, altruism, good life, ecology and morality.[30] There are needs and issues which basic human rights, ethics and culture legitimate but the socio-political structure fails to implement.[31]

In this vein, Earl briefly notes: 'Many leading theorists have argued that NSMs [New Social Movements] are less directed toward policy outcomes and instead are more concerned with contesting cultural values and beliefs.'[32] Then, Koopmans – in pointing out that some movements 'by incorporating such innovations in their established repertoires [...] not only introduce an element of novelty in their interactions [...] but may also, if successful, establish a new recombination of identities, tactics, and demands that can in turn inspire other movements'[33] – draws attention to a very important dimension of the Gülen Movement's intercultural or educational repertoires of action and SMOs, its understanding of civil society, pluralist participatory democracy and their compatibilities with Islam, and its transnational altruistic services.

To sum up: there are contemporary social movements that do not restrict themselves to expressing a conflict, and/or do not push the contentious action or conflict beyond the limits of the system of social relationships within which the action is located – that is, they do not infringe the rules of the game; their objectives are by no means non-negotiable; nor do they contest the legitimacy of power or of the system in which they emerged. Such movements, which share the characteristic of being non-conflictual, may arise out of various religious or secular traditions.[34] They are not necessarily temporal, or discontinuous, or informal and non-institutionalized, or exclusivist with limited self-understanding. Conceptualization and description of such movements needs, accordingly, to be cautious and sensitive, especially in the case of multi-purpose or general movements which cannot be identified as class-based, materialistic and contentious.

No doubt, the differences and nuances can be explained by reference to the incompatibilities of the various theories, the different approaches by sociologists to their subject and a number of other interrelated historical, cultural, intellectual and political factors. The different roles played by movements in the political formation of societies, the different meanings given to the notion of movement in different political discourses, philosophies of history and theories of knowledge, have also affected the ways in which movements have been conceptualized. Another very important factor is the personal relation of the researchers to the movements under investigation, that is, the nature and degree of empathy/animosity that the sociologists bring to their subject-matter.

Since 1992, efforts by several European and American theorists have been underway to bring various theories of social movement together, and to bridge the gap in understandings and find a common ground. In doing this they found that they were limited to 'research rooted in core democracies' and 'comparing cases across this relatively homogeneous set of polities'.[35] The subject of this study, the Gülen Movement, is a collective actor that has emerged outside those 'core democracies'. In the effort made in subsequent chapters to explain its rise, operations and outcomes, I hope to show that it is necessary, and possible, to go beyond the approaches that can only deal with collective action that is restricted in location, politically oriented, contentious and adversarial, and with narrow material objectives. Indeed, approaches that characterize and explain social movements in those terms may be seen as over-generalized for many cases, not just the particular movement studied here. It is then possible to hope that this book may highlight the aspects and dimensions of collective action that have typically been understated or ignored altogether.

2

Historical Background

2.1 INTRODUCTION

This chapter recounts in chronological order the socio-political developments of the Republican era. The narrative provides the background material necessary for the analysis that follows in later chapters. Interspersed within it is a *parallel narrative*, offering a very summary outline of the formative events in the history of the Gülen Movement. I shall point in particular to

- the ideas, attitudes and events of this period that have shaped and influenced the various kinds of mobilization in Turkey;
- the distinguishing characteristics of the socio-political context in which the Gülen Movement emerged and has worked; and
- key events in the period up to 1994 that directly affected Gülen and the Movement as collective actor. (For reasons that will become clear, the events after 1994 are best treated separately.)

Connecting the rise of movements only to their immediate socio-political context does not adequately explain the full range of collective action – very different kinds of movements can and have emerged from the same background conditions. Also, it is unsatisfactory to study a movement in one context in terms derived from the study of other movements in a different context, because variations in structure, laws, policies, and culture lead to differences in strategy, leadership styles and resource mobilization. With respect to the emergence, dynamics and outcomes of any social movement in Turkey (especially in the case of the kind of multi-purpose civic action that characterizes the Gülen Movement), the political system, its institutions and processes, and the larger social and cultural ethos, constitute highly significant material factors. That is why it is necessary to trace the seeds of collective action in Turkey to the early Republican years, when a new state and society formed. To understand contemporary social phenomena in Turkey, we need to understand the changing circumstances in which the attempt was made to establish, and then hold on to, a nationalist, laicist, and Westernized republic after the end of the Ottoman Empire.

2.2 CRISES AND CONFLICTS; DEMANDS FOR MODERNIZATION

2.2.1 The Republican era: one-party rule

In July 1923, the Turks won sovereignty over eastern Thrace and all of Anatolia. In August, the delegates in the national Parliament fell to infighting over the political course and nature of the future regime. After lengthy disquisitions and eventual intimidation by Mustafa Kemal,* Parliament abolished the sultanate and deposed the sultan but retained the caliphate with no political authority. However, many in Parliament did try to invest the caliphate with such authority, aiming thereby to retain influence with other Muslim lands and populations. Then Mustafa Kemal proposed an amendment and, on October 29, 1923, transformed the nation into 'the Republic of Turkey'.[1] In 1924, at his urging, Parliament abolished the caliphate, the Ministry of Religious Endowments and the office of Shaykhulislam (the highest religious authority) and assigned their responsibilities to two newly established directorates under the government. It abolished the Ministry of the General Staff, and shut down sharia courts and madrasas. The Law on the Unification of Education placed religious secondary education under the Ministry of Education, reorganized the madrasa at the Süleymaniye Mosque (Istanbul) as a new Faculty of Divinity and enforced co-education at all levels.

These changes put the military and religious cadres under governmental control and the potential for an Islamic state (the most likely challenge to the legitimacy of the Republican regime) was thereby quashed. In addition, Parliament accepted that Turkey was no longer a world power – its frontiers were to be bounded by the Turkish-speaking population of the Republic –

---

* UNESCO, 1963:128–9; Lewis, 1965:258. (Mustafa Kemal Atatürk said: 'Sovereignty has never been given to any nation by scholarly disputation. It is always taken by force and with violence [and] some heads may roll in the process.')

and it would not entertain any vision of transnational leadership in any respect. The initial, occasional and individual, reactions to these changes were suppressed by the state apparatus. When, later, 32 parliamentarians, not happy about the changes, broke with the party and formed the Progressive Republican Party, Mustafa Kemal's People's Party changed its name to the Republican People's Party (RPP).[2]

The partition of the state at Sevres, the invasion by the Allied Forces, and the British influence on Kurdish nationalist aspirations, nurtured a peculiar Turkish nationalism and aggravated relations with the Kurds, who previously had for the most part supported the Turkish nationalists. A law passed in 1924 forbidding publications in Kurdish widened the chasm between the Turkish nationalists and the Kurds. When a Kurdish nationalist rebellion in religious garb, led by Sheikh Said, erupted in 1925,[3] the Turkish government issued a law on Maintenance of Order, granting itself extraordinary powers to ban any group or publication deemed a threat to national security. That threat has been used repeatedly ever since by defenders of the system and vested interests. A good example was the establishment in 1925 of the Independence Tribunals (ITs). Enabling the execution of 1,054 people, the ITs played a significant role in suppressing rebellions – the Sheikh Said rebellion, for instance, was ended quite quickly with his arrest and execution.[4]

ITs also snared many others, including Said Nursi,[5] the most important Islamic thinker of the Republican era. Nursi was an Islamic modernist whose writings mapped out an accommodation between the ideas of constitutional democracy and individual liberty and religious faith. During the war years, he had fought against the foreign invasion and for independence, and spoken out against both modern Islamic authoritarianism and economic and political backwardness and separatism. His ideas for a modern Islamic consciousness emphasize the need for a significant role for religious belief in public life, while rejecting obscurantism and embracing scientific and technological development. Although he was not involved in any rebellions, ITs sentenced him, along with many hundreds of others, to exile in western Anatolia.[6]

In 1926, the government declared that it had uncovered a conspiracy to assassinate Mustafa Kemal and, in the next two years turned the ITs on all its enemies. All national newspapers were closed and their staff arrested on grounds of compromising 'national security'. The Progressive Republican Party was shut down, its leaders accused of collaborating in the conspiracy and arrested for treason. Under public pressure several prominent figures were released but others, though they had once worked closely with Mustafa Kemal, were executed.[7]

2.2.2 Laicism

A strongly Kemalist Parliament – for all practical purposes a one-party state – enacted a series of measures between 1925 and 1928 to secularize public life. Mustafa Kemal believed that Turkey must renounce its past and follow the European model of progress.[8] He accordingly set about eliminating all obstacles to a laicized and Westernized nation-state.[9]

Dervish houses were permanently closed, their ceremonies, liturgy and traditional dress outlawed. Kemal publicly denounced the fez[*] and the hijab (veil) as symbols of politicized Islam, as the headgear of a barbarous and backward religiosity, as a foreign innovation. Asserting that Turkish peasant women had traditionally worn only a scarf around their hair, he depicted the hijab as representing subordination of women by a reactionary political ideology. Parliament passed a law requiring men to wear brimmed hats and outlawed the fez. Women were given the right to vote and stand for election. The day after Christmas 1925, Parliament adopted the Gregorian calendar, in place of the Islamic one, as 'the standard accepted by the advanced nations of the world', and it changed the Muslim holy day of Friday into a weekday, and instituted Sunday as a rest day.

The following year (1926), Parliament repealed Islamic Law and adopted a new Civil Code, Penal Code and Business Law, based on the Swiss, Italian, and German codes, respectively. In 1928, it deleted from the constitution the phrase 'the religion of the Turkish state is Islam'. The constitution did not yet state that Turkey was a secular state – that was to come in 1937 – but the intent was clearly to secularize, and to make Westernized forms of social order more visible in, the public sphere.[10]

In 1928, the new alphabet based on the Latin was accepted instead of the Arabic script. It was argued that the new alphabet would help raise literacy. If conceivably true, the low literacy rate could hardly be blamed on a

---

[*] In fact, the fez had barely existed a hundred years in the Ottoman Empire and was associated with the state and its functionaries, not with the religion, whose dignitaries traditionally favored the turban.

script that had served written Turkish well for about a thousand years. The low levels of literacy were more particularly the result of the prolonged wars, an ineffective system of public education and the belief that having an effective one was an unnecessary luxury during wartime. Rather, reform of the script had historical, cultural, and political intent: use of the Arabic script had identified the Turks as belonging to Islamic civilization and history; use of the Latin characters would identify them with the direction of European civilization and modernity. At a stroke, the new regime totally renounced its past and embraced the revolutionary concept of history. In not learning the Arabic script, the children of the Turkish revolution would also not learn Islamic tradition and, indeed, would be unable to read its greatest literary monuments, or the documents produced only a few years before in the Ottoman Empire.[11]

In the 1920s, the State looked to develop an indigenous, elite entrepreneurial class that would be loyal to and defend the new status quo – a nationalist bourgeoisie. In 1927, it provided to these privileged private citizens transfer of state land, tax exemptions, state subsidies, discounts on transport, and control of state monopolies. During the 1930s these citizens formed the core of the statist-elitist-laicists, whose actions will come up in the arguments in this and later chapters [chapters 3 and 4]. They were also the first of the protectionist vested interests to exploit State-owned Economic Enterprises[12] (SEEs) and other state resources.

The shift to protectionism and statism hardened as the 1930s wore on and deepened the effect of the ensuing economic woes: agricultural prices collapsed causing peasants to fall into severe debt; industrial wages stagnated. The Republican revolution had reached a deadly plateau. Government economic policy drew fierce criticism and occasionally led to violent public reaction. The state centralized economic planning and organized several investment banks as joint stock companies to provide credit to agriculture, develop the mining and power industries, and finance industrial expansion. It also monopolized communications, railroads, and airlines.[13]

2.2.3 Cultural revolution

The Republican regime was both deliberate and selective in what it remembered and appropriated of the past. It linked the emerging national identity to Anatolian antiquity. The history and language reforms were part of a sustained campaign to erase the pre-existing culture and education. Mustafa Kemal personally directed the scientific and literary activity of the later 1920s and 1930s.[14] In 1932, he founded the Turkish History Research Society* and charged it with discovering the full antiquity of Turkish history. He theorized that Anatolia had been first settled by Sumerians and Hittites, whom he claimed as Turkic peoples that had migrated from the central Eurasian steppes carrying with them the underlying building blocks of 'Western civilization'. Also at his command, a Turkish Language Society was established in the same year. The 'Sun Language Theory' was developed, asserting that Turkish was the primordial human tongue from which all others derived. These theories made a deep, enduring impression on the generations that grew up on the textbooks teaching them. Education was designed to make pupils and citizens proud of their Turkish identity and suspicious of the Ottoman past, while also countering Western prejudices about Turks and Turkey. The explicit aim of the Turkish Language Society was 'to cleanse the Turkish language of the accumulated encrustations from the Arabic and Persian languages' and from the conceptual categories of the Islamic intellectual tradition. In the following decades the Society's officials made a concerted effort to introduce substitute or newly coined words. They were largely successful. The current generation of Turkish speakers find works from the early Republican era – including, ironically, the speeches of Mustafa Kemal himself – unintelligible unless translated into contemporary Turkish. Publication in languages other than Turkish was forbidden. In the 1920s, eighty percent of the words in the written language derived from words of Arabic and Persian origin; by the early 1980s the figure was just ten percent. By providing historical roots outside Ottoman history, the Republic's ideology combined the goals of Westernization and Turkish nationalism, claiming that Western civilization really originated in a Turkic Eurasian past, which the Ottoman Empire had obscured.[15] As political scientist Binnaz Toprak sharply observed, these policies produced 'a nation of forgetters'.[16]

In 1933, a law reorganized the Darulfunun (literally, 'home of the arts', an Ottoman university founded in the fifteenth century) into Istanbul University and purged its faculty in favor of those supportive of Mustafa

---

*   Renamed as 'the Turkish Historical Society' in 1935.

Kemal's program for national education. In 1934, the State required all citizens to adopt and register family names. Many potentially useful administrative advantages might well be imagined from a system of alphabetized family names, but the change expressly required that the names be authentically Turkish: names derived from Arabic or Persian roots, or from other ethnic origins (Jewish and Armenian, for example), were not permitted. The measure thus reinforced the national, ethnic identity of the citizens, as distinct from (in particular) their religious identity. The state effectively bound the personal destiny and identity of its citizens to that of the nation-state.* In 1936, the government monopolized the authority to broadcast. At the same time, nationalists were advocating the use of Turkish in Islamic liturgy. Parliament established a fund to produce the Turkish version of the Qur'an; Atatürk encouraged the use of Turkish for mosque prayers, Friday sermons and for the call to prayer. After some public resistance (and violent reactions from the state to this resistance), the prayer liturgy remained in Arabic, but the call to prayer began to be done in Turkish, and this was made compulsory in 1941.[17]

The Republican People's Party (RPP) established 'People's Houses' and 'Village Institutes'. By 1940, more than four thousand People's Houses had been founded to facilitate the development of popular loyalties and to communicate to citizens their mission and values as formulated by the regime. In 1935, Mustafa Kemal demanded a new strategy for education, which went nation-wide in 1940 through the Village Institutes. The graduates were expected to teach and emphasize techniques of agriculture and home industry, and to inculcate the fundamental ideology of the Republic. These Institutes were widely resented. The people accused the mastermind behind the Institutes of being a communist and the Institutes of being agents of one-party rule and atheistic. They mistrusted the system also on account of its control rather than transformation of their affairs, as it consistently failed to realize land redistribution or relieve them of the power of landlords.[18]

In 1931, Mustafa Kemal had outlined his party (RRP) ideology in six 'fundamental and unchanging principles', declaring it to be 'republican, nationalist, populist, statist, laicist, and revolutionary,' concepts incorporated into the constitution in 1937 as definitive of the basic principles of the state.

---

* In 1935, Parliament gave Mustafa Kemal the family name Atatürk, 'Father of the Turks'.

While the political system and 'ideology' of Turkey remains *Kemalism* or *Atatürkism*[19], the last three of the six principles became contentious over time. 'Etatism' or 'statism', meaning the policy of state-directed economic investment adopted by the RPP in the 1930s, was not universally accepted as a basic element of Turkish nationhood and eventually abandoned. 'Laicism' or 'secularism' has been variously interpreted by those at different points on the Turkish political spectrum. It refers in fact to the administrative control of religious affairs and institutions by the state – rather than to separation of 'state' and 'religion' – and to the removal of official religious expressions from public life, but it also implied in principle freedom, 'within these bounds', of religious practice and conscience. 'Revolutionism' – in much later years replaced by the term 'reformism' – as one of the least articulated principles, suggests an ongoing openness and commitment to change in the interests of the nation. In reality, as Turkish history since the early days of the Republic has repeatedly shown, some things can hardly be discussed, let alone changed.[20]

Sociologist Emre Kongar considers the Turkish social and cultural transformation as unique – in the totality of its ambition and in its success in replacing, with a synthesis of Western and pre-Islamic Turkish cultures, the previously dominant Islamic culture of an Islamic society.[21] However, the drastic reforms – from grand political structures to the everyday matters of eating, dressing and celebrations – pushed through in such a short period of time, would need a longer period for assimilation. They were not all welcomed but, to the contrary, provoked hostile reactions, which has had the effect of enduringly politicizing certain issues in Turkey.[22]

2.2.4 İnönü, 'the National Chief' and 'Eternal Leader'

After the death of Mustafa Kemal Atatürk in 1938, his reforms were consolidated by his successor, İsmet İnönü. Parliament granted İnönü the titles of 'the National Chief' and 'the Eternal Leader', with enhanced powers in anticipation of possible challenges to the regime, powers much greater than those of the last two Ottoman sultans.[23] The Second World War began a year later. İnönü's forceful use of the crisis ensured, through imposition of martial law in much of the country, the maintenance of the Kemalist structure, and it kept Turkey out of the war.[24]

During the war years there were shortages of basic goods and cash, as well as inflation. The government imposed an extraordinary 'capital-wealth

tax' on property owners, farmers, and businessmen in 1942. The tax sched-
ules were not prepared with formal income data but left to the personal es-
timates of local bureaucrats, who divided taxpayers according to profits, capacity, and religion – Muslim, non-Muslim, Foreigner, and Sabbataist (Jewish converts). Many were financially ruined by this tax, against which no
appeals were admitted. Resisters were, after arrest, deported or sentenced
to hard labor. The Turkish financial world was severely shaken.[25] In 1944,
İnönü suppressed student protest movements against his policies. Prominent figures were arrested and charged with 'plotting to overthrow the government'* and to bring Turkey into the war on Germany's side.[26]

Turkey was still underdeveloped: there were shortages of tractors and
paved roads; a mere handful of villages had electricity; barely a fraction of
the country's agricultural potential had been realized. Villagers resented the
increased state control, the increased taxation, and the symbols of state-im-
posed secularization. Wartime price controls destroyed their profits. In addition, while already poor and over-taxed, villagers were forced to build
schools, roads, and facilities for masters who often turned out to be aloof
mouthpieces of the hated regime. The military police violently suppressed
dissent. In the towns, the appalling economic conditions, censorship of the
press, and restrictions on personal freedom, fed a growing exasperation.
Even after signing the UN Charter,[27] Turkey prolonged martial law for
more than a year, press censorship remained heavy, and no labor union activity was tolerated. Anti-government sentiment grew accordingly: state
civil servants who had suffered heavily from inflation, and businessmen,
both Muslim and Christian, who had carried the burden of the capital tax,
united in opposition to the single-party authoritarianism.[28]

Four parliamentarians, Celal Bayar, Refik Koraltan, Fuad Köprülü, and
Adnan Menderes, formally requested that the constitutional guarantees of
democracy be implemented. Köprülü and Menderes published articles in the
press critical of the RPP. They and Koraltan were expelled from the party;
Bayar resigned his membership. Following domestic and external pressures,
İnönü in 1946 allowed the four dissidents to form the Democrat Party

---

* What is meant by 'the government' is the single-party establishment (including parliament
and government) identifying with and defending the regime. Whoever questioned or
opposed this establishment was perceived as and accused of 'overthrowing the state or
regime', a recurring theme in the history of the Turkish Republic.

(DP). The DP served as an umbrella under which all who mistrusted or opposed the RPP government sought refuge and voiced the resentments that had been building up over previous years.[29] Then, before the DP was able to organize fully, the RPP called early elections in May 1946, which it won.

However, the victorious RPP all but split in a tussle between its single-party statist and its reform-minded members. The RPP leader was forced to resign, and the party adopted a new development plan. Turkey joined the IMF (International Monetary Fund) and then implemented some economic and political corrective measures. The hated founder and head of the Village Institutes was relieved of his duties. The Education Department decided that religion could be taught in schools, and a Faculty of Divinity opened in Ankara in 1949. Under international pressure since signing the UN Charter, the RPP also relaxed its attitude toward popular Islam. Even so, in the 1950 elections, it won only 69 seats as against the DP's absolute majority of 408.[30]

It is during this period, in 1941, that Fethullah Gülen was born, in a village in Erzurum, eastern Anatolia. His parents took charge of his early education and religious instruction. There were few opportunities for a general secular education for ordinary Turkish people at this time. Gülen's parents sent him to the nearest state primary school for three years. However, because his father was assigned by the state to a post as preacher and imam in another town, one that had no secondary school, Gülen was unable to progress to secondary education. Although at this time mosques and congregational prayer were allowed, all other forms of religious instruction and practice were not. Even so, Gülen's parents, like many other ordinary Turkish people, kept up the Turkish Islamic tradition and made sure that their children learned the Qur'an and basic religious practices, including prayer. They avoided confrontation with the authorities and the regime, concealing the fact that they were providing elementary Islamic instruction to their own and their neighbors' children.[31]

2.2.5 Democrats, 1950–1960

In 1950 power passed from a single-party dictatorship to an elected democratic government. But then something happened that would recur in different guises to haunt Turkey right up to the present: top army officers offered to stage a coup d'état to suppress the elected government and restore İnönü to power. For fear of an international intervention, İnönü declined. The Democrat victory was received with jubilation; Bayar became the President, Menderes the Prime Minister.[32]

From 1948 to 1953, production, especially in the agricultural sector, GDP and economic growth, all boomed. More than 30,000 tractors were imported, which farmers could finance through credits; dams were built; cultivated land increased by more than fifty percent and total yields swelled; major cities were linked to a national highway system for the first time; the miles of paved highways quadrupled and improved feeder roads made it easier for thousands of newly imported trucks to get farm produce and goods to market. In these years the DP presided over a period of lower cost of living, increasing production and employment, tax reform, customs reforms, and support of private capital and foreign investment.[33]

Then, from 1954, overall economic growth slowed. The expansion had been financed with borrowed money and fuelled by splendid harvests. With low levels of hard currency, the country was left with large trade and balance of payments deficits. In 1955, import restrictions returned and foreign investors refused requests for new loans. The privatization program never got off the ground. The largest firms were still the SEEs. The government's building of cement plants, dams, and highways all at the same time was simply trying to do too much. In September, the attempt of Greek Cypriots to unite with Greece caused riots in Istanbul and Izmir. When thugs attacked Greek merchants, martial law was declared. Some of the media began to act the role of an opposition party. The government threatened to prosecute the publication of news that could 'curtail the supply of consumer goods or raise prices or cause loss of respect and confidence in the authorities'. Two daily newspapers were closed for doing just that.

The largest industrial conglomerates in today's Turkey[34] had their origins in this period. Mechanization of agriculture forced surplus laborers to migrate to the cities in search of work. Urban traders and businessmen accumulated enormous wealth and clamored for political leverage proportionate to their economic standing. The Confederated Trade Unions of Turkey also expressed the desire for greater political participation. As the DP identified with free enterprise and free expression of religious sentiment, it attracted many of the successful entrepreneurs and the conservative peasants. However, the rapid economic growth had had social consequences, in particular rousing political envy among those who felt threatened, that, in its enthusiasm for the boom, the government had failed to foresee.[35] The later years of the period were characterized by thugs, students and security forces fighting on the streets, with media galvanizing discontent on certain issues in favour of vested interests – recurrent motifs in the country's modern history.

Particularly ominous was the growing resentment of the established 'Republican' bureaucratic, military, and intellectual elites, whose laicist and statist assumptions about national life were being challenged by democratically oriented policies. The ostensible reason for the military officers' resentment was that their salaries did not keep up with inflation. In 1950 the DP government, wanting to purge the revolutionary core in the army general staff, discharged the top brass with ties to İnönü. Then in 1953, uncertain of the goodwill and potential neutrality of the university faculties, it prohibited university faculties from political activity by law. A 1954 law introduced an age limit which forced faculty members and some judiciary to retire – these were the Republican cadre, then over sixty, who had been in post for twenty-five years.

Democrats looked to thread a way between the pressures from constitutional secularism and their electoral base. In 1950, they ended the twenty-seven-year ban on religious broadcasting with twenty minutes per week of Qur'anic recitations on radio, and introduced religious teaching into the public school curriculum. More Imam-Hatip schools* were opened and the call to prayer (*adhan*) was once again made in Arabic. The unloved People's Houses and Village Institutes were closed.[36] Defaming Atatürk was made a criminal offence after a few busts of him were smashed. The courts found the recently organized Nation Party guilty of using religion for political purposes and dissolved it.

In spite of the DP's concessions to the secularists and statists, conditions became strained. The defenders of the status quo in Turkey (who will come up again in the later parts of this narrative) counter-mobilized against

---

* These are, despite the name, secular state schools, entirely within the national secular educational system. The cost of their construction has never been met by the Turkish state but through donations by ordinary people, who then handed them over to the Ministry of Education. The schools follow the national curriculum with extra basic courses on Islam for the training of preachers and Qur'an teachers by state trained, assigned and paid teachers.

the elected government and civil society. Citing the economic downturn, displeased businessmen and academics withdrew their support for the DP. A dean at Ankara University delivered a 'political lecture' and was dismissed; students were mobilized for protests; some academics resigned. From 1955 onwards, officers in the armed forces began noticeably to conspire against the government.[37]

Discontent in the military stemmed from complicated social roots. Since the end of World War II, the prestige of a military career in Turkey had slowly declined. Democratization had marginalized those accustomed to playing a central role in the country's affairs. A small number of officers within the army formed a kind of oppositional, reactionary movement against the elected government, incorporating revolutionary ideology into the training of cadets and junior officers. Menderes, wary of the influence of the officers and İnönü, made a military reformer his minister of defense, but opponents among the military top ranks managed to have him dismissed. After that, Menderes ingratiated himself with the generals, but he was ill-informed about the junior officers frustrated by the hierarchy of the officer corps and hungry for economic and political power. After Turkey joined NATO in 1952, those officers started to receive advanced training in Europe and the US, and to interact with the American and NATO officials based in Turkey after 1955. They complained about 'purchasing power' and 'standards of living' in Turkey. In the 1957 elections, the DP, despite taking almost 48 percent of the vote, lost its majority. The RPP meanwhile found new support among intellectuals and businessmen defecting from the DP. Two months later, nine junior army officers were arrested for plotting a coup.[38]

Through 1958–59, the DP government implemented some economic measures, rescheduled its debt, and received further loans from the US, OEEC (Organization for European Economic Co-operation), and IMF. In 1959, it applied for membership in the European Economic Community (EEC). A partial recovery began. However, discontent among state servants and the elite persisted. The RPP went on the offensive. İnönü's tour of Anatolia became the occasion for outbreaks of violence along his route. Menderes ordered troops to interrupt the tour by İnönü in 1960, but İnönü called their bluff and embarrassed the troops into backing down. Student protests and riots started in April. On one occasion, police opened fire, killed five and injured some more. Under their top officers' direction, cadets from the military academy staged a protest march against the government but in solidarity with the oppositional student movement. Some elements of the armed forces openly displayed their opposition to the elected civilian authorities. Martial law was declared. On May 14, crowds demonstrated in the streets. On May 25, Parliamentarians fought within Parliament leaving fifteen injured. On May 27, the armed forces took over the state.[39]

During this decade (1950–60) Fethullah Gülen completed his religious education and training under various prominent scholars and Sufi masters leading to the traditional Islamic ijaza (license to teach). This education was provided almost entirely within an informal system, tacitly ignored and unsupported by the state and running parallel to its education system. At the same time, Gülen pursued and completed his secondary level secular education through external exams. In the late fifties, he came across compilations of the scholarly work Risale-i Nur (Epistles of Light) by Said Nursi but never met its famous author. In 1958–9, he sat for and passed the state exam to become an imam and preacher. On the basis of the exam result he was assigned by the state to the very prestigious posting in Edirne.[40]

Throughout this service he maintained his personal life style of devout asceticism while mixing with people and remaining on good terms with the civic and military authorities he encountered in the course of that service. He witnessed how the youth were being attracted into extremist, radical ideologies, and strove through his preaching to draw them away from that. Using his own money he would buy and distribute published materials to counter an aggressively militant atheism and communism. He saw the erosion of traditional moral values among the youth and the educated sector of Turkish society feeding into criminality and political and societal conflict. These experiences were formative influences on his intellectual and community leadership and reinforced his faith in the meaning and value of human beings and life.[41]

2.2.6 Military coup d'état

Some circles in Ankara and Istanbul welcomed the military coup; much of the general public accepted it with sullen resignation. Declarations of non-partisan objectives notwithstanding, the military's actions confirmed the general perception that the coup was an intervention against the DP government on behalf of the RPP. The DP was denounced as an instrument of 'class interests' aligned with 'forces opposed to the secularist principles of Atatürk's revolution'. DP Parliamentarians were arrested and the party closed down.[42]

Calling itself the National Unity Committee (NUC), a junta of 38 junior officers exercised sovereignty and declared a commitment to the writing of a new constitution under which Parliament would resume its role. General Cemal Gürsel, nominal leader and chairman of the NUC, became President, Prime Minister, and Commander-in-Chief. The NUC grouped into three factions, which from the outset disagreed about aims and principles. One faction comprised old school generals (pashas) who wanted to restore civil order and civilian rule. The second faction, more interested in social and economic development, wanted a planned economy led by SEEs and to hand power to İnönü and the RPP. The third faction, made up of younger officers and communitarian radicals, advocated indefinite military rule in order to effect fundamental political and social change from above, a sort of non-party nationalist populism on the pattern of Nasser's Egypt.[43]

The power struggle among these factions continued until the pashas dissolved the NUC and formed a new NUC, exiling fourteen radical junior officers to Turkish embassies abroad. The pashas only later realized how far the radicals had disseminated revolutionary views among the junior officer corps. They purged some of those, but sub-groups reformed, conspiring to seize control and overhaul the whole political and social system. Aware of the continued danger and wanting to prevent their 'economic marginalization', senior officers formed OYAK and the AFU. OYAK was a pension fund for retired officers financed by obligatory salary contributions; it developed very quickly into a powerful conglomerate with vast holdings.[44] AFU (Armed Forces Union) was set up to provide a forum for discussing issues of concern under the supervision of the top ranks: the pashas intended to gain control over the junior officers and to ensure there would never be another military rebellion that they themselves did not lead and direct.

Meanwhile, those who favored a return to a single-party system deadlocked the Constitutional Commission. After a purge, the Commission eventually produced a document. However, a rival group of professors submitted another draft and convinced the NUC to appoint an assembly made up of the NUC and 'some' politicians. The compromise constitution, written by two professors, passed in a deeply divided referendum in 1961.[45]

The constitution brought significant structural changes to society and government. It established a bicameral legislature. The upper chamber Senate was directly elected for six-year terms, but members of the NUC and former presidents of Turkey became lifetime senators and fifteen others were appointed by the president. The lower chamber was popularly elected by proportional representation. Legislation had to pass both chambers. The national budget was reviewed by a joint commission of the two chambers. A Constitutional Court (CC) was established, fifteen members of which were drawn from the judiciary, parliament, law faculties, and presidential appointments. The CC reviewed laws and orders of Parliament at the request of individuals or political parties.* The president of Turkey would be elected by Parliament, from among its own members, for a single term of seven years. His office maintained a certain independence from the legislature. The constitution guaranteed freedom of thought, expression, and association, which the 1924 constitution had not included. Freedom of the press was limited only by the need to 'safeguard national security'. The state had the power to plan economic and cultural development advised by the State Planning Organization. The National Security Council (NSC) was institutionalized by law, chaired by the President and made up of the chief of the general staff, heads of the service branches, the prime minister, and ministers of relevant cabinet ministries.[46] The NSC would advise government on matters of domestic and foreign security. Through its general secretariat and various departments, the NSC was gradually to develop into a decisive political force, as ever greater portions of political, social, and economic life came under the rubric of 'matters of national security'.[47]

The coup was a grave error, set a bad example to the rest of the military cadre about ignoring the military hierarchy, and also aroused their ambitions for the successive military interventions in Turkish domestic politics, especially in 1971 and in 1980, which halted the democratization pro-

---

* The chief editor of the *Turkish Daily News* Ilnur Çevik maintains: 'For quite some time the Constitutional Court, the supreme judicial body of Turkey, was regarded as a tool of the conservative establishment, which rejected reforms and did its best to maintain the current order, where our country has been reduced to a semi-democracy with a rather dismal human rights record.' (Çevik, 1999a).

cess so that Turkey lost valuable time in its economic as well as democratic modernization.[48]

2.2.7 After the executions: 1961–1970

Hundreds of DP deputies were tried on charges of corruption and high treason. The trials and executions of DP leaders during the national elections of 1961 made obvious the junta's true political ambitions. Partly in response to public appeals for clemency, the sentences of eleven of the fifteen condemned to death were commuted to life imprisonment. The former president was spared on account of his advanced age and ill health. Prime Minister Adnan Menderes and the Foreign Minister Fatin Rüstü Zorlu, and Finance Minister Hasan Polatkan were hanged in September.[49]

In the general elections held a month later, İnönü's RPP won 73 seats. The core of the DP reformed as the Justice Party (JP) was only three seats short of a majority in the lower chamber. Cemal Gürsel, the coup leader, became President. The election results[50] could well be interpreted as a repudiation of the new regime and its constitution. Political instability marked the next several years, as a series of short-lived coalition governments headed by İnönü, with the support of the army, tried to implement the constitution. In late 1961, workers began demonstrating in the streets demanding their right to strike. Junior officers, determined to prevent a new Democrat take-over, plotted a coup in February 1962 under Colonel Talat Aydemir. Aydemir, a key conspirator in the 1950s, had been unable to participate in the coup due to his posting in Korea. This time he took part and was arrested. Circumstances forced the JP and RPP into a brief coalition until May. When it collapsed, İnönü formed another coalition that, thanks to concessions, managed to last more than a year. Meanwhile, a second coup attempt by Colonel Aydemir was thwarted, and he was executed in May 1963. Local elections in 1963 made it clear that the governed no longer gave consent to the RPP. İnönü resigned. The winning JP, however, failed to form a new government. Once again, İnönü managed a coalition with the independents, which survived for fourteen months, thanks largely to the Cyprus crisis preoccupying everyone throughout 1964. In February 1965, the budget vote brought down the government, and the country limped to elections in October.[51]

Social and economic goals of public policy were never achieved because vocal opponents to development planning were in the cabinet after the first coalition. For instance, the cabinet rejected proposed reforms for land, agriculture, tax, and SEEs. The State Planning Organization advisors were forced to resign. The government's lack of political commitment to its work, the increasing politicization of appointments and its partisan protection of vested interests, instead of those of the whole nation, weakened state institutions.[52]

In 1965, Süleyman Demirel's JP won the elections with an outright majority. Demirel assured the generals that he would follow a program independent of the old Democrats. He reconciled with the military, granting them complete autonomy in military affairs and the defense budget. However, the irregular economic growth of the 1960s gradually alienated his lower middle class constituency. The JP began to fragment, some following Colonel Alparslan Türkeş into nationalism, others following Necmettin Erbakan into religious pietism. Türkeş, a key figure of the 1960 junta, had returned from exile abroad in 1963, retired and later took over the chairmanship of the Republican Peasants' National Party[53] (RPNP). Under his direction the RPNP adopted a radically nationalist tone. Erbakan formed the National Order Party (NOP) in 1970, the first of a series of political Islamist parties in Turkey.[54] He gained a reputation as a maverick for freely airing intemperate remarks and advocating a role for Islam in public and political life.

In the 1960s, the RPP argued with the same old rhetoric that Demirel's policies had forsaken the principles of Atatürk* and would ruin the peasant and worker. Bülent Ecevit, who had been the Minister of Labor in the three RPP-led coalitions till 1965, asked the RPP to shed its elitist image and trust the common people to know what was best for them. Some deputies did not like his suggestions and left the party. However, Ecevit had understood that the voters had supported Menderes and later Demirel because they felt alienated by the RPP's arrogance and because the other parties' programs were better.[55]

By 1970, Turkey faced a mounting crisis whose origins lay generally in deteriorating economic conditions, the massive social changes since the 1950s, a loss of confidence in the State, and the circumstances of the Cold

---

* This remains the gravest accusation in Turkish politics against any person or group considered a symbolic or direct political challenge to the protectionist vested interests in the establishment. It is highly significant that, at rather predictable junctures in events, this accusation has also been directed against the country's prime ministers and presidents.

War. On the other hand, there were some successes in Turkish-foreign joint ventures: an oil-pipeline, a dam, two irrigation projects, and associate membership of the EEC. By the end of the decade, the state monopolies, the publicly owned banks, and the recently founded OYAK had become fairly successful and sizeable enterprises. Mechanization pushed labor to western Europe: the migrants' cash remittances from Europe were Turkey's most important source of foreign exchange.[56]

In 1967 leftists formed the Confederation of Revolutionary Workers' Unions (DISK). Its president was Kemal Türkler, a founding member of the (communist) Turkish Workers' Party (TWP). DISK was anti-capitalist and politically radical activist, encouraging street demonstrations and strikes to achieve its objectives. Proportional representation brought such small parties into Parliament, with the result that public life became increasingly influenced by the activities of small extremist groups of the left and right. Throughout the late 1960s and 1970s, they exerted an influence on politics beyond their numbers. The milieu in universities enabled leftists to form on-campus 'idea clubs' with agendas anticipating the imminent radical transformation of society. Spreading outward from the universities, politicization and polarization increasingly infected public life. National dailies, language, music, art, and festivals came to be known as leftist or rightist; people could be identified on the political spectrum by the vocabulary they used in everyday speech.[57]

One of the most notorious extremist groups that emerged in this period was Revolutionary Youth (*Dev-Genç*). It grew out of an effort to link the 'idea clubs' at universities nationally under Marxist leadership. It advocated the violent overthrow of the state. The left in general stressed opposition to imperialism, to the West, and to American bases. Americans and their interests represented, to the leftists, subservience to international capitalism and militarism in Turkey. The correspondence in 1964 between American President Johnson and then Prime Minister İnönü, published in 1966, in which Johnson threatened not to back Turkey in the event of a Soviet attack, turned public opinion dramatically against the US. For leftists, the letter confirmed that the US had no real interest in Turkey beyond a cold calculation of its place in the international power balance.[58] They accused Demirel and the JP of being 'American stooges'. Demirel announced a government and police crackdown on 'communists.'

The leftists were also targeted by the right, which, in general, coalesced around a common anti-communism, in many (but not all) cases, advocating conservative Islamic piety and values as normative for Turkish society. A large portion of the Turkish populace was indeed socially and religiously conservative – a fact not lost on Demirel, who was not above occasionally manipulating traditional Islamic social values or fears of the Soviets for political purposes. More virulent forms of nationalism and anti-communism became evident in the late 1960s. There was sporadic anti-American violence: in 1966, rioters attacked the US consulate, the office of the US Information Agency and the Red Cross; increasingly violent demonstrations accompanied the visit of the US Sixth Fleet; the US Information Agency in Ankara was bombed. Leftist and rightist groups both took part in demonstrations that turned increasingly violent in late 1967.[59]

In 1968, leftist students seized the buildings at Ankara University demanding abolition of the examination system and fee structure. In May 1969, a rector and eleven deans protested against the government and resigned. In August, demonstrators belonging to the leftist unions occupied the Eregli Iron-Steel plant. Riot police were unable to evict them. Airport employees went on strike in September. Fighting took place all over the country during the elections in October. The JP maintained a shaky Parliamentary majority. The RPP was still in its identity crisis. Six other parties entered Parliament, though none won even seven percent of the popular vote. Then, in 1970, because of economic problems, unpopular corrective measures and a three-month-late budget, JP dissidents forced Demirel to resign.[60]

In 1961, Fethullah Gülen began his compulsory military service in Ankara. By chance he was in the military unit commanded by Talat Aydemir. However, not being a professional soldier, Gülen had no contact with Aydemir himself or with the military cadets and high-ranking officers who took part in the conspiracy. On the day of the coup, he and his fellow troopers were confined to barracks and thus only witnessed the coup and its aftermath through radio announcements and briefings from officers. After the coup, Gülen was sent to Iskenderun, where he would do the second posting that completes compulsory military service. Here, his commanding officer assigned to him the duty of lecturing soldiers on faith and morality, and, recognizing Gülen's intellectual ability, gave him many Western classics to read. Throughout his military service Gülen maintained his ascetic lifestyle as before.[61]

In 1963, following military service, Gülen gave a series of lectures in Erzurum on Rumi. He also co-founded an anti-communist association there, in which he gave evening talks on moral issues.[62]

In 1964, he was assigned a new post in Edirne, where he became very influential among the educated youth and ordinary people. The militantly laicist authorities were displeased by his having such influence and wanted him dismissed. Before they could do so, Gülen obliged them by having himself assigned to another city, Kırklareli, in 1965. There, after working hours, he organized evening lectures and talks. In this phase of his career, just as before, he took no active part in party politics and taught only about moral values in personal and collective affairs.[63]

In 1966, Yaşar Tunagür, who had known Gülen from earlier in his career, became deputy head of the country's Presidency of Religious Affairs and, on assuming his position in Ankara, he assigned Gülen to the post that he himself had just vacated in Izmir. On March 11, Gülen was transferred to the Izmir region, where he held managerial responsibility for a mosque, a student study and boarding-hall, and for preaching in the Aegean region. He continued to live ascetically. For almost five years he lived in a small hut near the Kestanepazarı Hall and took no wages for his services. It was during these years that Gülen's ideas on education and service to the community began to take definite form and mature. From 1969 he set up meetings in coffee-houses, lecturing all around the provinces and in the villages of the region. He also organized summer camps for middle and high school students.[64]

In 1970, as a result of the March 12 coup, a number of prominent Muslims in the region, who had supported Kestanepazarı Hall and associated activities for the region's youth, were arrested. On May 1, Gülen too was arrested and held for six months without charge until his release on November 9. Later, all the others arrested were also released, also without charge. When asked to explain these arrests, the authorities said that they had arrested so many leftists that they felt they needed to arrest some prominent Muslims in order to avoid being accused of unfairness.[65] Interestingly, they released Gülen on the condition that he gave no more public lectures.

In 1971, Gülen left his post and Kestanepazarı Hall but retained his status as a state-authorized preacher. He began setting up more student study *and boarding-halls in the Aegean region: the funding for these came from lo-cal people. It is at this point that a particular group of about one hundred people began to be visible as a service group, that is, a group gathered around Gülen's understanding of service to the community and positive action.*

2.2.8 Military coup II

Civil unrest and radicalization continued to grow in the 1970s. DISK orga-nized a general strike in the spring. In August, ominous news of a shake-up leaked from the General Staff. In December, students clashed at Ankara University. The Labor Party headquarters and Demirel's car were bombed. In February 1971, more than 200 extreme-leftist students were arrested af-ter a five-hour gun battle with the military police at Hacettepe University in Ankara. On March 4, leftist students kidnapped four American soldiers and held them for ransom. A battle ensued when police searched for the soldiers at a dormitory in Ankara University; two students died before the Americans were released. On 12 March 1971, the military seized control of the state, citing the crisis in Parliament, the incompetence of the govern-ment, and street and campus clashes between communists and ultra-nation-alists, and between leftist trade unionists and the security forces.[66] This was a sad repetition of their previous seizure of power (in 1961) and the same themes recurred in their discourse to justify their action.

The generals said they had acted to prevent another coup by junior of-ficers rather than because they had a specific program to lead the country out of its difficulties. Publicly blaming the political parties for the crisis, they selected a government that would implement the 1961 constitutional reforms. Under martial law, the military arrested thousands – party and union leaders, academics and writers; also they closed down Erbakan's par-ty, as well as several mainstream newspapers and journals. The National In-telligence Organization used severe repression, including torture, to extract confessions from suspects. The cabinet made no progress and was forced to resign. Constitutional amendments scaled back civil liberties, freedom of the press, and the autonomy of the Constitutional Court. Universities and the broadcast media lost their autonomy to supervisory committees. The National Security Council 'advice' to Parliament became binding. A system of State Security Courts (SSCs)[67] was introduced that, in the following years, would try hundreds of cases under the rubric of national security.[68]

Bülent Ecevit succeeded İsmet İnönü as the RPP chair. Erbakan put together a new party with much the same leadership and called it the National Salvation Party (NSP). Elections were held in 1973. Though they had very little in common, the RPP and NSP formed a coalition, the first of several that would govern Turkey with diminishing levels of success till 1980.

In Cyprus in July 1974, Greek Cypriot guerrillas, fighting for union with Greece, overthrew the Cypriot President in a coup and replaced him with a guerrilla leader. Killings began. Turkish troops landed in northern Cyprus to protect the Turkish-Cypriots and secured one-third of the island. There the Turkish-Cypriots organized what later, in 1983, became the Turkish Republic of Northern Cyprus (TRNC). Turkey paid a high price for this move: the substantial cost of assistance to TRNC; a 50 percent increase in its defense budget; diplomatic isolation and damage to its standing in the EC. Further, the US cut off assistance and imposed an embargo, which contributed to Turkey's grave economic position in the late 1970s. In 1976, Turkey signed a new four-year defense agreement with the US, but the US Congress did not approve it due to Greek and Armenian lobbying.[69]

Between 1972 and 1975, Gülen held posts as a preacher in several cities in the Aegean and Marmara regions, where he continued to preach and to teach the ideas about education and the service ethic he had developed. He continued setting up hostels for high school and university students. At this time educational opportunities were still scarce for ordinary Anatolian people, and most student accommodation in the major cities, controlled or infiltrated by extreme leftists and rightists, seethed in a hyper-politicized atmosphere. Parents in provincial towns whose children had passed entrance examinations for universities or city high schools were caught in a dilemma – to surrender their children's care to the ideologues or to deny them further education and keep them at home.

The hostels set up by Gülen and his companions offered parents the chance to send their children to the big cities to continue their secular education, while protecting them from the hyper-politicized environment. To support these educational efforts, people who shared Gülen's service-ethic now set up a system of bursaries for students. The funding for the hostels and bursaries came entirely from local communities among whom Gülen's service-ethic idea (hizmet) was spreading steadily.

With Gülen's encouragement, around his discourse of positive action and responsibility, ordinary people were starting to mobilize to counteract the effects of violent ideologies and of the ensuing social and political disorder on their own children and on youth in general. Students in the hostels also began to play a part in spreading the discourse of service and positive action. Periodically, they returned to their home towns and visited surrounding towns and villages, and, talking of their experiences and the ideas they had encountered, consciously diffused the hizmet idea in the region. Also, from 1966 onward, Gülen's talks and lectures had been recorded on audio cassettes and distributed throughout Turkey by third parties. Thus, through already existing networks of primary relations, this new type of community action, the students' activities, and the new technology of communication, the hizmet discourse was becoming known nation-wide.

In 1974, the first university preparatory courses were established in Manisa, where Gülen was posted at the time. Until then, it was largely the children of very wealthy and privileged families who had access to university education. The new courses in Manisa offered the hope that in future there might be better opportunities for children from ordinary Anatolian families. The idea took hold that, if properly supported, the children of ordinary families could take up and succeed in higher education.

As word spread of these achievements, Gülen was invited, the following year, to speak at a series of lectures all over Turkey. The service idea became widely recognized and firmly rooted in various cities and regions of the country. From this time on, the country-wide mobilization of people drawn to support education and non-political altruistic services can be called a movement – the Gülen Movement.

2.2.9 Collapse of public order

Ecevit resigned in 1974 in order to call elections that he thought, after the Cyprus action, his RPP could win. However, leaders of the other parties did not allow an election to be called. Ecevit's move brought governmental impasse until late 1980. A series of unstable coalitions followed, none of which possessed the strength to manage the economic problems, or control the political violence.[70]

Some enterprises that had taken advantage of foreign capital during the 1950s had grown tremendously in the 1960s. To maintain their position and leading role, and to lobby the government for support, in 1971, owners of the 114 largest firms formed the Association of Turkish Industrialists (TU-SIAD). However, the quadrupling of oil prices in 1973 raised the cost of the imports Turkey depended on and consumed about two-thirds of Turkey's foreign currency income. Inflation and unemployment climbed steadily after 1977. By 1978–79, there were even shortages of basic commodities.[71]

After the 1971 coup, the crackdown on radical leftists by the security forces started a spiral of attacks and retaliations to which there seemed to be no resolution. With Alparslan Türkeş's appointment as a minister of state from 1974 to 1977, the violent campaign of radical groups against all who disagreed with them escalated and contributed substantially to the collapse of public order by 1980. A 1977 May Day celebration by the leftist unions turned into a battle among themselves and with the police, leaving 39 dead and more than 200 wounded. Leftists retaliated with a wave of bombings, killing several people at the airport and railway stations. A state of virtual war prevailed between DISK,* the Turkish Workers' Party and other leftist groups on the one hand, and the Istanbul police force on the other. Clashes between rightist groups and leftists[72] killed 112 and wounded thousands in Sivas and Kahramanmaras. Ecevit declared martial law.[73]

Violence was at a peak on university campuses. In 1974–75, students disrupted classes, rioted and killed one another, forced the temporary closure of universities, waged battles, and carried out killings and bombings at off-campus venues frequented by students. Academics were beaten and murdered. At Ankara University in 1978, a leftist student, Abdullah Öcalan, formed the Kurdish Workers' Party (PKK) and began a separatist war in the south-eastern provinces. Americans and NATO personnel were targeted and murdered by the leftists. Although banned, May Day demonstrations organized by leftist labor continued. Clashes between rightists and leftists increased. Members of the security forces, journalists, party officials, labor union leaders, and ministers were murdered; strikes went on for weeks and months.

The divided government, meanwhile, did not take up an austerity plan suggested by Demirel's economic advisor Turgut Özal. In February, Fahri Korutürk's presidential term expired: for six months Parliament was unable to elect a successor. The economy was in tatters, with inflation running at

---

* The Confederation of Revolutionary Workers' Unions.

130 percent and unemployment 20 percent. Murderous confrontations between the radicals had taken 5,241 lives in two years. Erbakan's fundamentalist meetings in Konya stirred up the military. And again, for the third time in twenty years, on September 12, 1980, the military seized direct control of the state. Their discourse framed their action in exactly the same way as in the two previous coups.[74]

The constitution after the 1961 coup had restructured Turkish government and institutions in such a way that it caused the political system to fail. Personal and political liberties were not implemented, nor reforms to land, tax and the SEEs. The system crashed in insurmountable difficulties. Due to inability, or unwillingness, to revise the prevailing political culture for the needs of an open society, together with the consequences of economic crisis, deep fissures opened in society between those who had benefited from the rapid and haphazard social and economic development since 1945 and those who found themselves victims of the inflation, unemployment, and urban migration it engendered. There were those who had benefited from multiparty democracy through their links of patronage with powerful officials, and those who still lived with the residue of the one-party era with its authoritarian model of leadership, the equation of dissent with disloyalty, and party control of state offices. Turkey's standing in the Cold War contributed to the polarization of society and was also exploited to mask the sources of its problems, and made it impossible to achieve the political consensus necessary to adopt reforms. A major source of the political and social degeneration of the 1960s and the chaos and anarchy of the 1970s was the radical tendencies of students, militants, academics, unions, and officers of the state security apparatuses. Finally, the armed forces, which Parliament had failed to subordinate to civilian rule, put an end to that rule, which the armed forces had themselves established a mere ten years earlier.[75]

In 1976, the Religious Directorate posted Gülen to Bornova, Izmir, the site of one of Turkey's major universities with a correspondingly large student population and a great deal of the militant activism typical of universities in the 1970s.

It came to his attention that leftist groups were running protection rackets to extort money from small businessmen and shopkeepers in the city and deliberately disrupting the business and social life of the community. The racketeers had already murdered a number of their victims. In his sermons, Gülen spoke out and urged those being threatened by the rackets neither to yield to threats and violence, nor to react with violence and exacerbate the situation. He urged them, instead, to report the crimes to the police and have the racketeers dealt with through the proper channels. This message led to threats being made against his life.

At the same time, he challenged the students of left and right to come to the mosque and discuss their ideas with him and offered to answer any questions, whether secular or religious, which they put to him. A great many students took up this offer. So, in addition to his daily duties giving traditional religious instruction and preaching, Gülen devoted every Sunday evening to these discussion sessions.

In 1977, he traveled in northern Europe, visiting and preaching among Turkish communities to raise their consciousness about values and education and to encourage them in the same hizmet ethic of positive action and altruistic service. He encouraged them both to preserve their cultural and religious values and to integrate into their host societies.[76]

Now thirty-six, Gülen had become one of the three most widely recognized and influential preachers in Turkey. For example, on one occasion in 1977 when the prime minister, other ministers and state dignitaries came to a Friday prayer in the Blue Mosque in Istanbul, a politically sensitive occasion in Turkey, Gülen was invited to preach to them and the rest of the congregation.[77]

Gülen encouraged participants in the Movement to go into publishing. Some of his articles and lectures were published as anthologies and a group of teachers inspired by his ideas established the Teachers' Foundation to support education and students.[78]

In 1979, this Foundation started to publish its own monthly journal, Sızıntı, which became the highest selling monthly in Turkey. In terms of genre, it was a pioneering venture, being a magazine of sciences, humanities, faith, and literature. Its publishing mission was to show that science and religion were not incompatible and that knowledge of both was necessary to be successful in this life. Each month since the journal was founded, Gülen has written for it an editorial and a section about the spiritual or inner aspects of Islam, that is, Sufism, and the meaning of faith in modern life.[79]

In February 1980, a series of Gülen's lectures, attended by thousands of people, in which he preached against violence, anarchy and terror, were made available on audio cassette.

2.2.10 Military coup III

In September 1980, the military arrested and placed the prime minister, party leaders and 100 parliamentarians in custody. It dissolved Parliament, suspended the constitution, banned all political activity, dissolved and permanently outlawed all political parties, forbade their leaders to speak about politics – past, present or future – and seized, and subsequently caused to disappear, the archives of the parties of the past thirty years. Martial law was extended to all Turkey. Several thousand were arrested in the first week. The junta wanted in this way to signal its determination to institute a new political order.[80]

The coup leaders, the five commanders of the armed forces, formed the National Security Council (NSC) and gave themselves indefinite and unlimited power. General Kenan Evren became head of state and appointed a cabinet composed mostly of retired officers and state bureaucrats. Martial law commanders in all the provinces were given broad administrative authority over public affairs, including education, the press and economic activities. Return to civilian rule would follow fundamental revision of the political order. In the meantime, the 1961 constitution, where it did not contradict the provisions of martial law, would remain in effect until replaced.[81]

Evren said the country had passed through a national crisis, and separatist forces and enemies, within and without, threatened its integrity; that Kemalism had been forgotten and the country left leaderless; and that the junta would correct this and enforce a new commitment to Kemalism, with Evren providing the necessary national leadership. Much of the country viewed the coup with relief, expecting that near civil war conditions would soon end. Indeed the rightist–leftist street clashes ended immediately. However, within months, the army opened a new front against Kurdish separatists, which gradually escalated by 1983, and it also suppressed Islamic political activism.[82]

Turgut Özal was retained in the post-coup cabinet as Deputy Prime Minister and Minister for Economic Affairs. They decided to continue the economic policy he had planned under the former government. Özal negotiated with the IMF, World Bank, and EU. They released new credits and rescheduled former and more new debts. In this way, the state began a transition from an economy directed from above to an economy open to integration with world capitalism.[83]

2.2.11 New 'order'

The military regime forbade all strikes and union activities and disbanded the labor federations, imposed a strict curfew, and arrested more than 100,000 within eight months. Martial law authorities attempted to be even-handed, arresting the rightist and religious as well as leftist members. Several newspapers were closed for publishing articles critical of the regime. By 1983, about 2000 prisoners had faced the death penalty*. The trial of extreme rightist Mehmet Ali Ağca, who had tried to assassinate the Pope in 1981, revealed the extent of interactions between extremist groups and organized crime within Turkey and abroad.[84]

Universities were placed under the supervision of a newly created Council of Higher Education (YÖK).[85] The junta held the power directly to appoint university rectors and deans, and purged hundreds of university faculty. Over the 1980s, the number of universities rose from 19 to 29. The right of university admission was broadened, effectively diluting the power of the old university faculties and the traditional elite classes, whose children made up the student bodies. In 1981, the centenary of Atatürk's birth, the state arranged conferences, volumes of publications and the naming of numerous facilities and institutions – even a university – to commemorate 'The Centenary'. Evren's face next to Atatürk's on banners and in public ceremonies linked him and his military regime to Atatürk and Atatürk's regime.[86]

In the autumn of 1981, the generals nominated the members of a consultative assembly, directly appointed by the NSC and martial law governors, to draft a new constitution. Its mandate was to purge the country of the effects of the 1960 coup, including the 1961 constitution, which was partly blamed for the fragmentation and polarization of Parliament, the judiciary, bureaucracy, and universities, for needlessly politicizing all public

---

* Of these fifty were eventually executed and the rest, though spared the death penalty by later civilian governments, served life-sentences.

life, and for breeding the violence of the late 1970s. An annual holiday com-memorating the 1960 coup was abolished.[87]

The new constitution was approved by referendum in 1982. While rec-ognizing most civil and political rights, it laid heavy emphasis on the protec-tion of the indivisible integrity of the state and national security, extended a measure of impunity for the extensive use of force during riots, martial law or a state of emergency, strengthened the presidency, and formalized the role of the military leadership. The president was charged with ensuring 'the implementation of the constitution' and 'functioning of the state organs' and would become the guardian of the state, serving a single seven-year term with potentially wide powers. He would appoint the cabinet, the Constitu-tional Court, the military Court of Cassation, the Supreme Council of Judg-es and Prosecutors, and the High Court of Appeals. He would chair the Na-tional Security Council (NSC), now made a permanent body with the right to submit its views on state security to the Council of Ministers, who were required to give priority to the NSC's views. Parliament again became a uni-cameral legislature. Any party short of ten percent of the national vote would not receive parliamentary representation. A new discretionary fund was cre-ated and put at the personal disposal of the prime minister, outside of the parliamentary budgetary process. Restrictions were placed on the press and labor unions. The State Security Court would rule on strikes, lockouts, and collective bargaining disputes. The government lost its mandate to restrict private enterprise. By a 'temporary article' appended by the NSC, General Evren became President, without being elected.[88]

The NSC forbade more than 700 former parliamentarians and party leaders from participating in politics for the next ten years. It shut down several newspapers for some time for failing to observe severe restrictions on political articles. Due to the brokerage firm and bank crisis in 1982, Özal left the cabinet. In 1983, the NSC permitted the formation of new political parties. Some new parties that looked like reincarnations of the old parties or were directed from behind the scenes by former leaders were barred from the elections and closed down. The NSC approved three par-ties: the Nationalist Democracy Party (NDP), led by a retired general, the Populist Party, headed by a former private secretary of İsmet İnönü, and the Motherland Party (MP), formed by Turgut Özal.[89]

President Evren did not hide his dislike of Özal but this only made his party an early favorite with a public very tired of the military. Evren's stated preference for the NDP probably condemned it to a third-place finish. The MP won 45 percent of the vote and an absolute majority in Parliament.[90]

In 1980, on September 5, Gülen spoke from the pulpit before taking leave of absence for the next twenty days because of illness. On September 12, the day of the military coup, his home was raided. He was not detained as he was not at home. He requested another leave of absence for 45 days. Then the house where he was staying as a guest was raided and he was detained. After a six-hour interrogation, he was released. On November 25, he was transferred to Çanakkale but, due to illness again, he was not able to serve there. From March 20, 1981, he took indefinite leave of absence.[91]

By the third coup, the Turkish public appeared to have learnt a lesson. There was no visible public reaction. The faith communities, including the Gülen Movement, continued with their lawful and peaceful activities without drawing any extra attention to themselves. Gülen and the Movement avoided large public gatherings but continued to promote the service-ethic through publishing and small meetings. At this point, the Movement turned again to the use of technology and for the first time in Turkey a preacher's talks were recorded and distributed on videotape.

In the years immediately following the coup, the Movement continued to grow and act successfully. In 1982, Movement participants set up a private high school in Izmir, Yamanlar Koleji.

2.2.12 The Özal years

For the decade before his death in 1993, Özal dominated Turkish politics. He set his sights on a fundamental shift in the direction of economic policy, to encourage exports and force Turkish products into a competitive position in the world market. His policy instruments were: high interest rates to combat inflation, gradual privatization of inefficient SEEs, wage controls, and an end to state industrial subsidies. Through the mid-1980s, the economy grew steadily: whereas in 1979, 60 percent of exports were agricultural products, by 1988 80 percent were manufactures; the annual inflation rate was lower than it had been; and the government completed large-scale infrastructural development projects.[92] Privatization proceeded very slowly, although the government was successful in breaking up state monopolies. The size of the bureaucracy was still considerable.[93] Major cities grew as industry drew agricultural labor off the land. Economic liberalization rapidly benefited the largest industrial holding companies and some SEEs.[94]

Having a clear-cut economic policy, and executing it with relative consistency, Özal skillfully managed the bureaucrats and the economy.[95]

By mid-1985 Özal was determinedly pursuing political liberalization as well. Martial law had been lifted in fifty of sixty-seven provinces. Eight provinces in the southeast remained under a state of emergency, and anti-terrorism measures stayed in place throughout the country. Turkey's application for the full EEC membership that Özal championed was rejected in 1987. Economic liberalization did not automatically bring political liberalization with it. Özal succeeded in introducing new faces to political life in Turkey, but he was not allowed to normalize it completely or to exert civilian control over the military. By referendum, he let the former leaders of the former parties return to politics and called early elections for 1987. His Motherland Party won an absolute majority, 292 of the 450 seats; İnönü's Social Democrat Party[96] came in with 99 seats. Demirel's True Path Party took 59 seats. No other party, including Ecevit's or Erbakan's, reached the threshold.[97]

An aspect of Özal's liberalization was his encouragement of a role for Islam in public life. Özal understood that Islam was the source of the belief system and values of most Turkish citizens, and that it was excluded from the public sphere only with increasing awkwardness and artificiality. He said in 1986: 'restrictions on freedom of conscience breed fanaticism, not the other way around.'[98]

In 1984, seeking to recruit religious sentiment against the influence of communism, the military regime required compulsory instruction in Islam in all schools. Picking up an initiative of the Menderes government, the regime sanctioned construction of 34 public Imam-Hatip training schools in one year.[99] Özal's government permitted the graduates of these schools to go on to the universities. Also, members of parliament and the cabinet were visible in attendance at mosques on holy days and other religious observances. Parliament permitted university students to cover their heads in the classroom. Advocates of the headscarf presented it as an issue of civil liberty: in a democracy, they argued, the individual ought to be free to wear any clothing within the limits of public decency; since the constitution guaranteed freedom of religion, laws forbidding the wearing of headscarves violated the citizens' civil rights.[100] For its opponents, the headscarf was a reference to the veil that Atatürk had famously made a symbol of the 'reactionary' Islamic order. They claimed that wearing it was a political gesture directed against the secular state guaranteed by the constitution. In 1989, President Evren himself petitioned the Constitutional Court for a repeal of the new law permitting headscarves. Thousands of university students demonstrated throughout 1989 as the issue went into litigation, first being banned, and then re-permitted by an act of Parliament.[101] The Council of Higher Education (YÖK), in defiance of Parliament, banned it on university campuses.

Polarization became especially evident in the 1980s, as a new generation of educated but religiously motivated local leaders emerged as a potential challenge to the dominance of the secularized political elite. Assertively proud of Turkey's Islamic heritage, they were generally skillful in adapting the prevalent idiom to articulate their dissatisfaction with various government policies. Certainly, through the example of piety, prayer, and political activism, they helped to restore respect for religious observance in Turkey.[102] In reality, the controversy about the headscarf on campuses is the larger question of the role of Islam in Turkish public life. The visibility of a new consciousness in the public sphere was disturbing for some laicist-Marxists, like *Cumhuriyet* columnist Akbal (1987):

> If these young girls must cover their heads then they can quietly stay home and wait for a bigot husband like themselves! In that case no one would have anything to say against them. In her home she can cover her head, or any other part of her as tightly as she wants. What do we care, what does the society care! But those girls who say *'I want to have education, I want to become a doctor, a lawyer, an engineer, a chemist, a state official or a teacher'*, there is only one path we can show them and that is the path of modern civilization. [Emphasis in the original.]

Many of the new technocrats, diverse professionals, businessmen, and wealthy entrepreneurs started to emerge from outside the traditional classes of Republican elites. Personally religious or conservative, they were more willing than their predecessors to give open expression to that.[103]

For the unyielding laicists, Islam must be confined to the private domain. Since for them 'modern civilization' is at stake, any form of public visibility for Islam is perceived as a direct threat to, and loss of, the constitutive public sphere and system, and as a rebellious attack on Atatürk's reforms and the secular regime he established.[104] More objective commentators have argued, however, that it would be rash and senseless to assert that all women who adopt the headscarf or the new, urban Islamic dress in the city are supporters of the Islamist party or to associate it with politicized Islam in Turkey.[105]

2.2.13 President Özal

Following allegations of corruption, then inflation after 1987, electoral losses in several large cities and coming third in the local elections of 1989, and the defection of several MP deputies to other parties, Özal left party politics and ran for the presidency. He was elected the eighth President of Turkey in 1989.[106]

Iraq invaded Kuwait in 1990. Affirming Turkey's loyalty to the Atlantic alliance, Özal used his position to redefine Turkey's role in regional and world politics. He believed that the solutions to Turkey's economic problems lay in close co-operation with the US and full membership of the EU. He saw in this also the potential for a political solution to the Kurdish problem. Initially, his efforts paid off. The Gulf War, however, left Turkey in a complicated relationship with Iraq and the Kurds. The Kurdish autonomous zone in northern Iraq, seen from the Turkish military's perspective, constituted a potential incitement to the Kurds of Turkey. Since 1989, Özal had been seeking a non-military resolution of the conflict and advocating greater cultural liberty for Kurds. The end of the Gulf War in 1991 seemed a propitious time to carry that project forward. Özal directed the cabinet to repeal the 1983 law forbidding the use of languages other than Turkish. Two prominent Iraqi Kurdish leaders met with Turkish Foreign Ministry officials, twice with the Turkish military, and later with Özal. In October, Demirel came to power in a coalition government with İnönü of the SDP, which the Kurdish groups supported.[107]

After the 1980 military coup, Turkey's civilian politicians had never succeeded in gaining control of the military's actions in the southeast. Through the mechanism of the NSC, the generals had repeatedly intimidated politicians, including Özal and Mesut Yılmaz.[108] When, during demonstrations in 1992, more than 90 Kurds were killed by security forces, the

Kurdish deputies in the SDP resigned in protest: the chance of a negotiated solution receded. Meanwhile, the number of 'unsolved' murders in the southeast climbed. These killings were carried out by clandestine paramilitary groups, some of whom probably operated independently, but evidence began to mount of their being funded by the state.[109]

The conflict escalated in 1992 and 1993. Nearly 250,000 troops deployed to the region destroyed some 2,000 villages, displacing an estimated 2 million people, and themselves suffering more than 23,000 casualties. Local people fled to major cities all over Turkey. The Turkish army conducted a number of military operations across the border in northern Iraq to wipe out terrorist bases used against Turkey. In 1993, PKK leader Öcalan announced a unilateral ceasefire. Some were surprised but Özal had been directly involved. The military, however, interpreted this as a sign of the terrorists' weakness and, assuming final victory was close, intensified operations. Negotiating with Özal through Jalal Talabani,[110] Öcalan renewed the ceasefire. At this critical juncture, Özal died suddenly in April 1993, while still serving as president.[111]

After Özal, Turkey struggled to reconcile the changes of the 1980s and 1990s – the legacy of the late president – with the traditions of the Republic and the requirements of modern democracy. A strong, stable government seemed elusive as Turkey was beset by economic difficulties, political scandals, corruption, the ongoing battle against terrorism, and Kurdish separatism. In fact, each of these issues was as old as the Republic.

Within a month, Süleyman Demirel became President and Tansu Çiller Prime Minister. In 1993, the Kurdish ceasefire broke down and military operations against the PKK resumed as before. The PKK ambushed a bus and murdered 33 off-duty military personnel. Heavy new fighting erupted, and hope of a political solution to the conflict seemed lost. Neither Demirel nor Çiller was capable of opposing the wishes of the generals or prepared to risk a civilian–military confrontation by challenging the military's assumption of a free hand in dealing with southeastern Turkey. The ongoing struggle brought serious economic problems and estrangement from the EU. It also compromised the integrity of the state through the influence of organized crime.[112]

The government was unable to control spending, and consequently there was high public debt and an accelerated 'dollarization' of the economy in

1994. International agencies therefore downgraded Turkey's credit status. That prompted a devaluation of the Turkish Lira that cost Turkey an estimated $1.2 billion. An austerity package caused the Lira to lose half its value.[113]

In 1989, Gülen was approached by the Presidency of Religious Affairs[114] and requested to resume his duties. His license was reinstated to enable him to serve as an Emeritus Preacher with the right to preach in any mosque in Turkey. Between 1989 and 1991, he preached in Istanbul on Fridays and on alternate Sundays in Istanbul and Izmir in the largest mosques in the cities. His sermons drew crowds in the tens of thousands, numbers unprecedented in Turkish history. These sermons were videotaped and also broadcast. At the beginning of the 1990s, the police uncovered a number of conspiracies by marginal militant Islamists and other small ideological groups to assassinate Gülen. These groups also placed agents provocateurs in the areas around the mosques where he preached with the aim of fomenting disorder when the crowds were dispersing after Gülen's sermons. Due to Gülen's warnings and the already established peaceful practices of the Movement, these attempts failed and the agents provocateurs were dealt with by the police.

In 1991, Gülen once again ceased preaching to large mosque congregations. He felt that some people were trying to manipulate or exploit his presence and the presence of Movement participants at these large public gatherings. However, he continued to be active in community life, in teaching small groups and taking part in the collective action of the Movement. In 1992, he traveled to the United States, where he met Turkish academics and community leaders, as well as the leaders of other American faith communities.

By this stage, the number of schools in Turkey established by the participants in the Gülen Movement had reached more than a hundred, not counting institutions such as study centers and university preparatory courses. (Other SMOs set up by Movement participants, such as the different media organs – radio and TV stations, newspapers, journals, etc. – will be dealt with in later chapters, where this form of mobilization is discussed.) From January 1990, Movement participants began to set up schools and universities in Central Asia too, often working under quite harsh conditions. From 1994 onwards, following the establishment of the Journalists and Writers Foundation, of which Gülen was made the Honorary Chair, Gülen made himself increas-

*ingly available for comment and interview in the press and media and began
to communicate more with state dignitaries.*

*Later developments in Gülen's own discourse and the collective action
of the Gülen Movement will be raised in the following chapters as they become relevant to the discussion.*

2.2.14 Political Islam?

After Tansu Çiller's government lost a vote of confidence, the country
went to the polls in 1995. Erbakan's Welfare Party (WP) won the largest
vote, 21.4 percent, followed by Çiller's True Path Party (TPP) and
Yılmaz's Motherland Party (MP). Ecevit's Democratic Left Party (DLP)
and Baykal's RPP also won seats. Among the parties failing to reach the
threshold were the Nationalist Movement Party (NMP) of Türkeş and
the (leftist-Kurdish) People's Democracy Party, which showed strongly in
the Kurdish regions but less among Kurdish populations in the major cities. Erbakan was unable to attract coalition partners to form the government. In 1996, Çiller and Yılmaz formed a coalition government that
lasted only eleven weeks. Later, Çiller's coalition with Erbakan brought
the WP to power and made Erbakan the prime minister in 1996. Erbakan once again put political Islam on the Turkish agenda.[115]

An extended public debate about the role of religion and the meaning
of political Islam ensued. Erbakan's former campaign speeches were dug
out in order to heat up controversy – for instance, his 'either with or without blood' outburst during the 1994 municipal elections; his praise of Iran
for resisting the West; his pledges to take Turkey out of NATO; to set up
an Islamic NATO, an Islamic UN, an Islamic version of the EU, and an Islamic currency. These speeches carried more force as political gestures than
policies and were incapable of attracting broad-based support in the country. Nevertheless, similar or even more inflammatory posturing by other
WP deputies and mayors dominated national headlines. Perceptions of the
WP government were ambivalent: was it a thing to be feared, a threat to
secularism and the regime; or was it a sign of a healthy Turkish democracy,
that they had a right to hold, express and persuade others to share their position? The reason the WP had done as well as it did in the elections was
that it articulated a vision of the just society in Turkey through the use of a
commonly understood religious idiom, the traditional values – widely in-

terpreted as meaning Islamic morals and behavior. It also benefited from an 'anti-Ankara' sentiment, as voters reacted against a government and state apparatus riddled with corruption scandals and out of touch with common people. Nevertheless, a sizeable portion of the voting public did not like the WP's rhetoric and mistrusted their motives. Laicists opposed the WP's recruits in a variety of lower-level government positions.[116]

Erbakan made a series of visits to Muslim countries, which drew criticism from the laicists. In 1997 his government was brought down – not by its failure to lower the budget deficit or curb inflation, nor by various scandals, but by a rally in Sincan, a suburb of Ankara. Electoral success gave the Welfare Party (WP) access to the privileges (and responsibilities) of power as never before but they failed to use them in the service of the nation.[117]

2.2.15 'Post-modern' military coup

At a rally in honor of 'Jerusalem Day' hosted by the (WP) mayor of Sincan, the speech of the Iranian ambassador, anti-Zionist slogans chanted by the crowds and the posters displayed by Palestinian visitors, were enough for the army tanks to rumble into Sincan.[118]

A top-level military commission calling itself the 'Western Working Group' launched an investigation into the WP. On February 28, 1997, the National Security Council (NSC), projecting themselves as guardians of the Kemalist reforms, and in particular of secularism, released a public statement that: 'destructive and separatist groups are seeking to weaken our democracy and legal system by blurring the distinction between the secular and the anti-secular. [...] In Turkey, secularism is not only a form of government but a way of life and the guarantee of democracy and social peace [...] the structural core of the state.' The military's 'supervision' of Erbakan's government eventually forced its resignation in June 1997. Following this, the pressure on the Muslim communities increased, with some secularist leaders openly expecting a 'settling of accounts' with political Islam.[119]

In what the commander of the navy admitted was 'a post-modern coup', the politicians were forced by the military commanders either to implement the measures they proposed or put together an alternative government that would do so. Erbakan agreed to an eighteen-point plan to reduce the influence of Islam in Turkey, that is, to curb Islamic-minded political, social, cultural, and economic groups. The ban on certain faith communities, their SMOs and other religious institutions would be enforced, the 'reaction-ary' personnel in governmental positions and state posts would be purged, the spread of state Imam-Hatip schools would be stopped, and tighter re-strictions would be maintained on 'politically symbolic garments like wom-en's headscarves'. Many companies were denounced as 'backward', and state institutions and people were warned not to buy anything from those compa-nies. In addition, TUSIAD, the business federation, issued a report in line with the military's agenda, urging that the power of political party leaders be curbed. Erbakan was asked and agreed to sign an order purging 160 military officers for so-called 'Islamic' activities and sympathies.[120]

Since the military coup of 1980, nothing has been as divisive in Turk-ish political life as the NSC decisions of February 28, because those deci-sions affirmed the army's supremacy over political life.[121]

The reason the military did not take over the state administration was that they proved to themselves and to others that they could engineer far-reaching change in the political system and govern everything from their bar-racks. Through the NSC, the military possessed a constitutionally defined ex-ecutive authority that it had used since the 1980s to exert its power on a range of issues. This 'post-modern' coup caused the Turkish political scene to become even more confused and unpredictable. Erbakan resigned in 1997.[122]

The generals behind the coup 'asked' Mesut Yılmaz, the leader of the Motherland Party, to form a new government, and he did so. In 1998, the Constitutional Court closed the WP 'because of actions against the principles of the secular republic.' Six WP leaders, including Erbakan, were banned from political leadership for five years, and individual members also faced criminal charges of subverting the constitution. The mayors of Sincan, Kayseri and Is-tanbul* received prison sentences** for 'inciting religious hatred'. Within a few weeks, most WP deputies had joined a successor party, the Virtue Party, which subsequently became the largest in Parliament.*** In the end, for all its ac-complishments at the municipal level, the WP had fared no better than the

---

* The Mayor of Istanbul was then Tayyip Erdoğan, the Prime Minister of Turkey since March 14, 2003.

** Four years, 7 months; 10 months; 10 months, respectively.

*** This is another recurrent theme in Turkish politics. After all coups, the people has always voted for and restored into government positions the parties and leaders that the military overthrew or expressed strong dislike for.

other parties at finding solutions to the basic economic and political problems of Turkey. It had instead aggravated them.

Prime Minister Yılmaz pressed ahead with what came to be known as the 'February 28 Process' – the efforts to limit Islamic influence in public life. Parliament required pupils to complete eight years of primary education – a measure designed to eliminate students' admission to state Imam-Hatip schools and other faith-inspired communities' secular and state-inspected schools. During the military rule in the 1980s, the graduates of the state Imam-Hatip schools had been allowed to continue higher education in social sciences and other post-secondary institutions. The schools enrolled one-tenth of the eligible 'secondary education students'.[123]

The February 28 Process also enforced regulations banning headscarves from schools, universities and the entire public sphere. Asked about civil servants beginning to turn up for work wearing headscarves, one of the highest ranking military officers had called it 'the end of the world'. Public protests and hunger strikes broke out all over Turkey, but to no avail. The secularist circles and media, especially the radical secularist and leftist *Cumhuriyet*, tried hard to frame the public debate and spared no effort to reinforce the authority and power of laicism to define the terms of public discourse, including the meaning, style and judgment on head-covering, sometimes with pejorative top headlines or stories. The administration also moved against Islamic influence in other areas. The police detained twenty leading Muslim businessmen on charges that they had provided funding for Islamic activities, and in 1998 the chief prosecutor in Ankara's State Security Court asked for the closure of MUSIAD, the Independent Industrialists' and Businessmen's Association, and filed charges against its president for inciting hostility based on religion. All the people charged were eventually acquitted.[124]

When Yılmaz attacked Çiller on the grounds of corruption, Çiller's coalition partners, the WP, shielded her from prosecution. But before long, Yılmaz himself was implicated in revelations of corruption on such a massive scale that the foundations of Turkish democracy were threatened. It all came out as a result of a car accident.[125]

2.2.16 Crash and corruption

In a traffic accident that occurred in Susurluk in 1996, three occupants of a car lost their lives and one was injured. Since the identity of the victims and the story of how they happened to be riding together in the car came out, the case has gone on unfolding and remains an open file.

The three dead included Abdullah Çatlı, a criminal right-wing hit-man wanted in connection with the attacks and murders of leftist students in Ankara in 1978–79. He was also involved in the jailbreak of Ağca, the Pope's assailant. At the time of his death, Çatlı held a gun permit and, among his thirteen passports in various names, one Turkish diplomatic passport. The second passenger was Çatlı's girlfriend, a former beauty queen. The third was a senior security officer and deputy police chief of Istanbul, who had commanded police units in missions against Kurdish rebels. The survivor in the car, Sedat Bucak, was a True Path Party Member of Parliament with close connections to Çiller, and led a Kurdish clan receiving government funding to fight Kurdish separatists. Also found in the car were guns and silencers.[126]

At first, President Demirel denied government involvement in criminal activity. The Minister of the Interior resigned when it became clear that his initial statements about the crash were not only false, but that in fact he had had a long relationship with Çatlı. Newspapers published reports, based on police and intelligence documents, showing that state organizations had been hiring death squads to murder Kurdish rebels and 'other enemies of the state' since the mid-1980s, and that these death squads had evidently received a strengthened mandate in 1991. Türkeş, the former junta colonel and the leader of the Nationalist Movement Party, publicly acknowledged that Çatlı had been employed by the government to carry out clandestine missions on behalf of the police and the army. Another former Interior Minister Sağlam admitted that the National Security Council had approved the use of 'illegal' means to dispose of 'enemies'. The weapons used were in some cases traced back to the security forces. Funding for the death squads was raised through bank presidents, who in return received kickbacks from the drug trade that the squads were allowed to run, the profits being laundered through casinos licensed by the Ministry of Tourism.[127]

The published versions of official reports directed by Prime Minister Yılmaz were incomplete and misleading with respect to the period of Çiller's premiership. In fact, missing persons and mysterious murders dated back earlier than that, to 1991, Yılmaz's first term as premier. Yılmaz's statements, that outside the military police, the armed forces were unaware

of, and uninvolved in, the activities of the death squads, remained unbeliev-
able. New information became available almost daily, revealing the depth
and complexity of interrelationships between the police, military officers,
banks, the government privatization process, cabinet ministries and parliamentarians, business tycoons, organized crime and far-right gangs. It pointed to two ultimate sources of the problem. The first was the fanatical pursuit of the war against Kurdish armed insurgents in southeastern Turkey
and other enemies of the state, and the second was the corruption of the
ongoing strategy to privatize SEEs. Both the True Path Party and Motherland Party were implicated in the escalating spiral of scandals. But the issue
went even deeper. Bülent Ecevit and the chief of general staff had known
all about it since 1973.[128] Far-right nationalist and marginal fundamentalist
groups had apparently been secretly armed and used as paramilitary death
squads with the knowledge of the highest officials of the state. Investiga-
tions of Çiller's abuse of the prime minister's fund suggested that the account had been used to pay such hit men and squads.[129]

Three TPP associates were convicted while Çiller's associates defended
themselves throughout 1998 against charges involving their personal finances. Yılmaz's government collapsed in 1998 as Parliament investigated
his connections to organized crime.

The scandals of the 1990s were not evidence of anything wholly new
in Turkish politics. This was how the Turkish political system had worked
for decades, as an elaboration of systems of patronage. This is the result of
political patrons' access to dramatic sources of wealth in the form of control of the formerly state-owned industrial ventures and businesses (the
SEEs). Beginning in the early 1980s, a very large portion of Turkey's industrial capacity was put up for sale. The stakes were enormous, and it is
hardly surprising that, in the struggle for control of this huge financial potential, some of the darkest forces in Turkish society came out in ways similar to what has been seen all over East Central Europe since the break-up
of the USSR and the fall of the old Stalinist regimes. The ugliest aspect of
it all is that retired generals or military personnel took the highest administrative or consultative positions in such ventures, and that murderous gangs
were able to operate with the acquiescence of the Turkish military and bureaucrats, who found them useful against the separatists and other political
dissidents. These gangs included not only neo-fascist groups but also mar-

ginal fundamentalists. A police shoot-out with an illegal Kurdish fundamentalist group called Hizbullah (unrelated to the group of the same name in Lebanon) in eastern Anatolia in early 2000 led to the discovery of huge caches of weapons and the remains of dozens of persons murdered by this group, which had received state support for its opposition to the PKK, the separatist (leftist) Kurdish armed group.[130]

2.2.17 The return of Ecevit

After Yılmaz's resignation, Ecevit, head of the Democratic Left Party (DLP), became prime minister. He was virtually the only prominent political leader untouched by scandal, and he took the nation to early elections in April 1999. His victory in those elections was helped by the capture of Öcalan, the PKK leader. Ecevit formed a coalition with Devlet Bahçeli's* NMP and Yılmaz's MP. As prime minister, Ecevit confronted issues, some as old as the Republic, and others unexpected by earlier generations.[131]

In 1999, Öcalan was captured, tried, and sentenced to death for treason for his role in leading the Kurdish separatist struggle against the Turkish state. Öcalan made some statements of reconciliation, calling for an end to the separatist war and pleading that the Turkish and Kurdish people were in the end indivisible. The Turkish military interpreted these remarks as evidence of PKK weakness.[132]

In 1997, EU member states did not offer Turkey a pre-accession partnership. This stunned Turkey, which had held associate member status since 1964. Some EU member states feared that Turkey's large population, cheap labor, and agricultural and industrial products might outbid the comparatively high-priced European labor and products. They also raised political objections to Turkey's membership, such as the relationship with Greece, abuses of the civil rights of political dissidents and minorities, the use of torture, the military's influence over elected government, and its very rigid attitude towards religion.[133] Dutch parliamentarian Arie Oostlander reported (on Turkey's accession to the EU):

> The underlying philosophy of the Turkish state implies an exaggerated
> fear of the undermining of its integrity and an emphasis on the homoge-
> neity of Turkish culture (nationalism), an important role for the army,

---

* Türkeş's successor in the Nationalist Movement Party.

and a very rigid attitude towards religion, which means that this underlying philosophy is incompatible with the founding principles of the European Union.[134]

In 1999, an earthquake struck the most heavily industrialized Istanbul–Izmit corridor. The aftermath of the quake showed both the weaknesses and the strengths of Turkey. The state was completely inadequate and ineffective and came to people's assistance too late and too slowly after the disaster. One dimension of corruption emerged with the death of more than 17,000 people: contracting procedures had allowed construction companies to put up shoddy structures that ignored building codes.[135]

By 2000, the generation of men who had led the country since 1961 was passing from the scene. The coalition government failed to amend the constitution to enable Demirel to serve a second term as President; rebellious deputies urged Demirel to retire in spite of the potential for political and economic destabilization; the Supreme Electoral Board barred Erbakan from participation in politics; Türkeş died; after Demirel, Supreme Court Judge Necdet Sezer became President. A younger generation was calling for a more democratic, open, liberal, and humane public regime, for their leaders to translate the nation's enduring values, potentialities, and aspirations into a form that could be meaningfully articulated in present conditions and carried forward to the future.[136]

President Sezer did not merely disappoint the younger generations; he proved to be the staunchest protector of the status quo and, through his continual vetoes and unilateral actions against the government and parliament,[137] a most vigorous opponent of the efforts for modernization and accession to the European Union.

2.2 IMPLICATIONS OF THE HISTORICAL BACKGROUND

Like all the Ottoman intellectuals in his generation, Mustafa Kemal was brought up on the revolutionary, democratic, and nationalist ideas of the Young Turks, the Committee of Union and Progress and, through them, the French Revolution.[138] The War of Independence primed Mustafa Kemal to come to power, to eliminate the sultanate-caliphate, and enable his socio-cultural and political ambitions to radically Westernize Turkish society. He was convinced that the only way to save his country was a radical change in the political system along the lines of the western European nation-states. He worked his strategy through the representative bodies authorized by local communities, the Republican People's Party, the government, parliament, the institutions which these bodies set up and, later, through the statist-elitists. He controlled and guided the political power and cadre of a new laicist nation-state that would necessarily establish the conditions for the revolutions he had planned.

However, with and after Atatürk, the emergence of a protectionist bureaucracy, then of an intelligentsia, and the subsequent transformation of both through a broadening of the bases of their recruitment, education, and politicization, have deeply scarred Turkish history and society ever since. Domestic and international developments have not influenced the role and leadership of the protectionist elitists, namely the military, civilian bureaucracy, and academics. There is little recognition, on their part, that there might be a variety of models of social organization that could serve as a platform for Turkish society and interests in particular, and for global society and humanity in general. They do not see or appreciate that internal motivations and desires lead people, not political and external pressures. Inevitably, the road that the protectionist elitists paved in collaboration with vested interest groups only polarized society, increasing societal tension and unrest.

In any case, the radical reforms of the one-party era touched only some segments of society. Some segments did not take part in those top–down directly induced changes; also, some lived far away from the urban centers, or had little exposure to the reforms, or rejected and remained outside them. In short, the reforms were not as complete or extensive as some celebrated statist-elitist-secularists claim or wish to believe.[139] Of course, some writers (notably, Daniel Lerner and Bernard Lewis) have lauded the resounding success of modernization in Turkey. On the other hand, its critics argue that 'Turkish modernization, when examined from alternative vantage points, contained little that was worth celebrating'. So influential was their demur that by the end of the seventies 'modernization' had become a dirty word, and authors such as Lerner and Lewis were cited only as examples of the 'wrong' way of studying the late Ottoman Empire and republican Turkey.'[140] Divisions between those who unreservedly admire (even revere) the radical modernization and those who question it are mirrored in divisions between the urban and the rural, and between the east and the west of the country, which influence political views and trends in today's Turkey:

Before anything else, the new republic would use all the power and energy at its disposal towards the substitution of Western culture for the
Islamic. The insistence on changing Islamic institutions and structures
prevented the modernizing elite of the Kemalist era from turning their
attention to broader definitions of systemic change.[141]

The governing ideology in the one-party period also necessitated its
favoring an authoritarian, tutelary attitude towards the public, and its interventionist economic policy. There was little accumulation of wealth except in the hands of the state, no wealth-owning class that would protect
and support the revolution and lead progress. That is why, in the 1930s,
state-owned conglomerates were formed to carry out the state-planned industrialization and economic development.

The State-owned Economic Enterprises (SEEs) came, over time, to
dominate business, economy, and politics. Through political patronage,
government officials and former military officers staffed the bureaucracy
of the new republic, saw the opportunities to create and build state-sponsored personal fiefdoms, and seized control of the SEEs. Further, taking
advantage of tax exemptions, state subsidies, low-interest capital, priority
access to scarce resources, foreign exchange and trained personnel, state
officials and officers increasingly turned the SEEs against private sector
competition. They became a real elite, a protectionist, republican class,
with a strong grip on economic and political power.[142]

When some politicians and parties sought to make reforms in the system, they could not do so without disturbing a protectionist elite unwilling
to accelerate the democratization and economic liberalization that would
harm their interests. Authoritarian rule and its suppressive measures, and scar-
city of basic necessities, alienated people from the elitists' ideas and attitudes.[143] The role played by faith (Islam) in the identity and lives of the majority of Turks was undeniable.[144] When the elitists tried to revolutionize and
Westernize (as well as the material aspects of the state's relations with its citizens) the inner dimensions of individual, family, societal, and religious identities, aversion and resistance were inevitable – as was the oppressive authoritarianism of the RPP in response to resistance, and its kindling, in turn, an
even stronger desire for a free society and a liberal economy.

The invested sinecures – in theory for the people but in reality against
them – facilitated and engineered the conditions for the protectionist elite's

interventions and military coups. Through the coups they sought both to re-establish state authority according to their own understanding and to restructure the political and economic system. Everything in society came to be institutionalized around a set of static norms imposed from above. Military power, constitutionalized and thus embedded in the state structure, defined the boundaries of civilian power. The arrangements of key political actors, prior to or during transformations, established new rules, roles, and behavioral patterns, which became the institutions upon which the new regimes consolidated. Accords between the political elite and the armed forces drew the parameters of civilian and military spheres that would later become persistent barriers to change and, thus, democratization. Before the transition to civilian rule the rules of the game were set by the military. New constitutions were drawn up by consultative assemblies largely appointed by the military. Thus began the period of 'guided democracy' with its 'licensed' or 'accredited' political bodies and parties, under the direct supervision of the National Security Council.

Political liberalism, which would gradually expand civil society, promote democratization, protect human rights and prevent destabilizing political responses, has never been fully achieved. In practice, elitist or military interventionist counter-mobilizations have allowed very little movement towards full democracy in Turkey – a fact acknowledged by European countries and authorities and, unfortunately, condoned by them 'at all costs' – even the cost of disenfranchising those elements of the Turkish population, 'however moderate', who support other political approaches.[145]

The primary justification for the three coups in 1960, 1971, and 1980 was that rampant corruption and civil discord paralyzed the operation of parliamentary democracy.[146] No coincidence then that the February 28 Process occurred at a time when bribery and corruption were endemic features of the economy.[147] International records clearly put Turkey high in the list of most corrupt countries (57th out of 91 countries, according to *The Corruption Perceptions Index 2001*). The loss to the nation, as publicly declared by the Corruption Investigative Committee of the Turkish parliament, was 150 billion US$ through bank graft and plunder by their owners.[148] It is noteworthy that some CEOs and top advisors of the banks concerned, and of the holdings that owned those banks, are retired senior generals.[149]

The office of the president, the inter-parliamentary committees and other institutions clearly had, and through the Constitutional Court exercised, the power they needed to prevent the incumbent government or parliament from carrying out the reforms the nation needed. Since the leadership could not overcome opposition from other institutions and had to abide by the rule of the Constitutional Court, it could not carry out policies like economic and political liberalization, and so progress to democratic and political efficacy was stifled.

After the collapse of the USSR and the Eastern bloc, and the end of the Cold War, Turkey's statesmen and civil societies worked to establish close commercial and political relations with the Balkan, Caucasian, and Central Asian states. A thin sort of culturally Islamic revivalism came into view. However, there was little prospect of any movement for an Islamic state gaining wide popularity in Turkey in the 1980s. Islamist fundamentalists occasionally staged dramatic acts of violence, but numerous polls of the general population have found that no more than between two and seven percent of Turks favored the establishment of a political order based on Islamic law. Throughout the 1980s, electoral returns gave Erbakan's Welfare Party no more than ten percent of the popular vote nationally. Sometimes the specter of an Iranian-style Islamic revolution was raised, but Turkey was not Iran. No one in any way resembled Khomeini.[150] The majority of Muslims in Turkey are consciously resistant to any sort of radical or fundamentalist Islamist movement. Even those who may be considered or consider themselves to be conservatively religious have grown up as citizens in a secular order and accepted its basic premises. Accordingly, Turkey's Islamic or faith-inspired movements accept the fundamental premises of democracy.

Since the 1950s,[151] there has been strong public demand for transformations in different sectors of the state apparatus. Societal changes and the demands for organizational autonomy have brought to light widespread issues and crises in the functioning of the country's bureaucratic institutions. The normal functioning of those institutions has been instrumentally subordinated to the dominant interests. Political scientists Dorronsoro and Massicard observed: 'Organizations controlling – directly or indirectly – the Parliament have increased in the last decades.'[152] Another political scientist, William Hale (1999), summed up the political system in Turkey as 'amoral partyism' or a 'system of neo-patrimonialism' in which a party's 'clients' ignore any fiscal irregularities and political inconsistencies as long as they are benefiting – party leaders can therefore change alignments without any justification in terms of the party's supposed ideology. So, democracy in Turkey is 'characterized by state dominance over civil society, political patronage and corruption, and political parties that operate as spheres of intra-elite competition'.[153] The traditional protectionist leadership in Turkey has been based on a strict nationalist, secularist and bureaucratic-authoritarian understanding.[154]

Several social and political scientists have detailed the particular features of the control and management flowing from this bureaucratic-authoritarian understanding over the last thirty years as: special interventions under pressure of particularist demands; clientelistic management of power; compromise with the traditional (protectionist) elites and with speculative and exploitative interests; unabashed spending of public funds for political purposes; the apportioning, by political entities, of publicly owned industry, SEEs, state agencies, and the banking system; and partisan control of information and the media.[155]

As this chapter has also shown, given the logic of the dominant elitist-statist-secularist attitudes, questions have rarely been asked about certain issues, such as the heterogeneous block of interests mobilized around certain parties, the rationale of Turkey's model of development, the imbalances between the east and west of the country, and between ethno-religious communities, the separation and exclusion between the protectionist and modernizing groups, the people's need for faith and for a role for it, the place and significance of civic initiatives, the place, weight and status of Turkey in Europe and the world, and so on. Sociologist Ali Bulaç comments on the resulting waste of energy and resources:[156]

> The governing elite in Turkey, as a hard core, is resistant to any development, reform, or legitimate democratic demands [...] Democratic developments and increases in civil initiatives carry the accumulated energy from the periphery towards the centre, but resistance at the core continues to cause a waste of social energy.

In terms of the capacity to govern, the response by the Turkish political elite has consisted of the introduction of restricted reforms along with a resort to repression and counter-mobilization against its own people. In terms of capacity to represent, the reaction has taken the form of hyper-politicization and under-representation. This system of relationships has resulted in distorted modernization and the breakdown and transformation of collective actions, the hyper-politicization of all issues, short-term interest, patronage, and nepotism, societal conflicts and tensions, sectarianism and terrorism, and embezzlement, massive graft and corruption.[157] Political analyst Heinz Kramer sums it up well:

> Turkish society, therefore, needs to be directed to and transformed by institutionalization; the selection and renewal of modernizing personnel in organizations; democratization; globalization; the disengagement of old antagonistic elites and demands; and the acknowledgement of Islam as a guide to the spiritual well being of people.[158]

2.3 CONCLUSION

We have seen in the foregoing that the protectionist group within the Turkish establishment collaborates with other ideological, media and interest groups to their reciprocal advantage and (nearly always) to the disadvantage of ordinary citizens. The templates of organization and repertoires of contention in Turkey and the Turkish societal context are very different from those that obtain in western Europe and North America. Although the Gülen Movement and other contemporaneous movements are similarly situated collective actors, it draws only on the available templates of organization, while other collective actors draw on repertoires of contention. Cultural stock and repertoires of contention are not static; they grow and change – something that has been demonstrated also in the accounts of state-sponsored organized crime, that is, the unfolding entail of the Susurluk incident and the February 28 Process.

The Gülen Movement introduced into the cultural space a new understanding that contentious or adversarial, conflictual or violent action, is not the best course, that it is no longer a valid or viable option and its effects tend to be both negative and, at best, short-lived. Then, on the basis of that understanding it offered an alternative, an option that was new and familiar: *hizmet*. Through faith-inspired but not faith-delimited service-projects, participants in the Movement committed their time and effort for the well-being of their fellow-citizens and the larger society; in so doing they have demonstrated practically that, rather than conflictual and violent action, the peaceful service ap-

proach, educational projects and co-operation, make a substantial and enduring difference in the life of individuals and communities.

In relation to contemporary discourse on collective action and social
movement theories, I conclude that, while political opportunity structures are
a factor and a link, and helpful in understanding how and why movements
develop in Turkey, they cannot be said to be the only or sufficient determining factors for the emergence of either disruptive and violent collective action
or of peaceful, altruistic community services. Findings from other socio-political contexts cannot be safely generalized or applied to the conditions, actors
and counter-actors in Turkey. We may not assume that similar movements,
operating in what appear to be similar political opportunity structures, will
necessarily develop along similar lines. (The previous chapter reviewed examples showing that, despite similarities between the American and European
political systems, movements developed quite differently in terms of tactics
and impact, and after some time lag.) Nor may we assume that the availability of political opportunities necessarily and directly translates into increased
collective action, whether contentious or peaceful.

Reliable description of the nature and identity of a collective actor
must follow from careful, attentive focus on specific features, outcomes and
framings of mobilization and counter-mobilization in the local societal context. Also, we need to give due weight to the ideas and sentiments, the discursive and interpretive processes, that have led to growing discontent, to
violent or peaceful responses. Sound analysis needs to take into account a
broader system of relationships, within which the actors' goals, values,
frames, and discourses are produced, facilitated, and constrained.

Societies differ in the amount of social movement activity they have,
in how such activity is structured, sponsored, and controlled. In Turkey, it
is largely either the state apparatus or the civil society that sponsor both
movements or counter-movements. By contrast, in western Europe or
North America, states often act or arbitrate neutrally, even though some
state apparatus and democratic processes might look quite similar on other
grounds. Accordingly, imputed or constructed meanings, especially in our
case within the sociology of social movements, are not fixed or static but
subject to change and variation with the social context. Meanings, concepts,
societal conditions and resulting action are indeed different, albeit overlapping. The complex, symbolic, ideational, and inter-subjective factors associ-

ated with movement mobilization and dynamics are intermittently constructed, modified, and changed in the process of contestation, and they are also manifested, accepted and interpreted differently in different cultures.

Mobilizing and counter-mobilizing actors do not have equal access to the same cultural stock. Even if they do or claim that they do, the reality constituted by the skills, orientations, styles, interests and supporters or collaborators of the groups is sure to be somewhat different from what it appears or they claim it to be. How the socio-political elite, media, and interest groups conceptualize the nature, identity and outcome of mobilizations and counter-mobilizations is highly dependent on local conditions and context.

In the next chapter, we turn to the themes of the mobilization of the Gülen Movement in Turkey and the counter-mobilization by its opponents. We will focus on the period after which the Movement came to be perceived as a new, distinctive collective actor in social, cultural and symbolic contexts. We will give particular attention to the Movement's means and ends – how it mobilizes and what for, how it frames both its own mobilization efforts and those directed against it; how it is mobilized against and to what ends; and how both mobilization and counter-mobilization are situated in relation to particular conjunctions of events and circumstances.

3

Mobilization and Counter-mobilization

3.1 INTRODUCTION

In this chapter I examine the competing perspectives within the social field in Turkey and try to understand mobilization and counter-mobilization in terms of the motives, beliefs, and discourses manifested by the actors. I focus on how frames are produced and utilized in different real situations – sometimes utilized quite systematically in fact to mask realities – and on how ideas, beliefs, and culture affect the repertoires of action and contention. The discussion particularly illustrates the relevance of language, leadership, SMOs, and the media, in framing events and processes. I aim to avoid reductionism in the analysis by allowing the plurality of relations and meanings to appear: these are *visible*, i.e. readily accessible to an outsider-observer, and *multiple*, in that the dimensions and processes of mobilization and counter-mobilization overlap and intertwine, requiring a wide array of analytical and conceptual tools. Failure to deploy a sufficiently wide array of such tools can only result in a sterile and repetitive stereotyping of either or both of the mobilizing and counter-mobilizing actors.

It is precisely the intellectual and political sterility in the societal context of Turkey in this period that the service-ethic of the Gülen Movement has labored to address. It has done so without at any stage or in any form challenging the legitimacy or authority of the interests, structures and institutions that have mobilized against it. To the contrary, it has persevered in advocating approaches and techniques for the building of consensus by providing new insights into how people can develop their capacity for positive action, for locating mutuality of interests so that individuals and groups can interrelate and co-operate in terms of shared space, shared goals and universal values.

The themes developed within contemporary social movement theories, if applied separately, are not adequate to explain the kind of multi-form civic action undertaken by the Gülen Movement, which requires a quite different mode of analysis within a *syncretic* framework. This framework will evolve and expand as the discussion progresses in the following chapters. In this chapter, the principal themes picked up within that framework are: the contested social field; bringing new issues to public space and making them visible; symbolic and cultural production; production of and access to information and the media; vertical and horizontal social mobility and professionalism; reflexivity or symbolic potential; transnational projects and international recognition; altruistic action and its symbolic challenge; definition and redefinition of democratic process; consequences of the success of mobilization; intervention in the decisions of the public authorities and, as a sub-set of such intervention, the February 28 military coup and irregularities. Discussion of these themes will establish how certain collective actors, seeking support and legitimation, deploy ideological masks to distract attention from their real interests and intents; it will illustrate the strategies of mobilization appropriate to the construction of an open civil space conducive to peaceful negotiation of social, cultural, political and religious encounters.

3.2 THE GÜLEN MOVEMENT

3.2.1 Cultural mobilization:
public space and making new issues visible

Mobilizations with political strategies seek primarily to alter external realities and often have defined material objectives; they tend to focus on change in particular political or economic relations, or particular policy directions or outcomes. Mobilizations that are culturally oriented tend to look to an interior transformation as a means (and goal) of change in value systems; aiming to preserve or restore and revitalize a culture, they focus much more on ideas and beliefs, on values, norms and identities.[1]

The cultural dimension, Gülen affirms, is a necessary component of collective or national consciousness, without which a people cannot move forward along a path recognized and valued as their own. He argues that a close relationship obtains between the harmony and stability of the ways in which a people conduct their affairs and their cultural resources. Refusing to see the underlying principles and the components that constitute one's culture is 'blindness' and 'trying to remove them from society means total confusion'.[2] Turkish society is a complex one, whose needs cannot be articulated without intelligent reference to the cultural resources of its people. The Gülen Movement therefore attempts to mobilize the universal cultural elements within the traditions, codes and idioms of the past to evolve new symbolic systems that can, in important ways, stand out as independent and free of control and standardization by the traditions, codes and idioms that at present dominate in Turkey and elsewhere.[3] This cultural understanding is by no means exclusivist as it expressly moves out, from within a psychologically secure, well-established heritage, towards global integration:[4] 'Originating in Turkey but becoming increasingly transnational, the Movement represents novel approaches to the relationship between faith and reason, peaceful coexistence in liberal democracies with religious diversity, education and spirituality.'[5] The approach contrasts sharply with the attitudes, demanding forgetting and selective memory, that were described in the sections on 'laicism' and 'cultural revolution' in the previous chapter. Sociologist Hendrick concludes that the Gülen Movement, as a 'service movement' is 'a civil/cosmopolitan mobilization [...] in which Islamic morality and ethics might fuse with, rather than combat, the financial and political institutions of neo-liberal globalization".[6]

An approach that is resolute and consistent in its commitment to 'fuse [...] rather than combat' most particularly requires opening up new channels of representation and winning access to hitherto excluded themes, projects and services. In an order open to civil society, initiatives like this should lead to reform and improvement of local and national decision-making processes. For the present, that is not the order that obtains in Turkey: rather, the state, with its internal combination of public intervention and private interests, generates pressures for standardization of the cultural space. These pressures affect all groups. The outcome is the reverse of 'fusing' or social cohesion; the segmentation or isolation of groups, the near impossibility of constructive encounters in the public space, has long had severely negative impacts on the nation's development towards participatory democratic processes and distributive justice in respect of economic and social and political opportunity.

The Gülen Movement has systematically shunned contentious, political or direct action, preferring to remain, in principle and practice, non-adversarial. It has, instead, in order to form and inform the public space, and to consolidate and revitalize participatory democratic processes, exerted itself in constructive efforts to draw contending individuals and groups to collaborate in a common spirit of service. A prominent example of these efforts is its establishment in Turkey of the Journalists and Writers Foundation (JWF), which brings together academics, scholars, statesmen, and journalists who hold different, even conflicting, worldviews.[7] Under the JWF a number of specific platforms were set up – for example, the Literature, Dialog Eurasia, and Abant platforms. These platforms were a pioneering venture when they started: 'In regard to those attending and arrangements [this kind of association] had not been seen before in Turkey'.[8] One sociologist commented appreciatively: 'Scholar-scientists, people of religion, members of the arts, and state officials, who until recently would never have imagined coming together, shook hands, embraced, and sat side by side.'[9]

The platforms continue to bring urgent matters to the fore to be engaged with in a constructive spirit. They lead the public space in starting negotiations on issues that have caused tensions and clashes for decades. The 'Abant Platforms' in particular have been widely appreciated as an effective forum for airing dilemmas that many people in Turkish society longed to have openly discussed and resolved. The Movement has thus contributed to the training of a potential for coexistence, for a common sense of citizenship, without the need to clash and with the hope of mutual respect and compromise.[10] Moreover, since the issues aired enter the public space they are presented to decision-making, which transforms the JWF initiatives into possibilities for social change without confronting (still less, seeking to invalidate) the legitimacy and authority of the decision-making apparatuses themselves. As spaces for speech and spaces for *naming*, these initiatives permit new words to be spoken and heard, different from the words that the dominant power groups in Turkey want to impose, and coming out of a rationale different from theirs. That is not naively ignoring the tendency of those dominant groups to assert hegemonic control over political mechanisms and processes; rather, it is seen, from within the Movement and outside, as teaching wisely and by example the proper role of social institutions, and thereby helping to define what participatory democracy in the country could become.[11]

The JWF platforms generate and disseminate ideas, information, knowledge, and thereby contribute to an improved level of awareness of controversial issues. Through media outlets and other institutions – which will be described fully below (§3.2.3 and 5.2.4) – as well as the JWF platforms, Movement participants demonstrate a competence to redefine the problem field (*spannungsfeld*). Intellectuals from a wide spectrum of perspectives are engaged in this effort to improve awareness, and to contribute to the process of *naming*, of making distinctions, based on information. There is a difference between people being manipulated through the consumption of meanings imposed by external and remote powers, and their being able autonomously to produce and recognize meanings for their own individual and collective lives – only the latter constitutes a communicative action, 'a consensual co-ordination of individually pursued plans of action',[12] making visible new powers and possibilities of handling systemic conflicts and new forms of social empowerment and responsibility in a complex society.[13]

Some of the controversial issues aired had been 'hidden', in the sense that there was no accounting of them within the rationales of the decision-making apparatuses in Turkey, issues such as the 'analysis of our social structure, religious consciousness and the international community', and Turkey's right to have a say in international affairs.[14] As sociologist Vergin put it, people 'always wanted to know and hear such things, but they came from a preacher and Islamic scholar, in such a simple but profound and intense way.'[15] The Movement's addressing these 'hidden' issues helped to focus collective attention on the critical choices that the society needs to discuss and decide. Gülen has spoken and written on a wide range of such matters – the individual, government, democracy, religion, culture, diversity, integration, alienation, the past and future, tradition and modernity, ethical values, education, tolerance, conflict or co-operation on current events, and so forth.[16] However, Gülen's style of speech and the way he handles these themes is special. Political scientist Ateş commented that Gülen 'dwells more on what should be rather than what is'; Ünal and Williams conclude that he 'deal[s] with problems or crises that are plaguing Turkey, not specific people, parties or the State'.[17]

Indeed, others in Turkey who assume civic and political leadership, to the extent that they have been able even to broach the themes on which Gülen has opened discussion, have done so by touching upon only the outward symptoms of the deeper conflicts and anxieties that affect the societal field. Doing that attracts and inflames collective attention, which has led at times to the development of opposition among different social groups, or counter-mobilization by the protectionist interests in power. Because the issues lie deep, an inappropriate framing of them does not engage the deeper resources of the society to gather and resolve them in ways that do not generate divisiveness and aggravate problems.

The Turkish public space or symbolic field has witnessed a growing tendency to assimilate some of the complex issues – ethnicity, religious observance, secularism, the role of the military in politics, societal cohesion and peace, work ethics, universal values – into the narrower arena of political competition. However, hardly any change has been witnessed, as a result of this politicization of the issues, in the way that public institutions actually function and operate. The long-term dimensions and entail of the underlying problems therefore continue to perplex the nation. Among the collective actors that take on such problems, the Movement has a marked difference in style and strategy. Agai (2002) notes that the Gülen Movement 'is not ideological but rather seeks to educate people through flexible strategies'.[18] Aslandoğan and Çetin (2006) make the same point more directly:

> Rather than dealing with daily politics, the Gülen Movement makes the latent and dormant power in Turkish people visible and forces it to assume a shape in terms of educational, health and intercultural and interfaith services and institutions.[19]

That is to say, the Movement does not contaminate its cultural and educational purposes with political tactics or political ambitions. It gives appropriate expression to the issues that need to be addressed, and calls for change through taking responsibility and dealing with individuals and their needs, rather than with (or against) political and governmental positions.

The Gülen Movement acts as an engine of transformation in the mindsets and attitudes of people. The cultural emphasis of its work raises awareness for the recognition of cultural production and its representation.[20] As a by-product of that, it exposes the contradictions and the silences that the dominant apparatuses of the political system seek to camouflage. The processes of modernizing institutions and making them proficient and effective have undoubtedly gained in strength through the services provided or mediated by Movement participants, but, as Melucci has pointed out, the vested interest groups who need to hide their own neglect in these areas of service, and to hold down the status quo, artificially contrive new problems and new areas of conflict.[21]

3.2.2 Cultural and symbolic production

Contemporary systems of production and management increasingly intervene in internal processes, in the formation of attitudes, desires and needs, in relational networks and symbolic structures across the whole socio-cultural field – this includes the construction of meanings, codes, public spaces, relations and needs in the lived world, and does not exclude the domains of the imagination and of spiritual reality.[22] Large management projects require extensive control of systems of information, symbols, identities and social relationships. Tension and conflicts arise due to the ways in which management purposes and outcomes are conceived, and to the ways in which tensions and conflicts, and identities and needs, are defined. On the one hand, individuals must have substantial discretion over symbolic resources so that they can express and achieve their potential for autonomy and self-realization. On the other hand, the management effort, seeking (at least cost) to maintain cohesion, integration and order, looks to exert control across the very domains in which the meanings and motives of individual behavior are constituted. It is a dilemma of complexity. The dilemma is resolvable only through a virtuous circle of mobility and exchange (of information, ideas and personnel) between the managers and the managed, and a relationship between them of sustained mutual vigilance combined with mutual good faith and patience – the willingness, on occasions of unusual difficulty, to give each other benefit of the doubt. If a social order fails, overall, to provide for this individual autonomy along with harmonious integration of complexity and multiplicity, it results in exclusion and marginalization, and the fracturing of society into conflicting interest groups – a few very powerful ones, most others relatively very weak, all operating in a climate of distrust and hostility.

Viewing the recent history of Turkey in regard to the issue of faith, Bulaç observed: '[it is] a history of tension between people of faith, who would like to have a voice in the civil area, and the state society, which would like to transform the rest of the society in an authoritarian way.'[23]

Viewing the same history in regard to political life and aspirations to democracy, it is clear that there has been substantial, repeated breakdown and failure: the country has experienced four military coups (in 1960, 1971, 1980, 1997) and several other interventions short of an overt coup; destructive and long-lasting armed conflicts of political left and right; ethnic and sectarian terrorism; severe segmentation between the elitist-statist-secularists and the grassroots of Anatolian society; and corruption on a world-beating scale among top state officials.[24] The dismay and heartache this produces was well-expressed by sociologist Vergin (1996):

> The poverty of ideas shaping Turkish political life; the shallowness of the world around us; the empty, hollow, sterile, short-sighted games being played in the name of political struggle and democratic competition; and the display of superficial politics here have both saddened and angered me for a long time... The roads to Turkey's ability to be governed and to taking its rightful place in history have been blocked (or cut), and its political philosophy and foresight have atrophied.[25]

In short, Turkey's recent history has witnessed no virtuous circle reliably linking the state with its people, the managed with their managers. The Gülen Movement's positive service-ethic can be understood as an offer to mend the broken circle, to re-unite the society, and to heal divisions between society and state. Former President Süleyman Demirel said about Gülen that he is striving to 'strengthen the Turkish nation's unity and solidarity'.[26] Through its discourse and actions the Movement has aimed to reawaken collective consciousness and direct attention to the radical social, cultural and spiritual dimensions of human needs, which the nation's 'politics' systematically ignores or obscures.[27]

The authoritarian elite's approach to the management of the nation's development has been consistently exclusionary – they have sought to impose in Turkey an order and a reality solely of their own making, often expressing it with impatient disdain for the doubts and reservations of those concerned about the ensuing loss of cultural integrity and historical continuity.[28] The Gülen Movement as a collective cultural action symbolically reverses the *naming* imposed by the dominant protectionist interests, and it reveals the arbitrariness of that *naming*. It restructures reality using different perspectives, which lead to the crumbling, in the symbolic domain, of the monopoly of power over that domain exercised by a few. Some hopeful shifts in attitude have been observed as a result, both in the political arena and among the people as a whole. Political scientist Barton (2005), reflecting on the work of the Gülen Movement, concludes that it is 'the sort of movement that offers Turkey's (and the entire Muslim world's) best hope of uniting Islam, modernization, and secular, liberal democracy'.[29] Turkish society views 'the new trend as the expression of a collective conscience and collective sentiment, common thoughts and feelings'.[30] As the Movement's discourse gained influence through the visibility of its actions and platforms, there was a change in public perception of Islam. Hitherto, there had been efforts, in the service of short-sighted interests, to propagate and manipulate negative images of Islam. Yet, these images were gradually modified. People – from left to right politically, from observant Muslims to ardent secularists, from elder statesmen to ordinary citizens, and from ordinary members to leaders of the non-Muslim communities in Turkey – came together in beginning to question the recent past, to see a different reality, and become open to change and renewal.[31] Armenian Patriarch Mutafian said: 'People who shared the same religion could not get together in this country [Turkey] until recent times. Now, people from different religions come together at the same dinner.'[32] He added: 'The person to thank for this [development] is Fethullah Gülen and the Foundation [of Journalists and Writers] of which he is the honorary president. We followed the path opened by him.'

A prominent example of Gülen's personal participation in intercultural affairs (and of the concomitant opposition to it by the protectionist elite) was his meeting Pope John Paul II.[33] Çandar (1998) interprets the Gülen–Pope meeting as a major 'development' and sees the activities of the Gülen Movement as 'closely related to Turkey's future'. Commenting on the opposition to the meeting and the Movement generally, Çandar wrote:

> At any rate, inside Turkey there is no 'foundation of legitimacy' in the public conscience for opposition with this intent. If it continues this path, Turkey will have chosen to be fully an isolationist–totalitarian regime. Those who follow such a path will be assumed to be guilty of having decided to destabilize Turkey or continue its ongoing instability. In this respect, the Gülen–Pope meeting is a very important security measure for Turkey's democratization. Indirectly, it is an important contribution toward Turkey becoming a stable country.[34]

Modernity has accelerated fragmentation of identities and break-down of unitary symbolic space. It has radically drained and emptied the individual's life of the symbolic functions which used to enable (and condition) social expression, imagination, and aspirations for successful integration into the social fabric. Individuals and groups are forced into an anxious state of 'rapid change, flux and uncertainty'.[35] Sociologist Göle (1996), reflecting on two decades of confusion and uncertainty among her generation, wrote:

> We who have lived in Turkey during the last twenty years have been in a state of shock. We have been swinging back and forth between the desire to catch up with the new age and to know ourselves; wavering among ambition, anger, and excitement; and trying to open a path by hand between our spirit and the world. We are fighting over our unofficial identity and unclear design.[36]

She adds that Gülen 'made [this modern condition of ours] meaningful by a deep mixture [of] conservative thought and liberal tolerance'. Gülen's work indeed focuses on precisely this symbolic reintegration, taking on the task of healing the breach and remaking one's world. It encourages people to adopt new ways of *naming* and perceiving reality. It enables people to recompose the various parts of the self and orient their strategies towards recovery of the dimensions of symbolic existence and presentation. It teaches both the theoretical and practical aspects of how to become a rounded human being, how to educate the mind, heart and spirit in order to lead a fulfilled life and be oneself while being with and for others.[37] Göle maintains that 'Gülen's thought favors individual modesty, social conservatism and Islam in the founding of civilization', and that 'his thought gives examples of [both] modest and tolerant people who have not lost their connection with God, and of the individuals worn down by the suppression of tradition and modern excess'. Another sociologist, Özdalga (2005) argues:

> Turkey is a country where the nation state has so far not been able to fully integrate its citizens or to meet the demands of society at large; for various reasons – poverty, education, ethnic or religious difference – large sections of the population still experience alienation in relation to the institutions of the nation-state. This is often compensated for through ethnic, local and/or family ties.[38]

Besides such ties of family and ethnicity there are other relational networks, as Özdalga's analysis shows, through which the Movement acts to counter alienation – such as weekly neighborhood meetings, professional associations, parent-school associations and so on – and operational values such as consultation and collective decision making, collective ownership, and community.[39] In interpreting and tackling the problems of modernity, the Movement helps to formulate solutions at the level of individual autonomy that can prepare for the development and integration of the individual into the modern nation-state and the twenty-first century global habitus.[40] The importance, in Gülen's understanding, of a commitment to dialog, plurality and peaceful coexistence has been ably summarized by Paul Weller:

> Gülen's thought offers intellectual and spiritual resources that enable us better to understand the one world in which we all live, as well as to engage with the challenges that living in this world brings. Such resources are needed for understanding the nature and dynamics of the world, and for enabling us to resist the kind of disastrous outcomes which some argue are inevitable, which many others fear, and which all of us have a responsibility and a possibility to do something about.[41]

The Movement affirms the need for autonomy and meaning; it calls for awareness of the limits of human action and life; it requires recognition for the spiritual dimensions of human experience and aspirations, strongly commending the search for a new scientific paradigm to accommodate those aspirations; and it demands respect for different cultures and historical and cultural continuity, peaceful coexistence, and religious broad-mindedness. The strength of this discourse is demonstrated through practical actions, whose outcomes in turn reinforce (and through feedback help ameliorate) that discourse. For just that reason the Movement is strongly mobilized against – namely, that it seems to succeed in challenging and reversing the logic of the dominant instrumental rationality. Social movements, as Melucci explains, by revealing the negligence in power (and the shadowy side of its dealings – misuse of office, authority and resources) enable people to take responsibility for their own action. Movements strive symbolically to *name*, to elaborate codes and languages, in order to define reality their way. They reverse the representation of the world served up by the dominant models, refusing the latter's claim to uniqueness; and they offer, through social practices and lived experiences, alternatives to replace the predominant communicative codes and objects of thought. Thus, social movements, of which the Gülen Movement is one particular example, introduce a new paradigm, a redefinition of public space, for norms of perception and production of reality beyond what is inscribed in (or prescribed by) the hegemonic discourse.[42]

3.2.3 Information and media

Symbolic and informational resources are a new kind of power. Inequality used to be explained and measured primarily as an outcome of the unequal control and distribution of economic resources. It is now also explained and measured as an outcome of having, or not having, a substantial and specific control over the codes and symbolic resources that frame information. There are organizers of information directing its flow and targeting a widening range of social or administrative fields. Their access to the codes and symbolic resources corresponds to a distribution of social positions, power, and interests. Dependence and manipulation are ever present, and symbolic multipliers render the effects of communication unpredictable and disproportionate, and deeply influence politics in critical areas of social life. Being deprived of information is not the problem – even in the shanty-towns of the poorest cities in the world, people today are widely exposed to media output – the problem lies in their not having any power to organize this information to serve their own needs. Thus, in the modern world, being dominated is being excluded from the power of *naming*. It is the un-reflected consumption of the *naming* which frames human experiences and relationships and thereby exerts control over their meaning.[43]

From 1995–2001, the elite and the media in Turkey functioned as a close-knit team,[44] deliberately and systematically distorting reality. About this period, when Turkey was counted among countries with the most corrupted state systems, the Center for Strategic and International Studies (CSIS) in Washington reported that 'the powerful Turkish media barons praised and protected politicians with whom they enjoyed close and profitable business relations, [and] jointly cultivated' the impression of an unusual 'economic stability with success and determination. [...] The corrupt quadrangle of businessmen, media, politicians, and bureaucrats, with its tentacles in Turkish political and economic life' played a key part in manipulating and misreporting news; they transformed public and political life into a field of tension and conflicts and 'produced an atmosphere of crisis in Turkey'.*

On a 'Live TV' discussion program on Kanal 7 on May 5, 2006, media and bank owner Dinç Bilgin confessed to how this many-tentacled quadrangle, of which he was a member, became instrumental in smear campaigns against journalists and other civilians, how they received military memos and commands from certain generals among the chiefs of staff, how 'a media cartel' was instrumental in the fall of the government and a party to interference in tenders for government contracts. In essence, then, the problem concerns the greater or lesser visibility of codes, the pertinent decision-making processes, and a complex game of interactions between the vested interests and ideologically motivated protectionist groups.[45]

Through its skills, the autonomy of its language, and the complexity of the exchanges and organizational strategies that characterize its work, the Gülen Movement has been able to influence the debate about the ways in which reality is constructed by the Turkish media. By filtering imposed messages, activating everyday communicative networks, exercising choice among the various media available, and professionally interacting with the media system, Movement participants have themselves become a new medium in the construction of public discourse.

In terms of electronic communications and the internet, the Movement was the first Turkish social actor to make itself available online and free to the masses.** Gülen was also the first preacher to have his lectures made available in audio and video cassettes to the general public in Turkey. He encourages the use of mass media to inform people about matters of individual and collective concern. When talking about the qualities of the new type of people who would strive to extend altruistic services to all humanity, he says:

> To stay in touch and communicate with people's minds, hearts, and feelings, these new men and women will use the mass media and try to establish a new power balance of justice, love, respect, and equality among people.[46]

---

* Aliriza, 2000:2–4; id., 2001:2; see also the confessions made by the media and bank owner Dinç Bilgin. For details, check several National Turkish media from May 5 onwards to the end of the month. Also, see footnote 1 on page 72.

** The caption to the logo of the daily *Zaman* reads: 'First Turkish Newspaper on the Internet', at www.zaman.com.

Gülen communicates to a broad cross-section of people through media set up by Movement participants since the early 1980s.[47] He regularly contributes editorials and other writings to several journals and magazines. He has written more than forty books, hundreds of articles, and recorded thousands of audio and video cassettes. Gülen has given speeches and interviews covering many pressing social, cultural, religious, national and international issues. These have then been serialized in different dailies or compiled into books that are best-sellers in Turkey.[48] His writings are available in translation in the major world languages, in print and electronic form through numerous websites.[49]

Movement participants established a national and international television station – Samanyolu Televizyonu (STV), a major news agency – Cihan Haber Ajansı (CHA), an independent daily newspaper (*Zaman*) with a daily circulation of over half a million copies nationally,[50] several leading magazines,[51] and a prominent publishing house, The Light, Inc.[52]

Zaman was established in 1986 and was 'the first to publish a special US edition in North America. Worthy and unsensational, *Zaman* is the only newspaper to print local Turkic language editions all over the Turkic world'.[53] It was the first Turkish daily newspaper to make itself available online, which it did in 1995. Special international editions for other foreign countries are printed in local alphabets and languages[54]. The paper is acknowledged for its serious, fair, and balanced reporting. It has won national and international awards[55] for its modern page layout and its contributions to intercultural understanding through its foreign editions.[56]

The media outlets all report on and disseminate educational and cultural activities as well as news and the perspectives of Movement participants. They are formally independent of one another; however, they are informed of each other's activities through diffused, multiple, educational, cultural and professional networks of volunteers, who set a good example for one another, provide alternative perspectives and forums that can be emulated or improved on by others.[57] These media outlets have proved to be very effective during times when the values, services, and institutions of the Movement were misreported by others. They aim to be visible to the decision-making apparatuses, which govern the major media networks and define the political agenda, so that the controversial issues and debates dividing society should not be 'muffled and veiled behind the facade of formal neutrality and apparent self-referentiality'.[58] In addition, they respect and encourage the public discourse which is created in everyday networks by citizens.[59]

Turkey came to know the 'contradictions between media–military relations', as well as the centers and interests which decide on the language to be used and the information to be organized and broadcast, during the most politically and economically turbulent years* before and after the February 28 'soft coup'.** There were centers controlling language and related information technologies; and there were financial decision-making centers which moved enormous amounts of economic resources through the production and manipulation of information.[60] This was the time when 'impropriety was maximized. Some of the people in power at the time, both in the civilian and military bureaucracies, took advantage of the situation'.[61] Columnist Bilici lamented: 'only a small section of our media can stand on [universal] principles in the face of a major crisis, such as the […] February 28 Process […] once again journalism gives way to ideological blindness.'[62]

What became visible at this time were new forms of domination, whose principal power rested in the power to provide patterns of thought for the people. New centralities and marginalities were defined by this privileged control over the production and diffusion of information, as the power behind the media system attempted to impose patterns of cognition and communication which would work far beyond the specific contents diffused as news.[63] A smear campaign against certain prominent journalists and intellectuals was initiated to inflame public opinion. Some journalists were alleged to have provided support for a terrorist organization in exchange for money.[64] A draft proposal for a law that would 'purge the state institutions of thousands of civil servants who want to destroy the state' was prepared by a group of chiefs of staff who had masterminded the Feb-

---

* As a result of the illegal, fraudulent practices of the collapsed private banks owned by media tycoons, the practice of public banks of lending to themselves, the exposure of billions of dollars of the public banks controlled by the government, and the flight of billions of dollars overseas, the stock market plunged by one-quarter in two days and the Turkish Lira lost one-third of its value.

** Birand, 2001; Özel, 2003:80–94. The February 28 military intervention will be discussed in detail later within the chapter, see §2.2.15 and §3.2.8. Here, we only touch upon one aspect of it – how information was manipulated by the interest groups.

ruary 28 coup and who later held senior positions at the companies charged with embezzlement and corruption.

> Later on, it was discovered that the entire affair was based on a military article that was called ANDIÇ, prepared by Deputy Chief of General Staff General Çevik Bir and General Secretary Major-General Erol Özkasnak. The same duo was instrumental in ensuring that the conspiracy made the headlines and many journalists were dismissed. Bir and Özkasnak personally took part in pressuring the media.[65]

Political scientist Kuru lists the negative effects of the February 28 coup for the faith communities:

> The WP–TPP* coalition collapsed [...] the WP was dissolved by the Constitutional Court. The [...] process was very destructive for Islamic education and practicing Muslims in Turkey [...] the headscarf was strictly banned at universities, the [state-run] Imam-Hatip secondary schools were closed [...] teaching the Qur'an to children under age twelve became illegal. The military expelled allegedly Islamist and avowedly pious officers. [...] pro-Islamic corporations and financial institutions faced official discrimination.[66]

Among the individuals attacked, Gülen was made the most prominent target. The media group owned by Dinç Bilgin, Atv, which was grossly engaged in the improprieties, broadcast two recordings of Gülen. These had been crudely doctored to make him appear to be suggesting that Muslims should infiltrate state institutions. The broadcasts were made not on account of their 'intrinsic' news value, but according to the hidden priorities of interest groups and institutions.[67] The intention was to divert public attention onto a prominent figure and thereby distract the masses, meanwhile rampant embezzlement, graft, and apportioning of SEEs, lands, banks, resources and wealth could go on unchecked.[68] In conveying the doctored discourse, the media outlets concerned were exploiting the trust of the people and attempting to shape the attitudes of neutral parties who had hitherto looked favorably on Gülen and the Movement.[69] Ergun Babahan, chief editor and director of the media outlets of Dinç Bilgin, later gave a number of interviews to the media and press and wrote several articles about the events. He detailed how they became embroiled in the corruption schemes

---

*   Welfare Party and True Path Party.

and attacks on faith communities at the request or command of certain military staff, who were driving the February 28 Process.

Gülen Movement participants, through the efforts of the media organs they had set up, proved themselves, and enabled neutral parties, no longer to be mere consumers of information, receivers of pre-fabricated news. They could no longer be wholly excluded from the discussion about the rationale that organizes the flow of information. They now have some measure of competence to influence that flow of information and the power to shape reality that it carries. Without denying the imbalance of power in this regard, the Movement as collective actor shows itself able at least to render that imbalance visible.[70]

Today, smear campaigns are still used.[71] The Movement attempts to remedy the situation through a growing skill in setting the formal preconditions for any discourse and practice. Every day more is being revealed by the Turkish media as a whole about the ideologically motivated schemes of generals ambitious for power and wealth.[*]

Institutional actors claiming to play 'the rules of the game' and simultaneously undermining them is a profoundly anti-democratic characteristic. The rules by which the institutions are supposed to play are the necessary condition for holding the complexity of the social order together. The rules may be discussed and redefined as one goes along, but as long as they remain the rules, they must be respected; otherwise violence, in a subtle form, becomes the de facto rule, as was the case during the February 28 injustices. The state conservatism of those who masterminded the February 28 'soft coup' is clearly represented in their unscrupulous manipulation of images and information. It is very much manifest in content, verbal violence and schemes to kill,[72] and behind it lies the conviction that, as far as great concentrations of power and wealth are concerned, there are in fact no rules with which they feel any obligation to comply against their will.

---

[*] While this section was being revised, a prominent leftist weekly, *Nokta*, was closed after police raids at the command of a military judge following its news report on a retired admiral's notes about a possible military coup plan. All its archives and electronic files were taken by the authorities. In its last issue published April 19, *Nokta* magazine used the coverline 'We will not stop until absolute democracy'. For more, see nos. 24 and 25 of the magazine (April 13–26, 2007) and contemporaneous reports in the national and international media.

The contempt for such attitudes in the public space proves that they do not draw on a groundswell of general opinion or correspond to attitudes widespread in society.[73] Rather, it reveals the limitations and narcissism of those institutional players' worldview and their contempt for the rules. Unlawful dealings and interference with and subversion of proper procedures are still being gradually revealed in Turkey.[74]

Journalists Birand (2001, 2006a) and Gülerce (2006) concur that '[those who] dared to engage in an unprecedented smear campaign' went on to act in a way that '[did] not honor the armed forces'; instead of honoring and preserving its traditions, they had been 'causing harm to that significant institution'. Such institutions do 'not keep those [who are] not abiding by the established traditions or [who are] going beyond the mark, even though they are very much applauded for a while'. When the schemes planned and acted out by those generals and their team were later disclosed, and it became known that they did not act in accordance with publicly espoused military traditions, the military had to retire them, and they became an object of contempt in the eyes of the overwhelming majority of the public. Gülerce also makes the point (as did others) that such individuals and the teams under their command have damaged the good name of state institutions.*

The columnist Kamış said of the working group within the military (self-styled the 'West Working Group') which masterminded the February 28 Process:

> The group said this name epitomized their adherence to Western values because Westernization is one of the fundamental principles of the Turkish Republic. However, we now see that they don't care about Western values. [...] They are dreaming of a West devoid of democratization, individual rights, human rights, freedom of worship and civil initiative.

The task of safeguarding democracy means playing the democratic game to its fullest extent: it means demanding that all political players make the reasons for their positions and policies known to the public; it means ensuring that 'the rules of the game' are respected; it means struggling against the

---

* There are applications by Ahmet Altan, Cengiz Çandar and Nazlı Ilıcak (see above, §2.2.15) to the prosecutors to start necessary legal proceedings against the generals engaged in the February 28 Process, but they still retain their immunity, or the prosecutors for reasons they cannot control or explain, have turned down the applications. See *Zaman*, 2006c, 2006d and other Turkish national media in May 2006.

monopolization of information; it means opposing government policies con-structively, i.e. by offering credible alternative policies. It means also that the autonomy of civil society actors must be respected, not by collapsing their concerns into the political arena, but by taking the trouble to respect their distance from that arena. Regrettably, the culture of special interest groups was, on February 28, ill-prepared to undertake the task of safeguarding de-mocracy, for those groups have always sought to reduce everything produced in civil society to political in-fighting, threats or manipulation.[75]

In the 1990s the production and dissemination of information in Turkey and the majority of Turkish media were monopolized by vested interests. When the Gülen Movement joined in the discussion in the media and in the production and dissemination of information, the one-sided game was spoiled. Media outlets set up by Movement participants have gained the trust of the masses and become positively influential in the construction of information and public space. This helps greatly to get nearer to the truth of issues and to rupture the façade behind which the vested interests scheme their schemes.

Vested interest and protectionist groups counter-mobilized during and after the February 28 Process, at the expense of the Turkish public. They collaborated to steal billions of dollars of public money behind a smoke-screen of imaginary threats to the regime. They deployed the national secu-rity argument without scruple, combining with it accusations that their op-ponents were 'reactionary' and/or 'subversive'. They got rid of the public servants who would not collaborate with their schemes and protectionist ideologies. They abused their authority and positions, which they claimed were to serve the nation, in order to eradicate its faith and faith communi-ties. They seemed to be winning for some time; eventually, however, their true intentions and wrongdoings came out and, to their further embarrass-ment, continue to be revealed.*

3.2.4 Social mobility and professionalism

If the formalized institutions of the state do not deliver the services or stan-dard of services for whose management and regulation they are responsi-

---

* Only the media and information aspect of the February 28 Process are discussed here. Further details of this 'soft' or 'post-modern' coup d'état, and how Gülen, the Movement and other civil society members reacted, will be dealt with in a later section §3.2.8.

ble, collective (or, rarely, individual) actors take on the relevant tasks. The reason for that is need: society, especially complex modern society, cannot function effectively without those services. To the extent that collective actors are successful in delivering the needed services, it puts pressure – as we noted in the previous section – on the state and its formalized institutions to assimilate the themes and ideas and the operational values associated with the successful delivery of services. To the extent that a socio-political order is open, this results in amelioration and modernization of the state institutions and agencies concerned – political, economic, cultural – indeed, in some open societies, voluntary local actions have even led to improvements in police functions and practice, a service that almost universally operates as a state monopoly. However, to the extent that a socio-political order is not open, the success of collective actors in managing and providing needed services is perceived as a threat to the authority (perhaps even the legitimacy) of the state, which may then act to disparage and shut down the SMOs engaged in service provision. To understand and evaluate the impact a social movement has on society and state in this regard, cultural codes and the movement's ability to produce meanings for society as a whole are highly relevant. In the previous section, we discussed some aspects of that in relation to framing of information and media activity. Here, we look at the relationship between collective action, professionalization and social mobility.[76]

Social mobility is important for a number of reasons, the most relevant of which for the Gülen Movement is that: 'the more mobile a society is, the more open and fairer [it is shown to be], and that mobility affects the way networks and SMOs are formed, and their size and shape, and the professionalism in them.'[77] Movement participants have long been engaged in non-formalized, philanthropic or altruistic services,[78] which has entailed an extensive, albeit partly invisible, cultural training in new (mostly vocational) skills and intellectualization. The Movement has also been strongly committed to professional services, including retraining processes aimed at better-employed actors in the market and SMOs. Well-educated and qualified members doing proficient work incidentally helps promote the image of the Movement within the larger social field.

In all domains, the Movement has consistently rejected the use of confrontational or direct action tactics.[79] It has instead focused its energies on establishing new enterprises and co-operatives, agencies for personal development, in-service training, and job placement. '[It] has proved able to unite and mobilize large numbers of people from many diverse backgrounds to work on significant social projects.'[80] This is evident in sectors such as education, journalism, television production, radio broadcasting, co-operatives, the accommodation industry (building houses, hostels and hotels), health therapy, and banking/finance.[81] Accordingly, one of the effects of the Movement has been modernization of the society through the expansion of innovative occupational sectors, with notably high turnover of personnel in communications, education and welfare services.

The work of the Gülen Movement, as demonstrated by its sustained outcomes, leads steadily and reliably to modernizing innovation, to more balanced distribution of opportunity and effective welfare services. The scale and professional quality of the services managed by Movement participants, outside as well as inside Turkey, have been widely acknowledged. Their administrative and operational successes have been achieved in extremely competitive environments, and sustained for over thirty years. The successful secular education provided by the Gülen-inspired secondary- and tertiary-level institutions, the service-ethic mind-set associated with universal moral values grounded in Islam, combined with the cultural and professional training gained in both the receiving and the providing of education, has led to a marked horizontal and vertical social mobility in Turkey. It has contributed, in short, to a *modernization* of society – that is not something that could have been anticipated by the protectionist and vested interest groups within the power establishment in Turkey; it is an outcome that runs counter to their assumptions (and prejudices) about any mobilization that strives to make an intelligent, enriching use of the human and cultural resources indigenous to the lands and history of the Turkish people.

The positive outcomes of the Gülen Movement's work – and that of other collective actors similarly concerned to, and engaged in, trying to make things better – can hold only so long as the state does not impose a bureaucratic centralist approach on society as a whole. Such an approach extends arbitrary controls*, impedes participatory processes (and the democratic rights expressed in those processes), and strengthens the protec-

---

* For example, raids into civil society SMOs by legally unauthorized military personnel.

tionist mechanisms and exclusivist values that make society less and less 'open' (in the sense explained above).[82] (Just how protectionist mechanisms function in Turkey will be illustrated in the section on the February 28 Process, pp. 89–95.)

The success of the Movement's mobilization has in some quarters, perhaps predictably, evoked considerable hostility. Leaving aside envy, which is simply a psychological issue, there are a number of political, ideological, and financial factors motivating this hostility.[83] First of all, *any* collective mobilization – not only or particularly the Gülen Movement – not initiated by the protectionist groups within the power establishment is viewed with disfavor by the establishment, because it tends to regard any independent collective action as a potential threat to itself as establishment. If an independent collective mobilization proves its success or efficacy, the power establishment mobilizes against it because it encroaches upon territory that the vested interests groups need to monopolize in order to pursue particular projects and schemes they have in hand and in order to retain their hold on the levers of power. The Gülen Movement's projects and activities have educated and trained many thousands of people, provided them with moral orientation and guidance that makes them orderly, law-abiding citizens, an effort that has improved and modernized society, widened opportunity, etc. In doing all this, the Movement has systematically avoided contentious or adversarial action, so that its work should strengthen public order and social cohesion, and not be used (or construed) as a threat to the power or authority of the state and its institutions. Nevertheless, the Movement constitutes an independent mobilization, moreover one that draws on cultural codes and traditions that the protectionist groups within the establishment wish to suppress. That is why they particularly and very publicly chose to target Gülen himself and the Movement as a smokescreen to distract public attention (and legal scrutiny) away from their own financial and ideological schemes.[84] Political scientist Yavuz explains:

> Gülen represents a major threat for these people, because they want to see a backward, radical Islam, in order to justify repression – whereas with Gülen, you do not get that. [...] Gülen tries to educate the periphery by teaching them foreign languages and providing scholarships for study in foreign countries. This angers the establishment as well, because they want to control the country and not to share the resources with the rest of the population. [...] Gülen was on the side of the poor, while the

establishment did not want to see his movement opening up educational opportunities for the marginal sectors of Turkish society. This frustrated militant secularists in Turkey.[85]

3.2.5 Reflexivity or symbolic potential

An action is said to be generative of reflexivity or symbolic potential if it enables individuals, within the limits set at any given moment by the environment, to affirm and express their autonomy, their being different from other actors within a system, and to own, produce and represent to others the meaning of their action. Symbolic potential is distinct from the specific content of the action itself and constitutes the collective identity. It is enhanced by belonging to organizational and communications networks, since such networks yield solidarity and build resistance against impositions (of identity or meaning) from above by remote, impersonal power.[86]

The reflexivity of the Gülen Movement is very high, as its collective identity is not based on primary associations – gender, age, locality, ethnicity or religion[87] – but on projects and services for the common and collective good. As Kebede and colleagues (2000) explain: '[Reflexivity is] both the product and the cause of collective action [...] created in the midst of collective actions, and the process of maintaining [it] stimulates further collective action.'[88]

Being in the service of the common good, not in the service of a private cause, is a particular emphasis of the approach and actions of the Gülen Movement, and a major theme in its discourse. Without reciprocal recognition between collective actors, there can only be oppression and repression, emptying the social field, in which collective identity is produced, of meaning and the potential for positive, fruitful interactions.[89] The Gülen Movement affirms its belonging to the shared culture of the society and its acceptance of the political and cultural diversity of Turkey:[90] '[It] can live fruitfully in and contribute to secular and religiously plural democracies.'[91] It does not deny others' identities. It refuses adversarial discourse and contentious action, whether lawful or unlawful. Nevertheless, according to Özdalga even though 'the Gülen community neither socially nor economically differs markedly from the established elite', that elite does not recognize the Movement except as 'the adversary'.[92] This indicates a failure of political (as well as moral) imagination, and a readiness to conceive difference only in terms of conflict. The harm in this attitude lies in the tendency of conflict – whether it concerns material or symbolic resources – to transgress the system's shared 'rules of engagement'. An example of this is when Gülen and the Movement were attacked, apparently by the Atv media group.[93] In this attack the Movement's opponents, hiding their identity and motives behind the Atv coverage, sought to create a distorted picture of Gülen's and the Movement's motives and actions. Thus, 'Gülen himself and his community find themselves in a conflict to affirm their identity, which has been denied them by the opponents'.[94]

The protectionist political elite within the Turkish establishment collaborates with the interest groups mostly formed out of the so-called '[19]68 generation'. The experiences of that generation resulted in ideological readings of reality – dogmatism, separatism, sectarianism, violent clashes and armed conflict – that still haunt and prevent the elite's thinking from keeping abreast of the changing terms of social, economic and political realities in Turkey.[95] The statist, elitist, leftist, militant secularists in Turkey failed to produce either political ideas or the tools with which ideas can be put into practice. They failed to deliver, in other words, not just an alternative point of view but also the means whereby it could be made practicable. They were unable to produce a political design that comprised instruments and models of transformation compatible with the historical, economic, and social context. Also, the effects of their actions at the systemic level did not enable cultural innovation or institutional modernization. Eventually, that inability reduced them to 'opposition' in the Turkish Parliament and a minority voice in the wider society; their position and programs are mostly articulated and projected from within the Republican People's Party, or simply 'the left' in Turkey. Political scientist Ergil has summed up the intellectual sterility of 'the left' in this way:

> First, there is no opposition in the political parties that claim to be the 'opposition'. Secondly, the opposition does not have a language of its own other than merely criticizing the government for whatever it does on a daily basis although they would do the same when and if they are ever in power. Thirdly, none of the opposition parties or institutions, including the secularist bureaucracy, has an alternative economic program to back up their alternative political positions. Fourth, most of the opposition parties do not have a definite or definable social basis (supporting social-economic groups).[96]

So this group did not contribute much to the development of reflexivity in the larger societal context or social cohesion. It has become a means and source of polarization, segmentation and tension in Turkey. The 'opposition' has in practice decayed into a counter-mobilization against all except themselves. That counter-mobilization is especially targeted on religion, religious people, and all modernizing efforts and projects originating from the faith-inspired communities. That is the context of their making Gülen and the Movement their major 'adversary'.

Not all of the '68 generation have remained intellectually stuck. Some have come to approach certain issues, and especially religion, differently. One of them, political scientist and columnist Alpay said: 'our eyes opened a little more', 'society could not be understood without understanding religion', and 'religion is not the people's opiate, but it might be society's mortar'.[97] Denying the secularists' 'conspiracy theories' about Gülen, he affirms that Gülen separates religion from party politics and the state:

> I perceive Hodjaefendi* [Gülen] as a man of religion who separates religion from politics, opposes a culture of enmity that can polarize the nation, and contributes to our understanding of Islam with his tolerance. His efforts should be respected.[98]

On the accusation that Gülen aimed to turn Turkey into a religious state, the leftist-liberal editor-journalist Çevik commented:

> All these [allegations] are absurd. Everyone knows Gülen has been preaching tolerance and goodwill. He has always encouraged dialogue not only between the believers and non-believers but also among [members of] religions. That is why he met the Pope and sowed the seeds of inter-religious dialogue. [...] Is it wise to push around a person who is obviously not a terrorist? Are we doing a service to our country by discouraging his followers to push ahead with Gülen's project to raise a new generation of well-educated Turks who respect moral values as well?[99]

Morris, writing in the *Guardian* (2000), said about the leftist Bülent Ecevit, who resisted suggestions by the generals who masterminded the February 28 coup that Gülen was a threat:

---

* An honorific meaning 'respected teacher'.

> The Prime Minister Ecevit, who has made his reputation as a staunch secularist, is one of Mr. Gülen's many fans. In particular, Mr. Ecevit has spoken of his admiration for the network of schools and colleges that [the] Gülen [Movement] has established across Turkey and [abroad].

At the World Economic Forum in Davos in 2000, Ecevit stressed in his speech, as a matter of pride and prestige, the importance of Gülen-inspired schools being all over the world, and how these schools contribute to the cultures and well-being of Turkey and other countries.[100]

It says much of the Gülen Movement's reflexivity, and its success in weakening or removing barriers between people, that it received recognition from such unexpected sources. It had enabled even those who have no part in its work to reflect on the irrational polarization, rigid separation and closure between different collective entities in Turkish society. The term used to denote such polarization is 'segmentation'. It takes account of the degree and size of barriers that separate social groupings to explain mobilization: the higher the degree of segmentation, the denser the resulting network of associational and community affiliation that takes place behind them; the more intense the collective participation in this network of relations, the more rapid and durable will be the mobilization of a movement.[101] It is instructive to note how and by whom the segmentation in Turkish society is produced and sustained and how third parties react to that.

The February 28 coup is referred to, by Turkish and non-Turkish scholars, as Turkey's 'witch hunt' period, or its 'McCarthyism'.[102] Even before that period, *Sabah* columnist Mengi (1995) maintained that what Gülen started

> can lead to a much sounder deterrence against religious fundamentalism than that which the state has produced. The door he opened can be a stage on the road to having the chance to live Islam within our own national identity. To open the people's way and secure peace and tolerance, religion must be protected by contemporary thinkers and institutions. If the developments of the past few days* have taught us about this need, how fortunate we are.[103]

In an article written in 2000, rhetorically titled 'Wasn't Gülen Supposed to Be a Saviour?', Birand queried the logic of what was going on:

---

* Gülen-initiated dialog and reconciliation meetings and their positive repercussions.

> Up until only a few years ago, Gülen was portrayed as a major bulwark
> against religious extremism. Now, an 'elimination' operation has been
> launched. Something strange is going on. [...] If Gülen was a 'hazard', if
> his schools were providing the kind of education that conflicted with the
> secular system, then why was he treated as a 'saviour' at that time? If he
> was not a 'hazard', why are efforts being made to 'eliminate' him today?
> There is something strange about all that.[104]

He concluded with the question: 'If Gülen had committed a crime,
why did the authorities wait until today? [...] To sum up, a highly dangerous process has begun.'

Gülen and Movement participants restructured and revived collective
energies through the formation of new platforms, identities and new collective services. They activated everyday communicative networks, and succeeded in raising new elites and intellectuals. Their antagonists, by contrast,
were being questioned, even mocked, by some formerly from among them.
Social scientist Yılmaz has shown that Gülen's discourse and practice have
obtained the support of many well-known liberal intellectuals and former
Marxists and listed a good number of them.[105] All those people now affirm
and accept that the solution to Turkey's problems depends on reaching a
consensus. Moreover, some influential scholars, deemed to be 'Islamist' and
known as such among Western academic circles, have also modified their
discourse and action in line with Gülen and express ideas and attitudes different from their earlier positions. Journalist Yagiz (1997) pointed out that
Gülen had aimed at, and succeeded in, bringing different segments of society together for the common good, in contrast to those who divide and
keep people in their different camps in tense opposition:

> Gülen wants to bring secularists and anti-secularists, who have been arti-
> ficially separated on this issue, together on common ground. He says:
> 'Secularism should not be an obstacle to religious devoutness, nor should
> devoutness constitute a danger to secularism.'

While the reflexivity or symbolic potential of the Gülen Movement is
increasing and playing a reconciliatory and mediating role between strongly
segmented communities or groups, the reflexivity of the protectionist group
is failing and the rifts they cause enlarging. Özdalga (2005) affirms that the
Gülen Movement plays 'a mediating role in the civilizing process' and pre-
dicts that 'what the group or movement represents' may lead some to

'counteract'.[106] 'By attacking Gülen from all such fronts, they must also be trying to frighten those intellectuals and politicians who give support to the activities that he has recommended.'[107]

3.2.6 Transnational projects and recognition

Part of the reputation of the Gülen Movement is owed to the success of the collective services and symbolic potential produced by institutions and SMOs outside Turkey. Its transnational and joint projects have yielded significant recognition and co-operation from foreign sources.[108] That success in part motivates the counter-mobilization in Turkey.

The business, educational and interfaith organizations operating across economic, political and cultural boundaries work within a common rationale based on knowledge, skills and shared ethical values.[109] The core of the Movement is an educative mobilization which addresses time, space, relations between people, the self, and the affective deep structure of individual behavior. Its rationale therefore does not exhibit change, whether in Turkey or anywhere else.[110]

Gülen encourages people to serve humanity through education, intercultural and interfaith activities and institutions, in order thereby to lessen the gaps between peoples and to establish bridges for the common good and peace. He has explained that society's three greatest enemies are ignorance, poverty, and internal schism, which knowledge, work-capital, and unification can eliminate. Ignorance is the most serious problem, and it is defeated through education, which has always been the most important way of serving others. It is the most effective vehicle for change – regardless of whether it is in Turkey or abroad, and whether or not people have systems working or failing – as the solution of every problem in human life ultimately depends on the initiative and capacities of human beings themselves.[111] Poverty is mitigated through work and the possession of capital, justly deployed in the service of others; and internal schism and separatism are vanquished by striving, through forbearance, tolerance and dialog, for unity.[112] These principles apply equally outside Turkey as within it. The Movement's non-violent and peace-making approach and vision have been widely acknowledged and appreciated.[113]

Now that we live in a global village, Gülen argues, the best way to serve humanity is to establish dialog with other civilizations, to come together on some common ground, with mutual understanding and respect, and thus to work for peace, the co-operation of diverse peoples, and the prevention of the predicted clash of civilizations. Gülen has stressed this consistently in his writing:

> We can, by coming together, stand up against those misguided souls and skeptics to act as breakers, barriers if you will, against those who wish to see the so-called clash of civilizations become a reality.[114]

To ensure the understanding and tolerance necessary for securing the rights of and respect for others, Gülen particularly urges the social elite, community leaders, industrialists and businessmen to support quality education.[115] This has enabled the Movement to establish several hundred educational institutions in Turkey and other countries.[116] It is important to be aware that 'the schools inspired by Gülen's educational understanding are not religious or Islamic. Instead, they are secular private schools inspected by state authorities and sponsored by parents and entrepreneurs. They follow secular, scientific, state-prescribed curricula and internationally recognized programs'.[117] The students and graduates of many of these institutions, in Turkey, the Balkans, Europe, Africa, Central Asia and the Far East, continue to take top honors in university placement tests and consistently finish at the top in International Science Olympics, producing a number of world champions, especially in mathematics, physics, chemistry, and biology.[118]

After some initial disquiet on the part of some commentators, the schools became a means for the Gülen movement to gain recognition for its identity. When doubts were raised about the effects of the schools in 1999, Metin Bostancıoğlu, the National Education Minister of the leftist coalition at the time, said: 'There is no problem in the Turkish [Gülen-inspired] schools, but there are problems at home [in the state schools in Turkey].' He noted that 'there is not a single school in the records of the National Education Ministry which is registered in the name of Fethullah Gülen'; rather, 'they are all registered in the name of foundations'. He stressed that 'the ministry carries out the necessary controls in the schools and the hostels' in partnership 'with local authorities', and that 'mathematics, physics, and English courses are good at the schools'. Moreover, Bostancıoğlu made a particular point of affirming that the schools have no hidden agenda:

> I believe that the children are grown up well at [these] schools. The children are successful in the university entrance exams. The schools follow the curriculum. I do not know any hidden targets of schools.[119]

Columnist Özgürel stated (2000) that 'Ankara [i.e. the Turkish state] cannot find a concrete complaint or crime by which it can take over the schools'.[120] Faced with the concerns raised by a few about the schools, Gülen promised that if anyone could should show that the schools were teaching anything opposed to modern Turkish and democratic values, he would immediately advise people to close the schools.[121] In a letter sent to the secretary of Chief of Staff General Çevik Bir* of Turkey, he wrote: 'If the Turkish State and authorities would give guarantees on covering the expenses of continuing [the] education and on keeping the standard of education at those schools at least as high as it is, the schools would be handed over to the State.'[122] Cenk Koray, one of the journalists who visited the schools outside Turkey, concluded:[123]

> Instead of binding these schools to the Ministry of Education, we should allow Gülen to administer the state schools in Turkey! A flower is not easily grown in a swamp. We are trying our best to pull up the flowers, make them fade and destroy them! What a shame! [...] A Russian official** succinctly stated the essence of this work: 'There are two important events in Russian life: One of these is Gagarin's being sent into space before the Americans, and the other is the opening of these schools.' If foreigners are thinking like this, what are we doing?[124]

Under the headline 'Ambassadors back Gülen schools in Asia', The *Turkish Daily News* reported (in 2000) the positive effect of the schools outside Turkey on the country's foreign relations:

> In order to give a new impetus to Turkey's relations with Central Asian and Caucasian countries, the Turkish Ministry of Foreign Affairs held advisory meetings in which Turkey's ambassadors to these countries participated, and then a report was prepared. The report said that Gülen schools in those countries had been playing a positive role in Turkey's relations with those governments.[125]

---

*   One of the two masterminds of the February 28 Process.
** In charge of education in Moscow at that time.

In the same year, Birand reported: 'Gülen[-inspired] schools were being praised, even the children of military personnel were enrolling in those schools abroad, [and] the reports our ambassadors abroad sent home on these schools were full of praise.'[126] Many other people from all walks of life have also visited these schools and witnessed the quality of education and the positive change in those students and the peoples affected, and expressed their approval.[127] The Kyrgyz Constitutional Court President Bayekova described Gülen as a person of science, peace, and tolerance. Remarking on the international importance of Gülen's work, Bayekova said:

> We saw in Gülen an example that, if a person wants, he can achieve as much on his own as a government does. We can establish peace and dialogue if we want. We, as Kyrgyz, work hard to fulfill Gülen's goals.[128]

The Romanian commission of UNESCO presented Gülen with an award for his remarkable efforts in activities concerned with dialog and tolerance and his efforts toward co-operation and peace between the nations of the world.[129] In a 2003 report prepared for the RAND Corporation, public policy expert Cheryl Benard stated:

> Gülen puts forward a version of Islamic modernity that is strongly influenced by Sufism and stresses diversity, tolerance, and non-violence. His writings have inspired a strong multinational following and have proven attractive to young people.[130]

So much positive acknowledgement and recognition outside Turkey of the success of the services and SMOs inspired by the Gülen Movement has provoked anxiety in the protectionist elite and vested interest groups. These groups prefer to isolate Turkey from world realities, as it is then easier for them to impose their control and authority on Turkish society. While they are not recognized for their contribution to any international achievement, they counter-mobilize against others who are, in order to retain their status, in Turkey and the international arena, as the single voice and authority acting on behalf of Turkish people. The capacity of the participants and SMOs in the Gülen Movement to outdo the elite in educational, intellectual, scientific and cultural services and to participate effectively in the international arena has symbolically revealed the elite's limitations. This hurts the elite's standing in the eyes of the people (within Turkey and abroad), something that it finds an intolerable irritant.

3.2.7 Altruistic action and its symbolic challenge

Altruistic action is dealt with here briefly and only in relation to counter-mobilization: how mobilization is encouraged and framed through altruistic services and why it is taken as a symbolic challenge by the protectionist vested interests. The concept of 'offering' and symbolic challenge will be further dealt with in §4.1.5.

Gülen's understanding of duty, to serve humanity especially in the field of education, 'permits no expectation of material or political gain. Sincerity and purity of intention should never be harmed or contaminated.'[131] Educationalist Woodhall (2005) explains further:

> Gülen's philosophy of education is not utilitarian, nor a social and political activity which can be divorced from the rest of his philosophy or faith, but a firmly integrated and well-developed component of his world view. [...] He indicates that the means must be as valid as the end, apparent or material success is not the only measure [...][132]

In the same vein, Tekalan, another educationalist, also confirms that the purpose of the movement 'is to ensure respect for objective and universal human values, to never have ulterior motives to seek material interests nor to impose any ideology or to seize power through politics in any country'.[133]

For over forty years, Gülen has urged his audiences 'to achieve the right balance of social justice between the individual and community; to develop and advance in every individual and the whole nation feelings of love, respect, altruism, striving for the sake of others, sacrificing their own material and non-material benefits and aspirations for the sake of others'.[134] Sociologist Tarcan (1998) asks rhetorically why anyone should be disturbed by altruistic services and so vehemently oppose them:

> Who can object to raising youth who use science and the technology it gave birth to for the good of humanity, scientists respectful of moral principles, administrators who serve people sincerely, and officials and managers who do not steal and abuse their position but rather understand administration to mean serving people?[135]

This understanding of service is geared primarily to 'offering' in Turkey and abroad. It is a mobilization that presents alternative models of a kind that state systems cannot replicate. That is why it has attracted broad attention, in favor and against, within a short period of time.[136] Melucci explained that 'offering' represents a symbolic challenge to the dominant cultural codes and the customary (so-called 'rational' self-interest) basis of strategic and instrumental logic in complex societies; the unilateral power of giving (for nothing, sometimes in defiance of immediate self-interest), and thereby generating and providing cultural models, constantly results in a movement's predominance in societies. The reason is that the autonomous and gratuitous ('for nothing') production of cultural models is neither motivated nor regulated, nor can be side-tracked, by cost–benefit calculations.[137]

In the eyes of those who for years have exploited and usurped Turkey's wealth and resources, the generations raised and those yet to be raised among the Gülen Movement are a challenge to their way of thinking and rationale. They have found their logic upset. For, while they seek to siphon money and resources illegally from the state and people's pockets, others have begun instead to construct alternate modes of behavior and generate alternative meanings. This offers a symbolic challenge to the rationality of calculation, established bureaucratic routines, and means-end relationships (the cost–benefit calculations mentioned by Melucci). The challenge arises from the given-for-nothing nature of the 'offering' and the directness of personal commitment, which demonstrate that sharing with others is not reducible to instrumental logic. In essence, it reminds us of the limitations of a system's power over people and events, calling into question the system's sway over us, and inviting us to assume greater responsibility for our choices and actions. In so doing, it becomes a vital component in the renewal of civil society and the reinforcement of social cohesion.[138] For precisely those reasons there is counter-mobilization by vested interests.

3.2.8 The February 28 process and its aftermath

A complete account of the February 28 Process which followed the 'soft coup' of that date is not relevant here. An outline of the coup events and pertinent issues was presented in the historical narrative in the preceding chapter, §2.2.15–16 (see pp. 45–50). Here we intend to explain and understand why Gülen and the Movement were targeted during the February 28 Process, and how the Movement was able to come through the crisis without resort to negativity, to any counter-action or conflictual or coercive means. Before doing so, it may be well to remind readers that the opposition from certain ideological interest groups within the power establishment in Turkey is directed towards *any* collective actor that is perceived to endanger their schemes and vested interests; however, there are particular reasons why those vested interests made the Gülen Movement a major focus of their counter-mobilizing efforts. The discussion following should bring out those reasons.

Even as this explanation was being written, further exposures about the February 28 Process continued to reveal the main actors, their schemes, wrong-doings, ulterior motives and means, greatly strengthened by revelations by state personnel and organizations, and confessions by the major actors in the Process. (None of the major figures who masterminded the February 28 coup has denied what they are alleged to have done. On the other hand, none of them has yet been subject to legal process. Çandar, Altan and Ilıcak have made individual applications to the courts, so far to no avail.* Since major state institutions were exploited in the February 28 Process, Gülen has not taken any action against individuals involved so as not to further damage or bring shame to the institutions concerned.)

Before February 28, the Susurluk scandal and its continuing fallout had already revealed the existence of the 'deep state' and the extent of political and military malpractice in the country. It had shown that security officials were involved in illegal operations with right-wing gangsters and politicians associated with some military commanders, ministers and Prime Minister of the time.** During these decades, the country has witnessed how 'democracy is suspended or forced into the background every time its results are not acceptable to the powers that be'.[139] Kramer states that this suspension of the political rules causes acute distress, since the system cannot be trusted to provide the people with the means and risk-reducing fa-

---

* I talked to Ilicak and Altan in London in 2007. Ilicak told me that she won the case she took to the European Human Rights Court but had not pursued it further in Turkey. Altan told me that Çandar tried to bring a case on their behalf in Turkey, but the military courts did not allow their case to proceed.

** Former Special Forces chief İbrahim Şahin was jailed for his involvement in the Susurluk scandal. He has had close relations with retired army Captain Muzaffer Tekin who is believed to have instructed lawyer Alparslan Aslan and orchestrated the gang for the murderous attack on judges in a Turkish Council of State in 2006 (*Turkish Daily News* 2006). Sahin and Tekin had close relations with retired Major General Veli Küçük, another key name in the Susurluk scandal and court assaults. For an attempt to define such gangs and 'the deep state' phenomenon, see Birand (2006b); and Appendix 1.

cilities with which to overcome the consequences of far-reaching uncertainty.[140] The condition of acute uncertainty went much further, after February 28, when there was no longer agreement on the rules, value orientations, communal ends or collective goals.[141] It was called a 'soft coup' because 'the coalition government was ushered out of power with strong pressure [...] from the Turkish military and secular elites' and they did not hang fifty people as they did in the 1980s.[142] As the crisis deepened, emergency laws and martial regulations further suspended rules, values, and goals, and thereby affected the capacity of individuals and groups to respond with certitude to the question of identity: who we were before, and who we are now.[143]

On February 28, 1997, the National Security Council (NSC), presenting themselves as guardians of secularism, released this public statement: 'destructive and separatist groups are seeking to weaken our democracy and legal system by blurring the distinction between the secular and the anti-secular. [...] In Turkey, secularism is not only a form of government but a way of life and the guarantee of democracy and social peace [...] the structural core of the state.'

In what the commander of the navy, Admiral Güven Erkaya, called on national TV 'a post-modern coup',* the military commanders had pressured politicians by explicit threats of violence, and political and economic pressure, either to implement proposed measures or fashion an alternative government that would do so.[144] Prime Minister Erbakan agreed to an eighteen-point plan to curb Islamic-minded political, social, cultural and economic groups. Later, in June 1997, the military's supervision of Turkey's democratically elected coalition government resulted in its forced resignation. Following this, the pressure on the Muslim communities increased, with some secular leaders hoping for a settling of accounts with political Islam.[145]

Nothing in Turkish political life since the military coup of 1980 has been as divisive as the National Security Council (NSC) decisions of February 28.[146] Political scientist Cizre-Sakallioglu thinks that 'No major element of Turkish politics at present can be understood without reference to the February 28 process'. She adds:

---

* In a January 2001 television program, a former military commander Özkasnak labeled this intervention as a 'post-modern coup', too.

> The February 28 process indicates not only the far-reaching implications of
> the NSC decisions, but also the suspension of normal politics until the sec-
> ular correction was completed. This process has profoundly altered the for-
> mulation of public policy and the relationship between state and society.[147]

The February 28 Process not only altered the relationship between
state-bureaucracy and civil society but also between Turkey and its democratic partners and supporters. The assessment of journalist and author
Howe is that 'In the process, basic democratic norms have been violated,
which has spawned deep resentment within the country and led to strains
with Turkey's democratic partners.'[148]

Until columnist and Parliamentarian Ilicak (2000) published a memo
which had been issued from the General Staff's Intelligence Bureau, most
people remained unaware of the details of the smokescreen of the February
28 coup. The military memo, dated April 1998 and titled 'Special Action
Plan', revealed an order for 'a smear campaign' to silence opposition voices
among intellectuals, journalists, politicians and civil society members. According to the memo, just after February 28, Cengiz Çandar, Mehmet Ali Birand
and the former Human Rights Association Chairman, Akin Birdal, were
among the campaign's targets. Soon after the apprehension of Şemdin Sakık,
the second-in-command in the armed wing of the separatist Kurdish terrorist
organization, the PKK, Sakık allegedly 'confessed' that these individuals had
financial and organizational links to the PKK. Given the apparent source of
the information it was likely that most of the public would believe this story.
Even graver, an assassination attempt on Birdal followed, which left him seriously disabled. Soon afterwards, it became clear that Sakik's statement was
not genuine. The memo points to the responsible individuals in the Chief of
Staff's office: Former Deputy Chief of General Staff General Çevik Bir and
Chief of General Staff General Secretary Erol Özkasnak.

Journalist Incioglu (2000) interviewed Çandar to uncover further details of the memos. Incioglu comments:

> The incident was telling about the journalism ethic and had a financial
> aspect as well, because it coincided with the investigation of the Sabah
> management for their shares in the bailed-out Etibank. Sabah columnist
> Çandar says: 'My newspaper sold me out.'*[149]

---

*   Çandar attempted to report on the illegal activities in which the owner of Sabah was involved.
His report was not published and he was laid off by the newspaper's management.

Against the accusations that some from the state used the daily *Hürri-yet's* editor Ekşi and gave him instructions to write his column accordingly, Ekşi (2000), in his article entitled 'Character Assassination' confesses:

> In the Sakık incident, the state* has deceived the members of the press, including me. I am publicly condemning those who have deceived the press and caused me to write things against fellow journalists...(who were implicated as being on the payroll of the outlawed PKK).[150]

The General Staff Secretary *confirmed* that the memorandum had been issued by its staff. Some analysts interpreted the army's willingness to confirm its involvement as a sign that the current commanders did not approve of their colleagues' or predecessors' actions. Others simply hoped this controversy would be an opportunity to lay the past to rest: 'The army has admitted the facts,' said Birand.[151]

The Turkish Journalists' Association (Türkiye Gazeteciler Cemiyeti) issued a press release on August 10 stating:

> It has been observed that the media is involved in a number of conflicts of interest and is furthermore under the influence of certain power centers, and this is reflected in media policies. In light of this, it is not possible to speak of editorial independence.[152]

During this period, some marginal but like-minded people – special interest groups, ideologically motivated individuals, staunch militant secularists (who were anti-Islam), and a few people abusing their judicial authority or military ranks – jointly fabricated news and threats. They selected certain columnists in the press and media to ensure that information spread widely among the public.[153] They aimed to influence public opinion and decrease popular confidence in certain journalists, members of parliament, human rights activists, academics, intellectuals, and civil society members. Gülen became the highest profile target. Behind a smokescreen of accusations against him of seeking to overthrow the regime, creating national security issues, and presenting threats of reactionary fundamentalism, those orchestrating the coup tried to conceal their dishonest dealings, graft and plunder of state wealth and resources.[154] For some then, an environment of constant conflict in Turkey was seen as favorable to their interests.[155]

---

* In fact, not the state but a few generals and their friends at the Chief of Staff.

The suspension of rules and values becomes even more evident if we examine the emotional side of the situation. The experience of some individuals involved with the faith communities in Turkey was ambivalent because of the degree of shock produced by the rapidity and unpredictability of the event. It was accompanied by fear and anxiety over what had been lost and the new situation created. *New York Times* reporter Frantz (2000) wrote that the war of attrition during the February 28 Process 'sent a chill through his [Gülen's] circle of admirers and raised anxieties among liberals who are not associated with his movement'.

There are always different outcomes to the collective processes that follow an emergency like the February 28 coup. Certain groups in the community may assimilate or suffer more from the negative, destructive and depressive components of the event and may thus be contained within a state of shock, impotence or inertia; others might disintegrate. And yet, once people had recovered from the immediate shock, the aftermath of the coup with its revelations about unlawful, undemocratic practice, also suggested hope or a will for renewal.[156]

The adaptability and reliability of the culture of the Gülen Movement then became an invaluable resource in accommodating to the new situation, whereas more rigid and exclusive cultures would have experienced greater difficulties in coping with the acute uncertainty.

A number of explanations can be suggested for the capacity of the Gülen Movement to respond to such a situation positively and peacefully, instead of retreating into passivity or a sort of collective psychosis at the cultural and group levels (as Melucci has argued can happen).[157] The first is the reliability and legitimacy of the authority that Gülen and Movement participants already enjoyed. The second is the density and vitality of their networks of belonging, all the heritage present in the Movement, and the ability to restructure and redirect these in new situations. The third is the Movement's ability to listen to society at various levels – something that the masterminds of the February 28 injustices had never done.

Kinzer[158] (2001) notes that the incompetence and apparent unwillingness of the army and state apparatus to assist people in the immediate aftermath of the Izmit earthquake in 2000 led, three years later, to the mass disillusionment of the populace with institutions such as the army, the government and political parties. On the continuing growth of this disillusionment, after the assassination at the Supreme Court of Appeals in 2006, one of the victims of the February 28 Process, Çandar (2006) pointed out:

> As the haze around this organized gang lifts, we're coming across perpe-
> trators who have connections to the notorious Susurluk affair that covert-
> ly triggered the developments that led to the post-modern coup of 1997
> which removed the Erbakan government through military coercion.

The February 28 Process was not limited to Turkish citizens either. Kinzer was among five foreign correspondents who were singled out as having been especially responsible for feeding 'distortions' to the world. He was charged by the Chief of Staff and expelled from Turkey on grounds that he along with the other journalists had placed himself at the service of unnamed subversive 'interests'.[159] Over the decades, Turkish or non-Turkish individuals, whose actions do not suit the protectionist interests, have consistently been accused in the same idiom of posing a threat to the state or national security.

Gülen was attacked by some who were marginal in the establishment, and by their extensions in the media and other sectors of the civilian sphere.[160] On the other hand, as Gülerce observed, support for Gülen and the Movement within society did not diminish as a result of this war of attrition: 'Even during periods when Gülen was subjected to planned attacks carried out by certain circles, it was observed that he had 85 percent of public support.'[161]

An effective democratic system must be able to absorb the tension between the structures of representation and the demands or interests of those represented therein. It must also devise social and political measures to reduce the distance that separates power from social demands, without ideologically neutralizing the problem. The mere fact that a direct command from certain generals is replaced by representation, mediation, and the capacity to produce negotiated decisions, does not necessarily lead to a process being 'democratic'; it may result, instead, in non-representative institutional arrangements, as was clearly witnessed through the Susurluk scandal[162] and the military memos related to the events of February 28.

Political scientist Ataman argues that 'the traditional leadership of Turkey [is] based on its strict nationalist, secularist and bureaucratic-authoritarian understanding. [...] Leadership groups first try to maintain their interests and then secure national interests. In many cases, the interests of the leadership group are proposed as national interests.'[163] Another political scientist, William Hale had reached a similar conclusion earlier:

> Turkey has so far not been able to shake off the inherited notion and institution of the authoritarian state and the transmitted undemocratic and non-egalitarian habitus of its military-bureaucratic elite. Around this institutionalized core of the rule of the military-bureaucratic reformers, a new modern elite has emerged in the Turkish Republic. Based on a cartel of interest and legitimized with the Kemalist ideology, this elite controls the resources of the modern sectors of Turkish society. However, whereas the social structural background of this elite is modern, their behavior is characterized by an authoritarian and elitist habitus.[164]

Anthropologist Eickelman points out that 'the militant secularism of some governing elites – the Turkish officer corps, for example – has been associated until recently with authoritarianism and intolerance more than with "enlightenment values".'[165]

It is against this background, and within this context, that one can understand why the Gülen Movement was particularly targeted. It was targeted because it operates as a 'symbolic multiplier'.[166] By the sheer scale and success of the services it provides, it lays bare the weaknesses of the protectionist apparatus and obliges it to justify itself. The articulation, by the Movement as collective actor within the larger society, of collective needs and democratic demands makes it possible for dominant protectionist relationships, interests and privileges to be lawfully questioned, and for decisions taken by the apparatuses to be subjected to measurement against collective needs. Also the hope remains that those decisions can be checked by due process of law.

3.2.9 (Re)defining democracy

Contemporary social movements concern themselves with 'a redefinition of what democracy is, can be, and ought to be'.[167] Individuals and groups wish to construct their identities 'instead of remaining simply recipients [of identities] assigned them from the outside'. Political institutions in a democracy open up a field of participation compatible with the system. They also allow social demands to transform into a collective opportunity to exercise rights and to voice opposition, and an 'open society is possible where political actors assume a non-totalizing role as mediators of demands'.[168]

After the establishment of the Journalists and Writers Foundation, Gülen met with a few political leaders and some government members.[169] A retired general (who would later take part in the February 28 Process), and some from the protectionist elite, criticized these efforts by Gülen. In response to the criticism of his meetings, Gülen replied:

> In a democracy, a system with a fully civil character, popular participation in the administration is encouraged to the extreme, as summed up in the saying, 'The nation owns unrestricted and unconditional sovereignty'.[*] I have never even thought of going into the street to demonstrate and openly criticize the system, although democracy permits this when necessary. In fact, as such behavior could lead to anarchy, I always approach it with caution. For this reason, not only as a right but as a responsible citizen, citizens meeting with political and state leaders, or state leaders and politicians meeting with people from every social segment, should be appreciated and encouraged.[170]

Gülen's response is strictly in line with what participatory or pluralist democracy requires. He also drew attention to the fact that his meetings 'operate fully within the legal framework of the Turkish Republic'.[171] In another interview, Gülen stated: 'If we are to proceed to an even more perfect democracy, that can again be achieved through democratic processes.'[172]

Democracy in complex societies consists of more than the competition for access to governmental resources and more than elections. It means the creation of conditions which allow social actors to recognize themselves and be recognized for what they are or want to be. In this sense, democracy means the freedom to belong, to construct social spaces of recognition, and to express oneself in systems of representation. Non-authoritarian democracy accommodates a dualism: the right to make one's voice heard through representation and the right to modify the conditions in which it is heard. The Gülen Movement contributes to the achievement of the conditions necessary for an effective pluralist democracy through formal and informal networks such as conferences, platforms, relational and associational neighborhood meetings, and media outlets.[173] Similarly,

---

[*] Quoting the aphorism of Atatürk, displayed in the Turkish Grand National Assembly Hall (Parliament).

the premises of a pluralist theory claim that participation signifies acting to promote an actor's interests and needs, and being part of (or belonging to) a system, thus identifying with the 'general interests' of the community. Political participation involves the action of private citizens, aimed directly at influencing the selection of the government personnel and the actions of those personnel.[174]

If, as Gülen says – 'the majority of [the Turkish] media support the [Movement's] initiatives, regardless of their origin [and a]lmost all state and political leaders and intellectuals have expressed their approval and appreciation'[175] – how are we to understand the logic of those who oppose his efforts?

The Turkish political system is subject to various degrees of internal manipulation within the system through the constraints imposed by a structure of dominance anchored in social relationships. Although the boundaries determining what issues can be submitted to the decision-making process are structurally set,* control over the rules and mechanisms of decision-making itself are assumed to be the privilege exclusively of those representing the dominant protectionist interests[176] – as has already been pointed out by the Turkish Journalists' Association press release.[177] The protectionist elite, as Kramer and Alpay concur, 'was reluctant to give up its tutelage of the masses', even though it 'had hardly any relations with the masses'.[178] For members of that elite, any initiative that does not originate from amongst them and any attempt to shift power relationships within the political system or to acquire influence over decisions, is either a threat, a matter of crisis for the regime, or a national security issue.[179]

Gülen holds that this understanding or notion of democracy runs into problems because the world is a culturally diverse place and no single group, nation or culture has the monopoly on democratic ideas and practice:[180]

> Democracy, though it still needs to be further improved, is now the only
> viable political form, and people should seek to modernize and consoli-

---

* The founding principles of the Turkish Republic are written within those parts of the Constitution that 'cannot be changed'. Özgürel (2000), 'Gülen and the Threat of Subversion', states: 'We have seen that the principles of law, democracy and social justice can be neglected, but the most sensitive principles, those of the republic, secularism and national security, are bound up tight'.

date democratic institutions in order to build a society where individual
rights and freedom are respected and protected.

The problem, then, is how to give precise definition to the parameters
of pluralist participatory democracy. Undoubtedly, social relations influence such participation in both directions. From the perspective of the protectionist ruling groups, political participation serves to confirm the priority of their own interests and to secure the subordinated consensus of other
social groups; participation takes place within the confines and rules determined by their dominating system, thus – to a greater or lesser extent –
promoting their interests. To them, the subordinate groups participate politically so as to increase their influence in the decision-making processes or
to alter institutional power relationships. However, as these groups are always more or less excluded from involvement in decision-making, their effort is manifested through non-institutional forms of action.[181]

However, the activities of the Gülen Movement take place within the
confines and rules of the political system as it is. They do not aim to maximize the advantages of the actor in political decisions. No matter how their
worldview or services might empirically affect the political system, they do
not threaten to disregard or infringe the rules of that system as given, nor do
they transgress its institutional boundaries. The services given by the Movement are not a contest among adversaries for the distribution of control over
the allocation of social production and of imbalances of power among social
positions. Rather, all the efforts of the Gülen Movement need to be analyzed,
using analytical categories other than political ones, as *collective social altruism*. Özdalga attempts to explain this using Weber's notion of 'worldly asceticism', and attributes the protectionist groups' suspicion about the Movement
to their underlying power interests:

> Rather than advancing political ambitions, his [Gülen's] objective is to
> foster an ethic that comes very close to what Max Weber described as
> 'worldly asceticism,' an activist pietism with a tendency toward the ratio-
> nalization of social relationships.[182]

To intolerant reactions, which allege that he is after political gains or
seeking a new political formation – albeit that would be, in any event, quite
lawful, permitted under Turkish law and the constitution – Gülen responds:

> I have absolutely no political aspirations and expectations. I have never been involved in any political effort or activity. [...] But I see myself as a genuine member of this nation, as one of the threads in the lace of this culture. So as long as I live, if I have an opinion about an issue related to it, I won't hesitate to express it.'[183]

On another occasion, Gülen commented:

> I consider such speculation as a great insult for me. My path consists of searching for God. It is wrong to portray a man who found something in his life according to his own measures as still looking for something. Those who found God have found everything. All other yearnings are futile in life. I always had meetings with political figures but my attention has never wavered from the ultimate goal of my life, that is, searching for God.[184]

The reason that there has been counter-mobilization against Gülen and the Movement is that – as columnist Ipekci argues[185] – the dominant protectionist group assume that social, cultural and political representation in Turkey, as well as the identification of any societal problems and their solution, are their sole and exclusive prerogative.

This is, again, best seen in the counter-mobilization during the February 28 Process against SMOs and civil society. It was not based on democratic procedures or political consensus but was and is realized and secured through ideological interpretation. The protectionist system propagates itself and permeates daily life and existential choices. It filters and represses some demands by presenting them as an absolute, existential threat to the very structure of society. When the counter-mobilizing actor cannot compete with any alternative in argument, action and services, the requisite stigmatizations are ready to hand: as we have mentioned earlier, the protectionist system simply assimilates any suggestion or advice, any alternative or opposition, under the familiar rubric of a threat to national security, or some variation thereof.

Despite the fact that such interpretation and counter-mobilization is anti-democratic and anti-egalitarian, it is legitimated in terms of conjunctures and the exploitation of segmentation, radicalization and tension in society. It resurfaces at different conjunctures as improprieties, corruption or concealment of other vested interests. One way for protectionist actors to seek a reduction in the risks involved in a decision is to secure for themselves a preventive consensus through the use of ideological manipulation. This preventive consensus usually goes by the name of 'Kemalism'.

According to Hale (1999),[186] the decisions by the dominant protectionist system affect the rest of the social structure. Decisions are implemented only partially, not at all, or in a distorted fashion, according to the practical effect of the particular forces and interests intervening in the implementation process. Direct pressure on administrative bodies can also be used to distort the process or render a decision ineffective, or to secure an advantageous application of the new ruling. This produces a closed political system, in which transparency is minimized and impropriety is maximized.

Journalist Çevik (2002) considered corruption was 'also a vital issue to be taken up by the National Security Council'. He asked the generals and 'those who are concerned about the preservation of the Republic and the system [to] realize that under the current corrupt and deficient system, everything could fall apart'. In the same editorial, titled 'Corruption is Also a Top Threat', Çevik went on to argue:

> The sensitivity and determination shown in the fight against religious radicalism and separatism should also be displayed against corruption, which we feel is the number one menace. Corruption is at the root of many of the ills in Turkey. [...] We feel the military should also take up this menace and get to the bottom of the corruption and irregularities which have eaten into our state system.[187]

In the same vein, columnist Ülsever states: 'Some of the people in power at the time, both in the civilian and military bureaucracies, took advantage of the situation.' He questions those who claimed to love Turkey more than anyone else and yet held the most important positions during the February 28 Process. He states that those people 'did nothing at all about improprieties during their reign':

> The enemies of 'people's money' should surely have been captured when these lovers of the country held the most prominent positions. Instead they imposed a closed system where they had more rights than others 'to protect the country' and 'intervene' when the democratic system made mistakes. However, 'the economics of impropriety' was not solved, or even touched then![188]

Melucci argues that 'the execution of a decision requires the mobilization of both the administrative apparatus of the state and a sufficient quota of political consensus'.[189] The variable relationship between these two components settles the degree of legitimization attached to the decision. Continuous pressures, negotiations, and the power relationships among political parties and interest groups, play the major part in the legitimation and implementation of decisions. Therefore, the influence or efficacy of a decision cannot be assessed in the abstract but must, instead, be evaluated as part of the extant relationship between the forces and interests in a given society.

The efficacy of and support for decisions during the February 28 Process provide further evidence of whether such decisions were based on democratic values and procedures or to serve vested interests. The generals proposed a decree which would have allowed the dismissal of thousands of public employees 'suspected' of 'sympathizing' with Islamist, Kurdish or separatist leanings.[190] This decision and the subsequent dismissals demonstrated that the representation of interests within the political system is not realized through transparent replication. Instead, dominant social relationships set boundaries and determine both the potential and limits of action within the system. The coercive character of the decision was not a functional necessity founded on consensus, but illustrative of how dominating relations and interests manifest themselves within the political system. Alan Makovsky (2000) sees the insistence on the purge of all alleged 'Islamist' officials in governance, during which Gülen too was accused of being implicated, as 'the regime's effort to implement a draconian anti-Islamist program without clear public support'.[191]

By contrast with those overt and covert transgressions of the political rules, the discourse and actions of the Gülen Movement – their teaching and projects within Turkish social and cultural life – do not transgress any procedural or institutional boundaries. Their services and organizations do not break the rules of the political game.[192] To the contrary, according to the BBC's regional analyst, Pam O'Toole (2000):

> Gülen has been even feted by Turkey's secular establishment. [...] The message he preaches is one of tolerance, promoting a private, non-politicized form of Islam, which can peacefully coexist with Turkey's strongly secular state.[193]

Nonetheless, a repressive intervention was launched to re-assert the habitual limits of the system, with no excuses as to its blunt manner. Morris (2000) of the *Guardian*, argued: 'The case could split Turkish society. Some will regard the allegations as the fruits of secularist paranoia, while others will insist the threat is real and immediate.'[194]

That is indeed what happened during the accusation and trial of Gülen. The judge in the case rejected a request by several marginal ideologically motivated groups to be civil parties to the trial. Then certain military officers, the chief prosecutor, and some militant secularist associations attempted to intervene directly in the internal functioning of the political and judicial system. The reason, simply, is that, for them, the presence within the system of a new collective actor either strains the limits of their habitual operation and their dominant social relationships, or – through the success it has achieved in providing ideas, values and services – questions their rationality and efficacy. Whether by accessing the apparatus of the state and the media system or by influencing legislative decision-making, those who represent the dominant interests strive not to lose the structural advantages they enjoy within the political game.[195]

Another reason why initiatives or actions originating outside the protectionist group face exclusion is that they raise awareness so that the people begin to wonder what advantages follow to them from the particular dominant interests' exploitation of political processes and public resources. In fact, Turkey's primary problem was not Islamic fundamentalism, as a BBC report noted: 'Turkey's number one problem is the economic crisis and the difficulties the people are having in making ends meet. The agenda of the people and that of Ankara are incompatible.'[196] Nevertheless, the case the Chief State Security Prosecutor filed against Gülen claimed that he was the biggest threat to Turkey.

The prosecutor's repeated attempts to get an arrest warrant for Gülen were rejected by the courts for lack of substantial evidence.[197] That tells us a number of things:

First, it explains that the radically exclusionary protectionist ideology has settled in certain sections of the public bureaucracy. That, secondly, creates tensions between different forces and interests within the state's organizational bodies. Third, it also explains the conflicts that place different sections of the bureaucracy in opposition to each other, as well as the relative resistance to certain policies despite support for others. Lastly, it tells us that not all state apparatuses may be merely docile instruments in the hands of the dominant groups – rather, their operation also reflects a degree of autonomy, and the honesty, of some in the political system.

Melucci explained why ideology denies the 'adversary' any legitimacy. By deflecting all negative feedback onto the 'adversary', it maintains the legitimacy of its own action and widens its support base and the space within which it can act inside the political system.[198] The attempt to discredit Gülen and his services or to turn public resentment against the Gülen Movement and so legitimize repression is one of the essential components of the framing activity conducted by the protectionist vested interests after 1997. Greater control over the flow of information and the media guaranteed a structural advantage for the powers that be, as the game was never entirely open and positions were not those of parity.[199]

However, these interest groups failed to contend successfully for public consensus – partly because of the activities of media outlets inspired by Gülen Movement participants, and partly because the overwhelming majority of journalists, politicians and civil society leaders remained unconvinced by the arguments against Gülen, though some were compelled to silence. Çevik (1999b) comments:

> There are forces within the state which are trying to use Gülen for their own power struggle. Those who started the crusade against [Prime Minister] Erbakan now are testing their strength against Gülen, who is not only a moderate preacher but also a man who has won friends in high places. They want to show everyone that they can move mountains and, thus, that they call the cards in Turkey. Let us hope all this blows over with minimum damage to Turkey after the August reshuffling period ends.[200]

The August reshuffling period is the time when military officers are promoted or retirement decisions are taken in Turkey. Before and during this time, national security threats, and faith-inspired movements or communities are always made headlines by some likely-to-be-retired generals.

The allegations against Gülen were patently false, indeed absurd. Among those who never accepted the allegations is Bülent Ecevit, the prime minister of the time (between January 1999 and November 2002). Ecevit unwaveringly defended Gülen as a respectable spiritual leader and peaceful scholar. He stressed that, had it not been for Gülen and the schools he encouraged and inspired, communities and countries in Central Asia would have fallen under the influence of Iranian and Wahhabi fundamentalisms.[201]

3.2.10 Induced resolution

In 2003, Ankara State Security Court No.2 postponed taking a final resolution on the Gülen case. The court ruled that in the event that Gülen were to be involved in similar or graver acts requiring a jail sentence, the case would continue; and in the event that he were not, the case would be revoked. Attorneys for Gülen objected to the resolution, demanding continuation of the case in solicitation of acquittal. However, Ankara State Security Court No.1 stated that the resolution was final. Essentially he was cleared, yet only as long as he did not commit any further 'crimes', as defined by the state. The chief prosecutor opted to leave the case open for the next five years. Thus, if Gülen did not die by then, the case against him would finally collapse. So, he remained neither guilty nor acquitted, neither captive nor truly free.[202]

Four years later, in 2006, the Ankara 11th High Criminal Court revealed that it was unable to prosecute Gülen and therefore dropped the case, and thus Gülen was acquitted.[203]

Despite all odds, the Gülen Movement acts and operates fully in a form and field which is institutionalized and legal within the Turkish system and abroad. Even if their worldview or services might indirectly affect the political system, they do not in any way threaten to infringe Turkish laws, procedures or institutions. The services provided by the Movement are not a contest among adversaries. The Gülen Movement is an apolitical, philanthropic, inter-civilizational civil society movement, which is best characterized under the rubric of 'collective social altruism'.[204]

Those who are apprehensive that they might lose their exclusive, direct control over power and their interests within the system counter-mobilize aggressively against the Gülen Movement, in order to protect that control and those vested interests.[205]

3.2.11 Success of the Movement

It can be said that the Gülen Movement proves itself successful in the sight of communities in Turkey and abroad by mobilizing inactive, dormant, but innovative energies present in the Turkish and other societies. It absorbs conflicting pressures and eases tension within fragmented communities. It has transformed the potential to use coercive means to induce changes in political systems into peaceful efforts to produce beneficial services. It has, despite provocations and ill-treatment, never shown any inclination whatever towards violence or extra-legal tactics of any kind.[206]

The Movement has involved diverse people within a very short time over a large geographical area to achieve joint projects. It appears to have established the ideal balance between risks and advantages, so that millions of people are taking part in service-projects. By recognizing the outcomes of its actions and securing positive recognition from others, Movement participants compare and perceive its consistency and continuity over time and across borders. By comparing their investments with the results of their actions, they relate the rewards to the resources invested in the action.[207]

The Gülen Movement progressively modernizes its culture and organization. Along with support from the grassroots for the services provided, it connects with, and gains support from, influential people such as community leaders and industrialists, as well as small businessmen. By employing a sound rationality through the obvious neutrality of technical expertise, it is able to appeal to all. It socializes and transmits values and rules in order to oversee the development of personal skills.[208]

The Movement has formed a large number of organizations operating across economic, political and cultural boundaries. It circulates and diffuses ideas, information, new patterns of action and cultures. In this way, it is able to transfer latency into visibility through collective action and services, which are then institutionalized. Through associational and relational service-networks and through the media, the Movement participants harmoniously integrate and liaise between its many layers, formally and informally, as the need arises.[209]

The Movement participants and the service-networks see their own limitations through face-to-face discussions, availability of information and communication channels, skilled leadership in SMOs, the feedback from media and public, and consultation.[210] This makes them reflective. By generalizing and accumulating the results of their actions, the service-networks and SMOs access institutional mediation. This yields continuity between individual and collective identity, leisure and commitment, self-fulfillment and participation, particular and global.[211]

The Gülen Movement is also successful because it is a cultural and symbolic multiplier. It is a progenitor movement, that is, setting up original models and successful examples and establishing institutions, which other actors or movements can emulate and adapt.[212]

If the actions of the Movement are measured against the interests and objectives of that sector of Turkish society who are, as Eickelman has expressed it, 'militant secularis[ts] of some governing elites associated with authoritarianism and intolerance' then it proves itself successful. Gülen and the Movement do not have any aspirations to evolve into a political party or seek political power, as has been observed and repeatedly confirmed by many scholars and journalists.[213] On the contrary, as Karaman and Aras argue: 'Gülen represents the continuation of a long Sufi tradition of seeking to address the spiritual needs of the people, to educate the masses, and to provide some stability in times of turmoil. And, like many previous Sufi figures (including [...] Rumi), he is wrongly accused of seeking political power.'

What the Gülen Movement provides and accomplishes, comes up against strong vested interests, as well as the sinecures of protectionists in the Turkish establishment:

> Civility and tolerance will not prevail without struggle. The ideals of civil society, democracy, and open debate over basic values-ideals that are explicit in the works of [...] Gülen [...] are up against strong vested interests. [...] Not surprisingly, some efforts at reform have been met with threats of violence.[214]

In spite of counter-mobilization, the overwhelming majority of the Turkish public has expressed a favorable opinion about Gülen and the Movement in surveys.[215] The cable news company ntv-MSNBC conducted a survey (10,000 people) and showed that '96 percent of the public do not consider Gülen a threat to the country'. Ajan.net also conducted a survey (36,367 people) and found that '91 percent of the public accept Gülen as a moderate Islamic scholar and do not consider him a threat or the leader of a subversive organization'.

3.3 CONCLUSION

Whenever collective action openly addresses the central issues affecting society, it redefines the public space. This process affects political life, everyday lives, mental codes, and interpersonal relationships. But no sooner is the new theme raised in the public sphere, than it meets new limits. The mechanisms of the political system become selective, excluding and suppressing some of the dynamic components of the issue. What is excluded, however, remains stubbornly alive and either pushed into marginality or turned into a new voice for societal needs.[216]

So, any analysis of such relationships and participation which does not take into account the limits and exclusions imposed by the politically and ideologically oriented interests groups, or which downplays the reduction of services to politics or something else, becomes a pure apology for the existing situation, for corruption in the status quo, and for radicalization.

The protectionist groups, who are apprehensive that they might lose their direct control over power and their collective vested interests within the system, direct their aggression at the Gülen Movement at least partly in order to repair this loss in the eyes of the general public. However, when the reciprocity of recognition breaks down, aggressive feelings gain prominence and are redirected onto the 'adversary'. As also witnessed very clearly in the latest presidential election in 2007, and discussions related to these, the protectionist groups, which are in decline within the political system, and which have a common interest in keeping the system closed as far as possible, react predictably to hold on to their established position within that system by resisting the intended outcome, counter-mobilizing against civil society – in our case here, the Gülen Movement – and, wherever it is possible for them to do so, imposing selective and exclusionary restrictions on the criteria for social movement ventures and services.

The collective action of the Gülen Movement announces to the society that alternative definitions and dimensions of human experience are possible. It calls society to responsibility, to social construction, making good in tangible outcomes the social power that, over time, people can accumulate and exercise. The Movement's discourse and practice are a symbolic challenge to the dominant protectionist patterns of organization in the society, and, through innovative cultural and peaceful projects, it affirms basic rights, equality, and authentically participatory democratic processes.

The protectionist groups in the Turkish establishment seem to be incapable of bridging the rifts modernization generates, which the discourse and services of the Gülen Movement are capable of bridging. Through its work the co-ordinates of meaning, action and serving have been transformed; it proclaims a change which equally entails a change of the self. It affirms a non-contentious difference but does not renounce the validity of other perspectives or rationality. In this lies the strength of the Movement.

The collective action of the Movement may also put pressure on the political market. This pressure is not necessarily demand-oriented or antagonistic. In a manner most marked in the Movement, there appears the dimension of *offering*,[217] a kind of action in and through which new models of social rationality are developed and anticipated. This action concerns cultural codes, not confrontation and conflict with the political system. It allows a re-appropriation of the multi-formity of roles in service work. Indeed, the very identity of the Movement depends on its success in providing services for the community. This social centrality of the actor, the autonomous role in defining personal needs, the constant mediatory relationship between welfare, health, education and the individual, family, and community, gives everyday experience a function. This situates action along the continuum ranging from difference to innovation or change, to the creation of new arenas for positive action and culture which dominant groups and interests may neglect or may see as explicitly antagonistic in character.[218]

The Gülen Movement maintains a degree of distinction from the imposed cultural codes through the constitution and operation of SMOs which prefigure the goals it pursues,[219] and through its activity it visibly signals the societal and individual problems it addresses. Hence its character may constitute a challenge, but an indirect, symbolic one, not a physical, political or direct challenge.

Through educational initiatives, new media organs and networks, opposition to violent and coercive means and methods, intercultural and interfaith dialog, and co-operation on projects and services, the Gülen Movement has succeeded in its *naming* – framing new projects and services – thereby revealing the social and political nature of the definitions imposed by the dominant interest groups and their apparatuses. To date it has achieved some significant results in changing public attitudes.

In democracy in general, people are encouraged to 'participate, in order to have a voice'. However, despite the fact that Turkey is a democratic country, if and when someone other than one of the established actors within the political system does achieve something, the pervasive tendency of the protectionist groups is to start calling for silence, retreat, and isolation, or to solicit participation into its fold, rather than supporting communication, inclusion and socialization. The acceptance of one's assigned place in society serves as an effective and important processor of information. This tendency then becomes generalized at a cultural level, with the values it propagates manifesting one of the dominant protectionist codes expressed in a society. That is why, when Gülen has met with presidents, premiers, ministers, or other officials or authorities, local or foreign, the reaction of the vested interest groups has been vocal and contentious. To them, Gülen is merely a preacher who must lead prayers but do nothing more. They do not want to understand why he finds himself dealing with cultural and social issues, or why he is accepted as a partner in dialog by world leaders, such as the late Pope John Paul II.[220]

Gülen and the Movement started to bring to the surface, and act towards the elaboration of, precisely this neglected side of human experience: the need for meaning. The message of the Movement is embedded in its actions – not in what it states for the record or claims as its content. For, while it generally does not ask for goods, advantages, or reforms, it nevertheless brings these forward by making visible new meaning through its practices and services.

That effort is perceived by the protectionist forces as a challenge to the powers within the establishment. The Movement presents society with cultural gifts through its actions: it reveals new possibilities, another face of reality. When it acts, something has been said by that action – a message has been incorporated into the social arena, and a transforming debate can get under way. Whether or not the issues become topics for political contestation depends on the extent to which they may be taken up (or not) by politically relevant agents or otherwise translated into political agendas for the public. Regardless, the Movement proves itself capable of bringing about a change in the way people's experiences are perceived and *named*. Thus, it becomes the bearer of the hidden potential for change, and it announces new possibilities to the rest of society.

The institutionalization of the social understanding of the Movement indicates its cultural potential embedded in an issue or in a specific social field, and opens up more new arenas for innovation and change. The institutionalization of societal dynamics in a complex society is a more appropriate measure than simply asking whether or not the Gülen Movement is politically effective. The institutionalization of the services is a success and indicates that people in the Movement 'have gained new life for their activities via traditional not-for-profit foundations, which help legitimize them and represent an important method of linking society's past and culture. It is also an important indication of the culture's requests for unity and modernity'.[221]

One problem humanity faces at the global level has to do with the way in which we can coexist and develop common goals while respecting indelible differences. In order to act collectively at any given time, it is necessary to define a concept of 'we'; however, this definition is not likely to be set once and for all, but has to be agreed upon over and over again in a continual negotiation. The Gülen Movement's ongoing projects, the ever-increasing number of educational institutions, the cultural and dialog centers, and the non-profit, non-governmental organizations, are each important civic initiatives constituting this continual negotiation.

As stated earlier, in the context of any given political system, the capacity to create alliances, connections, and definitions of common goals becomes a central issue for the Gülen Movement and its successes. The Movement sees a radical form of 'identity politics' to be dangerous for society because of its intolerance, exclusivism, and self-defeating fundamentalism. Polls carried out by independent institutions and organizations indicate that the overwhelming majority of the Turkish public and other non-Turkish societies[222] approve of the works and deeds of Gülen and Movement participants, which implies acceptance of their values and goals.[223]

In short, the collective mobilization of the Gülen Movement continues to this day because the actor has succeeded in realizing – and through the course of action continues to realize – a measured integration or harmonization between many contrasting requirements:

> Modern Turkey is unique in the Islamic world [...] in its aggressive, totalizing approach to secularism and secularization. There is no question that the Gülen movement is deeply critical of the positivistic character of Turkish secularism. But to argue that it is opposed to secularity and democracy is to misread the Movement by projecting the dark anxieties and phobias of the more militant elements of the republic onto precisely the sort of movement that offers Turkey's (and the entire Muslim world's) best hope of uniting Islam, modernization, and secular, liberal democracy.[224]

In all circumstances around the world, Gülen and Movement partici-pants act meaningfully to reduce aggression, adhering to a simple maxim of paramount value: 'Peace is better.'[225] Gülen and the Movement prove de-finitively that they are 'on the side of peace at home and abroad [...] offer-ing Muslims a way to live out Islamic values amidst the complex demands of modern societies and to engage in ongoing dialogue and co-operation with people of other religions.'[226] Gülen himself has explained why this ap-proach is necessary, indeed may be the only one that can work:

> The peace of this (global) village lies in respecting all these differences, in considering these differences to be part of our nature, and in ensuring that people appreciate these differences. Otherwise, it is unavoidable that the world will devour itself in a web of conflicts, disputes, fights, and the bloodiest of wars, thus preparing the way for its own end.[227]

4

Conjunctural Factors

4.1 CONCEPTUALIZING THE GÜLEN MOVEMENT

T he questions discussed in this section are the ones most frequently asked about the mobilization by the Gülen Movement (GM) or about the counter-mobilization by its opponents at various conjunctures in Turkish history. The questions are:

1) whether the Gülen Movement is a civic initiative, a civil society movement;
2) whether it arises from a reaction to a crisis and/or is the expression of a conflict;
3) whether it is a sect or cult;
4) whether it is a political movement; and
5) whether it is an altruistic collective action.

These questions will be discussed to investigate how far epithets like civil, cultural, political, confrontational, conflictual, reactionary, regressive, exclusivist, sectarian, alienating, competitive, mediating, reconciliatory, pluralist, democratic, altruistic and peaceful can be appropriately used to characterize the Gülen Movement as collective actor or its action. The meanings of these terms are manifold and overlapping, but complementary and useful, and will help us to reach sound conclusions about the nature and potential of the Movement.

4.1.1 Is the GM a civil society initiative?

Civil society is described 'as an arena of friendships, clubs, churches, business associations, unions, human rights groups, and other voluntary associations beyond the household but outside the state [… providing] citizens with opportunities to learn the democratic habits of free assembly, non-coercive dialogue, and socioeconomic initiative'.[1] The terms 'civil society sector' or 'civil society organization' cover a broad array of organizations that are essentially private, that is, outside the institutional structures of government. They are also distinct from business organizations: they are not primarily commercial ventures set up principally to distribute profits to their directors or owners. They are self-governing and people are free to join or support them voluntarily.[2]

Despite their diversity, the services and institutions (SMOs) provided by the Gülen Movement share important common features that justify identifying them in the social civic sector. They are not part of the governmental apparatus, and, unlike other private institutions, they are set up to serve the public, not to generate profits for those involved in them.[*] In line with the definition given above, the SMOs embody a commitment to freedom and personal initiative; they encourage and enable people to make full use of their legal rights of citizenship to act on their own authority so as to improve the quality of their own lives and the lives of others in general.[3]

The SMOs are not primarily commercial. They emphasize solidarity for service projects and collectively organized altruism.[4] They embody the idea or ideal that people have responsibilities not only to themselves but also to the communities of which they are a part. Within the legal space as given, the Movement combines private structure and public purpose, providing society with private institutions that are serving essentially public purposes. The SMOs' connections to a great number of citizens and their multiple belonging and professionalized networks within the civil society sector,[5] enhance the Movement's flexibility and capacity to encourage and channel private initiatives in support of public educational purposes and philanthropic services.

The Gülen Movement is distinguished by its substantial and sustained contribution to the potential of citizens to apply their energies to discover and implement new solutions following their own development agendas. It has boosted voluntary participation, multiplied networks of committed citizens in mutually trusting relationships, pursuing, through respectful dialog

---

[*]   At the World Economic Forum in Davos, Prime Minister Ecevit recognized how Gülen-inspired schools as 'NGOs' contribute to the well-being and cultures of Turkey and other countries. See §3.2.6.

and collaborative effort, the shared goal of improving community services.[6] The Movement is thus an agent, on behalf of the country as a whole, for the accumulation of 'social capital'. In explaining the term, Putnam (2000) says 'social capital' refers to

> connections among individuals – social networks and the norms of reciprocity and trustworthiness that arise from them. In that sense social capital is closely related to what some have called 'civic virtue'. The difference is that 'social capital' calls attention to the fact that civic virtue is most powerful when embedded in a dense network of reciprocal social relations. A society of many virtuous but isolated individuals is not necessarily rich in social capital.[7]

Weller draws attention to the fact that 'although often overlooked in the social and political constructs of modernity', faith and faith-inspired organizations 'form a substantial part of civic society and […] contribute significantly to the preservation and development of both bonding and bridging social capital' in civic society volunteerism, the third sector and democracy.[8] The voluntary aspect of association with it is an important dimension of the Gülen Movement.[9] Individuals freely join associations and services of their choice, and they are also free to exit, without cost. Whether the underlying motivation for such voluntary participation is self-fulfillment, self-expression, self-development or something else, it is expressive of the individualistic nature of the concept of civil society.[10]

The fact that, as a thoroughly civic, autonomous initiative, the Movement is situated entirely *outside* the conventional channels of political representation – party, government, state, etc. – does not mean that it therefore stands in some way *against* the political, governmental or democratic system.[11] This would be a grave misreading of the reality of the diffused civic networks of collective action. Through the non-profit-oriented management of its educational and cultural institutions, the Movement distinguishes itself sharply from political actors[12] and formal state institutions and agencies. Its forms of collective action are multiple, variable and simultaneously located at several different levels of the social space. They do not contend with, or for space in, government or state institutions or agencies.[13] They deal with human beings individually in the public space through independent, legally constituted civic organizations.[14] The Movement's field of action – the origin, source and target of what it does – is the individual human being in the private sphere.[15] The natural consequences of this action extend to the civil–public sphere. Its approach is 'bottom–up',[16] namely, transforming individuals through education to facilitate the consolidation of a peaceful, harmonious and inclusive society as a result of an enlightened public sphere. It is not the 'top–down' approach characteristic of state or government agency.[17] That is indeed the rationale for Gülen's emphasis on the primacy of education among the Movement's commitments:

> As the solution of every problem in this life ultimately depends on human beings, education is the most effective vehicle, regardless of whether we have a paralyzed social and political system or we have one that operates like clockwork.[18]

In short, the Movement's work demonstrates a shift in orientation from macro-politics to micro-practices.[19] While the Movement's origin and services arise from a civil-society-based faith initiative, its discourse and practice affirm the idea that religion and the state are and can be separate in Islam, and that this does not endanger the faith but, in fact, protects it and its followers from exploitation and may strengthen it.[20] After his analysis of the transnational social movements originating from Muslim communities, Hendrick concludes:

> The Gülen Movement emerged as the most successful purveyor of Turkey's improvisation of Islamic modernity, a civil/cosmopolitan Islamic activist movement that seeks to realize its goals of global transformation via 'moral investment' in the global economy, 'moral education' in the physical sciences, and moral convergence with 'other' groups via tolerance and dialogue.[21]

The common features shared by its SMOs justify identifying the Gülen Movement as a civic initiative and a civil society movement.

4.1.2 Is the GM a reaction to a crisis and/or an expression of a conflict?

To answer that question,[22] it is necessary first to distinguish the terms 'crisis' and 'conflict'.

A crisis denotes breakdown of the functional and integrative mechanisms of a given set of social relations in one sector of the system or another. A crisis arises from processes of disaggregation of a system, related to dysfunctions in the mechanisms of adaptation, imbalances among parts or subsystems, and paralyses or blockages therein. A conflict, on the other hand, is a struggle between two actors seeking to appropriate or control resources regarded by both as valuable; the actors have a shared field of action, a common reference system, something at stake between them to which both, implicitly or explicitly, refer.[23]

Conflicts are conceptually distinct from crises. In conflicts the adversaries enter into strife on account of antagonistic definitions of the objectives, relations, and means of social production at issue between them. Whereas an antagonistic conflict manifests as a clash over control and allocation of resources deemed crucial by the concerned parties, a crisis provokes a subsequent reaction on the part of those who seek to correct the imbalance that has happened in the system. The difference between a crisis and an antagonistic conflict is a significant one,[24] one that can help to determine if the collective actor – in this case the Gülen Movement – is conflictual, contentious, reactionary, claimant or otherwise.

The research scholar Webb identified education and health as the major crises in Turkey since the period of the Ottoman state: the problems 'continually grew larger during the republican period and were even manipulated for political goals'. What aggravated these crises was, in her judgment, the fact that 'ideological and political concerns rather than logic and science ruled almost all the decisions made in the field of education'. During this time, Turkey did not achieve anything of note in this field in the international arena. 'To the contrary, the universities, which should have done high-level scientific work, each became a point of political focus and they were in the forefront of the three military coups d'état.'[25]

Interviewee Abdullah Aymaz argued that the dominant interest groups define movements in Turkey without referring to any crises, as if there had never been dysfunctions or faults in the operation of the system.[26] Yet, the Gülen Movement, in the face of the crises related to certain policies (or lack of policies) in Turkey,

> does not draw upon logic and action based on victim-blaming or system-blaming, or on the adoption of an injustice frame, or on opposition to the ruling system and the dominant interest. Rather than cursing the darkness, it prefers to strike a light against darkness, ignorance, backwardness, disunity, unbelief, injustice and deviations. So it does not concern itself with polit-

ically challenging the legitimacy of power or the current deployment of social resources.[27]

Therefore, for Aymaz, the Gülen Movement cannot be defined as a conflictual or confrontational reaction, and, in this sense, the Movement cannot be seen as a pathology of or antithetical to the social system.* Similarly, Ünal and Williams (2000:iii) hold that Gülen and the Movement do address and try to deal with problems or crises – problems such as the attempted politicization of religion, societal and sectarian tensions and exploitation thereof to keep Turkey off-balance, and undesirable activities such as fundamentalism, dogmatism and coercion – but not specific individuals or groups or political parties or the state.

On the other hand, might some crisis have *facilitated* the Movement's course of action, and contributed to its emergence or visibility in the public space? The appearance of the Movement has been linked by some commentators to certain conjunctural factors, the most frequent link[28] being to the economic and political liberalization policies of Turgut Özal, who dominated the Turkish political scene for a decade – first as prime minister (1983–89) and then as president (1989–93). Those policies led to socioeconomic processes, like the movement of people to new urban centers, and the establishment of new universities and consequent expansion of mass education. These processes are said to have brought a new consciousness into politics, which prompted people to 'question the state ideology, participate in formal politics and in the multiple networks of the faith-inspired communities'. Then, it is said, consciousness informed 'frameworks to discuss identity, morality and justice in society'.[29] While these explanations contain a small kernel of truth, they are reductive and miss the reality and meaning of the Gülen Movement in this period.

An example of such reductionism is Yavuz's claim that the emergence of the Gülen Movement is attributable to the increased migration from the countryside to the cities, the urbanization, industrialization and modernization of Turkey during the Özal decade.[30] This is at best a very partial expla-

---

*   Gülen in Ünal & Williams, 2000:21. If a social movement sees previously accepted status, pattern of relationship, or social practice as inexcusable, wrong or unjust, it starts systematically to alter the meaning of things from one frame to another, and thus it becomes and its actions are said to be 'antithetical'; see Goffman, 1974:44–5.

nation, and unsatisfactory because it fails to take account of or distorts key aspects of the Movement and its history.

Social scientist Jones has shown that what is common to all reductions is that one phenomenon is explained in terms of another of a different nature, one thought to be simpler or more fundamental, so that 'our desire for understanding at least the reduced phenomenon is satisfied.'[31] Although different kinds of reductionism do not proceed in exactly the same way, an example would be reducing the social dynamics of religions to economic conditions. 'This process may be a direct substitution of realities or the specification of the real causes at work in the phenomenon.'[32] Jones adds:

> Structural reductions of religious phenomena to non-religious sociocultural phenomena (even if established) cannot rule out that there may yet be more to religion – something other than being a purported sociocultural cause – and so cannot entail the substantive reduction of religion to only sociocultural phenomena. In particular, it would not rule out the possibility that religious experience involves an experience of other realities than those involved in social scientific theories.[33]

Similarly, Mellor maintains that social realities are much more complex than economic models allow, that the real social significance of faith or religion needs to be acknowledged as a causal power affecting people's views, choices and actions:

> Religious influences are located at the heart of all societies rather than in the private or epiphenomenal 'sub-systems' envisaged by secularization theorists. [...] This underlines the importance of the specifically religious differences for the development of society, and points towards some of the dangers in trying to explain away religious factors through forms of economic and political reductionism.[34]

It is surely obvious that a collective actor like the Gülen Movement cannot have come abruptly into being, with educated, trained adherents ready to seize on the opportunities presented by the opening up of the system or political structure at a specific time and place. Social movements take time to develop; they do not come ready made.[35] In any case, as sociologist Koopmans has argued,[36] the availability of political opportunities does not automatically and promptly translate into increased action and is *insufficient* to account for the emergence of a collective action and actor.

For an organized collective action as large as the Gülen Movement, there has to be, already in place, a sufficient contingent of people with the necessary intellectual and professional skills, and the readiness and will to be employed, *before* a particular historical conjuncture opens up a window of opportunity.

Linking the Gülen Movement to Özal's liberalization policies is, at best, an account of the structural conditions that define the action, it is a deficient, reductionist explanation insofar as it neglects to examine the actor itself – in terms of internal factors for example – and so fails to account for the types of behavior observed. In point of fact, the structural conditions explanation is itself of doubtful value, generally and particularly. Generally, because a collective actor or action does not automatically spring from structural tensions or conditions: 'Numerous factors determine whether or not this will occur. These factors include the availability of adequate organizational resources, the ability of movement leaders to produce appropriate ideological representations, and the presence of a favorable political context.'[37] And particularly, because the example of Özal invalidates the argument since Özal himself was from the faith communities,[38] from the multitude of people already educated, qualified and holding roles and status in Turkish society and the state structure at that time. A single individual could not, by coming to a higher position one day, have produced people like that in such a short period of time, let alone a movement like Gülen's, when there were already other state bodies functioning independently and when there was in place a large and strong protectionist opposition to what Özal said, planned and carried out.[39]

The hypothesis that political structure opportunities alone account for the existence of a particular group or collective actor is also disproved by asking the obvious question: If Özal and political conjuncture played such a formative role in the emergence of the Gülen Movement, why did the same opportunities not lead other actors to achieve comparable public visibility, resonance and legitimacy? As social scientists Edwards and McCarthy explain: 'the simple availability of resources is not sufficient; coordination and strategic effort is typically required in order to convert available pools of individually held resources into collective resources and to utilize those resources in collective action.'[40] The reality is that the faith-inspired communities had managed to utilize all the different forms of communication networks and media and, as entrepreneurs independent of state subsidies, had proved themselves successful and profitable in foreign-exchange-earning export industries.[41] Such financial and business acumen cannot be acquired all of a sudden following one person's accession to political power. In short, the explanation is not a careful evaluation of the conjuncture but social reductionism – it ignores the existence of informal networks, of everyday solidarity circles; it disregards 'the density and vigor of the networks of belonging, and the associative experiences that individuals have accumulated'.[42]

The mobilization resources of the Gülen Movement were present at the time, ready to be directed towards new goals because already in place. Had they not been, the situation could not have created them, nor could they have benefited from the situation to redirect and reshape their action.

The informal networks and resources, all the heritage, present in the movement need to be taken into consideration. Sociologist Kömeçoğlu (1997) highlights the role of non-visible networks – a movement 'incubates' before it emerges into the public.[43] He distinguishes between the discovery of the movement by the mass media and its organizational and cultural origins. Distinguishing between 'latent' and 'visible' phases in the formation of the Gülen Movement, he deems it necessary to explore the cultural networks that existed before its public appearance. Della Porta and Diani (1999) support Kömeçoğlu's claim with the argument that adequate organizational resources necessarily precede the mobilization of a collective actor.[44] Thus, prior to the 1980 military coup, Gülen Movement participants had already responded to the crisis in education and the contraction in the field for the expression of moral concerns by setting up institutions such as student halls of residence, university entrance courses, teacher associations, publishing houses and a journal (see the outline of events in Chapter 2.2.8, pp. 30–33). In short, the claim that the Gülen Movement emerged as a consequence of Özal's economic liberalization is simply a reductionist account and accordingly deficient even as a partial explanation or definition of the Movement.

The Gülen Movement did not emerge because of, or as the expression of, any conflict, let alone a conflict between the religious-minded and the secularists in Turkey.[45] Webb argues that although the protectionist interest group ideologically frames any effort from the faith-inspired communities as reactionary or fundamentalist, the Gülen Movement has never been mentioned in connection with any anarchy, terror or misuse of office. She adds that any such 'framing' has no concrete basis and has been rejected by the public, and indeed by the courts also.[46] Hendrick maintains that the Movement does not pose any threat to existing political or economic institutions: 'However conservative, however devout, the Gülen Movement is not fundamentalist.'[47]

A conflict, as we defined it earlier, is the opposition of two (or more) actors vying for control of social resources valued by them.[48] Gülen takes no part in this. He argues: 'for a better world, the most effective path must be to avoid argument and conflict, and always to act positively and constructively';[49] and: 'in the modern world, the only way to get others to accept your ideas is by persuasion'; 'those who resort to force as intellectually bankrupt; for people will always demand freedom of choice in the way they run their affairs and in their expression of spiritual and religious values.' While it still needs to be improved, 'democracy is now the only viable political system, and people should strive to modernize and consolidate democratic institutions in order to build a society where individual rights and freedoms are respected and protected, where equal opportunity for all is more than a dream'.[50]

Gülen himself neither approves nor ever uses the terms 'Gülen Movement' or 'Gülen Community'. He prefers the action to be called the 'volunteers service'* because this does not connote any contentious otherness, political separatism or conflictual front. He insists that the Movement does not and must not involve conflict; the volunteers service must be offered within the framework of the following basic principles: (1) constant positive action that leaves no room for confusion, fighting, and anarchy; (2) absence of worldly, material, and other-worldly expectations in return for service; (3) actions, adorned with human virtues that build trust and confidence; (4) actions that bring people and society together; (5) sustaining patience and compassion in all situations; (6) being positive and action-oriented, instead of creating opposition or being reactionary. Offered in this spirit, Gülen says, volunteer services can be said to be seeking only God's approval. He encourages all individuals in sympathy with his opinions to

---

* Gülen (2004a:210–14) also calls it 'a movement originating its own models'.

serve their communities and humanity in accord with this peaceful, non-conflictual, non-confrontational and apolitical stance.[51]

Ünal and Williams argue that many people from all walks of life and different intellectual backgrounds are attracted to and participate in this service because it permits no expectation of material and political gain and because it is not conflictual.[52] The types of service Gülen mentions – education, health, intercultural and interfaith dialog, cooperation of civilizations – require action, and concern relationships in the everyday lives of all members of society and humanity. The sociologists' term for this level is *the lifeworld.** If an action occurs that breaks the rules at the lifeworld level, it is described as *conflictual*. In conflictual actions or networks, action is taken by simpler and small 'cells' against the rules that govern social reproduction in everyday life. These cells go on to generate networks of conflictual social relations and a variety of forms of resistance.[53] Naturally there are forms of such popular resistance in Turkey, but this activity or behavior is absent in the Gülen Movement. Gülen[54] asserts that conflictual or reactionary action cannot reach its goals precisely because it typically offers extremism and violence and gets counter-extremism and counter-violence in return:

> Reactionary actions – or movements, no matter how powerful they are – cannot be successful [in] achiev[ing their] purposes, for balance and moderation cannot be maintained in them. Contrarily, they prove to be more harmful [...] as people fall into extremism. They thereby cause reactions on the other side. Violence ensures counter-violence from the others, too. What is essential, what ought to be, is positive action.

Aymaz maintained that none of projects in which Gülen Movement participants are involved ever break the rules of society, nor do they try to change "the rules of the game" in whatever field they concern. This is supported by the results of surveys conducted by independent organizations, by the recognition and acceptance of the Movement's educational institutions abroad, and

---

* The term *lifeworld*, which Habermas adapts from Schutz, means the shared common understandings, including values, that develop through face-to-face contacts over time in various social groups, from families to communities. The lifeworld carries all sorts of assumptions about who we are as people and what we value about ourselves, what we believe, what offends us, what we aspire to, what we are willing to sacrifice to which ends, and so forth. (Frank, 1996).

by the failure of the legal actions taken by the protectionist elite in Turkey against Gülen:

> The Gülen Movement does not do anything which prevents the system from maintaining its set of elements and relations that identify the system as such. Since the Movement participants and their projects do not breach social limits, the system can acknowledge, or tolerate, them without altering its structure. In this sense, the Movement has order-maintaining orientations. However, it does not come into being through consensus over the rules governing the control of valued resources. The intention of the Gülen Movement is not to protect the rules and procedures to protect the status quo governing the control of valued resources, any more than it is to challenge them.[55]

Interviewee Ergene stated that the Movement cannot be described as marginal as it did not come into being to react to the control and legitimacy of the system or its established norms, nor is it a consequence of the inadequate assimilation by some individuals of those established norms. Moreover, the Movement does not identify a social adversary and a set of contested resources or values. Within the Movement people express disapproval of actions or traits such as immorality, unbelief, injustice, provoking hostility and violence, and deviations, but disapproval or hatred is not expressed of the people who engage in them.* Ergene explained that the protectionist elite within the establishment have attempted to obscure this and the Movement's achievements and have thus been led into the reductionism of seeing the Movement's philanthropic services and innovative potential as subversive:

> Based on Islamic teachings[56] Gülen encourages people to services which are not an opposition [to] interests within a certain normative framework nor do they seek to improve the relative position of the actor so that the actor will be able to overcome functional obstacles in order to change authority relationships. This kind of [altruistic] behavior can be defined as competition for the good or better. It concerns not contending interests but presenting the likely best that can be done for the betterment of the conditions of society and humanity.

---

* Gülen in Ünal & Williams, 2000:260–1. In part this behavior is affirmative of the value of human beings, of always reserving judgment so as to remain hopeful for them; in part it reflects the formal doctrine that a sin, in the act or viewed prospectively, is a sin, but, once repented and viewed retrospectively, is a good since it led to the good of repentance and self-reform, which are among the human actions or conditions most loved by God.

Melucci[57] concurs with Ergene that such competition accepts the set 'rules of the game' and is regulated by the rights people are entitled to and by the interests that operate within the boundaries of the existing social order. Such competition is indeed different from those forms of solidarity action which force the conflict to the point of infringing the rules of the game or the system's 'compatibility limits'.

Interviewee Çapan also stated that the Gülen Movement does not breach the system limits in order to defend the social order, as in the case of ultra right-wing counter- or fascist- movements in history. The Gülen Movement does not claim, compete for, or raise conflict over, something within the state organizational or political system.[58]

> 'After 9/11, a lot of groups said they are moderate and changed their rhetoric,' said Baran[59]. [...] 'But the Gülen Movement for the last 30 to 40 years has been saying the same thing. They have not changed their language because they want to be okay now.'[60]

Since the Gülen Movement is not a struggle or mobilization for the production, appropriation, and allocation of a society's basic resources, nor engaged in conflict over imbalances of power and the means and orientation of social production, it is not materialistic or antagonistic. Any hypothesis linking the Movement to capitalist production or political positions and institutions obscures the cognitive, symbolic, and relational components that give the Movement its distinctive character.

The Gülen Movement does not dispute the shared rules and the processes of representation, or how normative decisions are made through democratic institutions. It aims for the internal equilibrium of society, for exchange among different parts of the system, and for roles to be reciprocally assured and respected so that social life, fairness and the material and non-material prosperity of individuals are maintained and reproduced through interaction, communication, collaboration and education. These relations allow individuals to make sense of themselves, of this world and its affairs, and of what lies beyond.[61]

Undoubtedly, relations and meanings, goals and interests transcend individuals. But the Movement takes no direct interest in institutional change or the modification of power relationships. Rather, it aims to bring change in the individual, in mind-set, attitudes and behavior. Many forms of the voluntary and altruistic community action undertaken by Movement participants correspond to everyday life and are strictly cultural in orientation, not political. Aymaz, when asked if the Gülen Movement could be considered a political movement, distinguished two types of actions or actors:

> The political one presses for a different distribution of roles, rewards or resources and therefore clashes with the power imposing rules within the structural organization of state; and the non-political one strives for a more efficient functioning of the apparatus or, in fact, for that apparatus' more successful outcomes, without exceeding the established limits of the organization and its normative framework.[62]

In this sense, Aymaz is saying, the Gülen Movement cannot be called a *claimant* movement either, since it is not seeking to defend the advantages enjoyed by a separate group or to mobilize on behalf of an underprivileged ethnic, religious, social or political group to get for it a bigger piece of the 'cake' of public funds or other resources.

Interviewee Çapan was clear that the Gülen Movement neither mobilizes for political participation in decision-making, nor fights against the state ideology, nor pretends to have a bias or tendency so as to get access to decision-makers. Movement participants have contributed to the opening-up of new channels for the expression of previously excluded demands like intercultural and interfaith dialog and co-operation (rather than conflict) between civilizations, yet in doing so, they do not in any way push their action of service outside the limits set by the existing norms and Turkish political system. Nor do they seek to change the direction of the state's development policy or otherwise intervene in its decisions or actions. Çapan added that not every public-spirited action is political or antagonistic; rather, there are social, cultural, cognitive, symbolic and spiritual dimensions of such action that can never entirely be translated into the language of politics.[63]

Snow and colleagues[64] class political actors as interest groups and define them in relation to the government or polity, whereas the relevance and interests of social movements extend well beyond the polity to other institutional spheres and authorities. Melucci holds that political actors engage in action for reform, inclusion in and redefinition of political rules, rights and boundaries of political systems; they therefore interact with political authorities, negotiate or engage in exchanges with them. They strive to influence political decision-making through institutional and sometimes partly non-institutional means. Non-political actors, by contrast, address issues in a strictly cultural form or cultural terms, and bring issues forward into the public sphere. They choose a common ground on which many people can work together. They *name* issues and then let them be processed through political means and actors.[65]

According to the definitions above, the Gülen Movement falls into the category of cultural or social actor rather than political actor. Although political action is legal, legitimate and indispensable for democracy in a complex system like Turkey, the Movement avoids formal politics, and acts at its own specific level within the limits to which it is entitled by law, aiming at well-defined, concrete, and unifying goals and services.[66] In particular, as Alpay (1995a) has argued, Gülen 'separates religion from politics, opposes a culture of enmity that can polarize the nation'.[67]

For the Gülen Movement, institutions and the market are not traps to be avoided but instruments to be utilized to the extent that they achieve the common good. In this way it strives to perform a modernizing role within institutions and societies. It contributes to the creation of common public spaces in which an agreement can be reached to share the responsibility for a whole social field beyond one party's interests or positions. Greek Patriarch Bartholomew confirmed this:

> In Turkey, Christians, Muslims and Jews live together in an atmosphere of tolerance and dialogue. We wish to mention the work of Fethullah Gülen, who more than ten years ago began to educate his believers about the necessity for the existence of a dialogue between Islam and all religions.[68]

The moral dimension of these issues and the successful provision of services that transcend any one party's interests or positions, raise awareness and so fuel reflection and discussion. That is, as it were, the herald of a cultural change that is already well on its way in Turkey and elsewhere. As Fuller points out, this change is perceived by some militant secularists in the army and the old elite structure as an assault against specific interests, an attempt to shift power relationships within the political system, and to acquire influence over decisions. However, Fuller argues, the Gülen Movement promotes an apolitical, highly tolerant and open regeneration of faith-inspired values, focused on education, democracy, tolerance and the formation of civil society: the Movement 'represent[s] a new Anatolian elite, comfortable with its Islamic heritage while striving to be modern, technologically oriented, and part of the European system as long as that does not mean a total loss of Islamic identity.'[69]

4.1.3 Is the GM a sect or cult?

What distinguishes Gülen and the Movement from cults and sects? If the distinction is clear why is it said that the Movement is a sect?

Turkey is a secular state in which freedom of conscience and association are conceived in such a way that religious communities and religious orders (because not regulated by the state) do not officially exist. The Turkish Constitution's commitment to laicism means that people can be (and many people have been) prosecuted for affiliation to and support of religious orders or sects.[70] Yavuz and Esposito argue that 'the sharp division between moral community and the political sphere is the source of many problems in Turkey. As the Turkish political domain does not provide an ethical charter, the moral emptiness turned the political domain into a space of dirty tricks, duplicity and the source of corruption'.[71] Politics in Turkey is, regrettably, based on what are euphemistically called 'protective relationships',[72] for the sake of which the concepts of both religion and secular democracy are misused.[73] Smith comments wryly, '[Critics] say that Ankara [i.e. the hub of establishment politics] has cultivated a seamless web of internal and external threats – some real some imagined – to keep the enterprise afloat.'*

The contraction of the field in which moral values can be expressed, combined with the inability or unwillingness of the authorities to deal with acute social crises, prepares people to turn to SMOs.[74] Because the people needed them, faith communities and religious orders not only survived, they have revived and gained prominence in Turkey. Alpay explained this succinctly: 'modern institutionalization and organization in Turkey remain behind, backward, whereas religious brotherhood and sol-

---

* Smith, 2001:3. Similar views are expressed in Ülsever (2001b), 'Will Turkey Demolish Her Fundamental Taboo? The Role of the Army', *Turkish Daily News* (August 14); Ülsever (2003), 'Status-quo Blocking Turkish Modernism, *Turkish Daily News* (February 4) argues: 'Thus, the so-called 'heritage of the revolutionary leaders of independence', i.e. the ruling military and civilian bureaucracy, have become the keepers of status quo especially after 1980s! [...] The [pro]claim[ed] heritage of the once revolutionary elite is now the most reactionary group of the country and they are blocking the way of Turkey before modernity i.e. "Westernization" in their definition.'

idarity, basic forms of social organization, continue.'[75] Indeed, those basic forms of organization, bottom–up, civic, faith-inspired initiatives, constituted the necessary social capital[76] and resource for modernization in the country. That success was nevertheless viewed by the protectionist elite with suspicion and described as a potential or actual threat to the foundations of the state.[77]

As the most conspicuously successful and popular effort to generate the social capital that the state was unable to generate, the Gülen Movement and Gülen himself have been particularly targeted. One of the devices to delegitimize them and their services is the accusation that 'albeit non-political' they are a sect, backward, and thus subversive.* Yet, while accusations of this kind have been plentiful, evidence of (under Turkish law) unlawful association, action or conspiracy has been non-existent. Not a single person from the Movement has so far been convicted of any of the false charges laid against them by ideologically motivated prosecutors and the protectionist groups behind them. Webb, after listing almost one hundred lower court hearings and judgments concerning Gülen himself, concludes: 'In the light of the relevant court decisions, and according to the verdicts given, experts appointed by the courts and the courts, the major conclusion is that the allegations and such similar claims [about him] are untrue, baseless and unsubstantiated.' Webb adds that the authoritative bodies found that there was no sign in his works of supporting the interests of a religious sect, seeking the establishment of a religious community, or using religion for political or personal purposes, or of any violation of basic government principles and order. Gülen's works consist of explanations of the Qur'an and Hadiths, religious and moral advice, writings that encourage the virtues of good, orderly citizens, what any government would approve and wish for.[78]

Aymaz explained why the Movement cannot be described as a sect:

> The Movement has never ever attempted to form a distinct unit within
> Islam. [It is] not a distinct unit within the broader Muslim community
> by virtue of certain refinements or distinctions of belief or practice.
> Neither is it a small faction or dissenting clique aggregated around a

---

* Murphy (2005): 'Radical Islamists revile it, saying it is too open to Western ideas and other faiths, and many military officials and secular-oriented intellectuals worry that Gülen and his devotees [sic] secretly want to establish an Islamic state in Turkey.'

common interest, peculiar beliefs or unattainable dreams or utopia. The Movement is already a well-established and transnationally recognized diffused network of people. The Movement has no formal leadership, no sheikhs and no hierarchy. They don't have any procedures, ceremonies or initiation [to pass] in order to be affiliated or to become a member.

Aymaz further explained that in the wider society, Movement participants are neither viewed nor act as any kind of closed, special group:

Movement participants, with their words, projects and actions, have proved themselves not to have any strongly held views or ideology that are regarded as extreme by the majority in Turkey and abroad. They have never been regarded as heretical or as deviant in any way by the public, in the media or in the courts. They have not been accused of being different from the generally accepted religious tradition, practices or tendencies. All movement participants are educated, mostly either graduates or post-graduates, serving voluntarily. These volunteers work by themselves, thousands of miles away from a specific doctrine or a doctrinal leader.[79]

Hermansen explains why the Gülen Movement *cannot* be called a sect or cult* in similar terms:

Tibi deprecatingly referred to the Movement as a Sufi tariqa including as a critique that Gülen functions as the shaykh (Sufi master). Agai concludes that this is a misrepresentation because unlike classical tariqa, there is no requirement of initiation, no restricted or esoteric religious practices, and no arcane Sufi terminology that marks membership in the Movement. Ergene also strongly disagrees with the characterization of the Movement as a tariqa in any classical social or organizational sense.[80]

---

*   In Turkey the terms 'sect' and 'cult' are used indiscriminately by laicist critics to disparage faith-groups or communities. The academic study of religion has tended to move away from the more classical sociological language of 'sect' to that of 'New Religious Movements'. See particularly, Barker (1982) and (1990). Populist use of the terms is not the same as their usage in classical sociological thought, where Weber and Troeltsch applied them to various forms of Christian community. Leaving aside the question of the applicability of this typology even to Christian organizations, use of such abstract terms to describe a faith-inspired movement that is not Christian would certainly have to be very tentative. I concur with Glock (1959:159–60), Hannigan (1991:314) and Beckford (1989:163–4) that Troeltsch's typology of church–sect forces every variety of organizational form into the typological scheme; it is a narrow view of religion rooted in outmoded and limited conceptualizations, which 'tends to inhibit further innovating ideas about the nature of religious organizations [or faith-inspired movements]'.

If the Movement cannot be labeled a cult or sect on account of its actions, can it be so labeled on account of participants' relations to its founding figure, Fethullah Gülen? This is the issue of 'charisma', and the associated process of 'charismatization'. Charismatization makes the group-leader in the eyes of its members a special, even a super-, being; it entails myths about his childhood, sacralized places, holy objects he has touched, etc. A picture is built up of this super-being who is nevertheless prepared to come down to the level of ordinary people. Charismatization makes the group-leader unaccountable, unpredictable, arbitrary in the exercise of authority and prone to abuse of power:

> the *authority* that is accorded by the followers [of the] charismatic [leader], insofar as it is not bound by rules or by tradition and the charismatic leader has the right to say what the followers will do in all aspects of their life – whom they will sleep with [...] marry, whether they will have children, what sort of work they will do, in what country they will live – perhaps whether they will live – and what toothpaste they will use. It really can cover anything; and it can be changed at a moment's notice.[81]

Gülen has been visible in public life through his speeches, actions, and projects since he was sixteen years old as preacher, writer and the initiator of civil society action. He has not led anyone into any absurdities, deviations, violence, killings, suicides or abuse of any sort. He has not presented any attitude of unaccountability or arbitrariness in his thoughts or actions.[82] In Turkey a very few marginal, ideologically motivated individuals and groups have opposed his worldview and projects, yet none so far has substantiated any accusation like that. This is a good indication that Gülen and the Movement are nothing like the sects, cults or new religious movements studied by Barker and others.

We set out earlier (§3.2.5, pp. 79–83) how and why the reflexivity of the Gülen Movement is so high. Movement participants have a clear definition of the services, the field of their action, the goals and the instruments used to achieve them, and as a result, what to expect and not to expect in return for what they are doing.[83] The Movement also has much accumulated experience, which it is very successful at imparting to its participants and to those outside the Movement. The Movement therefore does not experience a gap between unattainable goals and expectations and rewards.[84] The clarity about general goals and particular objectives – the attainability of its

projects – the stress on and the adherence to legitimacy of means and ends–
the accountability of how the projects are delivered – distinguish Gülen and
the Movement from cults and sects in a clear way.[85]

In the Gülen Movement, the rewards to be expected as a result of services provided are strictly 'from God'.[86] The Movement does not offer selective incentives (atomized cost–benefit calculations) to attract participants
in the pursuit of collective goals. Direct participation in the services itself
provides the motivation – to embody highly symbolic, cultural, ethical and
spiritual values, rather than to accrue worldly goods and material gains.[87]
Kuru notes: 'Gülen is against the kind of rationalism that focuses on egoistic self interest and pure materialistic cost–benefit analysis.'[88]

Gülen himself has said: 'If I were to prefer this world, to prefer to be
at the top of the State, I would have looked for a position in certain places
where such preferences could be realized.' He never did so, having lived his
whole life, including youth, as an ascetic. Recalling his youth when worldly
prospects were available to him, he said: 'If this person refused all the opportunities that came to his doorstep and rather headed for his wooden hut
in his youth, how could he have such desires now when he spends every
night "as if this were my last"? I think all of these accusations [of seeking
position or power] arise from [the accusers'] feelings of hatred.'[89]

Because motivation and incentivization are realized through the relational networks and the services provided altruistically alongside others, it
ties the individuals together.[90] The cohesiveness of the group, in contradistinction to cults, does not derive from belonging to it. Belonging is not for
its own sake, turned inward, but for the service of others, i.e. always looking outward. Gülen often refers to the maxim: 'An individual should be
among the common folks like any ordinary individual, yet with the constant consciousness that he or she is with God and under His constant supervision.' This means 'living among people, amidst multiplicity'.[91] Therefore, unlike sects or cults, Movement participants prefer being with and for
people, not avoiding them; they do not draw back into themselves and
break off relations with social partners, or sever relations with the outside,
nor renounce the relevant and feasible courses of action.[92] To the contrary,
Gülen stresses the current realities, the interdependency of communities
that has emerged with the modern means of communication and transpor-
tation – the world become a global village.[93] He teaches the awareness that

any radical change in one country will not be determined by that country alone because this epoch is one of interactive relations, and nations and peoples are more in need of and dependent on each other, a situation that requires closeness in mutual relations. Therefore, people should accept one another as they are and seek ways to get along with each other.[94] Differences based on beliefs, races, customs and traditions are richness, and should be appreciated for the common good through peaceful and respectful relationships.[95] Gülen adds:

> This network of relations, which […] exists on the basis of mutual interest, provides some benefits for the weaker side. Moreover, owing to advances in […] digital electronic technology, the acquisition and exchange of information is gradually growing. As a result, the individual comes to the fore, making it inevitable that democratic governments which respect personal rights will replace oppressive regimes.[96]

In another sense also, the Movement is not closed off from the world – it knows that it needs to be in the world in order to learn from it. Gülen explains: 'People must learn how to benefit from other people's knowledge and views, for these can be beneficial to their own system, thought, and world. Especially, they should seek always to benefit from the experiences of the experienced.'[97] It seems unlikely that individuals in a movement who have been reading and listening to Gülen would be in a sect-like relationship or structure.[98] Instead, Gülen urges inclusivity and openness to other people: 'Be so tolerant that your bosom becomes wide like the ocean. Be inspired with faith and love of human beings. Let there be no troubled souls to whom you do not offer a hand, and about whom you remain unconcerned.'[99]

The Gülen Movement does not have an ideology that posits an 'adversary' that it then makes an object of aggression, and to which it denies any humanity or rationality or potential for good. It systematically and consistently refuses to activate negative or destructive processes. It has for that reason sometimes been criticized for passivism. On the contrary, however, it encourages a higher motivational level and opens the way for individual and collective responsibility and mobilization. Gülen teaches that the principal way to realize projects is 'through the consciousness and the ethic of responsibility. [… As] irresponsibility in action is disorder and chaos, we are left with no alternative but to discipline our actions with responsibility. Indeed, all our attempts should be measured by responsibility.'[100]

This consciousness and ethic of responsibility nurtures individual upward mobility in the SMOs established with Gülen's encouragement. '[These] institutions have a corporate identity and their management is in the hands of real people. However, having been appointed as a manager through a social contract, these people are not allowed to utilize the institutions for their own benefits. Those who are now unable to work actively in the movement give over their role to the young people who will carry the torch of the altruistic services of the movement.'[101] Hermansen recalls how a senior participant in the Movement described its activism in terms of a relay race in which the current generations are running and passing the torch on to the next cohort to take it onward and higher.[102]

Individual upward mobility is for all and always possible in the Gülen Movement because entry and exit, or commitment and withdrawal, are always voluntary and always open.[103] A competitive spirit is also encouraged and predominates over the primary solidarities.[104] Individuals are employed at the SMOs on the basis of professional qualifications rather than on the basis of Movement experience or 'seniority'.[105] These features all prevent the rise of any dogmatic leaders, ideologues, rites, or exclusivist functions within the Movement. They also prevent the Movement from constructing an idealized self-image with exclusive values and symbolic resources and taking refuge in myth.

The Gülen Movement does not have or seek to have private sacred texts exclusive to itself, or develop special rituals and priestly functions, or special costumes or gestures or insignia, or other closed identity devices. It does not offer outcomes or rewards unattainable by the ordinary means of human effort in the real world.[106] It does not seek sacral celebration of the self in an abstract and anachronistic paradigm.[107] The Movement's action is not directed *against* anyone, real or mythical: it has no fantasized 'adversary' to blame if there is any shortfall in outcomes.* Rather, any failure must be socially defined within the actors' frame of reference and responsibility. Gülen identified the three major problems as the basis of all the trou-

---

*   In this way, the possibilities for a conflictual mobilization remain very remote.

ble in modern Turkey:[108] ignorance, poverty, and internal schism (social disunity). To these he added:

> Now to these have been added cheating, bullying and coercion, extravagance, decadence, obscenity, insensitivity, indifference, and intellectual contamination.[109]

> a lack of interest in religious and historical dynamics, lack of learning, knowledge, and systematic thinking [...] ignorance, stand as the foremost reason today why Turkey and the region is so afflicted with destitution, poverty.[110]

The limits of the reference field of the Movement (its principles and goals) do not permit any sort of aggressive and non-institutionalized mobilization, impractical and incompatible demands or expectations, or anything transgressing boundary rules – either in the Turkish or the international arenas – that could trigger conflict.[111] Movement participants are encouraged to reflect upon and compare their action in different situations at different times – an open process of working out costs and benefits, of measuring effort and outcomes, that enables them to criticize and amend policy, to predict likely outcomes, to learn from mistakes, etc. In this way, the institutions, the services given and their success, do not belong to any single individual and moreover remain oriented outwards to the real world.

Education, as we have emphasized, is the Movement's chief priority. In Gülen's view it is not only the establishment of justice that is hindered by the lack of well-rounded education, but also the recognition of human rights and attitudes of acceptance and tolerance toward others: 'if you wish to keep the masses under control, simply starve them in the area of knowledge. They can escape such tyranny only through education. The road to social justice is paved with adequate, universal education, for only this will give people sufficient understanding and tolerance to respect the rights of others.'[112] The education supported by the Movement is oriented to enabling people to think for themselves, to be agents of change on behalf of the positive values of social justice, human rights and tolerance.[113] This again sharply distinguishes the Movement from the tendency of cults to be oriented inward and to demand conformity from group members (of which the private rites, insignia, etc., are a badge).

The style and content of education is another distinguishing factor. Gülen holds that a new style of education is necessary 'that will fuse religious and scientific knowledge together with morality and spirituality, to produce genuinely enlightened people with hearts illumined by religious sciences and spirituality, [and] minds illuminated with positive sciences', people whose actions and life-styles embody humanity and moral values, and who are 'cognizant of the socio-economic and political conditions of their time'.[114]

Michel argues that for Gülen 'spirituality' includes not only directly religious teachings, but also ethics, logic, psychological health, and affective openness – *compassion* and *tolerance* are key terms. Gülen believes that 'non-quantifiable' qualities need to be instilled in students alongside training in the 'exact' disciplines. Michel considers that such a program is more related to identity and daily life than 'political action', and believes that it will yield a new spiritual search and moral commitment to a better and more human social life. Those dimensions of education can only be conveyed through example in the teachers' manners, disposition and behavior, not through preaching:[115] the Movement does not dictate the curriculum in the educational institutions its participants sponsor and manage. The institutions follow national and international curricula and students are encouraged to use external sources of information, such as the internet and the universities' information services.

The Movement, as we said, does not follow (as some cults do) an anachronistic paradigm. It does not romanticize the past. Yet it does emphasize 'cultural values'. Gülen has said: 'Little attention and importance is given to the teaching of cultural values, although it is more necessary to education. If one day we are able to ensure that it is given importance, then we shall have reached a major objective.'[116] Predictably, this emphasis has been seized upon by protectionist critics as a reactionary call to return to pre-Republican Ottoman society – in sociological terms, a kind of regressive utopianism. The term of abuse employed – *irticaci* – might well be translated in the Turkish context as 'reactionary'.[117] Gülen has always denied this accusation:[118]

> The word *irtica* means returning to the past or carrying the past to the present. I'm a person who's taken eternity as a goal, not only tomorrow. I'm thinking about our country's future and trying to do what I can

about it. I've never had anything to do with taking my country backwards in any of my writings, spoken words or activities. But no one can label belief in God, worship, moral values and [...] matters unlimited by time as *irtica*.

Melucci has explained how some movements, at their inception, define their identity in terms of the past, drawing upon a totalizing myth of rebirth with a quasi-religious content; their action involves a utopian appeal with religious connotations. This regressive utopianism reduces complexity to the unity of a single all-embracing formula; it refuses different levels and tools of analysis, and identifies the whole society with the sacral solidarity of the group. It translates the re-appropriation of identity into the language and symbols of an escapist myth of rebirth. Melucci adds that the predominant religious accent in these movements makes them susceptible to manipulation by the power structure, to marginalization as sects, and to transformation into a fashion or commodity for sale in the marketplace as a mind-soother. He further argues that contestation in such movements changes into an individual flight, a mythical quest or fanatic fundamentalism.[119]

Other theorists have called that description an over-generalization. Sociologist Asef Bayat points to the reductionism in Melucci's account, which considers all religious or revivalist movements, especially Islamist, as regressive utopianism.[120] For sure, it is not a description that can fit the Gülen Movement. Gülen's references to history contain no hint of a cultural politics, no attempt to disparage any historical epoch, especially not those moments associated with the origins of modernity in Turkey.[121] He does not evoke a past so as to express a wish to restore sultanate as a symbolic shortcut to unity and order, nor does he idealize 'homeland', 'religion', and 'family'. He is not seeking any ideological alibi to mask deficiencies in his understanding of the complexities of the modern world. Michel is very clear that Gülen does not propose 'a nostalgic return to Ottoman patterns'.[122]

To the contrary, since the inception of the Movement, Gülen has aspired to present models for self-improvement leading to social transformation.[123] He neither sees the past as a strategy for reinforcement of the present political order, nor considers that a new model based upon the past can or should be reinstated in the present. He has called that a grotesque anachronism, given that no sane person could believe that such a jump in time could come to fruition. He sees it as impossible for Turkey to recover the transnational hegemony it exercised before the First World War. The very idea of such cultural imperialism is incompatible with current economic, military and geographical realities. Michel observes: 'This is very different from reactionary projects which seek to revive or restore the past. [...] Gülen repeatedly affirms that "If there is no adaptation to new conditions, the result will be extinction".'[124]

Gülen looks to the past for examples to follow and mistakes to avoid, that is, for the means to go beyond what has remained in the past:

> Today, it is obviously impossible to live with out-of-date conceptions which have nothing to do with reality. *Continuing the old state being impossible, it means either following the new state or annihilation.* We will either reshape our world as required by science, or we shall be thrown into a pit together with the world we live in.[125]

Nevertheless, 'If keeping your eyes closed to the future is blindness, then disinterest in the past is misfortune.'[126] Historical consciousness clarifies the concepts of the present that are mostly shaped by the concepts and the events of the past. By presenting a very broad range of historical themes and characters, Gülen instills hope and creates access for his audience to necessary measures for reform and advance in globalized society. To him, knowing history is a feeder to an innovative and successful future in which you are able to know where you are going.

Gülen emphatically refuses the model of citizenship that reflects a certain kind of racial, ethnic, cultural and religious homogeneity based on some (often imaginary) society in the past.[127] In point of fact, none of the seventeen states that the Turks historically established were based on any such homogeneity. Consoling oneself with re-telling the heroic deeds of others indicates a psychological weakness peculiar to the impotent who have failed or are refusing to shoulder their present responsibilities to the present society:[128]

> Of course, we should certainly commemorate the saints of our past with deep emotion and celebrate the victories of our heroic ancestors with enthusiasm. But we should not think this is all we are obliged to do, just consoling ourselves with tombs and epitaphs. [...] Each scene from the past is valuable and sacred only so long as it stimulates and enthuses us, and provides us with knowledge and experience for doing something today. Otherwise it is a complete deception, since no success or victory

from the past can come to help us in our current struggle. Today, our duty is to offer humanity a new message composed of vivid scenes from the past together with understanding of the needs of the present.

For the Gülen Movement identity is not something imposed by belonging and membership in a group; it is brought into being, constructed, by the individual in her or his capacity as a social actor. It is always in accord with social capacity. Relationship is formed at the level of the single individual, and awakens the enthusiasm and capacity of the individual for action. Through sociability people rediscover the self and the meaning of life.[129] The altruistic service urged by the Movement is this effort of human sociability and relationship.[130] Therein lies the core of the distinctiveness of the Gülen Movement. It does not lead to a flight into the myth of identity. It does not draw an individual into an escapist illusion so that he or she is magically freed from the constraints of social action or behavior. It reaffirms the meaning of social action as the capacity for a consciously produced human existence and relationships.

In the same vein, Gülen frequently talks about a renaissance, yet he does not mean by it any sort of magical 'rebirth'.[131] On the contrary, this renaissance is an active process, a toil – to 'prevent illnesses like passion, laziness, seeking fame, selfishness, worldliness, narrow-mindedness, the use of brute force' and to replace them 'with exalted human values like contentedness, courage, modesty, altruism, knowledge and virtue, and the ability to think universally'.[132] Acknowledgement of differences, multiplicity, the necessity of division of labor, and power relationships within the larger community, attach the Movement to a form of rationality geared to assessing the relationship between ends and means, to protecting people from the imbalances and divisions created by the forms of power required to govern complexity. 'Gülen's work is a constant exhortation to greater effort, greater knowledge, greater self-control and restraint.'[133]

Sects, by contrast, resist accepting difference and diversity within themselves and resist accepting their interdependence with the outside world. They lack a solution for handling difference within complexity. Their totalizing appeal does not take into account that people are simultaneously living in a system interdependently.[134] The Gülen Movement does not deny the interdependence of the social field in its worldview, values, or actual organizational frame. It does not have a totalizing ideology that possesses and controls the social field; and so it does not need to identify 'others' or 'outsiders' in negative terms.

By correctly and accurately identifying the true social character of conflicts, the Gülen Movement avoids producing unpredictable forms or expressions of collective action. Being socially, culturally and intellectually competent, Movement participants respond to the specificity of individual and collective demands, without allowing them to cancel one another out. They do not seek escape into a reductionism that ignores or annuls the individual for the appropriated identity of the movement. Utilizing this social capacity, it does not lapse into the pre-social, or withdraw into a sect or dissolve into a utopian myth. Gülen himself has said, in reference to being or becoming a sect, that he is 'personally not in favor of such practice', that Movement participants 'do not represent a separate and divisive group in society', and they 'are not associated with any group, nor have developed such a group'.[135]

The Gülen Movement is different from a sect in that it operates in awareness of its commitment to the social field where it belongs, interacts and contributes. It shares with the rest of the society a set of general issues, and seeks to find and form common grounds and references with others. Gülen writes:

> Gigantic developments in transportation and telecommunication technology have made the world into a big village. In these circumstances, all the peoples of the world must learn to share this village among them and live together in peace and mutual helping. We believe that peoples, no matter of what faith, culture, civilization, race, color and country, have more to compel them to come together than what separates them. If we encourage those elements which oblige them to live together in peace and awaken them to the lethal dangers of warring and conflicts, the world may be better than it is today.[136]

A sect by contrast simply breaks any such connection. It creates (ideologically and ontologically) separations, divisions and ruptures that cannot be overcome. Its identity politics and appeal tend to cover up or deny the fundamental dilemma of living a social life in complex systems.[137] Being an exclusive organization, a sect demands a long novitiate, rigid discipline, high level of unquestioning commitment and intrusion into every aspect of its members' lives.[138] The worldview or collective action of the Gülen Movement is not an isolationist withdrawal into a pure community-based or sect-like structure:[139]

> We should know how to be ourselves and then remain ourselves. That does not mean isolation from others. It means preservation of our essential identity among others, following our way among other ways. While self-identity is necessary, we should also find the ways to a universal integration. Isolation from the world will eventually result in annihilation.[140]

If the search for fulfillment within specific closed networks or a society is unable to handle information flow, it withdraws from social life and transforms spiritual needs into intolerant mysticism. A movement's identity claims pushed too far eventually evolve into a conflictual sectarian organization with an intolerant ideology, so that the movement tends to fragment into self-assertive and closed sects. If certain issues or differences become political and contradictory, and if the political decision-making is limited and incapable of resolving the differences, the movement breaks up into sectarian groupings.[141]

However, the Gülen Movement with its participation in the field of education, interfaith and intercultural issues, and of transnational altruistic projects and institutions, proves itself able to process information and emergent realities. Interviewee Aymaz explained how this works:

> The Gülen Movement acknowledges the fact that the common points, grounds, references and problems affecting humanity in general are far more than the differences which separate us. Gülen teaches that 'one can be for others while being oneself', and 'in order for a peaceful co-existence, one can build oneself among others, in togetherness with others'. The difference and particularism of an actor do not negate interdependence and unity with others. People can come together and co-operate around a universally acknowledged set of values. The way to do so is through education, convincing argument, peaceful interaction and negotiation.[142]

Aymaz emphasized that the Gülen Movement does not engage with identity politics. It does not seek to be different from other people, ethno-religiously, culturally or geographically. Movement participants accept and abide by Turkish and international norms, regulations and laws. They share the concerns and problems common to people all over the world, and work to contribute to their resolution. The worldview, intentions and efforts of the Movement are accepted and approved by the overwhelming majority of people in Turkey and by those who know their efforts outside Turkey. It is therefore able to become an agent of reconciliation between diverse communities around the world. These efforts are actualized through legal, formalized and institutionalized means and ends. The Movement is defined in terms of its social and multicultural relations; the intention of seeking consensus among communities legitimates its transnational projects,[143] so that it does not deviate into, or let others be led astray into, fundamentalism and sectarianism.[144]

Interviewee Ergene also argued that the Gülen Movement does not reduce reality to a small package of truisms. The service-networks are well aware of their capacity so they do not attempt to mask anything from the larger environment. The openness and transparency of its projects make the Movement effective and strengthen the confidence in it. The spirit of cultural innovation and the true spiritual seeking, alongside other faith-community members, within one's faith strengthens one's own sense of security and offers it to others. Interviewee Çapan made the point that, because the Gülen Movement responds to the need for cultural and social innovation, the collective search and engagement for worldly and other-worldly well-being within the Movement does not assume the character of a flight into militancy or sectarianism. Moreover, 'in over forty years there has been no case or accusation of crisis, greed, a different theology or drug use and suicide within the Movement'. The reason for this, Çapan explained, is that people do not experience frustration, isolation, disappointment and exploitation within the Movement; quite the contrary, they feel and find hope, a true human and humane identity, communication, compassion and peace.[145]

Finally, on the question of the Movement's charismatic leader, Ergene affirmed: 'Though everyone who knows and comes into contact with Gülen acknowledges and respects Gülen's knowledge, asceticism, piety, expertise and scholarliness on religious, spiritual and intellectual matters, this does not result in any sacral recognition or charisma for Gülen.' The common description of Gülen as the leader of the Movement – something that the man himself has never accepted or approved[146] – has not resulted in the emergence of an authoritarian personality or personalities. The Movement has remained committed to the establishment of collective reasoning, consultation and consensus, which prevents the emergence of or lapse into herd mentality or 'group-think'.[147]

4.1.4 Is the GM a political movement?

Emergent movements in complex societies – movements of all kinds: youth, women, urban, ecological, pacifist, ethnic, cultural – have been interpreted in basically two ways: (1) in terms of an economic crisis; or (2) as a result of deficiencies in political legitimation, that is, exclusion from institutions and access to decision-making.[148] Movements are studied and understood insofar as they are mobilizing against the authoritarianism of a system, struggling for equalization of rights, seeking inclusion in the system and political recognition, or reviving ethnic or religious accents in expressions of identity or behavior considered odd or bizarre by the prevailing social order. Those who would justify that social order then interpret the movements in ideological terms – that is, as a struggle (actually or potentially) to subvert or undermine that same order. This may cause a crisis in the day-to-day fabric of social life, a breakdown in norms, loss of identity and reactive violent behavior. However, not all forms of marginalization, reactions to crises, or efforts to adapt to imbalances necessarily generate a collective action or movement, and not all collective demands assume a political form.[149]

I argued in Chapter 1 that the dominant explanation for collective action and social movements hinges largely upon a particular understanding of the European New Left action and ideology in France, Germany, and Italy after the '68 generation and in the 1970s.[150] As a result of the closedness of political institutions, the radicalization of movements, the prevalence of sectarian Marxist organization in the New Left, and even the lamentable turn towards terrorism, the intellectuals of the Left, as the social movement theorists, preached revolutionary ideologies. They dignified social disorder and disruptive behavior with a revolutionary label. They often based their understanding on a reductionist analysis which tended to mask some of the features of collective action. They overlooked the presence of non-political elements in emergent movements. To them, that which was not directly political in nature was folklore and private escapism and only political representation could prevent collective demands from being dissipated into such.[151]

This arbitrary 'politicization' of demands constitute a reductionist interpretation in that it underestimated the specificity of the emergent movements. It channeled all collective demands within its scope into rigid forms of political organization of a Leninist type. Emergent collective phenomena in complex societies cannot be treated simply as reactions to crises, as mere effects of marginality or deviance, or purely as problems arising from exclusion from the political market. In reality social movements in complex societies share a number of prominent features as multi-form and diverse as are the areas of social life. The issues are not all objectives of low negotiability, nor are they entirely reducible to political mediation. Indeed, only a portion of collective demands can be mediated and institutionalized through the functions of political representation and decision-making. Demands can re-emerge in other sectors of society, the implications of which are often outside the official channels of representation, rationalization and control by the co-ordinated intervention of state apparatuses.[152]

Also in chapter 1, and again in 3, I pointed to a striking phenomenon in recent forms of collective action, namely that they 'largely ignore the political system. They generally display disinterest towards the idea of seizing power'.[153] New social movements are less engaged with social and political conflict than before because 'collective bargaining, party competition, and representative party government were the virtually exclusive mechanisms for the resolution of social and political conflict. All of this was endorsed by a "civic culture" which emphasized the values of social mobility, private life, consumption, instrumental rationality, authority, and order and which de-emphasized political participation'.[154] New social movements are, instead, characterized by open and fluid organization, inclusive and non-ideological participation, and greater attention to social than to economic transformations.[155] (See § 3.2.1–2.)

All of this raises questions about the relationship between the Gülen Movement and the political system in Turkey. For, as argued in earlier chapters and in §4.1.2 above, a notable feature of the Gülen Movement is that participants acknowledge and abide by the political system, and display disinterest towards seizing power and gaining control over the state apparatus. The Movement assumes forms of action and organization which are accountable and amenable to political mediation by the Turkish political system, without becoming identifiable with it. The Movement therefore does not act like an oppositional action which involves a minority, or which rejects the system in Turkey, or which resists the 'rationality' of decisions and goals imposed by the Turkish system.

To a certain extent, within different contexts and in response to different questions, the arguments have established that the Gülen Movement is what Melucci would call a cultural actor, or a social, *not* a political, movement. So, from here on, the discussion will focus on how the Movement as collective actor and its action are different from a political party, and the implications for Turkey, democracy, Islamism, subterfuge and dissembling, development or change in Turkey, and Turkey's integration into the international community.

The chief implication of the Gülen Movement is that political parties are unable to give adequate expression to collective demands. This is because parties are structured to represent interests that are assumed to remain relatively stable, with a distinct geographical, occupational, social, or ideological base. Also, a party must ensure the continuity of the interests it represents. When faced with the task of representing a plurality of interests, the traditional structure of a party may not be able to adjust itself to accommodate them. Indeed, it can hardly mediate between short- and long-term goals. For short-term gains and profits a party may act in favor of unstable, partial and hierarchical interests. In contrast, unlike political parties and bodies, the Gülen Movement's participation in social projects and in the specific areas of social life demonstrates no interest in hierarchism or short-term gains.

Moreover, the Gülen Movement represents its understanding through formal and institutionalized SMOs. As these institutions are mostly educational they do not take sides with political parties.[156] Rather than being distant to some, Gülen says, they are equally near to all.[157]

The social praxis of the Gülen Movement focuses on the role and needs of the individual.[158] It emphasizes individual needs for self-reflexivity and self-realization. Without straying into forms of narcissistic behavior, or the individualistic search for self-affirmation and instant gratification, the Gülen Movement testifies to a profound change in the status of the individual and his or her problems. Through socio-cultural efforts and services, the Movement addresses the individual dimension of social life, and thus with the products it provides, it may then affect the whole of society. Its space and the level where new forms of social action originate is not political space or power, nor government, nor regime.[159] It educates and socializes individuals without individualizing and politicizing the social. It acknowledges that neither individuals nor a system ever undergo change at all levels at the same time and in the same way. Change requires a lengthy period of time, enormous sacrifice, commitment and patience, and it can be achieved only through education, peace and co-operation of like-minded citizens and civilizations.

Barton reads Gülen's optimistic and forward-looking thought as a contemporary reformulation of the teachings of Rumi, Yunus Emre, and other classical Sufi teachers. He argues that Gülen emphasizes the self development of heart and mind through education, engaging proactively and positively with the modern world and reaching out in dialog and a spirit of co-operation between different religious communities, social strata and nations.[160] Weller makes the same point:

> Gülen has concentrated his efforts on establishing dialogue among the various ideologies, cultures, religions and ethnic groups of Turkey and of the wider world. While Gülen and his thought are rooted in a strongly religious vision of the world, his efforts for dialogue have extended beyond traditional religious circles alone.[161]

Like Barton and Weller, Michel recognizes the centrality of the religious and cultural vision of the Movement to its activities. The effectiveness of these activities depends on the openness, receptiveness, and efficiency of the available forms of representation.[162] The character of the services that the participants are engaged in providing keeps them away from the everyday, largely pointless partisan fights and rhetoric of political parties; they do not divert or exhaust their energies in political skirmishes.[163] This stands in contradiction to the dominant understanding of social movements as always contentious and conflictual.

This conscious avoidance of political contention is reflected in Gülen's evaluation of the failures in the last few centuries in Turkish history:

> Those who were in politics and those who supported them considered every means and action as legitimate and permissible if it were to gain them position for their own team or party; they devised and entered into complex intrigues and deluded themselves that by overthrowing the dom-

inant group and changing the party in power they would change everything and the country would be saved.[164]

Gülen adds that action should have been guided by thought, knowledge,
faith, morality, and virtue rather than by political ambitions and hatred.[165]

And yet, Gülen has been accused of politically-motivated subterfuge,
of concealing his true intentions, of hiding a political intent and agenda. In
2000 a state security court prosecutor accused Gülen of inciting his readers
to plot the overthrow of Turkey's secular government.[166] In a response to
questions from *The New York Times*, Gülen described the charges as fabrications by a 'marginal but influential group that wields considerable power
in political circles':

> 'Statements and words were picked with tweezers and montaged to serve
> the purposes of whoever was behind this.' He 'was not seeking to establish
> an Islamic regime but did support efforts to ensure that the government
> treated ethnic and ideological differences as a cultural mosaic, not a reason
> for discrimination. [...] Standards of democracy and justice must be elevat-
> ed to the level of our contemporaries in the West', said Gülen.[167]

Both Gülen and his opponents use the term 'political power' in their arguments. It will be worthwhile pausing to reflect on what this term and the
associated notions of 'political demands' and 'political participation' mean.

Political power is generally understood to denote the capacity of certain groups to exert privileged control over the processes of political decision-making, to take normative decisions in the name of society as a whole,
and to impose those decisions, where necessary, through the use of coercive means. In order of increasing generality the nature of 'political demands' are categorized into three: (1) demands regarding the regulation of
exchange between particular groups within the society; (2) demands that
call for the modification or adaptation of the rules of the political system,
so as to widen or restrict access to it; (3) demands regarding the maintenance or adaptation of the mode of production and distribution of social
resources. Political participation is also the defense of specific interests, an
attempt to shift power relationships within the political system, to acquire
influence over decisions.[168]

The Gülen Movement has not allied itself with any established political
party, and this has secured it a certain measure of success.[169] It sees that Is-

lam does not need a state or political party to survive, but does need the educated, the financially well-off and a fully democratic system:[170]

> Gülen's ideas do differ from political Islamists and other moderate
> Islamists by emphasizing the entrance of Turkey and Islam into main-
> stream global processes and a market economy [...] and emphasis on
> intellectual development and tolerance.[171]

Gülen believes that the main problem in the world is lack of knowledge, which involves related problems concerning the production and control of knowledge.[172] Producing, maintaining and disseminating knowledge can only be achieved through education, but not by party politics. Education is the key to becoming a better, productive and beneficial individual, whether one is Muslim or not.[173] He believes also that the sciences, humanities and religion enhance and complement one another rather than compete and clash.[174] Afsaruddin concludes that the effectiveness and spread of the Gülen-inspired schools within and outside Turkey are evidence of the success of Gülen's educational philosophy, which urges personal enlightenment and lays equal stress on the inculcation of ethical values and a sound training in the secular sciences.[175]

According to Tekalan, the primary purpose of the education in the Gülen-inspired schools is to ensure respect for objective and universal human values. The Movement has not had nor fostered ulterior motives to seek material advantages or impose any ideology or seize power through politics in the countries where it has SMOs. He adds that for the forty years since the inception of the Movement, no act contrary to these principles has been witnessed in any country. He affirms that the Movement has never aimed to seize power economically, politically or culturally inside or outside Turkey; its objective is to serve humankind without expecting any return and consideration for that service. Tekalan reports what Gülen said in 2002 in *Zaman* newspaper:

> Just as I did in the past, I am currently preserving the same distance from
> all political parties. Even if the power, not only in Turkey, but also in the
> whole world, is presented as a gift to me, I have been long determined to
> reject it with contempt.[176]

Rather than leave Turkey to remain a closed society, Gülen has supported initiatives for a democratic, pluralistic and free society.[177] He states that the role of individual morality is pivotal in this perspective to build, strengthen, and preserve 'a just political order'.[178] In the same vein, he has supported ties to the West – on the basis that Turkish society has much to gain from the achievements of rational knowledge there – whereas many from both the religious circles and the dominant secularist elite have been opposed to such rapprochement. Gülen was among the first and strongest supporters of full European membership and integration,[179] although some Islamist political groups criticized his remarks and opposed such membership. To them, the European Union is a Christian club and a threat to Turkish national and Muslim identity. Gülen was gradually able to bring about changes in the public mentality and attitude in Turkey.[180] He 'support[s] democracy and tolerance as the best way to govern and membership [in] the European Union as the best way of achieving economic prosperity'.[181] In addition, he has highlighted the need for peace, tolerance, and dialog with ethno-religious minorities within the Turkish community and between nations as an integral part of Islam and Turkish Muslimness.[182]

Gülen is 'critical of the instrumentalization of religion in politics', and has constantly opposed direct participation in party politics because the modern world exists in a 'pluralistic experience rather than within an assumed homogeneity of truth'. He is against those who have created 'a negative image of Islam by reducing Islam to an ideology'.[183] Through words and deeds he underlines the distinction between Islam, a religion, and Islamism, a profoundly radical political ideology that seeks to replace existing states and political structures, either through revolutionary or evolutionary means:

> *Hodjaefendi* [Gülen] opposes the use of Islam as a political ideology and a party philosophy, and polarizing society into believers and nonbelievers. He calls for those who believe and think differently to respect and tolerate each other, and supports peace and reconciliation. In my opinion, Hodjaefendi's efforts will help us put religion in its rightful place.[184]

Gülen has always been in favor of democratic institutions, free elections and other principles at the core of liberal democracy today. He maintains that the Qur'an addresses the whole community and assigns it almost all the duties entrusted to modern democratic systems, that people ought to co-operate by sharing these duties and establishing the essential foundations necessary to discharge them, and that the government is composed of all of these basic elements.[185] He says:

> Islam recommends a government based on a social contract. People elect
> the administrators and establish a council to debate common issues. Also,
> the society as a whole participates in auditing the administration.[186]

Gülen asks people to be careful not to erode the true values which the state or state organizations ideally stand for. He has been against those who cause chaos, societal tension and violence in Turkey or anywhere else. While dealing with tarnished politicians, crooked party politics and corruption, people ought to pay extra attention not to erode in public the true values, authority and respect for a state organization.[187] Gülen strongly holds that anarchic movements and activities destroy the atmosphere of peace, free exchange of ideas, and the rule and supremacy of law and justice:

> I have always stipulated that 'even the worst State is better than no State'.
> Whenever I voiced my opinion in words such as 'the State is necessary, and
> should not be worn down', I have never sanctified the State as some people
> have done. This preference is a necessity for me, because if the State were
> not to occupy a certain place, it is certain that anarchy, chaos, and disorder
> would dominate there. Then, there would be no respect for ideas, freedom
> of religion, and our consciences would be violated; justice would be out of
> the question. In the past there were times when our nation suffered from
> the absence of the State. Therefore, I regard supporting the State also as a
> duty of citizenship.[188]

'Although Gülen is not a politician, he is shaping the consciousness that will determine the future of Turkish democracy.'[189] His call for democratization, freedom, equity, justice, and human rights and the rule of law as the main basis for the regulation of the state–society relationship has symbolically confronted the privileged role and vested interests of the protectionist elite in Turkey.[190] He has brought about a shift towards civil society and culture, rather than party politics, as new reference points in the mindset and attitudes of Turkish people. (See § 4.1.1, pp. 111–14.)

Gülen's warning about mixing partisan politics and religion is teaching that politicizing religion ultimately does more damage to religion than to the state, and does it more quickly: 'Religion is the relationship between people and their Creator. The feeling of religion lives in the heart's depths. [...] If you turn it into a display of forms, you'll kill it. Politicizing religion will harm religion before it harms a government's life.'[191] Also: 'Religion focuses primarily on the immutable aspects of life and existence, whereas political, social, and economic systems or ideologies concern only certain variable social aspects of our worldly life.'[192]

Politicizing religion is always a reductionist endeavor: it turns the mysterious relationship between humanity and the Divine into an ideology. That does not mean cultivating indifference to what goes on in the public sphere, still less being indifferent to political or economic injustice:

> Gülen is not arguing that religious or spiritual people should stay out of the political arena or stop concerning themselves with politics. Indeed, such a recommendation would be no better than quietism and is a withdrawal from the responsibilities and obligations of citizenship and social participation. Rather, the lesson here is that confusing political involvement and advocacy with partisanship and party loyalty places the need for religion to speak publicly regarding political issues that affect human dignity and welfare, environmental stewardship, social justice and peace within too narrow a framework of competing power groups that divide, instead of build, communities. Truly religious people who are responsibly involved in their polis are not single-issue voters or single-party loyalists.[193]

Yet, even though Gülen has clearly stated and demonstrated that he has no political agenda, that he is against the instrumentalist use of religion in politics, that his emphasis is on the individual and so on, the protectionist elite still, in their ritualized way, accuse him and the Movement of being a potential 'threat to the state'.[194] Against this, Barton argues that 'Gülen is clearly not a fanatic; he is far too consistently moderate in everything he does and says for that to be the case'. He comments on why Gülen and the Movement are considered a political power and opposition by some militant laicists who see themselves as the guardians of the regime:

> His critics, most of whom appear not to be very familiar with his writing and ideas, see him as promoting a different kind of Islam to that recognized and approved by the state. This apprehension is largely based on a false understanding. In fact Gülen is not so much advocating a different kind of Islam but rather an Islam that reaches more deeply into people's lives and transforms them to become not just better believers but better citizens.[195]

Gülen refutes in his speeches and writings Islamist claims for an Islamic political platform: 'Islam does not propose a certain unchangeable form of government or attempt to shape it. Instead, Islam established fundamental principles that orient a government's general character, leaving it to the people to choose the type and form of government according to time and circumstances.'[196] He rejects the totalizing ideological character of Islamist political thought and activism[197] as totally foreign to the spirit of Islam, which advocates the rule of law and explicitly condemns oppression against any segment of society. He holds that Islam promotes activism for the betterment of society in accordance with the view of the majority, which complements democracy rather than opposing it:[198]

> This introduction of Islam may play an important role in the Muslim world through enriching local forms of democracy and extending it in a way that helps humans develop an understanding of the relationship between the spiritual and material worlds. I believe that Islam also would enrich democracy in answering the deep needs of humans, such as spiritual satisfaction, which cannot be fulfilled except through the remembrance of the Eternal One.[199]

This 'reading' of Muslims' responsibility to Islam is not, of course, peculiar to Gülen, as Eickelman has confirmed: 'thinkers and religious leaders like Turkey's Gülen [...] hold that democracy and Islam are fully compatible and that Islam prescribes no particular form of governance, certainly not arbitrary rule [...] and that the central Qur'anic message is that Muslims must take responsibility for their own society.'[200]

Barton explains that Gülen's rejection of Islamism is not due to merely strategic considerations or even personal preference. Rather, it is based on the argument that the Islamist claims to have found political guidance in Scripture represent a gross misunderstanding of the nature of the Qur'an that dangerously distorts the believer's approach to it.[201] Gülen himself says:

> Such a book should not be reduced to the level of political discourse, nor should it be considered a book about political theories or forms of state. To consider the Qur'an as an instrument of political discourse is a great disrespect for the Holy Book and is an obstacle that prevents people from benefiting from this deep source of divine grace.[202]

As well as Barton, Sykiainen and Eickelman[203] note that Gülen not only directly criticizes Islamist political thought in his many books and articles but also frequently argues in favor of democracy and the modernization and consolidation of democratic institutions in order to build a society where individual rights are respected and protected. He carefully makes clear his position that some forms of democracy are preferable to others and is cautiously optimistic about its development:

> Democracy has developed over time. Just as it has gone through many different stages, it will continue to evolve and improve in the future. Along the way, it will be shaped into a more humane and just system, one based on righteousness and reality. If human beings are considered as a whole, without disregarding the spiritual dimension of their existence and their spiritual needs, and without forgetting that human life is not limited to this mortal life and that all people have a great craving for eternity, democracy could reach the peak of perfection and bring even more happiness to humanity. Islamic principles of equality, tolerance, and justice can help it do just this.[204]

On the basis of Gülen's numerous and consistent comments in favor of modern democratic politics and against Islamist readings of the Qur'an and Sunna, Barton concludes that Gülen is neither an overt nor covert Islamist. He notes that, nevertheless, those who oppose Gülen insist that he is merely *pretending* to reject Islamist ideology – a tactic of some Islamists politicians and activists who do disguise their convictions and, in the name of political expediency, condone subterfuge and dissembling.[205] That is *not* Gülen's way. He has very properly clarified, and done so publicly in both print and broadcast media, that he and Turkish Muslims, like all Sunnis, do not have this concept of subterfuge or dissembling in their faith and practice, nor do they condone it*.[206]

Barton points out that we have good reasons for being confident that Gülen is not a secret Islamist and that he rejects Islamist epistemology.[207] For instance, in the struggle of ideas and contest for hearts and minds before and after 9/11, Gülen visibly provided intellectual and moral leadership, condemned all kinds of acts of terrorism with the most courageous and unequivocal public statements, and comprehensively explained related and relevant issues. He stated that the basic principles of religion are totally opposed to the political–ideological interpretations that underlie and motivate acts of terrorism; that these basic principles

---

* Interviewee Aymaz explained that the accusation of subterfuge is symptomatic of the grossest oversimplification of the socio-cultural and spiritual dynamics of the Gülen Movement; it contradicts the consciousness and clear understanding of the growing number of supporters of the Movement (now in their millions), which is very strict in its critique of conditions in the countries where Islamist groups condone subterfuge as a tactic.

should be taught to Muslims and other people through the education system; that administrators, intellectuals, scholars and community leaders have a responsibility to try to identify the originators and the motivating factors behind terrorist activities; that there are multi-national organizations which, overtly and covertly, have directed their efforts to destructiveness and the creation of fear in society.[208]

Gülen holds religion to be far above politics; he sees it as a source of morality and ethics, which are relevant to, not in conflict with, responsible politics. He does not want religion to become a tool of politics because when politics fails and goes awry people may blame religion. He does not want political aspirations to blemish religion or their potential for corruption to degrade it.[209]

Gülen's ideas and the Movement became the agent of a mass transformation in Turkey, bringing into the public space a new understanding of religion, science, secularism, and collective, social, altruistic, and educational services. Gülen realized that the development of politics and political institutions was lagging behind social and cultural change. He therefore revived the philanthropic tradition, the altruistic values and benevolence, of his Turkish fellow-citizens, and urged them to make up, through their services, the gap left by government policies and protectionist discrimination.[210]

Views, such as Gülen's, in favor of the consolidation of democratic and basic human rights, are repressed on account of the threat they are perceived to pose to the structural advantage of the dominant protectionist interests in the society. Such views face exclusion because they are seen as implicitly calling into question the privileges of those interests in utilizing political processes, and, by extension, of questioning their hegemony over the political system. The protectionists fear that certain understandings and demands may alter the balance of the political system and cause the criteria for selection and entry into it to be widened (see §3.2.9).

When new understandings are widely acknowledged and welcomed, and when people rapidly institutionalize for societal needs and cultural projects, this gives rise to new social models. The models provided by the Gülen Movement are cultural rather than political, they transform patterns of thought and relationship. These models survive because they follow a lawful political and institutional form. The rapid transformation of attitudes, efficient institutionalization of public needs and initiatives, collective or organized philanthropy for education, and apparently simple solutions to societal discord, achieved by Movement participants, were previously lacking in Turkish society, and never attempted by the protectionist political bureaucracy.

The Gülen Movement's societal projects have different meanings for different people in Turkey. In the eyes of those who look on the Movement favorably, the Movement recognizes that it belongs to the system and identifies itself with the general interest of the Turkish community, and acts – lawfully and properly within the boundaries of the legal rules and social norms of the country – in the pursuit of collective shared objectives. However, for those opposed, this participation and contribution are the covert claims of particular competing interests, an attempt to exert influence over the distribution of power to the benefit of 'the others' in Turkish society – a claim asserted despite the fact that collective cultural and altruistic services differ in nature from political participation or contention.[211] This reveals not only that the response of the political system in Turkey can vary markedly according to different cases, but also that it differs especially from cases that have been studied in western Europe or North America.

From that observation two outcomes follow. The first is to recognize that social movements like the Gülen Movement provide incentives for the modernization of a political system, consolidation of civil society and pluralistic democracy, and, in the case of Turkey, alert people to the urgent need for institutional reform. Secondly, we can recognize that the prevalent conceptual frameworks are inadequate (in some ways, even, biased) as approaches to faith-inspired communities, especially to peaceful, mainstream Muslims, and cultural Islam. Restricting analysis to the purely political dimensions of the observed phenomena (such as a clash with authority) constitutes a surrender to reductionism[212]. Such reductionism ignores the specifically social dimensions of a collective action and focuses exclusively on those more readily measurable features which, because of their high visibility, attract the attention of the media.

> Contemporary Social Movements' modus operandi is to fashion new meanings for social action and serve as vital engines of innovation. The political dimension often represents nothing more than a residue.[213]

The Gülen Movement sees that the needs of the individual, culture and society, come before politics.[214] This should not be in any way confused with naïve culturalism that may ignore rights and guarantees recognized by political institutions. The issue then is a redefinition and re-shaping of what democracy is, can be, and ought to be. Gülen does not ask individuals to remain passive recipients, just accepting whatever is fed to them from the outside. Rather, he advises them actively to seek possibilities and alternatives to construct themselves. Both means and ends must be non-confrontational, non-violent and non-coercive; they must be grounded in love of human beings and the creation, in reliable information and understanding through education and communication, and in freedom, collaboration and peace.[215]

Enabling people to make better use of their resources, to free themselves from material and other inequalities, and to become reflexive and beneficial to others is achieved through prioritizing knowledge and education rather than party politics or partisanship. Gülen teaches that, for a better future, humanity needs more tolerant and more altruistic individuals with magnanimous hearts and genuinely open minds that respect freedom of thought, that are open to science and scientific research, and that look for the harmony between the Divine laws of the universe and life.[216]

Sociologist Saribay describes Gülen as non-political, as someone who does not want to politicize Islamic values.[217] Agai sees him as a reformist thinker rather than a revolutionary.[218] Karaman and Aras conclude that he 'seek[s] to address the spiritual needs of the people, to educate the masses, and to provide some stability in times of turmoil. And [...] he has been wrongly accused of seeking political power.'[219]

Change is possible through the establishment of fairness, equal opportunities, freedom and justice, which enable needs to become rights without abrupt or violent change in the political setting. If people are given access to cultural freedom and sound educational opportunities, they will be wise enough not to fall prey to the schemes of vested interests or privileged elites who harness public discourse in order to maintain their established control over languages and codes and so mask the aggravation of injustices and inequalities. A society consisting of well-educated, vocationally well qualified and trained people, culturally cognizant of their needs, values and rights, will not slip into the risks of mere folklore, private escapism or terrorist desperation.

The Gülen Movement looks for answers to the questions all people living in complex modern societies face: 'how to develop humane qualities, good behavior, love for others, enthusiasm for self-improvement, and an active desire to serve others, make a difference in the world, and to persevere in this desire in the face of setbacks and failures.[220] It therefore assumes a non-totalizing role as mediator of demands. It invites and allows society to take responsibility for its own actions within the legal boundaries. It helps to create common public spaces in which an agreement can be reached to share the responsibility for a social field, beyond party interests or positions. This generates innovative energies, keeps the system open, produces innovation and new SMOs, develops elites, brings into the area of the decidable that which has been excluded, and illuminates the problematic areas of complexity in a system. Such a movement is indispensable for the healthy functioning of an open democratic society.

Gülen holds that it is through the democratization of Turkey that the possibility of keeping the goals of industrialization and economic development together with a form of nondependent participation in the world system may be achieved. He assigns equal importance to democracy and development, which in his opinion are interdependent, but democracy precedes development.[221] He works for the development of a society freed from hunger, poverty, striking inequalities, and suppression of civil rights. This can be reached only if, along with economic development, society guarantees improved forms of civic as well as political participation, equal rights, and respect for civil and cultural freedom. He does not want change to lead to decreased participation and deeper isolation in the current world system. Without democracy, Turkey cannot conceive development in any meaningful sense. To Gülen, efforts to bring about transformation in institutions and the established mind-set in Turkey should be made through education, interaction, collaboration and consensus, without resort to violent or coercive means and ends.[222]

These non-confrontational, non-conflictual efforts must persevere without modification, despite peculiarly difficult conditions or adverse situations.[223] This will allow Turkey to participate in the world system, not in a merely dependent position but with some capacity to exert influence and engage in dialog and negotiation.[224] By the same token, it is a condition also for making a contribution to democracy on the world scale.[225]

The democratization process may thereby draw attention to a critical weakness and inadequacy of political initiatives for the problems and issues facing us today. It is one of the roles of social movements to bring these issues to public attention, through the proliferation of information and its novel forms. Cultural activities and non-violent forms of action, provided they find the proper channels, can sometimes reach out to address the world and make the difference.[226] Today, such positive change can only be brought about partially and in a piecemeal fashion.

In his sermons and lectures, Gülen speaks a new language, an idiom that is his own. He draws on the heritage of those that preceded him, rooting his arguments in the memory of the past. He then takes the humane attitudes and reasoning he derives from the intellectual and spiritual enlightenment of the mainstream traditional sources and interprets them in accordance with current and predicted needs. He does not adopt the language of previous struggles because he is able to define his own identity. He does not use the symbols, organizational experience, and forms of action, of the movements that preceded this one. He bases his understanding on tradition to convey new meanings. Yet, this does not necessarily imply that he is backward-oriented; rather, his approach embraces modernity without fear.[227]

The Gülen Movement transforms itself into new institutions, providing a new language, new organizational patterns and new personnel. The meanings and motives for behavior that the Movement attempts to constitute and the internal processes of the formation of attitudes are not merely material and political. Against the imposition of lifestyles which no longer provide individuals with the cultural bases for their self-identification, the Movement deals with human needs at the cultural and spiritual level. It brings collective energies into focus so that deep-seated dilemmas and critical choices can be addressed. It asserts that the individual can only be educated, cared for, and informed, within a healthy environment and sound institutions.[228]

Gülen motivates people for purposes other than those imposed by dominant interests. He speaks for freedom of speech and consolidation of democratic institutions so that actors will not seek to bend multiple meanings to their goals, so that they will not lend meaning to their own vested interests. He calls for the redefinition of social and cultural objects. Behind these words we can detect a plurality of meanings congruent with the true nature that constitutes a civilized human being. Michel expresses it aptly[229]:

> Gülen holds that the true goal of nations must be civilization, a renewal of individuals and society in terms of ethical conduct and mentality.*

4.1.5 Is the GM altruistic collective action and voluntary philanthropic service-projects?

Social Movement theories overlook the presence, in contemporary collective action, of 'philanthropy, altruism and voluntarism',[230] which are the core dynamic of the SMOs and services the Gülen Movement provides. Here I discuss how self-motivated philanthropic service-projects and contributions differ from financially motivated ones, and how they address the need for cultural empowerment. I try to answer the questions: How has Gülen urged individuals to contribute to and serve society constructively? How is the relation of education and altruism framed in the Gülen Movement and imparted to the wider public? How did the authorities of other countries learn about the services? What is Gülen's role, interest and wealth in the services provided? What is the humanitarian, social, or religious dimension of altruistic services? Is there any difference between the Movement's understanding and the secularist humanist understanding of altruism? How does altruistic action perform and establish civic and democratizing (empowering) functions?

In Turkey up to the 1980s hyperpoliticization of all issues in society and artificial divisions between people were prevalent. Extremist and ideological issues were raised around the partisanship between rightists and leftists, around the sectarian division between Alevis and Sunnis, around the ethnic distinction between the Turkish and Kurdish, and later around differing definitions of secularism between the laicists and the religious-minded. Such issues so far dominated society that tensions, conflicts and fights be-

---

* See also, in Kurtz (2005:382), this optimistic observation '[Gülen] cultivat[es] a holistic peace through his non-violent lifestyle, the condemnation of terrorism and violence, and his mobilization of a movement for spiritual and social change in the world. [...] Perhaps his innovations in cultural paradox will inspire others to help us find a way out of our global conundrum.'

gan to undermine its security and stability, even indeed its survival. Thousands of people were killed.[231]

Throughout this period, Gülen, as scholar, writer, preacher and civil society leader, strove to draw people out of societal tensions and conflicts. His message reached the masses through audio and video cassettes, as well as public lectures and private meetings. He appealed to people not to become part of on-going partisan conflictual issues and ideological fights. He analyzed the prevalent conditions and the ideologies behind the societal violence, terror and clashes. He applied his scholarship and his intellectual and personal resources to convince others (notably, young university students) that they need not resort to violence, terror and destruction to establish a progressive, prosperous and peaceful society. He maintained that violence, terrorism, death, ignorance, moral decay, and corruption could be overcome through forbearance and compassion, through conversation, interaction, education and co-operation.[232] He reminded them not to expect everything from the system because of its backwardness in some respects, its stifling bureaucratic, partisan and procedural stagnation, and its lack of qualified personnel. He urged people, instead, to use their constitutionally given rights to contribute to and serve society constructively and altruistically. And he convinced them that such service is both the means and the end of being a good person, a good citizen and a good believer.[233]

Gülen has always seen education as being at the center of social, economic and political modernization, progress and welfare. Individuals and society can only be respectful to the supremacy and rule of law, democratic and human rights, and diversity and cultures if they receive sound education. Equity, social justice and peace in one's own society, and in the world in general, can only be achieved by enlightened people with sound morality through altruistic activism. Therefore, education is the supreme remedy for the ills afflicting Turkish society and humanity in general.[234]

A higher sense of identity, social justice, and sufficient understanding and tolerance to secure respect for the rights of others, all depend on the provision of an adequate and appropriate universal education.[235] As so many people are unable to afford such an education, they need to be supported by charitable trusts. For these trusts to function well needs the right human resources – dedicated volunteers who would enter and then stay in the field of service. The volunteers should not be making a gesture (however worthwhile) but a long-term commitment rooted in sincere intention – their motivation should have no part in it of racial or tribal preferences; and their effort should be both patient and persevering and always lawful.[236]

Gülen started to talk to people from all walks of life in Turkey. He visited individuals, groups, cafes, small villages, towns and metropolitan cities. From peddlers to industrialists and exporters, from secondary school students to postgraduates and faculty, from the common people to leading figures and elites, he imparted the same message to all: sound education and institutionalization, and to achieve that, altruistic contribution and services.[237] He appealed to values that are present in all traditions and religions: duty, moral obligation, disinterested contribution, voluntary philanthropism and altruistic services.[238]

In this way, student hostels, accommodations, primary, secondary and high schools, universities, study centers, college-preparatory courses, press and media organs, publishing houses, student bursaries and research scholarships came into being.[239] The Movement participants performed a modernizing role in the educational field, while their behavior towards the outside world translated into institutional support or an advanced form of cooperative social enterprise, 'alternative entrepreneurship'[240]:

> Gülen genuinely believes in and encourages free enterprise. According to him, believers both in Turkey and abroad must be wealthy. He emphasizes education arm-in-arm with development, and economic and cultural togetherness for the future. [...] He recommends the dynamic of knowledge against ignorance, work against poverty, and solidarity and wealth.[241]

Gülen's well-defined, concrete, unifying and constructive goals have made his projects, the institutions established on his inspiration, visible at specific levels. The successes and accomplishments of the students and schools of Turkey at national and international levels, in scientific and research contests in theory, practice and projects, drew positive attention from the authorities of other countries. (See §3.2.6.) The disintegration of the Soviet bloc revealed the need for these educational services in various areas and cultures. Education was the best and most meaningful way to contribute to their growth and development.[242]

Educational institutions established by charitable trusts inspired by Gülen presented solutions to areas with ethnic–territorial problems. These institutions accepted differences and rendered them valuable, rich and negotiable. It invited students and other people to coexist peacefully in diversity. It called for tolerance, dialog between different spheres of society and different nations of the world, peace and love, and firm commitment to openness of mind and heart. Students worked to achieve this civilized disposition through the sound education offered them. With the sponsorship of Movement supporters, hundreds of such successful institutions have been set up in over one hundred different countries.[243]

Movement participants have mobilized previous affiliations into a new system of relations in which the original elements have gained deeper meanings. They have encouraged transfer of pre-existing dormant resources to the benefit of a new objective. At the same time, the Movement has transformed itself into a new transnational social unit capable of creating new resources for education and societal peace through altruistic action.[244]

As Gülen himself has noted, he owns nothing and has no ambition for worldly wealth.[245] His sincerity, clarity, ascetic life-style and practiced example of altruism have successfully motivated teachers as well as parents and sponsors for the common good. As a man of profound scholarship and wisdom, a highly gifted writer and speaker, Gülen could well have had a very satisfying career as a community leader and author.[246] However, he has concentrated his effort on motivating the masses to invest in sound education, and he has led by example.[247] He has always remained aloof from financial management of the institutions and instead encouraged their sponsors actively to oversee the use of their contributions.[248] This has built enormous confidence, not just in Gülen's honesty and integrity but also that of the people employed at the Gülen-inspired institutions.[249] Furthermore, the students he has educated and his relatives have followed his example.[250] Aside from never accruing any personal wealth, Gülen is reported to have prayed for his relatives to remain poor so as not to raise any suspicion of their having gained from his influence. Those relatives, it is said, smile and say: 'As long as *Hodjaefendi* is alive, we have no hope of becoming wealthy!'[251]

One of Gülen's arguments invited people to live and act not for their own present but for the future of the next generations. He maintained that people in the present and future generations will pay dearly and not know comfort and contentment if people today do not exert the necessary efforts for the coming generations. Giving examples of characters and events in the past, from Turkish and non-Turkish or from Muslim and non-Muslim history, he succeeded in awakening a sense of moral duty and obligation, of selfless generous concern for others. He has used the analogy of a candle, consuming itself but illuminating its surroundings. If people are not financially able to contribute, he asks them to give their time, thoughts, energy and moral support to collective services. Among the examples he frequently gave were the Biblical Prophets and the Messenger of Islam, their companions and disciples, saintly and scholarly people from global communities, or scientists and community leaders – it is common to encounter names like Newton, Pascal, Sir James Jeans, Kant, Gandhi, Iqbal and Rumi in his writings and teachings.[252]

In this and similar ways Gülen persuaded people to take part in altruistic services and educational projects. He presented the world as a market for humanity's and God's pleasure and said people should compete in righteous and beneficial services without ulterior motives. He urged them to combine their efforts, resources and energies into charitable trusts, in which no one benefits from what the institutions earn except the students themselves.[253] Citing a saying attributed to Ali, the fourth caliph in the formative era of Islam, Gülen holds that 'all human beings are one's brothers and sisters. Muslims are one's brothers and sisters in religion, while non-Muslims are one's brothers and sisters in humanity. [...] Human beings are the most honorable of creatures. Those who want to increase their honor should serve this honorable creature'.[254]

'Altruism'[255] a term coined by Auguste Comte, is an ethical doctrine that holds that individuals have a moral obligation to help, serve, or benefit others, if necessary at the sacrifice of self-interest.[256] Most of the world's religions affirm it as a religious or moral value and advocate altruistic behavior alongside self-discipline and containment of one's own interests and desires. However, psychologists, sociologists, evolutionary biologists, and ethologists have their different perspectives on altruism.[257]

The Islamic tradition does not equate altruism with the sort of mutual behavioral manipulation seen in certain parasites that can alter the (biochemical) functioning of other organisms. It does not see it as a tactic used in the competition for limited resources within society, as suggested in analogies with sexual or evolutionary selection. It does not see people as by nature incapable of doing anything to violate their preferences but only doing so as a sort of culturally masked (and therefore unconscious) assertion of self-interest. Nor, in the Islamic tradition, is altruism a form of consequentialism, the idea that an action is ethically right if it brings good consequences. Altruism, in the Islamic perspective, does not hinder individual pursuit of self-development, excellence, and creativity, and it is not an ideological fabrication by the weak for the weak or by the weak to sponge off the strong. It is not like game theory which discusses, for a given situation, the available strategies for each player and calculates the average, or expected, outcome from each 'move' or sequence of 'moves'.[258] What Islam teaches is quite different from what is argued by thinkers who see altruism as a variant of individual or species mechanisms for survival or self-projection.

Gülen's approach to altruism is mainly formed by the perspective of Islamic teachings, the Qur'an and the Sunnah. The source, origin, consequences and implications of the ideational and social praxis of the Gülen Movement are accordingly also quite different from those in movements hitherto explored in social movement theory. The question then arises: Why has such a widespread willingness to engage in altruistic action arisen in the Gülen Movement? What is the moral dimension of such educational services and voluntary forms of action?

In terms of political structure and social policies, voluntary forms of action emerge as alternative answers to the shortcomings, deficiency or crisis in the governmental or welfare system in a society. Whether in man-made crises or natural disasters, mis-direction or absence of welfare provisions and services leave people to their own devices. They act to provide adequate public goods or services when a system is unable to overcome structural shortcomings by means of governmental institutions. Such conjunctures or opportunities create a feeling that individuals are bound by duty and morality to work towards the common good and common goals. Forms of action then concentrate especially on the issues and fields relating to health, caring, religion and education.[259]

Bar-Tal notes that altruism, in general, is a kind of behavior which a) benefits another person, b) must be performed intentionally, c) the benefit must be the goal itself, and d) must be provided without expecting any external reward.[260] With respect to the Gülen Movement, Çapan explained that altruistic service outweighs the other dimensions of the Movement and thus gives it its particular character. That service, Çapan added, has never combined with or been 'infiltrated' by marginal and deviant groups present in the societies where the SMOs are located, nor have any aggregate behaviors formed and coagulated within it – the educational services have never dissolved into mere claimant behavior or violent rupture, nor lost capacity to tackle educational issues for the common good.[261]

Interviewee Cahit Tuzcu[262] emphasized the role of religious teaching and inspiration:

> The belief that to act for the benefit of others is right and good and the moral duty to treat others fairly justify voluntary action in the Movement. This moral or philanthropic feature comes from religious inspiration, 'serving people, serving God' or 'The best amongst you is the most beneficial to human beings'. Being charitable is a way of life, a way to purify one's intentions, wealth and life.

In the same vein, Bahaddin Eker[263] argued:

> It is undoubtedly the faith that inspired in people and implemented in Turkish society philanthropy and paternalism through *sadaqa* [charity] and *zakat* [the prescribed annual alms] and the *vaqifs* [endowments]. Helping others and providing resources are the duty of the well-off, the affluent, towards the weak, unfortunate, under-privileged, wayfarers, orphans, widows and students. The rich person must concern himself or herself with the poor because he or she is responsible for them before God. Apart from being a religious duty, this is an act of generosity, an innate feature of being a true human.

Eker went on to explain that philanthropy may assume a number of forms: 'one's allocation of time, energy, money, property or a simple smile, care or prayers.' He sees such provision as 'an alternative and barrier to egoistic interests at the expense of the others', and as 'a remedy for societal discord, conflicts and violence'.

Both Tuzcu and Eker are echoing explicit teachings of Gülen, for example his saying that the path to earn eternal life and the approval of the Giver of Life

> passes through the inescapable dimension of servanthood to God by means of serving, first of all, our families, relatives, and neighbors, and then our country and nation, with finally humanity and creation being

the object of our efforts. This service is our right; conveying it to others is our responsibility.[264]

Another aspect of altruism is that an actor ought voluntarily to support and contribute to collective provision of appropriate services. Faced with the immensity of the problem to be tackled, a single individual freely and voluntarily joins a form of collective solidarity and from personal choice enters a network of relations.[265] Such a choice is marked by unselfish concern for the welfare of others. Altruistic action is characterized by the gratuitousness of the giving – the *pricelessness* of the resources or the time or whatever it is that is given for nothing in return. In order for an action to count as altruistic, its gratuitousness must also encompass the relation that binds together the actors involved in the collective action. Melucci (1999) distinguishes such action from what may be confused with it, a form of private solidarity regulated by interpersonal exchange. He illustrates the latter with the example of a person who voluntarily and without compensation helps a neighbor with gardening chores. Both of these features are important to understand the nature of the altruistic social services provided by the Gülen Movement. First, the gratuitousness, that the action is done with no expectation of direct benefit or compensation; second, that the action is done through voluntary participation with others in the collective organization and delivery of the service– as Melucci puts it – by the entering into 'a voluntary bond of solidarity'.[266]

Absence of direct benefit or direct economic rewards does not mean that the workers for the voluntary action do not receive any payment in a work relationship. However, it does mean that economic interests do not constitute the basis of the work relationship among those involved. Also, economic benefit is neither the cause nor the effect between the voluntary actor and the recipients in the performed action. The voluntary action specifically aims at producing benefits or advantages for subjects other than the volunteers or workers. Therefore, its gratuitous nature lies in the free fruition of its product by the recipients. That is why the Gülen Movement is generally acknowledged under the form and name of *hizmet*, service provided for others.

However, beyond the immediate interest of the actor or workers, other 'rewards' (symbolic advantages, prestige, self-esteem, authority) are present in altruistic action, just as much as they are in any other form of social exchange. Altruistic action may also yield indirect economic benefits, insofar as the participant acquires useful skills (e.g., professional skills in a certain occupation), establishes networks of influence (professionally advantageous contacts), or learns leadership qualities.* Moreover, it is in the nature of such services and of their objectives, that there may be a multiplicity of secondary or tertiary objectives pursued by individuals. Yet, these sorts of instances are rather infrequent and do not invalidate the altruistic services undertaken and the collective objectives shared by all those involved to achieve the common good. After all, the inner contentment or repute attached to individuals after such services is not what they aim and work for – these are simply an unlooked-for grace which may (or may not) ensue from doing such altruistic work.[267]

Another feature of altruistic action (as noted by Melucci) is that it requires some form of organization for its effective performance, and this organization ought by no means to coincide with an institutionalized, formal, associative structure and hierarchy.[268] Its ends can be achieved by informal, diffused, decentralized, permeable networks of friends, business associates or philanthropically like-minded people gathered around a single project, as in the case of the Gülen Movement.[269] That is how so many projects, services, institutions and initiatives of the Movement have come to be supported by such a wide range of individuals, companies and organizations.

Interviewee Aymaz[270] pointed out another equally important feature of voluntary forms of altruistic action, namely its civic aspect, alongside its faith-inspired and humanitarian aspects. He argued that this action provides far more opportunities for participation than political activities. Altruistic action expresses membership in a far larger civil community than a political party. It provides people with purpose, a sense of belonging, responsibility, commitment, accountability, with incentives and the inner contentment of trying to be useful and beneficent. Also, since people must reach a consensus on the details of any new social, cultural or educational project,

---

* This can be illustrated from the history of Christian churches in the West. For example, the Methodist church in England has often been seen as the 'training ground' for early Labour Party politicians in that it had a tradition of small meetings and lay preaching etc., all of which, in the context of a faith-community group, developed skills that could then also be deployed in the wider civic society. The same may be observed in the case of the mainly Black-led church traditions in the USA (the Revd. Dr. Martin Luther King and Revd. Jesse Jackson, among others, are from this tradition).

altruistic action performs a distinct civic and democratizing function – people learn how to negotiate and persuade, to present convincing arguments, to be accommodating, flexible about differences, to negotiate, generate and accept consensus.[271]

Aymaz said that the Gülen Movement presents to the wider society new cultural, organizational, and relational models. It teaches individuals to use their constitutionally given rights to contribute to and serve society positively. In general terms, he described the Gülen Movement as 'a form of collective, purposive, and organized social altruism that has arisen from civic society'. This description is supported by DiMaggio and Anheier's explanation of how non-profit services are sources of diversity and innovation, which provide, to both people and policymakers, the vehicles, models and solutions to deal with social ills.[272]

Finally, there are orientations of altruistic action whose presence in the public domain discloses the existence of hidden dilemmas deeply embedded in the structures and operation of complex societies. Altruism involves putting the interests of others above one's own interests; it demonstrates that people are not inevitably driven by only evident and immediate or even long-term or undefined self-interest. That fact signals the persistence in complex societies of human needs and demands which cannot be reduced to bureaucratic routines and politics. Altruistic action invites us to seek change and to assume responsibility. It gives individuals a voice in society and a means to bring issues to light; it enables individual and public to accommodate a space for difference and to reinforce solidarity for societal peace and cohesion.

Using these accommodative, service-solidarity, organizational skills, and the trust it has earned from the people, for the benefit of the needy and the general good, the Gülen Movement has been extraordinarily successful at convincing the public to use its constitutionally given rights to serve humanity positively, constructively, and through self-motivated philanthropic contributions and charitable trusts. For this reason, the Gülen Movement has become, first, a vital component in providing an alternative and barrier to egoistic interests at the expense of others and a remedy for societal discord, conflict and violence; and, second, one of the most significant and leading actors in the renewal process towards a civil, pluralist, democratic and peaceful society.

4.2 CONCLUSION

Connecting the rise of movements to their socio-political context of origin seems too general an approach to explain the full range of collective actions that have emerged in Turkish society since the 1960s. That is not to deny the specificity of the causes of the various kinds of mobilization in the country, but merely suggests a key to interpretation of what was common to them and persisted beyond conjunctural variations.

In Turkey, the 1960s marked the beginning of the conjunction between the country's large-scale modernization and the emergence of antagonist movements. New pressures accelerated Turkey's change into a post-industrial society and clashed with the archaism of the state structure and a political system paralyzed by vested interests[273]. The predominance of protectionist, particularist interests smothered any attempt at economic planning, and the reforms themselves only grafted the new onto the old, swelling the bureaucracy rather than rationalizing it. This state of affairs has caused congestion and clogs in the political system.[274] The system's response to the emergence of new collective demands consisted of restricted reforms and repression, alienation,[275] and instrumental use of political wings for violence.[276]

The changes that began in the late 1960s contained in them a cultural and social aspect that was, and remains, irreducible to politics as such. Youth mobilizations, the transformation of lifestyles, the changed role of the media, the growth of voluntary action, new identity demands – all these contributed to a profound change in Turkish culture, mental categories, and everyday relationships. Yet, these significant features have been largely underestimated and attention has rather been focused on the political dimension, on electoral outcomes, on gains for this or that party. The impossibility of reducing society to politics is typical of complexity in general. But in Turkey, the primacy given to party-political struggle has thwarted the potential for innovation present in society; it has paradoxically prevented the development of an autonomous civic culture, and a deeply-felt identification with democratic institutions.[277]

Fethullah Gülen, as teacher and preacher, engaged actively with individuals embedded in the culture of Leftist and Rightist movements, although he was not himself involved in any political movements. He witnessed the demands and the ensuing clashes in the legacy of political forms of organization. He realized that the artificial hyperpoliticization of non-political issues distorted and dissolved many things into violence. He witnessed the resulting crisis of the movements that resulted in an escalation of terrorist activity. He maintained that in such situations where brute force is offered as a solution to problems, 'it is impossible to speak of intellect, judgment, rights, justice, or law. On the contrary, in their stead, [is] unlawfulness, injustice and oppression'.[278]

Gülen was fully aware of the richness extant in civil society, which had (and has still) to express its full potential. This richness had to be developed into a constructive and institutional form. He therefore tried to play a part in dealing constructively and peacefully with the tasks and issues pertaining to the predicament of a complex society.[279] He counseled and convinced individuals to transform themselves and to pool their efforts into forms of collective action, addressing issues like peace, education, dialog and cultural diversity. He has been responsible for a substantial modernization of public attitudes and thinking on these themes.[280] His efforts, along with the contribution of the people who listened to his message, resulted in the emergence of a generation of educated and skilled personnel in education and the media, and in the public services and business.[281] The Movement has become a meeting point and uniting agent which differs profoundly from the image of the politically organized actor.[282]

The particular form and content of this action was not and has not become conflictual or antagonistic. The Movement, when compared with the specific occasions of mobilization and struggle based on reactionary, political and antagonistic interests, has distinguished itself as an enduring form of service network. It interweaves closely with the daily life needs and identity of the wider community it serves. This has transformed a potential that was latent into visible collective action. Özdalga concludes that the civil society networks of the Gülen Movement prove themselves mediators and enablers, rather than blockers or retarders, of the civilizing process. They help to find solutions to the problems of modernity at the level of individual autonomy. This allows the development and integration of the individual into the modern nation-state.[283]

The Gülen Movement has reawakened the force for change that was dormant at the roots of civil society. It has managed to embody this apolitical potential in institutions in order to advance education and thus to revitalize and consolidate civic, pluralist and democratic institutions. It has acted as a barrier against actions that reduce everything produced in civil society to party politics. It has prevented the public space from being manipulated for cheap political gains and games. It has demonstrated that there are peaceful, non-confrontational, institutional channels for the handling of demands. It has opened new channels for individual and collective mobility, which certainly obstructs the formation of conflictual actions. The Gülen Movement is not affiliated with any governmental organization or state department inside or outside Turkey and has never induced its participants or others to breach the norms, laws and regulations enjoined there.[284]

The private initiatives and competitiveness which the movement encourages in support of public and philanthropic services are all based on free choice. They are grounded on voluntary participation and located simultaneously at several levels of the social space and system. The Gülen Movement has assumed a bottom–up approach to transforming individuals through education, communication and co-operation, rather than the top–down approach of government, state or regime[285].

The Gülen Movement therefore has not mobilized to claim a different distribution of roles, rewards and resources, nor clashed with the authorities and power. Through educational and intercultural efforts participants have not pushed the limits of the system. They wish, while holding to their identity and moral values, to be a modern partner and contributor to the European and wider global community.

The common characteristic of participants in the Movement is their acceptance of the scholarly authority of Gülen. They tend, in addition, to emphasize particular aspects in the practice of their faith, which emerge as distinguishing features or styles in their positive discourse and peaceful action. However, the Movement's consciousness of moral and religious values, and its ethics of responsibility towards Turkish and global human societies, the spirit of competitiveness and upward mobility, and the encouragement to acquire knowledge from multiple sources outside the Movement, are all factors disabling any sort of retreat into a closed group or sect. The Movement does not attempt to distinguish (and then sever) itself from the Muslim or secular global communities by virtue of a distinctive ideology, myth or utopian vision. The Movement has no special doctrines or dogmas, no private texts or procedures, no rites, ritual, insignia, costumes or ceremonies that mark people as having 'joined'.[286] Indeed, there is no membership, properly speaking, and certainly no exclusive one. Leadership is decentralized, resource management and decision-making diffused through

SMOs that are in regular informal touch with each other but which, formally and operationally, are independent. The institutions and activities of the Movements are open to all, providing scientific education, sound moral teaching based on universal ethical values, and they encourage peaceful, positive activism for one's community and humanity. The Movement is not linked to any sectarian tradition or affiliation. Networking, participation and affiliation in the Movement are not exclusive, alienating and sectarian because the Movement is not closed to the outside world – its very reason for being is collective engagement with the wider public. This is evident in its extensive transnational, intercultural and interfaith activities and organizations; in its having no closed orientation either of a geographical or communal or ideological kind; and in its open and fluid structure.

The Gülen Movement's discourse and practice demonstrate a consistent understanding of the separation between cultural efforts and actors that can bring an issue to light and the political efforts and actors that may then carry that issue into the political arena. Its worldview and social praxis demonstrate that it is not a political actor, and that it systematically differentiates between socio-cultural issues and political action. Through the outcomes of institutionalized social projects, it turns into a catalyst for societal needs to be seen and analyzed within new conceptual frameworks. Those outcomes prove that the level of individual meanings and cultural dimensions is more significant than the political level because such dimensions and meanings of issues are not immediately identifiable, and politics and politicians can ignore and eliminate them from their analysis between election periods. The Movement highlights the importance of an open civil society and public spaces, which provide an arena for the consolidation of democratic institutions and for the peaceful encounter between politics and social movements.

The Movement acts as a civic initiative with the moral duty to treat all others fairly and compassionately. It holds that altruistic service – in the way of education, health and welfare, interfaith dialog and peace – is inherent to being a true Muslim and a true human being. To eradicate ignorance, arrogance, hostilities and gaps within and between societies, the Movement fosters voluntary forms of altruistic action. This in return yields new cultural, organizational and relational models, projects and responsibilities for the common good. It awakens in people the disposition to accommodate diversity and multiplicity, to reinforce solidarity and humane co-

operation between different communities, and to contribute to civil, pluralist, democratic, healthy and peaceful societies.

The nature of the Gülen Movement has an altruistic, social, purposive
and collective orientation: altruistic, because participants do not pursue personal, material and political ambitions; social, because interactions are built
on social relations, on a one to one basis, and defined by the interdependence and the symbolic exchanges that tie people together; purposive, because individuals and groups act collectively to construct SMOs by means
of organized investments; and collective, because people define in cognitive
and affective terms the field of possibilities and limits and simultaneously
activate their resources and relationships to create meanings and services
out of their joint behavior, and also mutually recognize them.

The relationships, services and their outcomes give a sense to participants of being a 'we', and sustain an unspoken solidarity among projects
and the goals that their institutions pursue. This yields exchange and reciprocal recognition of the identity of the Movement as collective actor.

Rather than contention and confrontation with the state or its agencies and institutions, or with other non-state actors, the Gülen Movement
focuses on social renovations and transforming the mind-set of individuals
through science, education, dialog and democracy. Thus it cultivates a holistic peace through a non-violent lifestyle, and both implicitly and explicitly rejects terrorism and violence. It provides stability in times of turmoil
and inspires others to co-exist in diversity peacefully. It encourages reciprocal understanding and respect and so enables co-operation for the common
good. It instills hope in individuals and, through that hope, inspires voluntary commitment to sound education, institutionalization, and altruistic
contributions and services. These and similar qualities of the Movement
have made it into a phenomenon which is, in both theory and practice,
quite different from both traditional religious circles and from social movements as understood according to the prevalent conceptualizations.[287]

In sum, we conclude that the Gülen Movement is a civic initiative, a
civil society movement. It is not a governmental or a state sponsored organization. It did not emerge as a result of a governmental policy, nor a state
ideology. It is not contentious, oppositional, conflictual or political. It is
neither a sect, nor a cult, although it started as faith-initiated, non-contentious, cultural and educational service-projects. It is an apolitical, social, al-

truistic action. It centers on the individual, individual change and the education of the individual. Part of this education is also focused on raising consciousness about legality, lawfulness, human rights and one's constitutionally defined rights. It also works for the consolidation, therefore, of pluralist participatory democracy and equal rights. It has never condoned proselytization, coercion, terrorism or violence. It insists upon the lawfulness of both means and ends in its action and services. It supports state and church separation and Turkey's successful integration with international communities. In addition to its success as a provider of educational services, it has been positively acknowledged for its intercultural and interfaith services and organizations. Therefore, the collective action of the Gülen Movement is the result of the combination of its meanings, values, intentions, objectives, actions and outcomes. It presents itself to and interacts with the wider public, and works within limits and constraints, it has shown temporal continuity, and maintains a cohesive peaceful identity inside and outside Turkey.

In this and the preceding chapter, I indicated that, while no one owns the services and authority in the name of the collective actor, the Gülen Movement guarantees its participants access to immediate and verifiable control of the goods and services organized through their collective action. I have also shown that the Movement is strengthened by flexibility, adaptability, and immediacy – its availability as a channel for the direct expression of needs that state organizations, political parties or other more structured organizations cannot incorporate. The strength of the Movement's collective action and its SMOs lies in their ability to pursue general goals over the long term; in their insusceptibility to escapism, extremism or violence; in the simplicity of their decision-making and mediation; in their efficiency and effectiveness, and in their work ethics in which a variety of interests collaborate. These all account for the identity, nature and efficacy of the collective actor as evident to outsider observation. However, we have so far touched only incidentally on internal factors and conditions – participation, affiliation, goals; control, decision-making, accountability and other operational values; the potential for factionalism. To complement the analysis of the previous chapters, I turn in the next chapter to the discussion of these internal aspects of the Gülen Movement, using evidence from interviews and questionnaires conducted among participants.

5

Internal Organizational Factors
and Components

5.1 INTRODUCTION

In this chapter I discuss internal organizational factors and components of the Gülen Movement (hereafter abbreviated as 'internal factors') through the insiders' own framings and action in relation to the contemporary theories of social movements. The internal factors are presented in relation to issues concerning identity, relationship and participation, goals, intervention, power and authority, SMOs and commitment, leadership, incentives and rewards, and the potential for factionalism.

The discussion is based on in-depth interviews with three participants in the Gülen Movement (Abdullah Aymaz, Enes Ergene and Ergün Çapan), and two questionnaires that were distributed among the staff of institutions established by the Movement.[1] The two questionnaires are given in their entirety on the following pages and again at the end of the book, in Appendices 3 and 4.

The interviews and responses to the Questionnaires are also used to highlight the theoretical perspectives or diverse findings or assumptions of different researchers, and to assess the relative validity of alternative interpretations. The questions and answers are referred to as relevant to the particular theme under discussion, and to highlight important issues or arguments within the collective action and social movement theories. At certain stages of the discussion, it was convenient to group selected questions together and present them as tables. The different items on the questionnaires are identified by letter and number: 'A:1' means 'Questionnaire A, item 1';

'B:4 and B:5' means 'Questionnaire B, question 4 and its answers and question 5 and its answers'.

5.2 THE CASE OF THE GÜLEN MOVEMENT

5.2.1 Identity, participation and relationship

All three interviewees had very developed views on the theme of identity, participation and relationship. Ergene said:

> Individuals perform the greatest role in the process of becoming involved in the Gülen Movement. Relationships through social life facilitate involvement and make it easy and comfortable for individuals to join and contribute to networks of services. Within these networks, individuals interact and engage in negotiations as they produce the cognitive and motivational schemata necessary for action. People by their free will accept roles in accordance with their individual differences and personality traits. Individuals come into these service groups with a conscious decision to change and to direct their own existence[2].

Çapan argued that the relational networks are built and strengthened through interaction and through the value attributed to individual views, to contribution to philanthropist projects and to collective reasoning.[3] Participants are not looking for a communal identity, or to replace or relocate primary associations (gender, age-group, locality, ethnicity, etc.):

> The individuals are not previously isolated people. They do not see the Gülen Movement as a surrogate family. They do not instrumentally search for or center on identity or resistance to political power, either. They find an authentic relation to themselves and to others and therefore call one another and the whole society to responsibility.

Aymaz pointed out the significance of team work and collective effort when taking on responsibilities in service-networks:

> People within these networks of services understand that the vast potential to make a change in the lives of others is far broader than their own actual capacity for action. Through the establishment of social relationships, people become open to the personal realization that an individual is limited and not even sufficient unto himself/herself. On the other hand, they have opportunities to compensate for their limitations in community service through the potential of the collective actor.

When asked how this integration or affiliation in the service-networks is different from the susceptibility and submission of self-inadequate people to the authoritarianism in some political movements,[4] Ergene responded:

> The participants in the Gülen Movement, in contrast, are already educated, coming from a positively acknowledged background.[5] They are not misguided individuals. They are not beguiled by a utopia, an authoritarian coercive leader, or by any attempt at defying authority to bring a regime change in Turkey. The participants join the networks with the resolve that they can do something and it can really work. The intention is altruistic rather than selfish, rather than changing the direction of the development of the System. Furthermore, neither psychological nor political situational stress is the only necessary cause for joining a movement, and it is definitely not the case with the patterns of joining with the Movement.

These views are reflected in the responses to Questionnaire A grouped in Table 1 and B:11.

Table 1

A		SD	D	N	A	SA
7	The GM will turn into a political and conflictual movement.	978				
8	The GM will turn into a sect or a cult.	978				
11	The identity of the GM has isolated/alienated me from society.	956	22			
12	The GM reconciles and unites people on common grounds and references.				22	956
17	The GM is reducible to a linear and easily recognizable form.	952	20	1	5	
18	There is unity of ideas, means and goals in the GM.	956	22			
20	I can know if a person is associated with the GM by checking his/her discourse and action.		1	3	23	951
22	Identity changes over time and space in the GM.	901	76	1		
23	Identity is something given and taken.	963	14	1		
24	Identity comes with intentions, services and action.		15		24	939
40	The GM is located at several different levels of the social system simultaneously.		3	1	79	895

B:11

B:11 Where does your identity come from? List five elements only.

- deeds, action and intention
- deeds/work and its results
- community action, deeds and goals in the GM
- what the GM made me earn and gain through the services we give
- personal choice and character

When what the interviewees said is put together with what the participants replied in Table 1 and B:11 above, it indicates that identity in the Gülen Movement is not taken as something given. It is dynamic and always the result of an active process and has continuity. Since the participants willingly take on, own and retain it, the identity is not imposed. (See A:22, 23, 24 and B:11 and also the discussion in §3.2.5).

Imposition of identity tends to meet with reaction and defensiveness. In contemporary societies, people wish to assume responsibility for creating their own identity. Any forced identity is vulnerable, risky and does not guarantee continuity and stability. The real-world-oriented social service and project networks in the Gülen Movement could not serve to impose any kind of identity on participants. Recruitment into a social movement through psychological coercion or manipulation is unlikely to be as high and potent as critics allege:

> Since coercive persuasion or psychological conversion variables are zero in almost all SMOs, they can do little or nothing to [ac]count for most joining.[6]

Participants in the Gülen Movement confirm that identity involves continual investments. The Movement has learned to distinguish itself from the environment without leading to isolation from it or conflict (Table 1 and B:11). The Movement does not sever itself from society. The relational dimension of the collective identity of the Movement helps to form unity within the collective actor. (See A:11, 18, 25 and also the discussion in §4.1.3).

The Movement as collective actor proves able to recognize the effects of its action, its symbolic orientations and meanings (see §3.2.5). It attributes these effects to itself and allocates and exchanges them with others. This enables the Movement to establish over time relationship, links and bonds through services with the wider public. It also enables the solidarity that binds individuals to each other; this auto-identification and differentiation of the actor from others evokes social and mutual recognition with other collective actors (A:20 and 40; see also the conclusions reached in §3.2.5–6 and 4.1.3).

However, variations over time and the establishment of new relationships, organizational forms and institutions, and adaptations to the environment indicate something that at first appears contradictory. While the Gülen Movement tacitly affirms its difference from the rest of the society, it also states its belonging to the shared culture of society and its need to be recognized as a social actor for the common good. This seeming paradox is in fact a necessary prerequisite of a multicultural, diverse and pluralist society and presupposes a certain equality, a degree of reciprocity, and consolidation of democratic practice and institutions.[7]

Table 1 and B:1, 3, 4 and 11 indicate that Movement participants feel a bond with others because they share the same interests. This enables individuals in the Movement to make sense of what they are doing, and to affirm themselves as subjects of their action, and to withstand the breakdown of social relations during conflicts, as A:25 also indicates.

The February 28 Process[8] attempted to provoke the Gülen Movement into a situation of crisis or intense conflict. The unity and identity of the Movement as collective actor, and the firmness of its hold on its worldview, were severely challenged and tested. The Movement was able to respond positively and peacefully, and preserve its coherence in each of the spheres in which it provides services. This most serious situation failed to initiate a breakdown or fragmentation of the Movement or a breach of its external boundaries (A:7, 8 and B:9).

This indicates the capacity of the Movement as collective actor to produce and maintain a stable, durable self-definition over many years. Indeed, it has improved its capability of resolving problems posed by the environment and is becoming increasingly independent and autonomous in its capacity for action within the network of relationships in which it is situated.[9] The February 28 Process also proved that the Movement has the ability to produce new definitions and meanings by integrating the past with emerging elements and outcomes of a present situation into its stable identity, which in turn strengthens its internal cohesion and locates common ground outside itself (A:12). Therefore (see A:22 and B:9), while the methods and means to accomplish services may change or develop over time, the core of the identity in the Movement does not change with time and situation: it holds steady.[10]

Furthermore, the strong support for Gülen and the activities of the Movement, especially during that defamation period, from a very diverse and wide spectrum of politicians, statesmen, civil society organizations, thinkers and journalists corroborates the idea that the identity of the Gülen Movement is integrative rather than alienated (see A:11 and 12).[11]

B:1

B:1 What comes into your mind first when someone mentions the GM? List your first five ideas only.   • education and useful community services   • generosity – sacrifice   • altruism   • societal accord and peace   • world peace

Table 2

A		SD	D	N	A	SA
4	The GM devotes a considerable share of its resources to new projects, alternative openings and development.				39	939
5	The GM devotes a considerable share of its resources to the task of managing complexity, of consolidation of group solidarity, and of avoidance of disaggregation.	893	85			
7	The GM will turn into a political and conflictual movement.	978				
8	The GM will turn into a sect or cult.	978				
9	There is sacral celebration of Gülen and others in the GM.	970	8			
10	I have seen, heard of or experienced anachronistic and unrealistic things in the GM.	895	83			
30	My concern is for the self preservation of the GM and solidarity.	863	77		38	
31	My concern is for the alternative projects, new openings and new relationships.		18		78	884

Questionnaires A and B indicate that the collective identity of the Gülen Movement depends on how a multitude of choices, goals, relations, services and representations are held together, and is the outcome of conscious laborious processes. (See esp. B:1, 11; A:18 and 24.) However, collective identity patterns itself according to the presence and relative intensity of its dimensions. Some dimensions may be weaker or stronger than others, and some may be secondary and tertiary in priority. In our case, some (such as political power or governmental change) do not even make it into the classification (see B:1, 3, 4, 8, 9, A:7, and also §3.2.2, 4.1.1 and 4.1.4).

A:8, 9 and 10 reveal that the identity of the Gülen Movement is not shaped by transcendent, metaphysical and meta-social elements and entities, such as myths, legendary saints, idealized ancestors or sacral celebration of any individual. To the contrary, although the Movement is a faith-inspired initiative and the founding elements come from Islam and its universal values, it increasingly and progressively associates itself with purposive human action, culture, communication and social relations resulting from the services it provides (B:1, 3, 11; A:12 and 16).

In the light of the feed-back – criticism and praise – from outside the Movement, the collective identity is evidently becoming the product of conscious action, the outcome of self-reflection, and more than a set of given or 'structural' characteristics (A:16, 20, 23; B:1 and 11). The conscious collective construction of the identity within a widening transnational environment of social relations makes it increasingly self-reflexive, inclusive, integrative and universalistic (A:30, 31; and see the discussion in §3.2.6.

A:4 and 5 reveal another result opposed to what was postulated by Michels' ([1915] 1999) 'iron law of oligarchy', that all complex organizations produce self-interested ruling cliques and therefore any movement devotes a considerable share of its resources to the task of managing complexity, consolidating group solidarity, and preventing disaggregation.[12] This theory originates in the elite to rank-and-file relationship of the optimistic revolutionary and pessimistic non-revolutionary understandings of radical or socialist political parties and labor unions in the past. It is a highly deterministic and pessimistic understanding of organization and leadership, and based on the oligarchic tendencies of the trade unions of its own setting and on the way that organizational changes lead to changes in organizational behavior.[13] It may be valid only for certain kinds of organization and environment.[14] Many theorists have disputed Michels' argument for the inevitable transformation of organizations into oligarchy.[15] Such transformation is far from being universally observed among SMOs.[16] Cook maintains that the conceptual unity assumed by Michels' theory is no longer appropriate to the study of participation or membership in organizations.[17]

What Michels postulated might be valid for organizations with rigid forms of authoritarianism and charismatic leadership. However, it cannot be true for contemporary altruistic and cultural movements like the Gülen Movement.[18] Michels did not live long enough to see mass democracy or non-political SMOs,[19] expressive of individual or interpersonal relationships and pluralistic and democratic tendencies.[20] Contemporary collective action is not concerned only with revolt against leaders for economic reasons, and it does not consider individuals as 'cogs in the machine' of the organization in which they are members only as numbers.[21] Nor does all contemporary collective action develop a ruling clique of leaders with interests in the organization itself rather than in its official aims.* Within the Gülen Movement, there are no organizational tendencies or characteristics that make maintaining the organization the highest priority over and above every other possible goal. The Movement has little to do with goal displacement: this is clearly shown by A:5, 15, 21, 27, 28, 29, 35, 36 and 38.

The participants' emphasis on the services and their outcomes implies the inclusion of the social field as part of the construction of the Gülen Movement and identity within it. Beyond the definition which the Movement gives of itself and the recognition granted to it by the rest of society, the participants draw attention to interactive work among individuals, groups or service-networks. Rather than paying attention to the abstract and unsubstantiated accusations leveled at them by the ideologically marginal and vested interest groups in Turkey[22] – such as being sectarian, fundamentalist, reactionary – the participants shift their attention from rhetoric to the visible realities and concrete results of the Movement's collective action, they look to education and to useful, beneficial, altruistic communi-

---

* The elite or leaders, Michels argued, come to value leadership and its status and rewards above any commitment to the organization's goals. They tend to look after their private interests and, within the party, use their knowledge and know-how to influence decision-making processes; subsequently, ordinary members of the organization may be effectively excluded from those processes.

ty services and peace (see B:1).[23] Movement participants tend to differentiate themselves from political action and to mark off their cultural level from all others, especially from sects or cults (A:7 and 8).[24]

It could be concluded that dimensions such as those indicated in Table 1, Table 2, B:1 and 11 show the Gülen Movement to be action and goal oriented. This builds in the Movement a fairly cohesive and homogeneous identity and reality, which strengthens the physical and psychological interaction and, in turn, facilitates collective action of all kinds, including SMOs.[25] While the New Marxists' influence in social movement theory holds that representation of movements as largely homogeneous subjects is no longer feasible,[26] the reality is that many collective actions comprise different orientations, components and levels pertaining to different socio-historical levels or layers in a given society. When asked how to explain the apparent unity within the underlying multiplicity in the Gülen Movement, Aymaz responded:

> The collective actor of the Movement identifies and recognizes specific levels and a plurality of levels within the construction of collective action and identity. However, it does not negate and attempt to eliminate people's differences, but tries to bring them around the mutually acknowledged similarities and references to serve community and humanity rather than focusing on secondary, contradictory and ambivalent differences which do not have much significance for universally accepted projects, such as education. This carries in the message of the Movement a complex articulation of meanings, relations and values for peaceful coexistence and co-operation of civilizations. Reducing the Gülen Movement to just one of its many levels, all these into the unity rendered by ideologists or into dimensions of collective action that are visible at first sight, is either an error or reduction.

Recalling other qualities and components of the Movement as collective actor and its action, Aymaz explained the factors that facilitate its cohesiveness within plurality or multiplicity:

> The Movement stresses the reality and the projects not an/the actor. Starting from the present, it relates to the future, not to the world of fantasies. As the Movement establishes itself here and now with projects, and as it establishes its location, consistency, commitment and trust, the Gülen Movement gives people hope to think of the future. It does not oppose the idea that people should retain their values while changing. The retention of values and maintaining permanence should

not contradict continuity, progress and advancement. This draws many individuals into service-projects.

The factors Aymaz lists are labeled by McAdam and colleagues as 'micro mobilization contexts', namely the social contexts in which people already know one another: 'Prior interpersonal contact is the single richest source of movement recruits.'* In these social contexts, people can carry on discussion of appropriate action, and activate material resources, cultural capital and labor.[27] The social and cognitive processes in such contexts help develop a rationale that legitimates the SMO's formation and follow-up projects. In addition to the rationale, people also develop a belief that the SMO and its services are truly necessary and worth all contributions.[28]

Aymaz can be interpreted as meaning that the Gülen Movement does not give identity to people, but provides resources for them to construct their own identity, making them responsible for both that identity and their action. As there is not a single dimension to human behavior, all problems are first brought for solution to networks of people, into the ambit of communicative processes; the individuals only become informed within the collectivity, and then through collective reasoning voluntarily integrate into relational networks of educational, social, and altruistic services.[29]

Ergene also mentioned the importance of the service-networks in the Gülen Movement:

> Individuals themselves can construct the multiple social affiliations in everyday life, can easily adapt themselves to projects for the betterment of the conditions they live in, and can thus build direction and meaning for their existence in relational and professionalized[30] networks and services. Individuals do not see or sense the danger of losing themselves in the service-networks. They realize that their individual differences are respected. They do not cease to exist as unique and singular individuals but come to appreciate the use, value and centrality of network connections between persons. Their interaction and communication, the basic requirements of social life, are more easily maintained and mediated by networks of belongings. Through these networks, people orient themselves toward living at peace with the Movement and with the outside, wider public.

---

* McAdam *et al.*, 1988:708; for research supporting the argument that interpersonal interactions and affective bonds are the fundamental background to movement participation, see Lofland, 1996:234–6. B:5 also affirms this.

In everyday life, intimate interpersonal relations and also affective primary bonds allow individuals to make sense of their world through networks. People become more able to reach out to other systems, relations, meanings, goals and interests than was possible for them on their own.[31] Several researchers have measured self-efficacy and find that the more active the participants are, the more assertive, self-confident, energetic, and effective they are in using their capabilities, as compared to those who are less engaged in activism.[32]

Ergene went on to add:

> The Movement therefore exhibits a unified and homogenous identity agreed and based upon beneficial services for all. The relationships in the Gülen Movement are not hierarchical, mechanical or predetermined. One system, group or network does not impose on others a greater burden of limitations or liabilities. It is therefore a relationship of autonomy and interdependence.

Autonomy and interdependence may sound contradictory but are not so in reality. Autonomy comes from the fact that each SMO in the Gülen Movement already follows the rules and regulations laid down by the state or states in which it is working (the System), alongside which it has procedures and rules of its own that it has developed in everyday operation. Each SMO is governed by its own internal logic and constituted by specific relations, different societal ends, exchange and interaction between roles, and interpersonal and affective communication in lifeworlds. On the other hand, each of those dimensions can affect others through its outcomes: for example, the meaningfulness of primary relations, and the existence of equilibrium of the role system, and openness in decision-making mechanisms, all have impact on social relations, resources, or production. What is common to all SMOs of the Gülen Movement is that they are entirely located within the limits of compatibility of the System, and not oriented towards conflict or breach of those limits.*

When the regulations imposed by the state authorities – for example the prohibition of the obligatory daily prayers and the headscarf ban in all educational institutions – cause difficulties for individuals, the practice is to attempt to resolve the issues individually. Gülen-inspired institutions are

---

* As is stated by A:7, A:14, B:1, B:3, B:4, B:6 and B:9. See also §4.1.2.

never brought into a conflict with the state. While working within the limits allowed by the law and the System makes them autonomous, interaction, exchange and benefiting from collective outcomes, and recognizing these as their own and being recognized by others as such, make the collective actor of the Gülen Movement interdependent (B:10, A:20, 39 and 41). Individuals or service-groups are connected by interdependent relationships; any variation in one element therefore has effects on all the others in the Movement. The mutual relationships are negotiated, while institutionalized relationships are contractual. They adapt, negotiate, devise strategies, and restructure the field and adjust the means and future projects in accordance with their cumulative experience (B:10, A:4, 31 and 41).

That reveals another attribute, namely that the Movement as collective actor does not draw back into itself or break off relations with social partners in the wider public. The strategy or relationship of the Movement is therefore integration with and full commitment to the wider society through educational and cultural institutions and community work, rather than isolation, alienation and withdrawal from it: this is explicit in all the B:1 answers, implicit in A:5, 11, 31 and 40.[33] As the integration/partnership field enlarges, so too does the likelihood of forming new SMOs[34] – as we can infer from A:4, 25 and 31. The Gülen Movement co-operates with other legitimate and institutionalized organizations concerned with the same issues, and keen to develop joint initiatives based on compatible definitions. The activities of the educational institutions, such as science and knowledge Olympiads, student exchange programs, the activities of the Foundation of Journalists and Writers all around the world, and local and regional cultural and dialog centers are good, clear examples of such co-operation.[35]

As A:16, 24, 31, 40 and B:1, 3, 4 and 11 indicate, the Movement as collective actor identifies with all actors within the Movement and with their motivations, representations and the field of social relationships. This relationship is both direct and indirect or epiphenomenal: the outcomes that manifest through collective action are appropriated by other actors within the Movement. The relationships are constituted by their different orientations, and the various systems of social relations. Their sociability makes them visible and undeniable, a part of the larger society.

The service-networks in the Gülen Movement are not easily classifiable, as they are manifold and variable in density (see A:17). However, they are not deficient in division of labor. Çapan explained this as follows:

> Functions and responsibilities are duplicated among the various components of the collective actor. This prevents exploitation of the positions, authority and resources assigned to individuals. It provides some kind of inner supervision by all and makes one accountable to all. Also the individuals who have assumed any projects are continually supervised and supported cognitively, motivationally and, when it is necessary, materially to complete the projects. This provides people with strong incentives, solidarity, cohesion and exchange of experiences among components. Therefore none is accused personally of a failure but all marshal support, direction, consensus and resources necessary for the collective action.

In the Gülen Movement internal cohesion and sharing specific traits among the individuals and networks support collective action and make it easier for participants to mobilize. The existence of other mobilizations facilitated by these features is also described by Della Porta and Diani, Melucci, and McAdam and Rucht.[36] Also, the Movement reflects what Gerlach and Hine refer to as multi-faceted structure.[37] The structure has endured through time – through later developments and when the actors and issues have changed.[38]

B:10 (on decision-making) indicates that the Gülen Movement guarantees and provides participants with access to control of the resources and services pursued through collective action. This accounts for the strengths of the Movement as collective actor and nurtures social trust, honesty, flexibility, adaptability and immediacy.[39] It is something that more structured and formal organizations, especially political ones, cannot easily incorporate into their action.[40] This too does not fit with what social movement theorists lead us to expect. For them, a movement consists of diversified, autonomous units that devote a large part of their available resources to maintaining internal solidarity, often on the basis of primary relationships.* However, Aymaz was very clear that, with the Gülen Movement, 'solidarity is epiphenomenal. It is not the cause and primary goal of the formation and the collective action of the Movement. It is a secondary or a tertiary effect which results from the collective services and action.' Put simply, the Move-

---

* Such as age, gender, nationality and ethnicity, or an ideology.

ment and Movement participants do not *pursue* solidarity as a goal of their effort; rather solidarity *ensues* from their collective effort, their doing together what they collectively have approved as a good for themselves and wider society. Such solidarity might be considered a 'natural' output (as against 'politically contrived' or 'artificial' input).

Organizations needing to pursue and committed to pursuing solidarity have to, and do, hold people focused inward and 'safe' from outside influence or interpretation by the wider public. In the Gülen Movement, by contrast, communicated exchange of experiences keep the managerially distinct, quasi-autonomous networks in contact with each other and the wider public they serve. Information, know-how, and patterns of behavior circulate, passing from one network to another, and bringing a degree of homogeneity to the whole.[41] The service-networks in the Gülen Movement thus differ radically from the image of the politically organized actor. Service groups operate on their own, not from one center, although they maintain links to the collective actor through the circulation of information and professionalized people in the fabric of daily life.[42]

Also, the ensuing social cohesion or solidarity is cultural in character. To a certain degree, the solidarity of the group is inseparable from the personal quest and from the everyday affective and communicative needs of the participants in the network (B:7). Yet, it remains, as we have noted, epiphenomenal, not itself a goal pursued; rather, it accompanies action naturally as a result of experiences and memories gained and retained through the labor of accomplishing collective projects (A:30, 32 and 33).

Participation in services takes relatively stable, enduring forms of network. Individuals come and go and replace one another but the projects remain and continue. Individual needs and collective goals are not mutually exclusive; they are one and the same thing, and in daily life coincide and interweave closely with the action of the Movement.[43] The Movement thus becomes a vehicle, a means, for people to transform and nourish a latent potential into visible collective action. The participation in services around a specific goal and the tangibility of the products yield and strengthen solidarity. Externally visible aspects of the mobilization, and its rapidity, extension, and success, reflect the inner solidarity of the participants.[44]

The concept of 'membership' or 'participation' has been viewed as problematic by researchers.[45] As networks, rather than formal organizations, movements attract supporters or adherents, rather than members, although the former are often more committed than those who have formal membership in political parties.[46] Della Porta and Diani support the idea that social movements do not have 'members' but 'participants'. In the same vein, Melucci uses the notion of 'multiple belongings' for multiple affiliations or participation.[47]

What distinguishes the Gülen Movement is the multiplicity of its participants' affiliations.[48] There is no formal membership as such in the Movement. Individuals do not belong to any single community or network only. They participate simultaneously in a number of areas of social life and in associations of various kinds. In each of these settings only a part of the self, and only certain dimensions of the personality and experience, are activated.[49] In a religiously-motivated search, alternative affiliations are a journey for personal and spiritual development and meaning.[50] For service projects and networks, Aymaz exemplifies this:

> I am a teacher and a writer. I have commitments like my job and also voluntary extra contributions at the media organ I work for as a columnist. I also take part in neighborhood and community work where my family resides. I have interests in scientific issues and therefore take part in the editorial board and the selection committee of a popular scientific monthly. My children attend a high school and I take part in the family group of the school to improve the educational level of the school. I also engage in interfaith dialog and visit and receive people from different faith communities. I also attend meetings and networks of people from my own hometown and former places I lived in. In short, I participate in several networks due to my place of residence, job, interests, hometown, children's education, and so forth. Likewise, there are thousands of people attending more networks and doing more community services in the Gülen Movement than I do.

What Aymaz says means that being an actor in the Movement integrates a manifold set of affiliations and interests (A:16). Participants who gain access to the general media and have previous mobilization experience contribute to the network of services, and more specifically in the professionalized cultural or media market and with public institutions. This brings effectiveness, rapidity, and extension into the organizational capacity in the Gülen Movement, and ensures diffuse forms of leadership.[51] According to circumstances, therefore, people respond to the multiplication of interests, of opportunities to contribute, and of choices of affiliation. Being part of a network means keeping open the range of opportunities for self-recognition, being useful and beneficial to others, and also avoiding conflicts (B:4).

Being part of a network in the Gülen Movement is not due to lack of choice but out of choice (B:8). It is by conscious decision that individuals become part of the Movement and then enact and experience self-fulfillment in it (A:13 and B:2). Therefore, the collective action of the Movement proves for many a call, a vocation, and through the multiple belongings they often find further inspiration and incentivization in the ideas and tactics espoused and practiced by other participants.[52] Responding to the call to take part enables people, through different channels, to experience a passionate optimism:[53] they want to experience now what it is possible to accomplish or what they must do that is meaningful in itself for others and coming generations. What is done on a small scale in one context creates meaning and repercussions within a broader compass. What people engage in may appear not to affect themselves directly, but it feeds and promotes something essential for the collective actor to realize an effective mobilization or rapid and widespread diffusion for a service-project through multiple affiliations.[54]

Multiple affiliations in the Gülen Movement also facilitate diffusion. 'Diffusion[s] can be either direct or indirect depending on whether they come about through unmediated contacts between participants or are mediated by the mass media.'[55] Sociologist Whittier (2004) confirms that cultural representations and news coverage shape the practices of other activists through diffusion and that activists, even when they share no network connections, learn about movement innovations, actions and successes through the mass media.[56]

The Gülen Movement has spread beyond Turkish national borders, developing contemporaneously and displaying significant similarities in different countries. Diffusion has been strongest in the neighboring countries, which are geographically and culturally close, but also very strong in others with no historical ties or similarities in social and political structure. The peaceful cultural–educational and collaborative understanding brings different social entities together around common meanings and values. Diffusion has been through personal orientations, literature, conferences, the media,

aid and relief agencies, educational and cultural SMOs, interfaith and dialog organizations, and travel and visits.[57]

Geographical proximity, historical ties and structural similarities have
facilitated the services offered by the Gülen Movement. Linguistic similari-
ty also constitutes a tie and has been a powerful catalyzing factor in diffusion among the Turkic countries. However, the Movement does not attempt diffusion through recruitment among strangers, in private places, or
by means of door-to-door canvassing.

Multiple affiliations bring up the question of 'the free-rider' and totalizing commitment, and how these are handled in the Movement.

Interviewee Çapan argued that the negative effects of the 'free-rider'
attitude are contained by the internal factors of the Gülen Movement – self-
willed choice, self-fulfillment, altruism and vocation.[58] In addition, face-to-
face discussions, availability of information and communication channels,
skilled leadership in SMOs, and self-willed choice of a network and freedom to exit or withdraw from service-networks in the Movement obstruct
the development of such a free-rider problem in the first place.[59] In faith-
inspired service-projects, expectation of reward from God alone, the purity
of intention, or the accountability to God for one's deeds and intentions,
which may all be called piety or God-wariness, help prevent, or at least
minimize, the free-rider problem.

Multiple belongings in the Gülen Movement are a result of the complexity of human relationships. Individuals pass from one service-network
to another. Individual commitment to a specific project or a specific service-network is not therefore a totalizing commitment. It does not demand
a life-term involvement. Involvement may be temporary. This permits individuals to look for and take up practical opportunities for the self-planned
integration of personal experience in everyday life. Self-fulfillment is
through self-willed formation of meaning, and self-planned integration and
experience (see A:35, 37, 39, 41, and B:11).[60]

The nature of participation, commitment and personal fulfillment
through multiple belongings reveals another distinctive dimension of the
Movement: 'continuity', that is, continuity between individual and collective identity, and between leisure and commitment. The multiple, mutable, and overlapping relations of belonging to service-projects form the
basis, cohesion and continuity of the Gülen Movement. In these network

relations, individual needs and collective goals, and individual and collective interests, are constantly negotiated and served. Individuality and collectivity are not mutually exclusive. While the individual and diverse contributions enrich community, what is done for and to the wider community, ultimately benefits individuals. Secondly, people commit themselves to service-projects both within leisure time and committed time. The continuity between leisure and commitment, by presupposing a close connection between self-fulfillment and participation, enhances a great deal of feeling and meaning, and forms the basis of material and immaterial resources in collective action.

When asked if such integration or participation in any way prompts participants in the Gülen Movement to breach the limits of the System, Ergene explained that, while seeking integration to the Movement or into the multiple belongings, individuals are not required, or allowed, to challenge the constraints established by law or the general public, and that the history of the Movement so far has not shown any illegality.[61] Moreover – see B5 – it is through micro-relational mechanisms (that is, friendships, acquaintanceships, kinships, and associational networks) that people are motivated to join the Movement. These mechanisms reduce the cost of participation and encourage people to mobilize themselves.

B:5

B:5 How did you join the GM?
- exemplary friends from the GM and their conduct and sincerity
- reading Gülen's works and listening to his lectures
- the overall meaning and the message of the altruistic services
- the worldview of the GM
- people at my immediate environment, neighbors, and relatives

---

The low or zero cost of entry into, and exit from, project-networks also explains the tendency of participation to become temporary, short-term and not totalizing. Aymaz commented on this as follows:

> Participation in a specific project might be short-term but an individual's commitment to values and meaning in the collective action of the Gülen Movement is not. Individuals do not go out of the Movement but will to substitute themselves for another project. This substitution is not hindered by the project-networks in the Movement if one wishes so. The

plurality of other projects and networks available for the individual facilitate straightforward substitutability of the individual for another service-
network or -project. The sharing of short-term goals means that only one
segment of individual experience is placed at stake. In this way, any individual or people in any service-network do not have a connotation or
false assumption of individual failure, exit or betrayal.

Aymaz's clarification points out that plurality of goals and resources
allow individuals to change networks with only minor consequences for the
improvement and effectiveness of either their contribution or the network.
In addition, leaving a group becomes less dramatic an event for the individual, as the range of possible service-networks of choice expands with the increase in social differentiation (see A:4, 5, 40 and 41).

B:5 also tells us that participation in the Gülen Movement is not isolationist or atomized – individuals do not join the service-networks on an individual basis alone, nor act or work in them out of self-interest. They do
so through relational channels, such as friends, neighbors and professional
associations. Individuals have the opportunity in service-networks to come
to know one another as human beings. This informal fellowship develops a
common sympathy which contributes to intimacy and social cohesion or
solidarity. The Movement therefore does not need any formal ceremonial
behavior, ritual, symbols, slogans, costumes or badges to foster identity or
unity.* Newcomers keep their former and extant relations outside the
Movement. Participation in the Movement is based on information-sharing, exchange, interaction and taking an active role in the collective action.
It takes the form of friendship-based circles. It is contextualized: people in
it have simultaneous and multiple interests and friendships, and professionalized and altruistic commitments. Losses that may arise for any reason are
therefore not borne by the individual in loneliness.

By way of conclusion on this theme, it can be said that there is a certain degree of social, cultural, cognitive and emotional investment or construction within the inter-relational networks, or networks of relationship, in
the Gülen Movement. Through these, individuals feel part of a common
unity, a social coherence and cohesion. This interactive and communicative
construction is socially and cognitively framed through active relationships

---

* As is also expressed directly by A:19 and indirectly by A:35, 36, 37, and 38. See also
§4.1.4 on sects and Lofland, 1996:241–2.

in different areas of social life, which maintains the collective identity and action of the Gülen Movement over time.

When the collective actor proves able to handle assaults and counter-mobilization cognitively and intellectually, while remaining within the limits of the System, and while remaining unaffected by environmental and conjunctural changes, the actor or the identity has gained a certain stability and permanence over time. Then, the collective actor starts to be easily recognized by friends, opponents and third parties. The ability to recognize and to be recognized over time distinguishes the Gülen Movement from other collective actors and highlights its potentiality. Its identity is an interactive process. It is what and how the individuals in service-networks perceive themselves to be, and how they define themselves in a certain way, relative to others. Therefore it needs to be treated at both the individual and collective levels because human beings are 'essentially relational creatures [...whose] identity consists not simply in their separateness from others, but in the myriad affiliations that link them with a shared lifeworld'.[62]

As discussed above, in light of the responses in the questionnaires and interviews, identity is constructed through a combination of rational exchange, affective connections and bonds, mutual recognition, purposive calculation and meaningful action. Personal choices, meaning, emotion, and expectations and interactions are all measured against the collective actor's field of operation and reality. This assessment comes from the possibilities and limits of action, which help the collective actor to define itself, its environment and relationship with that environment. The identity of the Movement is also a collective interactive process because many individuals or networks take part in defining the meaning of their action, in maintaining their ongoing relationships with other individuals and groups, and in calculating the field of opportunities, constraints, costs and benefits for any action.

This collective and continuous process in the Gülen Movement cannot be visible to a short-term, transitory researcher-observer. It is manifested in forms of organization, internal rules and procedures, and professionalized leadership relationships, all of which in return feed back and crystallize the identity of the Movement.

At the moment of joining the service-networks, individuals might not bring a profound personal investment. Rather, their commitment and contribution increase as their knowledge of the field in which they have come to contribute grows and matures. This investment progressively strengthens the participant's bond with a service-network or SMO, and is a cultural and symbolic investment.

Relationships so constructed – quite unlike participation in actions and organizations with totalizing accents – are far deeper and more binding than, and outlive, short-term participation. Coherence comes from the self-reflective capacity and the quality of direct contribution or participation in the collective action. This cultural, symbolic and plural form respects individual differences and needs, and does not welcome sectarian solutions, marginalized ambitions or the actualization of interests formed and pursued in conflict with the System.

In sum: relationships in the Gülen Movement are *affective:* interpersonal, social, informal and integrative; *professional:* formal and contractual; *cultural:* educational, self-reflective, altruistic and apolitical; *locational:* project-based and inclusive; and *transnational:* – peaceful, collaborative and civilizing.

5.2.2 Goals

In social movement theory 'goals' is a central term which often includes and relates to plans, schemes, projects and strategies. In their varying conceptualizations researchers select certain elements in or out of their discussion.[63] We looked at the goals of the Gülen Movement in Chapter 2 from a particular perspective; here we examine the relevant internal factors. However, it will be helpful to take note first of two points raised by interviewees Aymaz and Çapan. Aymaz said:

> The first thing to discuss might be the overtness of the goals of the Gülen Movement. Since the decisions and goals are set in open-to-all service-networks, in the full light of publicity without concealing the existence or objectives of the Movement, without keeping the identities and participants secret, the Movement does not establish and protect a separate existence or intention free from outside control or supervision. The goals are taken through rational public discussion and decision-making.

Çapan pointed to another characteristic of the Movement's goals – that they are consistently positive, constructive and non-disruptive:

[The goals] are non-violent, non-coercive and peaceful in theory and practice. The fact that Gülen was unanimously acquitted in 2006 of the lawsuit filed against him in 2000, the fact that the accusations against Gülen to wear him and the Movement down 'were not proved and no elements of crime came into being', emphasizes the overtness, lawfulness and legitimacy of goals inspired by Gülen and pursued by the Gülen Movement.[64]

Bearing those points in mind, I turn to the pertinent internal factors. In B:9, below, participants list among other things, types of goals which are not permitted in the Gülen Movement including, political, personal and violent goals and any action taken without consensus.

B:9

B:9 What is <u>not</u> permitted in the GM? (List five things only.)
- politics, violence and reactionary action/attitudes
- conflictual–oppositional action, violence
- personal and material gain by means of services
- any action/initiative without any collective reasoning, discussion and consultation
- extremism, immorality, bad habits

Given the heterogeneity of the social basis of the service-networks, the Gülen Movement focuses on general, precise, concrete, unifying and constructive goals rather than mutable and unattainable goals and passing interests.[65] This produces within the Movement an understanding of 'a permanent hierarchy of interests' in society.[66] Education, interfaith dialog, and non-political, non-conflictual and non-violent community services, improving oneself and developing social and cultural potential take priority in the Movement (as discussed in previous chapters, and see responses A:4, 12, 31 and 41). The projects are selected for their practicability, legality and effectiveness. They are not exploited for a 'politics of signification',[67] that is, in order to gain ascendancy over others or to move up in some existing hierarchy of constituency, class, politics or credibility (see A:15, 18, 27, 28, 36, and 38). The reason for this is explained by Gülen very simply:

If each individual in a network tries to impose himself or herself as the only authority in a certain field and some others imitate him or her, discipline is destroyed, confusion engendered, and the community is divided against itself.[68]

Social movement theories postulate that the social heterogeneity of participants and geographical dispersion inhibit collective goals and action.[69] Again, this does not prove valid for the Gülen Movement. On the contrary, the social heterogeneity of the participants in the Movement, alongside geographical dispersion, formalization and institutionalization in over ninety countries, become motivational factors for them.[70] Individuals perceive their identity, affiliation and Movement services to be in a high degree of accord and correspondence within their life space and the world at large. Their own and the Movement's orientations, interests and values are congruent and complementary. Moreover, as the Movement's goals and worldview do not depart much from mainstream or pre-existing prospects at hand, participants readily incorporate their energies into the Movement's collective action. Almost a thousand educational and cultural institutions world-wide contradict what the theory postulated.[71]

However, if specific issues are connected with universal values (peace, human rights, poverty relief, and so on), short-term projects can be taken up, allowing an immediate and correspondingly transitory mobilization. Examples are earthquake relief for Pakistan and Peru, Far East tsunami aid, African famine and poverty relief, and other relief efforts in disaster-hit countries. Such action is, again, patterned according to cultural and institutional choices within transnational consensus and legality.[72] Different components converge in such mobilizations – institutions, the media, luminaries from the art world, and foreign authorities.[73] What is striking about these short-term service-projects is that the Gülen Movement draws especially upon local service-networks, leisure time and also professionalized commitment. In this way, the collective actor of the Movement establishes relationships and co-operates with the institutions or professionalized sectors of the market for short-term mobilizations such as the football match organized between a world team and the Turkish national team for Bosnian orphans, whose education had been interrupted for lack of facilities and finances after the war.[74]

Those not identifying themselves in the Movement but supportive of these initiatives have not identified, or complained about, the initiatives as being mobilizations solely based on an ideological or political commitment of the organizers. For many, belonging finds meaning in action, voluntary commitment, vocation; it is heterogeneous and integrative. It starts with short-term projects and objectives but in time turns into long-term commitment and affiliation, and the foundation of future altruistic community services. When asked about short- and long-term goals in the Movement, participants gave a variety of answers (see B:3 and B:4 below). The short-term goals were all characterized by the desire either to improve the quality or extend the range of the services offered by the Movement. The long-term goals included self-improvement and earning God's pleasure through such services. Interestingly, some of the short- and long-term goals are the same.

B:3

B:3 What are your short-term goals in the GM? (List the first five only.)
- far better and higher quality educational services
- more educational institutions
- appealing and responding to many more people
- becoming more successful and more active
- getting more people to hear the community's message

B:4

B:4 What are your long-term goals in the GM? (List the first five only.)
- to be useful/beneficial to all, to take services to many more
- to become the best, to do the best
- to earn God's approval and pleasure
- to become more knowledgeable, successful and active
- to qualify to serve at better institutions

In addition, the goals of participants in the Gülen Movement relate not to an instrumental objective alone, nor only to a particular community and network. The joint effort of the collective actor with the outside and the combination of service/vocation with professionalism give continuity to the Movement: namely, continuity of relationship between individual and community, between the Movement and society, between the past and the present, between the Movement's goals and universal values, between the particular, local goals and issues the Movement deals with and the global concerns of the people of the world.[75] This continuity is strengthened by the Movement's observing the legal and normal boundaries wherever it works, thus affirming its citizenship in the System: this secures for it attitudinal support for its values and goals.

When asked (B:1 below) what they commonly associate with the Gülen Movement, participants did not refer to leadership, ideology, or material or political aspirations.

B:1

B:1 What comes into your mind first when someone mentions the GM? (List your first five ideas only.)

- education and useful community services
- generosity-sacrifice
- altruism
- societal accord and peace
- world peace

B:1 indicates a homogeneity of intention, goals and action amid the heterogeneity of people and conditions. This gives greater specificity to the collective identity of the Movement. It shows that relationship in the Gülen Movement is not based only on temporary interpersonal bonds, discontinuity of action or totalizing principles and values, for these, in the highly differentiated societies of today, cannot provide a sustainable identity for any collective actor. The relationship expressed by responses in B:1 is instead framed by the conjunction of global and universal concerns and by the ever broader horizons close to individual, everyday and human experience. Therefore, the Gülen Movement emerges as congruent with the requirements of peaceful collective action in modern societies.

That may raise another question in terms of social movement theory. If many diverse people are led to participate in the movement by their personal life experiences or contradictions in the wider society, there should arise correspondingly diverse layers or diverse internal cultures coexisting within what emerges as one and the same collective action, which would seem to require that the movement must have a political entity or super-network connecting and co-ordinating (managing) the diverse elements. When this was put to Çapan, he responded:

> That question is related to politics, not to community service. The loci of political action and community service are different. Political groups with different political outlooks, worldviews and goals, work for their distinction, separateness and superiority over others. They work self-righteously for positions in a political environment, to be seen and elected. Their separateness and superiority should not be confused with service-networks, which operate altruistically to offer what is lacking in a society, [and] in which people or groups eliminate their selves and work without being named or acknowledged. The intention is not to be seen or elected. Quite the contrary, people contribute anonymously.

Compared to political action,[76] the type of community service and the various orientations of the Gülen Movement involve the high degree of flexibility of a very adaptable organizational form and the elasticity of interpersonal relationships. This lets the networks fulfill simultaneously self-reflective functions and produce cultural codes. It enables an easy shift or 'bridging' from one function over to another. This collective identity structure with adaptable networks and self-reflective resources supports public mobilization and provides the energy for projects. That in turn feeds the networks with new participants, trains new skills and redefines issues and the public space.[77] It is one of the reasons why the Gülen Movement has been acknowledged transnationally.[78]

Its symbolic appeal tends to prevent the Movement associating itself with or as a specific political individual or actor. By acknowledging everyone as they are, by giving everyone the chance to be different and respected, the collective actor cancels out its own separateness.[79] Through its inclusive and integrative action, the Movement proposes, in a paradoxical way, being for others while being itself; by contrast, a political actor proves its separateness, restrictedness or exclusivity and guarantees itself first. The political actor first guarantees being for itself, mostly in a contentious way, while being different, visible and separate from among others.[80]

When asked a more indirect question (B:8 below) participants indicated that even if they had the chance, they would not revise their original intentions in a more material or ideological direction.

B:8

B:8 What would you do if you came back to life again? (Answer in not more than 10 words.)
- would be the same and do the same job
- the same job – the same community/Movement
- not different but almost something similar in the Movement
- would wish to go to more poorer/undeveloped places to serve/to be useful
- not a director but a teacher at an educational institution

Table 3 below checks if and how far the participants detect any political or ideological purposes within or behind the activities or services of the Gülen Movement.

Table 3

A		SD	D	N	A	SA
6	We and the GM have an ideology.	971	7			
7	The GM will turn into a political and conflictual movement.	978				
11	The identity of the GM has isolated/alienated me from society.	978				
14	There exists an overt and covert challenge to the System(s) by the GM.	959	19			
15	All the services given by the GM are a means to reach other motives, goals and ideologies.	978				
27	There are differences between the organizational apparatus and the general interest of the movement.	973	5			
28	I believe there exist different interests in the GM.	971	7			
29	I believe different interests compete for power in the GM.	965	19	1	3	
34	There is a huge differentiation in the allocation of incentives, rewards and resources in the GM.	857	121			
35	Opinions, views and discourse are produced by and attributed to ideologues.	967	8		3	
36	The elites in the GM exploit opportunities and individuals to affirm themselves or to consolidate their positions.	971	7			

Table 3 and B:8 above can be summarized as indicating that the goals of the Gülen Movement are not focused on building internal solidarity through the device of creating a counterculture, and that the Movement is not an ensemble of networks and institutions within which participants can carry on their own activities (public or private), or pursue their own interests (political or commercial). Aymaz made the point quite explicitly: 'The Gülen Movement is not a means, substitute or subcontractor for some to establish their ideology, politics or economic interests. Neither is it a parallel society in which a commune or comrade-friends live in an increasingly radicalized way, closed off from the world and global communities.'[81]

The Gülen Movement is openly and concretely expressing a system of values in networks of relations, associations and in the wider environment. As we explained in §3.2.6, it has begun to be well-received by Turkish and non-Turkish societies and state authorities. Many of them indeed have begun to adopt the action and some of the perspectives of the Movement.[82] The relationship and direction is not towards radicalization through selective and solidaristic incentives but towards formalization and institutionalization of a civil, moderate, pluralistic, and progressive Movement.[83]

The Movement is in fact at the maturity stage of institutionalization or adaptation, although some of its opponents, the protectionist elite and bureaucracy, tend to portray it as if it were at the incubation stage (see §4.1.2). The pattern of development, phase and specialization of the Gülen Movement may indeed vary as to secondary details from country to country. However, its central theme or goal has consistently been never to turn into a political, ideological, oppositional, conflictual or violent movement.[84]

5.2.3 Intervention, power and authority

It is postulated that no SMO can meet its primary functional requirements without the intervention of an integrative authority, especially in political action. A bureaucratic or centralized structure is seen as central for the success of a movement and its SMO.[85] When this was put to Ergene, he said:

> There are channels through which collective social power establishes and maintains itself in the Movement. These are the role system in service-networks, consensual and adaptive exchanges among legitimate expectations and performances, progressive self-structuring according to local circumstances and ensuing mutable objectives, and flexible formal structure with mechanisms open to negotiation and transaction.[86]

And what about skilled people and Gülen's contribution to their work?

> There are people skilled in more mundane tasks of organizing and there are people more skilled in framing in service-projects. However, this way of working never nullifies or disregards the value and respect attached to Gülen's views and perspectives. The participants in service-projects organize themselves flexibly to accommodate and redefine their tasks and inner structures, if need be, in accordance with the feed-back coming from the wider public and with the alternative suggestions from Gülen's

counsel and [his] interpretations of current events through the media, should they be sought.[87]

Participants are clear that there are many sources of opinion and authority availale to them.

Table 4

A		SD	D	N	A	SA
35	Opinions, views and discourse are produced by and attributed to ideologues.	967	8		3	
37	Control is applied to people's routines by the apparatuses of regulation which exact identification and consensus.	899	75		4	
39	There is respect in the GM for different views and diversity.		2	1	83	892
41	The GM encourages the development of formal skills of action, decision making and continuous learning.				19	959

B:12

B:12 How do you make and take decisions in your unit? (Answer in not more than 10 words.)
- with my friends/colleagues at my department/in my professional unit
- colleagues and administration all together
- all people at the committee/institution together

So, consensual decisions, societal feed-back and the counsel and advice of Gülen and of other experts on specific issues are each a permanent component in the Movement's growth and efficiency, as Table 4 and B:12 indicate. The openness of the SMOs, their operating wholly within the boundaries of the System, and their capacity to absorb change and produce collective, consensual decisions attentive to feed-back from inter-actor transactions, constitute the specificity of the organizational life of the Gülen Movement as collective actor.[88] Also the combination of the division of labor and the formally institutionalized structure of the SMOs' management maintains the participants' readiness to deliver the necessary tasks in society.[89]

Following Gamson's terminology, the Movement is 'universalistic' in that it does not seek advantages only for its participants or constituents but strives to benefit society as a whole.[90] Profit is not the goal in the service-projects (see §4.1.5). A not-for-profit and foundational (*waqif*) basis provides the Movement with a resource-rich combination of decentralized bureaucratic or professionalized staff and non-bureaucratic sponsor-participants.[91] The degree of socialization among these, or the immediate dependence on dominant social relationships, and the will for services and modernization of SMOs, indicate an integrative, adaptive, progressive, complex social organization that is autonomous but does not ignore scholarly counsel and conventional wisdom (A:35, 37, 39, 41 and B:12).

To some outsiders, this may seem, again, an ambivalent aspect of the Movement's organization. According to their view and interpretation, the co-ordination or coherence has to be a result of dominant interests or power exercised within the Movement. They speculate that the coherence is not only constructed by technical, professional and human means or initiatives but also by norms, which define the forms by which predetermined goals are achieved, and – they add – norms must necessarily inhibit or restrict behavior and membership in the organization. Çapan responded:

> Such a perception ignores interaction, the need for internal coherence, functionality, the linkage between means and ends, and autonomy required for purposive and altruistic action. It also ignores organizational structures in the free competitive and political markets as if there were no functional rules, norms and stratification, nor segregation for their management and administration. It ignores the imposition and imbalance in their structure or organization, which does not require consensus for profits, finance or political positions and investments if need be.

> There is certainly no pressure to join, believe or conform in the Gülen Movement. All are voluntarily and consciously involved. There have been no instances or accusations of coercive persuasion, manipulation of consciousness, forced self- or ego-destruction, brainwashing or psychological punishment or duress. None of these account for joining the Gülen Movement.

Belonging to a community-based project or a service-network in the Gülen Movement signifies the integration of an individual into a collective, where there are appropriate channels for the expression of claims. Moreover, participation is open-ended and multiple, with intersecting and overlapping networks of affiliation. The service-networks can communicate with one another while each can be internally integrated but externally separated from the others by geography, objectives, local emergent realities or regional sensitivities. Individual mobility and multiplicity of affiliations are encouraged and available to all in the Movement.[92] The associative, occupational, communal and institutional channels to handle demands are always open and help prevent segregation and conflict.[93]

Then, what about the people who join the Gülen Movement at a later stage in their lives and have previous affiliations to other movements? Aymaz explained:

> People orient themselves towards new goals of transformation. Otherwise, they cannot recognize and be recognized by all constituent actors of the Movement. Unless they use the language, acknowledge and disseminate the worldview of the Gülen Movement, contribute in some way to the services, such a recognition can hardly take place. They will not forsake their previous communications and networks but utilize them to circulate the new messages and meanings.

An important point to note in Aymaz's response is that the interpersonal network relations precede individuals' becoming participants in the collective action of the Gülen Movement. Neither newcomers nor existing participants are disintegrated, excluded, marginal or rootless people.[94] Research shows that participants are from among those who are active and integrated into the community. This contradicts the common supposition that mobilization is a phenomenon involving those who are most affected by social disintegration and exclusion. In fact, availability for mobilization is weak among such marginal and rootless groups, while those who do become participants in a movement generally have a more solid collective identity and closer ties to a network of social affiliations.[95]

As for those who do not belong to the Gülen Movement but support its collective action, they are highly diverse and widespread.[96] The multiplication of roles and professions within the varied and widespread socio-economic groups who maintain a co-operative (but not participatory) relationship with the Movement makes it more difficult to identify specific social categories for the Gülen Movement.[97] Howard (2005) noted that the overwhelming proportion of educated participants in the Movement do not work in religiously-oriented occupations but in engineering, the sciences and business, and he observed that their moderate faith-inspired initiative was building a network of schools, universities, hospitals, media and businesses – a 'third way' between the forces of secularism and radical Islamism. That too is a factor encouraging more co-operative support for the Movement from non-participants or 'third parties'. A good example is the book, *Barış Köprüleri: Dünyaya Açılan Türk Okulları*, a compilation of twenty-seven articles written by 'third-party' statesmen, politicians, scholars, thinkers and journalists. The articles deal with more than 300 educational institutions and other efforts of the volunteers of the Gülen Movement in ninety countries.[98]

Student participation in the Movement is also of particular significance.[99] The overwhelming majority of participants are young university students, with the next largest group (almost as numerous) being graduates. Since those answering the questionnaire are all graduates employed in schools, it can be deduced (from B:13 below) that the average age in the Movement is 25–30. Most of the students or people in the service-networks are middle or upper-middle class.[100] They are from better integrated backgrounds, urban, with a high level of academic achievement (B:12).

B:12

B:12 What is your family background?
• urban-culture (78%)
• agricultural (22%)
• middle-class (44%)
• upper middle class, (20%)
• academic achievement (higher education) (18%)
• poor (18%)

B:13

B:13 How long have you been in the GM? (Number of years only)	
Years	Individuals
• 6–7	79
• 8–10	50
• 4–5	33
• 10+	5
• 2–3	13

The studies done on student mobilizations of the 1960s yielded a similar picture – the participants were upper-middle class youths of urban culture, with high, or prospects of high, academic attainment. In the case of the Gülen Movement, the volunteer–participants are educated and urban middle class, relatively privileged and better integrated: they have technical and cultural competence or economic-functional position that makes them more likely to mobilize because they perceive the contradictions of the system and their educational level and intellectual milieu foster the growth of egalitarian and anti-authoritarian values.[101] Yet, it is most important to note that, while participation among university students and educated newcomers from a wide variety of social experiences and backgrounds has grown, this has not radicalized the Gülen Movement, nor caused cleavages to emerge either in it or Turkish society. The participants in fact 'prioritize individual achievement in private, and expansion of freedom of expression, democratic participation, and self-government in the public domain'.[102]

Networks are the basis on which movements are built, and they perform different kinds of functions – as means of teaching people about the values of the movement, of reinforcing social cohesion or solidarity, of exchanging information and of organizing activities.[103] Networks (as we said earlier) attract supporters or adherents who are often more committed than those who have formal membership of political parties.[104] The efficacy resulting from this commitment is regarded as the source of strength in the Gülen Movement. Authority comes from the collective decision taking. Decisions on what to do are taken locally or in an individual project-network:

> As for the management of affairs, all these institutions are independent corporate bodies. There is no formal relationship among educational institutions or the other institutions, both within and without the country, except where there is a chain run by an educational trust. The institutions disperse news of their accomplishments through the mass media and promotions. In this way, ideas and thoughts that arise from a commitment to the same feelings are shared and owned by all.[105]

Supporters' efforts are not co-ordinated nationally. Autonomy is an important defining feature of service-networks and SMOs generally. This is achieved in the Gülen Movement through delegation, creation of a specialized body of representatives, and bureaucratic and non-bureaucratic boards based on equality.[106] For a whole range of matters related to the service-projects, decision-making is not concentrated at the top, with certain individuals only. There is a continual turnover of network or project leadership. Representatives within networks can be and are called to account at all times. The right to decide belongs to all who come to the network meetings. Free participation and self-motivated input, openness and responsiveness to technical and professional expertise overcome the risk of building up oligarchies and charismatic leaders. All these features are generative of power and authority in the Movement. They require and utilize autonomous conscious decisions and the kind of participation reflecting strong trust in democracy, which is a lever for positive transformation.[107]

5.2.4 SMOs and commitment

Sources of the frames of reference and the resources for the Movement are education, cultural experience and awareness, religious consciousness through knowledge and study, participation in social and communitarian representative bodies, responsibility and altruism, and belief in societal accord, peace, democracy, and co-operation (as opposed to clash) between civilizations (see B:1).[108]

Evidence shows that the more closely the individual is integrated into a group, the greater will be the degree of her/his participation. Participation is an expression of belonging to a certain social group, and the more secure the affiliation is, the more intense the participation.[109] Then, the more intense the collective participation in a network of relations, the more rapid and durable will be the mobilization of a movement or its SMOs.[110] This seems to be the case in the Movement's service-networks. The Movement facilitates and thus increases an individual's willingness to get involved in service-projects through her/his relationship with larger like-minded, similarly intentioned people (B:6; and see §5.2.1).

> Disciplined participation and co-ordination of strategies for achieving the movement's aims are achieved by creating a formal organization. The movement becomes an organic part of society and crystallizes into a professional structure.[111]

Social movements are known by and become a force for social change primarily through the SMOs they produce.[112] However, a social movement is never identified with a single organization; rather, there are various organizations, and sometimes even parties, which claim to interpret and pursue the aims of the movement.[113] Environment, strategic choices and tradition all have an impact on the model, size or magnitude of an organization.[114] However, the primary influence comes from the characteristics of the social group(s), after which come objectives, strategies, structure and resource constraints. Lofland (1996) argued that SMOs are on a macro-, meso-, or micro-scale of social organization, time and geography:

> The SM [social movement] is a diffuse, diverse, and broad range of upsweeping activism involving a great many SMOs. In contrast, the SMO is space and time focused. While it is often difficult (and contentious) to say when a SM 'began', the beginning of SMOs can commonly be traced to specific day, places and persons.[115]

According to McCarthy and Zald: 'A SMO is the complex or formal organization which identifies its goals with the preferences of a social movement…and attempts to implement these goals.'[116] About the SMOs of the Gülen Movement, Aymaz said:

> The Gülen Movement operates and focuses on education, health, media, publication, ethical finance and humanitarian aid and relief. There is no political wing, party or umbrella organization of the Movement. It is not based on, influenced by, affiliated with, or supporting the interests or policies of any single political party. It does not have cliques or a radical-flank effect, either.

The radical-flank effect is a mechanism triggered by the bifurcation of a social movement into radical and moderate factions.[117] Usually the more extreme and radical group frame the parameters of a movement and mostly have negative radical-flank effects in the movement or its SMO(s).[118]

In the light of what Aymaz said and the argument of the foregoing chapters, the SMOs of the Gülen Movement can be categorized as follows:

1. Education: pre-school – kindergarten; primary; secondary, high school (lycee- normal, science and vocational); higher education – university, language courses, computer courses, university entrance examination preparation courses; study centers for all ages; student dormitories and hostels.
2. Health: polyclinics, hospitals, health and diagnostic centers.
3. Media: TV, radio; and daily, weekly, quarterly (religious, social, literary, scientific, popular, ecology) journals; Writers and Journalists Foundation

4. Publishing: publishing houses, printing firms, bookshops, art-design and graphics companies.

5. Business and finance: a bank; an insurance company; businessmen's associations; bureaus of human resources and consultation; holiday resorts and accommodation.

6. Humanitarian aid and relief: local/regional, national and transnational aid organizations; study centers for the poor and under-privileged; women's clubs or foundations; cultural centers; interfaith dialog centers.

In explanation of the organization and effectiveness of the SMOs of the Gülen Movement, their service ethic and what makes them leading institutions in their field inside and outside of Turkey, Çapan said:

> The Gülen Movement is itself a complex collective actor, composed of many SMOs pursuing similar goals but different strategies. The interweaving of the service-project mentality with different integrative strategies makes the SMOs successful. Also what makes them leading institutions in their field inside and outside of Turkey is that employment is based on specialized training and on formal certification organized and issued by the States. Employment and advancement is in accordance with knowledge, achievement and professional expertise and competence rather than seniority or preference given to friends and relatives.

The service organizations cited above work on the open and competitive market and some became market-oriented. However – as discussed in §4.1.5 – they are not commercial enterprises in the sense that they do not privilege market presence and paid services for member-clients; the intention (rather than profit making) is to provide quality services and in this way answer in the best way the needs of people from all walks of life.[119]

In centralized organizations, power resides in a single leader, or a central committee, and local chapters have little autonomy.[120] However, the SMOs inspired by the Gülen Movement contribute to the educational, social, and financial wellbeing of the wider society (see §3.2.6 and 3.2.11). Some of them are formal chains of institutions but not centralized.[121] This decentralization is not a negative reaction to political or administrative centralization.[122] Table 5 below attempted to ascertain whether Movement participants perceive the existence of any centralized committee or organization and whether there is any rank–file relationship or discontent with such a committee.

Table 5

A		SD	D	N	A	SA
15	All the services given by the GM are a means to reach other motives, goals and ideologies.	978				
27	There are differences between the organizational apparatus and the general interest of the movement.	973	5			
28	I believe there exist different interests in the GM.	971	7			
40	The GM is located at several different levels of the social system simultaneously.		3	1	79	895

There is no community-*vs.*-organization or organization-*vs.*-community attitude (A:15, 27, 28 and B:1). However, since the various SMOs of the Movement grow and consolidate in widely varying environments (see A:40), this necessitates division of labor, plurality of models and functional specialization with more specific definition of roles and norms. Participants in the Gülen Movement modify SMOs in secondary details in response to stimuli and limits deriving from peculiarities in the local environment where they operate. However, the SMOs 'are all accountable to the local authorities [the State] and their own official inspectors, and comply with the state and international law':[123] their openness, visibility and accountability to the System legitimate the SMOs, and reduce the negative effects or avert the danger of suppression by potential opponents (see §3.2.6).

The grassroots participate in the formation of the Movement's culture and contribute to the concrete management of its action by exercising reciprocal control, by co-ordinating, and by utilizing the information broadcast by each of them through the media.[124] Different initiatives may overlap and different individuals may fulfill a number of functions contemporaneously due to manifold and inclusive networks. In most cases, these individuals (rather than institutions) act as informal intermediaries in various forms of inter-organizational relationships.[125] The Gülen Movement therefore does not need to have an umbrella organization to co-ordinate or to build a coalition of various SMOs for lobbying or collecting resources.

The other factor which renders an umbrella organization or leadership unnecessary is the degree of cultural development in the Gülen Movement. 'The greater the degree of cultural development, the higher are participant morale and, therefore, commitment and tenacity in the face of adversity, and retention of the movement participants.'[126]

However, this does not restrict competition among projects. Team work and competition along with co-operation and consultation among service-projects are encouraged; competition between individuals is not. Competition is not for differentiation but is a motivational device to reach for the best and progress within the confines of social and political order.[127] Özdalga interprets this as 'competitive struggle for higher profit and better academic results'. She adds: 'efficiency based on open competition, both within economic enterprises and educational institutions, predominates over solidarity with any specific group of family members, relatives, and/or fellow villagers.'[128]

In the Gülen Movement, division of labor is based on formal rules in institutionalized organizations while, in relational networks, tasks are allocated in an informal manner, and mainly according to the skills that each member proves able and willing to contribute to the projects.[129] Ergene explained that the forms of SMOs, as formal and institutionalized companies, have brought with them the development of professionalized management in the Movement:

> There is an awareness of the fact that division of labor, responsibility and managerial authority ought to exist. Social and professional control in any SMO is through direct supervision and formal standard rules or universally acknowledged sanctions. However, this inescapable condition assumes greater visibility and is also kept under constant supervision and control by extensive boards related to any SMO. This brings about a specific relationship between efficacy, the search for satisfactory internal relations and staying within legal boundaries.

As to the managerial positions, Çapan added:

> Being in a managerial position does not give anyone greater power or control over so-called strategic resources and it is not paid with greater material advantages or, more correctly, much differently than others either. On the other hand, it requires greater commitment, liaison and a compatible and holistic relationship with all.

From what interviewees Aymaz, Ergene and Çapan have said, and as the responses at A:27, 28, 30, 31, 34, 36, and B:1, 2, 3, 4, and 8, all show, it can be concluded that commitment is regarded not only as a practical day-to-day aim but also a long-term goal for all participants, not just administrators of the SMOs. Whether short-term or long-term, an undertaking does not provide any justification for differentiated control over resources of collective action. A division of labor and roles among the various groups results from the specialization of the activities of the various individual networks. This, of course, requires associative or professionalized expertise and information. Referral to professionalism and field expertise or information is always needed, and provides a greater capacity to intervene in the production and negotiation of the collective action of the Movement.* In this way, grassroots and professionalized participants formulate the proposals by consensus, and their efficiency or effectiveness are always broadcast through the media to all so that they can be emulated, improved on and get appropriate feed-back. Thus, while the grassroots provide a flow of resources, and the SMOs process and broadcast information and the outcomes, other networks are performing a kind of intermediate representational function.[130]

This collaborative framework tends to result in a diffusion of themes and experience, and a circulation of volunteers and expertise. Any service-network may initiate a project or brainstorm around a particular theme, and different service-networks may set up committees to study its feasibility without a formal or centralized authority. If any project proves successful, this is broadcast or circulated by volunteers, associates in the media or sympathizers in the periphery. The professionalized staffs at other SMOs take up issues and take them further. In this way, each SMO represents the collective purpose, but no single SMO can or does claim to be recognized as representing the Gülen Movement's collective interests as a whole. It is commitment to a rich and supportive culture, which keeps the SMOs of the Movement viable and continuing: this is a point also been made by Taylor (1989) and Lofland (1996) about social movements.[131]

About formalization or institutionalization of SMOs, there are a number of suppositions among some social movement theorists: institutionalization rarely occurs – in the first place few social movements survive, some dissolve because their aims have been achieved, some when the specific campaign for which they were formed is over, or when societies become more prosperous; leadership splits during downturns in mobilization caus-

---

* As A:35, 37, 39, 41, and B:10 and 11 all indicate.

ing a further downturn; the establishment of a working relationship with the authorities, access to decision-making processes, public recognition or even public subsidies, are considered to be integrating into the established system and impose limits on mobilizing capacity, alienating some of the movement's constituency, weakening it in the long run.[132]

In response, Lofland (1996) has argued that a quite considerable body of research literature finds little or no support for such claims. The reality is rather the opposite, as prosperity, as a feature of social organization, increases the availability of a wide range of resources that facilitate participation in social movements or SMOs.[133] In the particular case of the Gülen Movement, the foregoing discussions has shown that for the participants, primary loyalty is not to the Movement, or to themselves, but to action, to other human beings and to God; that the action is not a temporary instrument but a vocation, even a form of devotion. The multiple and simultaneous participations and affiliations, and the fact that projects formalized or institutionalized in the 1970s are still continuing today, invalidates the claims above. Lofland confirms that formalized SMOs tend to engage in institutionalized tactics and do not initiate disruptive direct-action tactics.[134]

Also, another factor which invalidates the social theorists' argument above is that some movements or their SMOs are 'enduring' as opposed to 'ephemeral' efforts to achieve social or personal change. Various forms of transient or ephemeral protest, violent action or, especially, 'mass insurgency' (Lofland's term) among the most economically deprived are not social movements or the action of SMOs. Social movements continue their action in either a moderate form after the regulation of their internal and formal procedures or a radical form after the adoption of less conventional means.[135] The simplest example is the clandestine and terrorist organizations that emerged from student movements and started to kill their political opponents in Europe after 1968 and in Turkey before and after the 1980s.[136]

In contrast, the Gülen Movement, since then, has endured and proved that positive transformations in individuals and society is possible without contentious, disruptive and violent action, and without a change in political settings. The Movement aims for people to be given access to cultural freedom and sound educational opportunities so that they will be aware enough not to fall prey to the schemes of vested interests, or to folklore, escapism or terrorist desperation.[137] In any case, all movements and organizations do not develop in the same or a linear direction.[138] Overgeneralization in terms of other movements does not help much in the explication of phenomena like the Gülen Movement. The existence and continuation of this Movement is necessitated by the way its SMOs are formed and operate and by the contemporary world conjuncture.* The conjuncture we are living through needs a far better educated, fairer and more peaceful world and the co-operation of civilizations. The world as it really is will continue to need human efforts like the Gülen Movement. Through its continual investment in alternative openings, continual search for individual and institutional improvement and development, consensual decision making, rotation of chairmanships in managerial positions, supervision and inspection of SMOs by boards, the tendency of its participants to come together, while attentive to expertise and good counsel, in response to local needs, so as to build and maintain effective and efficient SMOs, the Gülen Movement can answer these needs:

> Gülen's thought offers intellectual and spiritual resources that enable us better to understand the one world in which we all live, as well as to engage with the challenges that living in this world brings. Such resources are needed for understanding the nature and dynamics of the world, and for enabling us to resist the kind of disastrous outcomes which some argue are inevitable, which many others fear, and which all of us have a responsibility and a possibility to do something about.[139]

5.2.5 Leadership

The term 'leader' is used here to mean both leaders and organizers who originate, institute, inspire or urge forward.

The latest research on organizational models reveals a number of classifications of leadership, referred to degree of organization, distribution of power, levels of participation, public representation, articulation and effectiveness. A wide range of descriptions of leadership is offered but no single model or term. The models or terms center around roles or tasks. Leaders therefore may have numerous possible and actual combinations of the ideal-typical roles – charismatic leader, ideologist, formal, pragmatist, professional and recognized expert, etc.[140] Morris and Staggenborg, for example, define movement leaders as strategic decision makers who 'in-

---

* As indicated in B:3, 4, 7, 9, 10, A:4, 12, 14, 15, 16, 26, 31, 39, 40 and 41.

spire commitment, mobilize resources, create and recognize opportunities, devise strategies, frame demands, and influence outcomes'.[141]

A social movement can survive over a period of time if it can develop a relatively stable organization. Organizational structure is held to be essential to unify different components of a movement, institutionalize decision-making processes and dedicate resources to the achievement of goals. Organizational features vary greatly with the conditions of the social environment in which the movement operates and with its internal composition.[142] Discussion of this topic draws upon Weber and Michels who considered bureaucratic structure and organization to be the inevitable result of progress over time. According to them, this transformation in fact blunts the movement's initial conflictual thrust, substitutes its objectives or distorts its ends, turns it toward self-preservation and leads to an oligarchic leadership. Michels expressed it in a formula: 'Who says organization, says oligarchy.'[143] However, his findings as we commented earlier – have been strongly questioned: they have few referents in the real world, and as distinct intellectual premises are so far removed from reality as to lead to severe misinterpretations and anachronism on the part of contemporary readers.[144]

As a contemporary reader Chemers (1997) states: 'leadership is a group activity, is based on social influence, and revolves around a common task.'[145] As to the leadership within the Gülen Movement, the interviewees Aymaz, Ergene and Çapan were unanimous and offered strongly complement arguments. Departing from Weber's description of charismatic authority,[146] Ergene said:

> Gülen himself never assumes, accepts or approves of any leadership claim, charismatic revelation or moments, sinless start, being born anew, being given rebirth or a new sublime life, or adulation, on or around his name. Neither he himself nor anyone from the Movement has ever claimed superhuman powers of perception and ability to discern 'the truth'. The relationship with the Movement is not based upon intense love for Gülen in person, nor upon his attributes or characteristics, but upon the collective meaning, appeal and essence of the understanding, message, thought and action of the Movement. This does not deny Gülen's immense contribution to the thought and action of the Movement.

Gülen himself believes that 'single-person leadership is no longer viable':

> As everything has become so detailed, particularized, specified, and enumerated, the tasks now assume such forms that even unique, outstanding

individuals cannot accomplish them by themselves. That is why the place of genius has been now replaced by collective consciousness with consultative and collective decision making.[147]

Gülen says: 'Behind the institutions [...] are many people and companies from almost all walks of life regardless of their worldview, beliefs, and lifestyles [...] What I have done is only encourage people.'[148] That is confirmed by Aymaz: 'The assumption that almost a thousand institutions and millions of volunteers and participants in the Movement across the world are envisioned and governed by Gülen or any single individual else or a specific group of people, is absolutely untenable.' The leadership in the local service-networks supports this: different demands as they arise enter the local decision-making process, which can be open to the participation and control of various components of the network locally or regionally. Çapan explained further:

> As continuous, active, democratic, stable and enduring participation is encouraged, this does not let a large and inactive base finance a small number of managerial or active leaders, a primary cadre or main organization. This naturally prevents any leader or organization from having differing resources and differing degrees of power. However, this does not hinder various degrees of commitment, specialization, formalization and professionalization in the Gülen Movement.

Irvine's (2007:66) research in Germany confirms what Çapan maintains:

> Learning centers, intercultural centers and high schools are typically governed by an association, which is regulated according to German law. The members of the association, typically parents of children involved or members of the Intercultural Center, choose a board of directors, generally consisting of seven members. Members of the board of directors, which have a two-year term, are represented by a president who must approve all major decisions concerning hiring of teachers and educational curriculum and policy. The board generally meets once or twice a month.[149]

Irvine further argues that 'the relationship between Gülen and the institutions described above is loose and one more of inspiration than organization. As in Turkey, the Movement is extremely decentralized'. By way of example, she states:

There appears to be no central record-keeping office for the Gülen-related institutions in Germany; each city or town is responsible for organizing and maintaining its own schools and centers. Moreover, many of the participants in the centers and schools appear to have no idea that they are inspired in any way by the ideas of Gülen.

Quoting the head of an Educational Center, Irvine adds:

Eighty percent of the parents are unaware that the centers are connected in any way with the Gülen Movement since the staff does not typically talk about it with them. Indeed [...] most teachers are there because they believe in what the centers are doing, not because they are necessarily inspired by Gülen.[150]

Table 6

A		SD	D	N	A	SA
9	There is sacral celebration of Gülen and others in the GM.	970	8			
21	Those who speak for and stand for the GM in public are fixed individuals.	870	103		5	
27	There are differences between the organizational apparatus and the general interest of the movement.	973	5			
28	I believe there exist different interests in the GM.	971	7			
29	I believe different interests compete for power in the GM.	965	19	1	3	
34	There is a huge differentiation in the allocation of incentives, rewards or resources in the GM.	857	121			
35	Opinions, views and discourse are produced by and attributed to ideologues.	967	8		3	
36	The elites in the GM exploit opportunities and individuals to affirm themselves or to consolidate their positions.	971	7			
37	Control is applied to people's routines by the apparatuses of regulation which exact identification and consensus.	899	75		4	
39	There is respect in the GM for different views and diversity.		2	1	83	892
41	The GM encourages the development of formal skills of action, decision making and continuous learning.				19	959

B:10

B:10 How do you make and take decisions in your unit? (Answer in not more than 10 words.)
- with my friends/colleagues at my department/in my professional unit
- colleagues and administration all together
- all people at the committee/institution together

Table 6 and B:10 display responses to questions about the leadership style, decision-making, and allocation of authority, resources and positions at SMOs established by Gülen-inspired participants. From the interviewees explanations and the Questionnaires as above, three conclusions can be drawn.

First, the resources are not allocated among the collective actors of the Gülen Movement (A:34). This shows something in general, not only that people working in the Movement believe so. It should be noted that all SMOs in the Movement are formally structured so that resources cannot go unaccounted for or disappear in some way. There has been no evidence to the contrary since the Movement has been around, and the resources referred to are in any case under the control and supervision of the State and legal authorities, as mentioned earlier. That is what makes such institutions and their workers trustworthy and commendable in the eyes of ordinary people as well as the authorities.[151]

Second, no one individual has the right to distribute power. That does not imply the non-existence of an authority structure within the organization. Therefore, the forms assumed by the distribution of managerial power can vary within the SMOs. (A:21, 27, 35, 36 and 41)

Third, Table 6 and B:10 show that the leadership is decentralized: the degree of autonomy of the different components of the Movement is great and overlapping of influence can occur. While the Gülen Movement as a whole is decentralized, any of its SMOs has positions and authorities in its departments or managerial organization (B:10).

Aymaz and Ergene's description of the general principle of decision taking in the Gülen Movement makes clear the difference between the Movement and the cadre organization of Lofland's definition which is 'more fragile and temporary, highly absorbing, smaller in scale and likely less democratic than the mass membership organization'.[152] Ergene said:

> The general principle of decision taking in voluntary services and project-networks in the Gülen Movement is that a large number of participants

gather together in a single or different places and collectively undertake an interchange or consensus on new projects. All alternative actions and considerations are explicitly discussed and concluded by all participants as a whole. Collective decisions are taken either through consensus or voting.

Organizational forms can therefore be considered as a strategic choice made by the service-network on the basis of the principles and goals of the Gülen Movement. In contrast, according to the Resource Mobilization theory, organizational form and choices are made by leaders.[153] This is the opposite of the thought and action of the Gülen Movement.

Gülen himself expresses his unwillingness and detestation for any leadership, or even the mention of leadership, whether communal, religious or political.[154] B:6 asks how the participants in the Movement see Gülen.

B:6

B:6 What comes into your mind when Gülen is mentioned? (List the first five ideas only.)
- sincerity, love of God and people and creation
- scholar, intellectual / science, knowledge and wisdom
- enthusiasm to serve (God and people)
- integrity, profound insight, foresight
- concern, pain and sacrifice for others

As B:6 indicates, the participants in the Movement appreciate Gülen for his knowledge, scholarliness, sincerity, integrity, commitment to altruistic services, profound concern and compassion for others. It should not be ignored that all these qualities come from his Islamic education and upbringing. However, they do not result in a sacral celebration of Gülen or any other(s) in the Movement (A:9). Narrating a Prophetic *hadith*, Beekun and Badawi note:

> According to Islam, the two primary roles of a leader are those of servant-leader...First, the leader is sayyid al qawn khadimuhum[155], the servant of his followers. He is to seek their welfare and guide them towards [what is] good. The idea of a leader as a servant has been part of Islam since its beginning.*

They go on to maintain that what is essential in Islamic teaching on this subject has been conceptualized and developed as a leadership model by

---

* The Prophet emphasized a second major role of the Muslim leader: to protect his community against tyranny and oppression, to encourage God-wariness and to promote justice. See the same hadith in *ibid.*, 2–3.

Greenleaf, who defines the servant-leader as 'servant first', as one who has the disposition or 'the natural feeling that one wants to serve, to serve first'.[156]

Applying to Gülen ten characteristics of 'servant leadership' (drawn from Greenleaf and Spears), Çelik and Alan analyze his patterns of action and conclude that, rather than being a charismatic leader, he is a *servant leader*. Their list of the ten qualities that characterize Gülen as servant leader substantially confirms the responses of B:6. The ten qualities are: profound appreciation of the Islamic sciences and contemporary-modern thought; passionate activism; dialog competencies, communication skills and being an empathetic listener; dedication of his life to solving social problems; self-awareness or awareness of his personal responsibility; seeking to convince others rather than coercing compliance; effectiveness at building consensus within groups; promoting a sincere dialog among cultures, religions and civilizations; stretching his thinking to encompass broader-based conceptual thinking; seeking a delicate balance between conceptual thinking and a day-to-day operational approach; being goal-centered and project-oriented; ability or foresight to understand lessons from the past without ignoring the realities of the present; ability to evaluate the past, present, and future to reach a new synthesis; assumption of first and foremost a commitment to serving the needs of others; being earnest, dignified and modest; being always upright, truthful, trustworthy and just; recognition of the tremendous responsibility to do everything in his power to nurture the spiritual, personal and professional growth of all people within his community; and establishment of the principles of building a community of servant leadership.[157]

Rather than direct personal intervention, it is Gülen's intellectual and moral influence that is felt within the Movement. Irvine sees his relationship with the Movement as 'one more of inspiration than organization'.[158] Notably within the social organization or production of the service-networks of the Movement, as discussed earlier, the efficiency of decision taking is explained by the constancy and richness of the interaction of many individuals, its being multi-scaled and across multiple affiliations. This results in adaptive, spontaneous, self-organizing networks with representative leaders generated from the grassroots, from 'bottom–up'.

Ergene and Aymaz pointed out that in these networks there are no written rules, fixed procedures, formal leadership or fixed structure of bureaus. Yet, all three interviewees acknowledged that in the SMOs, which are institutionalized and professionalized – for example, the educational institutions, hospitals or the media – there are paid staff who are not active in the voluntary aspect of the Movement's activities but are nevertheless broadly sympathetic to its aims, and individuals from the grassroots of the Movement who are pursuing a career in those SMOs.

Ergene added that with legal constitutions, SMOs have obvious internal differentiation, functional division of labor, limits to the area of influence – working within a limited territory, the mechanisms of horizontal and vertical co-ordination, leadership and personnel selection criteria – and they keep written records. Except what is in the legal constitution of the SMO, there are no written or unspoken, overt or covert system(s) of accepted laws and regulations that govern procedure or behavior in particular circumstances, or within a particular SMO.[159]

> There is no hidden [informal] disciplinary procedure in any organization. However, in interpersonal social relationships, it is obvious that individuals share their perception of the issues and action, and this could have social–moral influence or implications among the individuals in a specific service-network, just as in any day-to-day social relationship anywhere in the world.[160]

From the discussion above, it is deduced that the norms within the networks guarantee integration, and provide the critical point of reference for every process of action and transformation. The selected managerial committee or board controls the transfer and redistribution of roles, resources and power through processes of collective reasoning. All those who constitute the service-network can intervene in the decision-making control of resources (B:9 and 10).

In addition to this democratic participation, Aymaz recalled the principle commonly accepted within the Movement – it originates in well-known Islamic teaching – that authority or power is not something to compete for, and is not allocated to one who asks for it. Beekun and Badawi (1999:3) point out:

> Generally, Islam discourages Muslims from actively seeking positions of authority. Campaigning for a position of power may imply that one is enamored with the position for one's own advancement or some other self-serving reason. [Citing the Prophetic *hadith*:]

> Do not ask for a position of authority, for if you are granted this position
> as a result of your asking for it, you will be left alone (without God's help
> to discharge the responsibilities involved in it), and if you are granted it
> without making any request for it, you will be helped (by God in the dis-
> charge of your duties).[161]

According to Aymaz, people in the Movement avoid seeking positions of power. (See also B:8 bullet point 5, which confirms Aymaz.) Therefore, the proper attention needs to be given to the prevalence of this attitude rather than to presuppositions about conflicts over power, resource distribution or succession.

Aymaz's point brings to mind the distinction between objective reality and its social construction.[162] Changes and interpretations in theories of social movements have no effect on a social movement itself unless and until perceived to be important by the movement itself.[163] Looking at structural arrangements/opportunities without considering the cognitive processes that intervene between structure and action can be misleading.[164] It is important to take account of the activists' own understanding of the opportunities available to them.[165] Aymaz used the analogy of a roadside observer trying to predict where a particular car was heading on the basis of what the observer already knew about the functional properties of the car – without knowing or taking any account of what the driver of that car had in mind for that journey. In fact, of course, trying to explain the social world of the Movement from the perspective of a researcher–outsider, without proper reference to what the Gülen Movement as collective actor is thinking and doing, is much more difficult – there are no up-to-the-minute road-maps, on the basis of which one might hope usefully to predict which route the driver might or might not take.

Aymaz's analogy is useful nonetheless. We take it to mean that some researchers' particular perceptions of the Gülen Movement are presented as the, or part of the, objective reality or common knowledge about the Movement. But what they present as the reality has not been mutually and socially constructed and shared between the collective actor and the researcher. On the matter in hand: rather than allocation of resources and power, the invisible resources behind the efficacy of the Movement should be studied – such as consensus, lack of competition for power and leadership, various forms of co-operation and exchange, reciprocal interaction, sacrifice, devotion, altruism, and working for and expecting only the pleasure of God. These are the variables by which the Movement achieves its objectives rather than individual or group leadership.

Organizational or managerial (not hierarchical) order is found within SMOs in the Gülen Movement. Extensive overlapping of roles and functions is directly tied to projects and a service-network of which people are a part. This brings about an action-oriented or project-oriented structure (B:1; A:12, 16 and 31). The purpose of having network leadership is not to obtain membership loyalty or generate propaganda, but to negotiate, mediate and facilitate co-operation among individuals and the wider society (A:34–39 and 41).

Constitutive norms include a definition of the relationship between the organization and society, in particular of the relationship between the Movement and the participants in its service-networks (B:11 and A:24). The actions of the Movement should not be measured against the interests and objectives of a certain political sector of a society (see A:15, 27–29). In the collective action of the Gülen Movement the norms *specify* the objectives, means, resources, forms and then roles. In the case of other types of organizations, the norms *form* first the organizational structure of the movement, which then, in turn, heavily affects the incentive structure.

5.2.6 Incentives and rewards

Resource Mobilization theory (see chapter 1, pp. 3–4) stipulates that individuals engage in collective action out of calculation of necessity and effectiveness. However, I have argued (in Chapters 3 and 4) that individuals participate in action for reasons other than sheer calculation and benefit. Edwards and McCarthy point out that these reasons include 'altruism, enlightened self-interest, compassion, religious conviction, or ideological commitment'.[166] Lofland lists reasons such as solidarity incentives, the rewards of status, positive regard, experiences of comradeship, fellowship, good times and the like.[167] Melucci analyzes the reasons as incentives that organizations offer to membership: 'material incentives' (economic goods, resources), 'solidarity incentives' (derived from participation, sense of belonging and relations among members), and 'value incentives' (related to aims of the organization and their realization).[168] Snow and Oliver prefer, for reasons or value incentives, the term 'purposive incentives', which come from internalized norms and values whereby one's self-esteem depends on 'doing the right thing'.[169]

Whether called value incentives, purposive incentives, or 'doing the right thing', for most participants in the Gülen Movement, internalized norms or values are defined by the service ethic, which mostly draws upon religious conviction and conscience and is maintained over time. Çapan said:

> The Movement does not set unrealistic and ineffectual objectives. It does not rely on incentives of solidarity, the self-preservation of the group and its solidarity. If incentives and solidarity became the sole reason for its existence, one could not explain its influence on people in the outside world. There are value incentives and these cannot be explained by self-interest.

In sharp contrast to what is stipulated by Resource Mobilization theory, norms and values in the Gülen Movement are not modified according to varying circumstances and ensuing cost-benefit calculations, self-interest, and financial success. In the varying circumstances that the Gülen Movement has found itself in, norms and values have always held steady over time, so that it has not suffered as a result of crisis or conflict in the face of new developments, but instead become stronger.[170] Ergene explained:

> The Gülen Movement has been able to respond to new developments, the requirements of the contemporary world, and its emergent realities and to defend or define the meaning of its action with respect to them. The entire normative structure of the Movement has already proved successful in response to the questions and pressures coming from the outside. So far, no crisis in any area of normative regulation has been witnessed throughout the organizational structure of the Movement.

Approaching collective action through only self-interest and cost–benefit calculations, or conflicts over allocation of goods in the political market, without referring to symbolic, normative and higher values and meaning, is a reductionist approach.[171] Turner and Killian affirm that 'altruism and personal dedication to valued causes (purposive incentives) are real and cannot be entirely reduced to self-interest'.[172]

What are the incentives in the Gülen Movement and how they are utilized in the relational service-networks and SMOs?

B:8

B:8 What would you do if you came back to life again? (Answer in not more than 10 words.)
• would be the same and do the same job
• the same job – the same community/movement
• not different but almost something similar in the movement
• would wish to go to more poorer/undeveloped places to serve/to be useful
• not a director but a teacher at an educational institution

Table 7

A		SD	D	N	A	SA
1	I have material, personal and other expectations from the GM.	965	12	1		
2	There is a difference between my expectations before and after joining the GM.	756	18		204	
4	The GM devotes a considerable share of its resources to new projects, alternative openings and development.				39	939
11	The identity of the GM has isolated/alienated me from society.	978				
13	The GM has become a source of privilege for me in society.			4	145	829
15	All the services given by the GM are a means to reach other motives, goals and ideologies.	978				
26	The GM has killed my speed and momentum in life.	951	27			
30	My concern is for the self preservation of the GM and solidarity.	863	77		38	
31	My concern is for the alternative projects, new openings and new relationships.		18		78	884
40	The GM is located at several different levels of the social system simultaneously.		3	1	79	895
41	The GM encourages the development of formal skills of action, decision-making and continuous learning.				19	959

From Table 7 and B:8 we see that individuals can change their cultural co-ordinates and relational networks. This opportunity for inner and upward mobility is one of the incentives the Gülen Movement provides in equity for all its members (see §3.2.4.) The existence of a network of associations facilitates and supports the development of new leaders for SMOs – socialization within such network serves as the training ground where skills necessary for the exercise of leadership can be learned, and network cohesion and values encourage the leader-to-be to assume the risks that would be associated with any position.[173] As Özdalga's research affirms, this enhances a strong urge for social mobility among participants in service-networks.[174]

Inside the Movement the leaders act as circulators of information, different perspectives and experience. In the outside world, they act as representatives of the network(s) and usually project an image of the services with which participants can identify and from which participants draw affective gratification and further incentive. Stephenson understands this as intending to 'raise an ethical and well-rounded generation that can be part of national and international leadership'. This leadership and representation provide and require an intensive exchange, interaction and socialization (A:11). For many in the Movement the very intensity of exchanges, interaction and participation itself becomes a reward[175] (B:8; A:1, 2, 13). Therefore, the symbolic and expressive function of a network leader is to gather and co-ordinate individuals, and to represent projects that the individuals collectively and altruistically work for. This function yields services which many people benefit from and which (according to the orientation of this Movement; see B:8) God will be pleased with. So the ultimate reward is from God alone and manifold.[176] This is because the participants become the initiator of prolific righteous deeds, as they express their willingness to serve in parts of the developing world[177] (A:1). This commitment does not lead participants to seek particularist rewards outside accepted norms and behavior, nor does it lead the network leaders to offer conditional compliance for different demands and isolate some participants (see A:4, 15, 31 and 41).

The organizational structure of any SMO maintains its unity, integration, consensus and motivation within itself. So, it gives its action a central direction to provide better, more useful and effective universal services. It does this by making the best possible use of the different resources and talents available to its boards and networks, pursuing shared objectives and adapting to a wider environment. To achieve this, if it provides a series of resources and rewards among its participants, it is done in accordance with a formal internal system for the allocation of resources, roles and the division of labor, and for the distribution of rewards and sanctions. This particular sensitivity about resources and their management leads to formalization, openness, transparency, lawfulness and legality. This further motivates the collective actor and individuals in its supporting networks to perform their functional roles within both the SMO's and the System's limits. In such SMOs, according to Melucci, incentives or rewards may range from material advantage, prestige, fraternal bonding, emotional gratification to spiritual gains.[178]

Resource Mobilization theory argues that individuals withdraw from a movement if their assessment of what the mobilization offers as rewards becomes negative. Then, the organizational structure utilizes its ideology to maintain the balance between the investment and rewards for the various members. So, ideology replaces rewards in order to maintain continued involvement, and manipulates the structure of social rewards through individual mobility and distribution of particular advantages.[179] While this could be true for some particular movement somewhere, it is not universally valid. It is, firstly, insufficient to explain the differing degrees of involvement of individuals in social movements. Finkel and Muller find private selective incentives to be incomplete, less relevant and highly problematic for social participation.[180] Secondly, individuals take part in action even though this would be costly, risky, and dangerous, and even though it could end in grave sacrifices, loss or even death.[181]

Other factors missed out by reductionist structural analysis are deeper personal motivations, individual emotional experience or mutual affective recognition.[182] Individuals identify and recognize one another on the basis on which they are mobilized (A:20). When they discover that other individuals and groups are going through the same experience, sacrifice, danger or loss, that supports their individual involvement or commitment. Personal effectiveness and development (mental, emotional, moral or spiritual) also become an incentive to continued participation.[183] Klandermans, distinguishing the social–psychological correlates of participation in social movements, describes participation as an attempt to influence the social and political environment, as a manifestation of identification with a group, and as a search for meaning and expression of one's views.[184] The differing degrees of individuals' involvement in social movements are indefinite – not fixed or static – and multifaceted, subject to change as social context changes. It is therefore an error to over-generalize about this involvement.[185] In any case, the Gülen Movement is quite unlike exclusive, ideological solidaristic organizations with limited material and ideational resources. In the latter, organization is based upon symbolic incentives – either ideological or solidaristic: we saw in §1.2.2–1.3 and 4.1.3 that such incentives prove a significant surrogate for lack of material resources. Such organizations are at any time liable to violent and coercive means, the more liable as the rigidity of the organizational model increases. For some forty years now, the collective action of the Gülen Movement has shown no such tendency, nor been tempted in that direction.* If any individual in the Movement has felt tempted to violence in response to provocation coming from outside agents, the Movement has successfully contained such impulses. Its verbal and written discourse of the Movement are available to all and show no sign of condoning or inciting even disruption, still less violence.

Chapters 3 and 4 argued that the Gülen Movement is not an exclusivist and ideological organization or movement heavily reliant on symbolic incentives. Such reliance increases the risk of internal conflicts and factionalism,[186] a theme to which I now turn.

5.2.7 Factionalism

In any society goods and values are allocated differently between different individuals. Insofar as the variation follows variation in functional importance (say, of particular divisions of labor), then the resulting hierarchy and stratification can be based on known (possibly also agreed and shared) values. Alternatively, hierarchy and stratification may reflect only structural injustices, effects of the distribution of power. Whatever their basis eventually they are 'likely to produce discontent and ineffectiveness in the usual ways'.[187] Lofland refers to gender, age, ethnicity, wealth, occupation, being able-bodied, education, geographical location, religion, and the like, as major bases of hierarchy. However, whether in a society or an SMO, some categories and dimensions of hierarchy 'are likely to be vastly over-represented and yet others to be extremely underrepresented or even absent altogether'.[188]

In a stratified system of roles, reciprocal expectations of behavior may display imbalances. The actor perceives inconsistencies among the various components of status (for example, in income, authority, prestige), or may be frustrated by a fall in relative to other positions in the

---

* B:9, A:14 and 15; see also §4.1.2.

hierarchy. This raises questions again about the differing interests, contentions or factions that complexity and heterogeneity of networks or their organization may generate. The degree of factionalism or propensity to schism is higher in exclusivist, conflictual and contentious organizations, which require the individual member accept subjection to organizational discipline and orders coming from others.[189] McCarthy and Zald give 'two major internal preconditions for splits and the development of factions: heterogeneity of social base and the doctrinal basis of authority'. They argue that factions form if the authority and the subgroups are concerned about the legitimacy or purity of doctrines or ideology and if the subgroups start questioning the bases of organizational authority, or the behavior of leadership, and if they disagree on possession of the prestige of success and material incentives.[190]

However, as I have argued in the foregoing discussion, the Gülen Movement does not have a doctrinal orthodoxy, is not an exclusivist organization, and has not revealed any internal disagreement over tactics, goals, or personalities. Moreover, as explained earlier ($5.2.1, page 175–6), solidarity is epiphenomenal and cultural in character and is located in the terrain of symbolic production in everyday life. It does need to be artificially generated. When asked about the existence or probability of any faction or schism in the Gülen Movement, Ergene responded:

> The different networks have specific tasks and interests. They therefore do not compete for power. However, they respond in different ways to the pressing needs of the environment. Also, in service networking there is not much significant differentiation of hierarchical roles, and few different parameters of the projects, or rewards for them. Besides, the tasks which require functional specialization are already carried out by professionalized individuals or networks for SMOs.

When asked about the effect of people coming from different movements and joining the networks in the Gülen Movement, Çapan said:

> They are in the Movement because they would like to be a part of an already working system. Imposition of any perspective which will not be in accord with the general principles of the collective action of the Movement will not be aired or much heeded. Those ideas or individuals who wish to impose themselves within the community will not integrate themselves into the majority anyway. There are enough venues

and channels to express one's opinion and convince people and come to a majority decision.

Asked about another common cause of schism, the choice of projects, Aymaz commented:

> People in the Gülen Movement co-operate for reasonable, feasible and promising projects. They do not go for and delude themselves with impractical, unrealistic, passing and untested whims and desires. The Movement has for years tested and proved their projects, such as all kinds of educational efforts and institutions. No one can say, 'We have enough of those, let's go and try something new in the uncharted murky waters'. In short, lack of such initiatives and people prevent the emergence of tensions and factions in the Gülen Movement.

What the interviewees are clearly recognizing here is that internal conflicts arise in a movement because of lack of fairness in distribution of resources and incentives, or deprivation of certain individuals, or the imposition of unrealistic, unpromising or obsolete perspectives or projects, and because of increased personal or collective risks.[191] The lack of internal communications and co-operation within an organization can facilitate conflicts.[192] However, due to the multiple belongings and participation in the service-projects and the media and press organs, to which Movement participants are affiliated, the interviewees felt that the Gülen Movement does not want for resources for communication, or for opportunities to pursue different but complementary strategies. Furthermore, the Movement is cognitively and ideationally able to provide its participants new explanations or perspectives for any emergent realities.[193] Therefore, internal conflicts, according to the interviewees, are less likely in the Gülen Movement.

Whittier and colleagues note that different groups or organizations dispute and contest for power and for different interests or meaning – that is, they aim, ideologically and strategically, to influence others in the organization so as to reshape the meaning, action, authority and outcome of the collective action.[194] Melucci explains how the rigidity of the ideological apparatus or orthodoxies within the main organization breeds differences in interpretation and application, that is, a faction. Factionalism obstructs the achievement of collective goals; it means that people have not been completely unified with the main body of the collective. The faction or subgroup usually forms around the presence of one or more sub-leaders, especially those with some personal charisma or different interests and agenda. These individuals work their way covertly through their personal interpretations, differentiation and ties with members. Eventually, the schism happens, and leads people to part from the main organization in order to set up a new one.[195]

Table 8

A		SD	D	N	A	SA
4	The GM devotes a considerable share of its resources to new projects, alternative openings and development.				39	939
5	The GM devotes a considerable share of its resources to the task of managing complexity, of consolidation of group solidarity, and of avoidance of disaggregation.	893	85			
6	We and GM have an ideology.	971	7			
27	There are differences between the organizational apparatus and the general interest of the movement.	973	5			
28	I believe there exist different interests in the GM.	971	7			
29	I believe different interests compete for power in the GM.	965	19	1	3	
32	There are dissatisfied elements in the GM because of its management.	961	15	2		
33	Factions exist in the GM.	978				
35	Opinions, views and discourse are produced by and attributed to ideologues.	967	8		3	
36	The elites in the GM exploit opportunities and individuals to affirm themselves or to consolidate their positions.	971	7			
37	Control is applied to people's routines by the apparatuses of regulation which exact identification and consensus.	899	75		4	
39	There is respect in the GM for different views and diversity.		2	1	83	892

In the light of the responses of the interviewees, the answers to Questionnaires, and the pertinent sections of §4.1.1–3, fragmentation and schisms are less likely in collectivities like the Gülen Movement. There are several reasons:

The Gülen Movement does not have an ideology.* What may be called the worldview or belief system of the Movement is not dogmatically attached to some fixed orthodoxy of interpretation of values and ideals handed on from the past, nor closed to fresh presentation of its own near reference-tradition or to ideas originating outside that tradition, still less to formulations and practices that open up (between different traditions) a large commons of compatible values and ideals.[196] As Sykiainen puts it: '[Gülen and the Movement are] occupied not by the dogmatic views touched on above, but by quite other values, such as compromise, stability, protection of the life, honor and dignity of the human being, dialog and consultation [and] justice, equity, and human rights, in our days.'[197] It follows that the Movement's SMOs cannot be demanding a return to the original purity of ideology, or something of that sort.[198]

The Gülen Movement, for its long-sustained positive, constructive and non-confrontational activism, relies on the social cohesiveness or unity of ideas, means and goals of its heterogeneous participants, and not upon some exclusivist solidarity separating some of them from others or all of them from wider society and the world.* What always matters most is not the numbers of participants but the quality of their inner commitment to the meaning of voluntary, altruistic service as broadly understood within the Movement.

The collective actor stays well clear of ritual or sacral affirmation of any ideological principles or leading personalities.** This prevents the radicalization of the image of the action beyond its factual meaning and contents.

The project-networks or SMOs of the Movement are not contentious subgroups, unresponsive to important needs in the wider social or political arena, inside or outside Turkey.***

Last but not least, there are no networks or SMOs that have broken off away from the Movement after deviating or opportunist leaders nor is there any likelihood of such an eventuality.****

All of that also prevents the Gülen Movement from turning into a fundamentalist or regressive sectarian organization and from breaking up into conflictual factions.

---

*   A:4, 5, 18, 30 and 37; see also §4.1.1 and 4.1.2.

**   A:8 and 9; and see §4.1.3.

*** A:27, 28, 29, 32, and 33; see also §3.2.6 and 4.1.4.

**** A:32, 33, 34, 35, 36 and 37.

5.3 CONCLUSION

Crisis has all but become the norm in Turkey – for reasons set out in the historical narrative in Chapter 2. For individuals in Turkish society it remains possible nevertheless to choose between crisis and development. They can, if they will, mobilize themselves into an action or movement that is non-conflictual and peaceful, and through it attend constructively to the branches and roots of the crises afflicting their society. Individuals and groups in Turkey have indeed done that. In this book we have been studying the most successful example of it, namely the Gülen Movement.

Individuals and groups have come together in this Movement to construct meaning, to make sense of their being in togetherness and in action. They have recognized, combined and sustained the meanings, values and plurality of aspects present in being and acting together. They share orientations that bind actors and the specific way of acting together through time. They share, within the opportunities and constraints, what is produced by their work. They share also the definitions of ends, means, field of action, investments and rewards. These continuous processes have become a network of active relationships between actors who interact, communicate, influence each other, negotiate, and make decisions.

The service-networks have increased in number and grown into a large, dynamic transnational movement. These networks construct models of decision-making and decision taking, leadership, and means and channels of communicating to third parties and the wider public. These networks of relationship produce and continue to share a service discourse, ethic and action specifically their own, which is shared by all who constitute the collective actor of the Movement. The set of practices, cognitive and cultural products, and the overall outcome of the collective action, are introduced into the society as a whole and incorporated into its language.[199] That is why the Gülen Movement is distinct and central in such fields as education, publication, media, culture, health, interfaith dialog and societal cohesion.

On the other hand, the Movement is rightly considered to be marginal in aspiring to access to the political system. It is also marginal in positive social recognition in the eyes of the very small, yet highly influential, protectionist elite and state bureaucracy. Correlation between the people, the electing many, and those promoted or assigned few, is neither automatic nor univocal. Small-group protectionist ideology and solidarity around vested interests has become a huge financial and political power that masks its agenda behind 'the state security syndrome'[200] or 'the strategy of tension'*. These mechanisms of intervention and control in the public space restrict the development of civil society, of collective experience and services, in Turkey, including (but uniquely) those of the Gülen Movement.

The Gülen Movement has been mainly organized through informal, everyday life cutting across interpersonal relationships, which has linked the participants of local communities to each other. Within these networks relationships are embedded in systems of relationships based on friendship, neighborhood, professions, and personal interests, and range through social, cultural and religious, communitarian and humanitarian activities. These activities exceed by far the sphere of overt political activities and link across localities and generations and have proven themselves capable of bridging ideological and social barriers through multiple participations, and strengthening mutual trust.

Although they seem relatively simple, the networks play a significant counseling role connecting individuals to broader social dynamics and diverse SMOs. New potentials in the society that that might be drawn to conflict and violence are thus transformed into productive, collective and useful actions and constructive projects.

The individuals who form the service-networks in the Movement includes a very high percentage of people from a middle class or higher socio-economic position. Their very open and visible engagement and integration in projects for education, culture, interfaith dialog, societal peace and civilizational co-operation, brings them recognition as bearers of universal ethical values or value orientations, which cannot be associated with ideas or orientations that are narrow, marginal or exclusive. They develop a certain vision of the world, become sensitive to particular and global concerns and causes, and acquire information and necessary skills and competencies to deliver service-projects that meet real social needs.

Availability of information, circulation and diffusion of messages and new initiatives for new service-projects, and the acquired experience and

---

* The strategy of tension is a way to control and manipulate public opinion using fear, propaganda, disinformation, psychological warfare, agents provocateurs and false flag terrorism actions. For more, see Celani, 2004.

professionalized expertise in the Movement, constitute its culture, its internal unity and cohesiveness. This enables the Movement to maintain the individual and collective need for self-fulfillment, for appropriation and communication of the meaning of action.

Benefiting from highly personal social relationships governed by the logic of SMOs, traditional solidarity, flexible ideational attachment and dynamic impulse, the Gülen Movement gives hope of achieving and preserving the meaning of human behavior along with the richness of diversity in a global society. It links collective goals and individual transformation and strives to retain respect for individual differences.

Altruism is elevated to a virtue of the highest standing in the Gülen Movement. The relationship of the individual to the others acting in the collectivity is encouraged, so as to be built in togetherness with others. This attitude implies different work ethics: gratuitousness, co-ordinated and effective services towards common goals, personal sacrifice in the interest of the collectivity, and working hard in the present for a happy future. Through interdependence and co-operation with all, and through the diffusion and proliferation of informational and educational institutions, the Gülen Movement renders seemingly weak, insignificant and local forms of action potentially able to exert an enormous influence far beyond their actual size and local effect.

As a result of wise, flexible guidance, awareness of the proper and efficient means for the achievement of particular objectives and general goals, and prudent concern for lawfulness or legality of both means and ends, the social and cultural practice of the Gülen Movement has come to involve all social categories and all age groups in different parts of the world. Its being to relate to the world in a global interaction turns it into a set of cultural referents and a life model.

The Gülen Movement equips people with cognitive, social, cultural and material resources to construct their present and future, as well as the language with which to design their experience in all of its dimensions. The codes of behavior and services enable people to make sense of their actions and to mediate between a plurality of conflicting demands and communities. The Movement does not intend thereby to annul all specificities and irreducible differences among people and social systems, but to educate people to respect and benefit from those differences.

The existence of inclusive and multiple participations and affiliations links and integrates different areas of the Gülen Movement. It also allows different individuals in service-networks to come into personal contact with one another. While establishing bridges between SMOs, individuals share and exchange experiences, resources and information. Private, cultural and social dimensions intersect in multiple but compatible (usually complementary) participations in the Movement. Such freedom of choice and action, with inclusiveness and flexibility, blurs boundaries between the Movement and wider society, and contributes to the growth of channels of communication, interaction and mutual trust. This in return saves the Movement from turning into a single, authoritarian, all-powerful, totalizing, sectarian organization or leadership.

The qualities of the SMOs of the Gülen Movement differentiate them from counterparts – in Europe for example – which on occasion defy the authorities with direct action and protest so as to disrupt official plans. For the Gülen Movement as collective actor, to defend truth and justice implicitly and explicitly is one thing, to defy established authorities and disrupt plans is another. To achieve right, clear moral understanding of an issue and then to follow a course of positive action in response is one way of dealing with it; being contentious and disruptive is quite another. The short- and long-term outcomes of the two are also quite different.

The dense, strong and multiple affiliations that individuals bring to or acquire through project-networks inspire, motivate and commit them to the services the project yields. Moreover, participants do not separate their private lives from those projects. Rather, they link their private lives to their public activities and their societal environment. This leads to harmonious and peaceful continuities rather than detachment, alienation, frustration and antagonism. There are also a great number of individuals who are sympathetic to the collective action of the Movement but do not become active in it. This indicates that the Movement is able to establish affective links with and among the wider public and is not an isolated actor. Indeed, there is no expectation in the Movement that participants should sever previous social ties, nor that they should have no other ties, or not make new ties while 'in' the Movement. To the contrary, such multiple affiliations are in principle and practice welcomed: loyalty centers upon effective delivery of service-projects and complementarity between them, it does not center upon the Movement as such: solidarity is epiphenomenal; it ensues from sharing work effort, from shared experiences and memories, and is not pursued as a precondition of doing the work at all.

That allows for diverse (usually complementary) levels of participation in the Gülen Movement. To be sure, a shared identity characterizes the Movement as a whole. But different levels of affiliation of participants and non-participants with the service-projects and SMOs make that identity of the Movement open and inclusive. This inclusiveness has no negative effect on the homogeneity or effectiveness of its service-projects. Being open to the outside world, not having or seeking a totalitarian organizational structure, but instead having and seeking compatibility with other collective actors and civil society bodies, and not being restricted to a certain time and place (or territory), all indicate that networking, participation and affiliation within the Gülen Movement are definitely not exclusivist, alienating or sectarian.

The majority of people who participate in the services are introduced by friends. The fact that it is not via relatives demonstrates the inclusive, transformative and lasting nature of Movement relationships. Also, the fact that introduction to and participation in the Movement or service-projects is through acquaintances of everyday life and through work colleagues indicates that the cultural perspective or worldview of the Gülen Movement is regarded as legitimate and rational. The participation of individuals who did not grow up within the Gülen community or its networks is also significant: it indicates purely individual choices and a strong subjective identification, an active rationalizing and reckoning of the decision to participate in the collective action of the Movement.

The links, relationships or co-ordination established by Gülen and the Movement as collective actor with already legitimized and institutionalized SMO leaders, communities and organizations reinforce the prestige and legitimacy of the collective action, the actors and the SMOs of the Movement. This can be particularly helpful when the collective actor is forced to respond to crises or emergencies.

The Movement as collective actor feels a sense of ownership over the action, and duty and commitment to it, but not ownership of the service provided, the outcomes of action or 'the object'. Therefore, there is no strife around 'the object'; the outcomes belong to all. This prevents the formation of factionalism and contentious vying for positions within SMOs.

The Movement does not envisage or intend an overall, sudden change in people and/or in the direction of the development of projects. The intention is to educate people with patience and dedication over time in order to enable them, in peace, to manage the complexity and plurality they have to deal with. That is why decision-making in service-networks is neither centralized nor invisible. Project development decisions are not taken by specific individuals or private groups. As participants are allowed to intervene in the decision-making processes, it is participatory.

Communication and interaction is free-flowing among individuals, networks and SMOs. Collective judgment and sensitivity are used to the full so as not to embarrass or upset participants and sympathizers of the Movement and others who are neutral to it. This is believed to be vital, especially for transnational educational services. This attitude has been mistaken for passivity or lack of assertiveness.[201] In fact, through forbearance and patience, skilled participants are able to transform conflictual potential into positive and productive resources for and through the services and projects they deliver. The Movement shows that mental, material, moral and spiritual transformative energies can be channeled into development without deviating into conflicts and violence. (That, incidentally, is evidence of capacity to learn from the experiences of political engagement of other collective actors, past and present).

The Gülen Movement does not advance an unrealistic claim to deliver overall transformation in systemic or global issues. However, its collective action responds, and offers workable solutions, to the local problems and issues arising from systemic inefficiencies and global concerns. The self-reflexive capacity, competence and efficiency of the Movement in developing effective approaches are plain to see. Their existence implies that the Gülen Movement possesses a mediating potential in addressing and tackling the problems of modernity, that is, in helping to formulate solutions at the level of individual autonomy, which is where the way needs to be prepared for peaceful development and healthy integration of the individual into the contemporary era.[202] Change amid the sheer complexity of modern contemporary societies can only be managed by education, information, interaction and co-operation – very little, if anything at all, can be achieved by unilateral action, coercive application of force and the wasting of human life either by bloodshed in war or by economic strangulation. Beneficial and sustainable change entails decisions, choices, accord and co-operation within and between societies and civilizations to achieve consensually valued projects and policies. That, person by person, project by project, is what the Gülen Movement has been working towards.

6

Summary and Conclusions

6.1 DEFINING THE GÜLEN MOVEMENT

6.1.1 On social movements generally

There is no scholarly consensus on what a social movement is. There are, in the literature, a number of classifications of collective actors based on their outcomes, structure, leadership, type of society and time-period in which they act, worldview or ideology. The differences in classification arise from the fact that movements have emerged in different social conditions, in response to different demands, and to variations in availability of resources and other constraints on opportunities for action. However, contemporary social movement theories have also been based on premises from earlier traditions within sociology and from earlier approaches to social theorizing. In addition, theorists bring their conceptions of their own political or ideological roles into the discussion – many of them very clearly influenced by experiences in the contentious movements of the 1960s and 1970s in western Europe and North America. This led to many divisions, even antagonisms, among the theorists – to the extent that some were advocating their approaches as if no other alternatives worthy of consideration existed.

In response to altered socio-historical contexts, especially since the 1980s, a new generation of theorists brought different experiences to their work and to the definition of their subject matter. These newer approaches omit some features or criteria from other theories or add a few new ones. Some criteria or metaphors are over-generalized; also the same terms are found used with different meanings, or different terms used with overlapping meanings. In Chapter 1, I reviewed the contemporary approaches in order to identify the differences among them, as well as recurrent themes and features. I argued that theories that in particular are applied to the explanation and analysis of contentious and conflictual movements are seriously deficient if applied to non-contentious and faith-inspired movements such as the Gülen Movement. I suggested that, instead, a syncretic approach, deploying a mix of analytical tools from the different theories, would yield better results for accurate description and analysis of such movements. I also underlined the need to take more careful account of the local specificities (historical, cultural, social political factors) before venturing to pronounce on the emergence, character, sustainability and likely outcomes of collective actions such as the Gülen Movement.

In Chapter 2, I set out, in the form of a chronological narrative, the main socio-political developments in contemporary Turkey. Going back to the early Republican years, this narrative explains the social, political and cultural processes that constitute the relevant conjunctural factors for understanding the emergence, nature, and sustainability of the mobilizations and counter-mobilizations on-going in Turkey to this day. It enables us to understand the specificity of their causes, what was and is common to them, and what persisted beyond conjunctural variations. It details characteristic problems of Turkish society and what the socio-political context permits and engenders by way of options for collective actors – the 'legacy' if you will of possible repertoires of action and templates of organization available to the people of Turkey. The narrative recounted the ruling elite's limited capacity for policy implementation, their use of repression, and bias in the judiciary and the media: what resulted was systemic blockages and crises, instability of government, acute cleavages and polarization in society, the solidification of vested interests and, in response, impatient, aggressive radicalism, widespread social disorder and violence, in turn vindicating further authoritarian repression by the elite. The negligible progress in democratizing institutions and modernizing the economy for the benefit of the nation as a whole led to new forms of collective action – some radical, militant, disruptive and ultimately ineffectual, but also to the very effective non-political and peaceful Gülen Movement.

Mustafa Kemal Atatürk worked his modernization and Westernization strategies through his Republican People's Party, which monopolized state institutions, centralizing state control of the military and civilian structures, expressly including all religious offices and education. This statist-elite shaped and guided the cadre of the new nation-state under what was in effect one-party rule. After Atatürk, this protectionist group collaborated with members of the media and business world for their mutual advantage; they formed a wealthy group which took control of State-owned Economic Enterprises (SEEs), turning them against private sector competition and dominating business and the economy, as well as politics.

As defenders of the status quo in Turkey, this protectionist group – eventually recognized and exposed as 'the deep state' – has proved itself an exclusivist conflictual movement, mobilizing consistently over the years against democratizing actors. Although always very few in number and not reflecting the views of the majority of the Turkish, they have been, through their hold on bureaucratic and executive power, more influential than democratically elected governments and parliament. Indeed, they have counter-mobilized as an ideological group against elected representation and civil society because a free and fully democratic society and a liberal economy would harm their vested interests. They have polarized society, increased societal tension and segmentation and facilitated and engineered the conditions for political intervention and military take-over.

The justification for the three coups in 1960, 1971, and 1980 was that parliamentary democracy had been paralyzed by rampant corruption and civil discord, and the state was threatened. The so-called 'post-modern' or 'soft' coup of 1997 and the ensuing February 28 Process were justified on the grounds that the state was under threat from 'blurring of the distinction between the secular and the anti-secular'. In fact this was a smoke-screen masking the massive bribery and corruption endemic to the political and economic system: it turned out that several chief executives and top advisors of the banks and corporations involved in the corruption were retired senior generals.

Each of these coups followed a pattern: civil unrest and radicalization grew; university chancellors and significant media figures would speak out against the Parliamentary government and civil society and call for strong action from the military to check the disorder; strikes, street violence, assassinations and terrorist bombings would occur; the protectionist elite would claim that the regime was under threat; the military would rise to do its 'duty' and take control of the state. Each coup restructured the political and economic system and set the limits of the civilian and military spheres. These limits were barriers to change and democratization. After every coup, before transition to civilian rule, the protectionist elite selected consultative assemblies to draw up new constitutions. These established new rules, roles, static norms and institutions by which the elite consolidated itself. Periods of 'guided democracy' with 'licensed' or 'accredited' political bodies and parties began, under the supervision of new presidents or the National Security Council.

Privatization and democratization efforts were nullified by heads of state, inter-parliamentary committees or by the judiciary appointed by the President. This negatively impacted the growth of the economy. It also demonstrated that other institutions exercised power over the elected government or Parliament. Since the elected leaders could not overcome opposition from institutions and had to abide by the rule of the judiciary, they could not pursue privatization, and therefore democratization and political efficacy were not achieved. That is why a liberal polity that would expand civil society, defend human rights, promote participatory democracy and so prevent destabilizing political responses, has never been realized in Turkey. Elitist or military interventionism has allowed very little progress towards real democracy in Turkey.

However, since the 1940s, despite some legal restrictions, peaceful, faith-inspired communities and civil society movements had continued to exist and expand their services to the public. By 1991, when the Eastern bloc was collapsing, President Özal and independent civil society organizations worked to establish close commercial and political working-relations with the Balkan and Central Asian states. A new cultural and faith-inspired service understanding came into view. By this time the Gülen Movement was already well-established as the most prominent and widely institutionalized of the movements with this understanding. Participants were mobilizing around a new synthesis of culture, education, dialog and co-operation for peaceful, non-partisan ends.

The Movement existed for over twenty years before it became the object of hostile media interest. Participants were already running secular private schools, university entrance courses, student hostels, a bursary system and publishing ventures. Since then it has gone on to establish more SMOs – TV and radio stations, newspapers and periodicals, hundreds of secular educational institutions from primary schools to universities, cultural centers and interfaith dialog institutions, hospitals, welfare and aid organizations. It has been widely acknowledged both inside and outside Turkey for the value of its work. This very recognition roused fears in 'the deep state' – they counter-mobilized by manufacturing crises about Islam or Muslims, inserting these fabricated anxieties onto the national agenda and using the resulting crises to hide corruption and law-breaking in their own activities.

In fact, several polls to date have shown that a huge majority of Turkish people do not wish for a political and legal order based on religious law. Turkey's population, including religious citizens and faith-inspired movements, have all been born into in a secularist, republican tradition and are quite comfortable with its basic premises. In the 1980s, Islamist political parties never gained more than a tenth of the popular national vote. Nevertheless, this meager showing was enough for 'the deep state' to raise alarm about an Islamist takeover. In reality, the faith-inspired service ethic expressed in contemporary Turkish society has not produced and was not derived from a movement to establish an Islamic state in Turkey.

The historical background presented in Chapter 2 demonstrated that the mobilization and counter-mobilization in Turkey do not neatly map socio-politically and historically onto the general paradigms of contemporary social movement theories. Chapter 3 therefore used multiple analytical tools from those theories to analyze the mobilization by the Gülen Movement and the counter-mobilization by its opponents.

6.1.2 The Gülen Movement as cultural actor

The dominant statist-laicist elite has stifled civil society in Turkey, concealed and obfuscated important issues, resisted necessary development and reform and repressed legitimate democratic demands. This has resulted in a waste of social energy and led to distorted modernization and the breakdown of civic initiatives and mobilizations. For an effective democracy to develop, the society needs modernized institutions, the selection and renewal of modernizing personnel to run them openly and efficiently, a competitive economy open to globalization, the disengagement of the antagonistic elite and an end to its political and cultural impositions, and intellectual and cultural freedoms, including the freedom, within a secure pluralist, secular polity, of religious association and orientation. The Gülen Movement has not responded to these needs through partisan political claims or actions, nor opposed the actions or schemes of the elite, nor in its discourse or its tactics challenged the authority or power of the state or its agencies. On the other hand, it has also not retreated from the mainstream of national life into a marginalized existence as an advocate of some anachronistic or otherwise utopian vision of how the society should be. It has, instead, sought to allow the latent potential of Turkish people to grow and articulate itself through a sustained program of educational, health and intercultural and interfaith services. This program is managed and delivered by a decentralized network of institutions (SMOs), informally linked but formally and operationally independent of each other. One result of the sheer proficiency of these SMOs – aside from the immediate benefits that accrue from the particular services locally provided – has been to strengthen the processes of institutionalization and modernization in Turkey. The Movement has consistently understood and stressed the role of civil society institutions in shaping the development of participatory democracy, and the special value of the *hizmet* ethic, the altruistic, voluntary provision of the services that local communities and the wider society need.

Through the work of its SMOs and a number of specific platforms, the Gülen Movement has refashioned the public space, and revitalized and consolidated democratization. These platforms have for the first time in modern Turkish history brought together people of different, even opposed, worldviews to discuss constructively issues that for decades have caused tensions, mistrust and hostility. This initiative has involved intellectuals in producing and disseminating knowledge and contributing to the process of *naming* based on information. It has thrown light on hidden issues that the rationality of protectionist apparatuses did not account for, and offered people a defense against manipulation through meanings imposed by vested interests. The platforms became a vehicle for the expression and discussion of pressing societal concerns and needs. The Movement has thus brought new approaches to the relationship between faith and reason, to peaceful coexistence with religious diversity, to the provision of modern education that combines training for the complexities of urbanized, industrialized societies with sound moral guidance based on universal ethical values and a deepening of personal faith and spirituality. This has constructed in Turkish society a taste and capacity for coexistence respectful of differences within a common sense of citizenship. The Movement has striven towards this goal without breaching the rules of the System, or questioning the legitimacy and authority of the state. Because of its primary focus on reforming cultural understandings, norms and identities – rather than material interests and economic distribution – it is right to describe the Gülen Movement as a *cultural actor.*

It deals with individuals and their needs; it aims at changing mind-sets and value systems, at *interior* transformation, in contradistinction to political strategies which seek to change external realities. The Movement has in this regard become an engine of social transformation that, as a by-product, exposes the contradictions and silences that the dominant apparatuses of the political system seek to hide. Its success in mobilizing on the basis of long-embedded cultural traditions of caring and service for others has created in the society symbolic systems and a focus for identification independent of the values imposed by the elite. The elite's attempt, through its authoritarian and exclusivist understanding, to impose norms and values that are solely its own, only alienated it further from society. The attempt at top–down cultural transformation stoked tensions and divisions within society, deepening the distrust and segmentation between the people and a state seeking to dictate to them what they should hold dear, what they should remember of their past and what they had better 'forget'. The Movement's tolerant inclusive understanding of culture contrasts sharply with the militantly narrow laicism of the protectionists. In contrast to them, the Movement has sought to mend the broken circle of communication and mutual recognition conjoining society.

Through discourse and action, the Gülen Movement alerts collective consciousness to the radical nature of social, cultural and spiritual needs that politics ignores, or which it mishandles by reducing them to arenas of contention between antagonistic political factions. By putting into practice constructive alternatives to the political approach to social problems, the Movement introduces to the public space a new paradigm, a redefinition of norms of perception and production of reality beyond the control of the hegemonic discourse. As collective cultural actor, it symbolically reverses the meanings inscribed in that discourse, and demonstrates the arbitrariness of those meanings and of the hegemony by which they are projected. Its success in seeing and shaping reality through different perspectives has led to erosion of the elite's monopoly of power over reality. That, in turn, has opened up new channels of representation, steadily reforming the decision-making processes and rules, with further effects on the forms of political democracy, distributive justice and segmentation.

While the service-projects, the collective action, of the Movement do not constitute an unlawful action nor a challenge (explicit or implicit) to the status quo, the Movement has been counter-mobilized by the protectionist interests because, on a symbolic ground, it challenges and reverses the logic of their instrumental rationality. Both to hold on to the status quo and to hide their failures in the service areas where the Movement is conspicuously successful, the protectionists open up new problems and new areas of conflict. They counter-mobilize in particular because the value of non-contentious civil society action – the efficiency of voluntary altruistic service and its role in modernizing institutions, in both developing the attitudes and mechanisms needed to build participatory democracy and motivating the people to become alert, active, law-abiding citizens (without whom a healthy democracy cannot be sustained) – emerged from a faith-inspired initiative inspired by a Muslim preacher, an Islamic scholar. Counter-mobilization took the form of efforts to manipulate the image of Islam, and denigrate Gülen and the Movement.

However, the service ethic of the Gülen Movement has successfully introduced into the public space a different image of Islam. Seeing that different reality, people from all segments of society in Turkey have become open to change and renewal, and recognized the value that faith can give to individual lives, and the importance for societal cohesion of cultural continuity alongside ability to adapt to change. As an example of that, the Movement institutionalized and revived the idea of charitable foundations, a valuable tradition successfully adapted for the benefit of present and future generations. The Movement offers intellectual and spiritual resources that enable people to construe the contemporary world in a more rounded way, as well as to engage with the challenges and responsibilities of building their future in it. An example of that is the commitment with which Movement participants set up television and radio stations, newspapers and other print media. This enables them to open up for the society a greater range of perspectives and forums, to contribute more effectively to cultural and intercultural understanding, and to be more active and visible in the processes which define the social agenda. As a result, controversial issues can no longer be hidden behind the facade of formal neutrality and the closed circuit of self-referentiality of the media outlets of the protectionist elite; also, the flow of information and connectedness within Turkey and between Turkey and the wider world has been hugely enlarged.

A major argument of the protectionist elite is that they are guardians and advocates of the modernization of the nation. However, here too, their policies and actions have not matched their rhetoric, and they have been outpaced by the achievements of the SMOs set up by the participants in the Gülen Movement. One of the effects of the Movement's work has been the expansion of innovative occupational sectors and higher turnover of personnel in communications, education and welfare services. The relation between the Movement, professionalization and social mobility emerges in the forms of vocational altruistic service work and cultural training in new skills and intellectualization, and professional re-training. The Movement has created new enterprises, cooperatives, and agencies for personal development, in-service training, and job placement. It has also created educational opportunities by teaching foreign languages and providing scholarships for study in foreign countries. This has attracted and mobilized large numbers of people from many diverse backgrounds to work on significant social projects. This mobility has made Turkish society more open and fair, and affected the way networks and SMOs are formed, their size and shape, and the professionalism in them. In short, the work of the Movement has led to modernizing innovation, more balanced distribution of opportunity, and better public welfare – without resort to confrontational or direct action tactics.

Another major argument of the protectionist elite is that they defend the nation against the threat of fundamentalism, of regressive, radical Islam. In fact, because they want sole control of the public space the elite need Islam to be seen as reactionary and radical, since that legitimizes their authoritarian control. It is the national and international recognition of the quality of the services provided by the Gülen Movement, their operational integrity and continuity for over thirty years in competitive environments, that prompts the protectionist group's envy and hostile polemic. However, the Movement is not only strictly non-violent and non-political, it also does not isolate and differentiate itself from the shared culture of society and unequivocally declares its acceptance of Turkey's secular polity. Gülen has encouraged people to serve humanity through education, intercultural and interfaith activities and institutions. All SMOs, whatever their field of action, have a common rationality based on knowledge, skills and shared ethical values. That rationality has not changed in different locations, within or outside Turkey. For example, no matter where situated, Gülen-inspired schools are not religious but follow secular, state-prescribed curricula and internationally recognized programs subject to state inspection. Successful transnational joint projects have brought recognition and co-operation from foreign officials and organizations. There is consensus among Turkey's ambassadors and local statesmen, intellectuals and scholars from the countries where the Gülen-inspired institutions operate that they play a positive role in relations between communities and states. Indeed, Gülen and Movement participants have received awards for their efforts in dialog, co-operation and international peace. The Movement's emphasis on diversity and non-violence, its active, sustained co-operation with other faiths and cultures has brought due appreciation of its peace-making vision, and functions as a most effective barrier against fanaticism, fundamentalism and any 'clash of civilizations'. The Gülen Movement has, in short, produced a much sounder deterrence against radical fundamentalism than the state has. Its vision allows people to live their faith within their Turkish identity in peace, tolerance and security. For participants, there is no inherent conflict between religious devoutness and secularism.

The intent of the polemic of the protectionist elite, by contrast, has been to polarize attitudes, to create tensions and anxieties, instability and division in the society. Yet, the deepest symbolic challenge to the elite comes from the Movement's service-ethic itself. This ethic is based on objective and universal human values – to care for others and serve them without ulterior motives, without any intent to gain material advantage, or to impose an ideology, or to accrue political leverage. This is a model of action that political systems cannot replicate. The cultural model produced by the Movement weakens the prevailing understanding that relationships between people (and indeed nations) must be governed by cost–benefit calculations based on self-interest. In open societies, the cultural models that a political system cannot replicate can nevertheless be tolerated, and ideally be learnt from so as to improve the system. That has not been the case in Turkey. The service ethic of the Gülen Movement represents a particularly potent symbolic challenge to the instrumental logic and rationality of vested interests in the country that have been siphoning money and resources from the state and people for many years. The Movement proves that its participants' direct personal commitment to and sharing with others cannot be reduced to instrumental logic. Since a system's power over people and events is very much dependent on what the people themselves accept or do not accept from the system, the Movement invites people, without confronting or challenging the system or breaching its laws, to assume responsibility for doing what needs doing. In this way it expresses the depth and potential of individual autonomy, and so motivates a civil society activism which, so long as it remains altruistic and non-conflictual, strengthens social cohesion. At the same time, necessarily, it exposes the inadequacies of the system, offering to the public sphere models of action and service which, eventually, may be taken up by political actors and influence policy- and decision-making processes.

During the February 28 coup, as in similar conjunctures before it, the protectionists and vested interest groups sought, through the media and information technologies under their control, to manipulate the political system to define new centralities and marginalities, to engineer anxiety, instability and conflict. Gülen was made the most prominent target of the media cartel operated by the elite, who hoped thereby to divert public attention from rampant embezzlement and graft, and illegal allocation of public and state resources. As well as reflecting their narcissism, this demonstrated their contempt for the rule of law and the norms of civilized political life. In attacking Gülen and his ideas, the protectionists intended to intimidate also intellectuals and politicians who, though not participants, are sympathetic to the Movement's vision and activities. This caused fear and anxiety even among liberals not associated with it. The Susurluk scandal and revelations after February 28 confirmed the existence of 'the deep state' and the extent of political and military malpractice in Turkey. During this period, democracy was suspended because its results were not acceptable to the protectionist elite; and democratic norms were routinely violated.

These divisive events had a profound negative effect on the formulation of public policy and the relationship between state and society. The protectionist elite have failed to produce a political design comprising instruments and models of transformation compatible with the economic and social realities in the contemporary world. In contrast to the Gülen Movement, they have not assisted cultural innovation and institutional modernization but caused many damaging divides in Turkish society. At this conjuncture, through responses from their media organs, Movement participants and third parties showed that they were no longer merely passive consumers of information. They could no longer be excluded from the discussion on the organization of the flow of information. They rebutted smear campaigns and showed a growing willingness and capacity to set the formal pre-conditions for any discourse.

Those orchestrating the February 28 coup fabricated national security issues and threats from reactionary Islamism. They used Gülen and the Movement to distract attention from their financial and ideological schemes and also as a warning to all supporters and sympathizers of the Movement. The Movement overcame this crisis without any counter-action, or resort to conflictual or coercive means. It was able to respond peacefully because of the trustworthiness and legitimacy of the authority of Gülen himself, the density and vigor of the Movement's networks of belonging and their long-demonstrated readiness to listen to society at various levels. Support within Turkish society for Gülen and the Movement did not decrease, because their work is widely appreciated as unselfish and non-divisive and their operational practice is consultative and transparent. By contrast, the dominant elite and the vested interests in Turkey *impose* constraints on the Turkish political arena and exercise varying degrees of influence from behind walls and closed doors. Also, if they demand control over the rules and mechanisms of decision-making, it is to serve their own interests, not the needs of society. Their attitudes and behavior are thus widely recognized as elitist and authoritarian, that is, as profoundly anti-democratic. Their attempt to discredit the Movement has been a key component of their framing of the public agenda, and is an obvious device to justify repression. No doubt, their greater control over the flow of information and the media gives them a structural advantage. However, they have failed to contend successfully for public consensus.

The Gülen Movement, by contrast, sees democratic norms and practice as the most, indeed the only, viable form of polity for contemporary societies. Its participants have been helping to modernize and consolidate democratic institutions so that individual rights and freedom are protected. The Movement holds that no single group, nation or culture has the monopoly on democratic norms and practice. It organizes conferences, platforms, relational and associational meetings and uses open media outlets inside and outside Turkey to encourage, through the exchange of ideas, the habits of discussion, negotiation and accommodation needed to underpin and secure democratic norms.

The Movement does not try to maximize the advantages of its actors in political decisions. It works strictly within the legal framework, whether in Turkey or abroad. Participants do not disregard or infringe on the system of rules nor extend beyond its institutional boundaries. The services they offer are not a contest among adversaries for control over the allocation of social production, nor for the creation of (new) imbalances of power. The Movement's work functions as a symbolic multiplier. The success of its services, as a by-product, obliges the dominant protectionists to justify their deeds – it exposes their weaknesses and calls into question their privileged access to state resources and political processes. If the protectionists' claims to be serving the nation were genuine, the struggle they advocate against religious radicalism and separatism would be matched by a struggle against corruption in Turkey. The Gülen Movement has, through its educational initiatives, its media organs, its determined rejection of resort to violence and coercion, its advocacy of intercultural and interfaith dialog and co-operation on projects and services, revealed the ineffectiveness of the definitions imposed by the dominant interest groups. Gradually over time, this has resulted in the public changing their attitudes to those definitions, and in the Movement gaining national and international acceptance. This inevitably vexes the protectionists: they assign to everyone in Turkish society a place, a 'meaning'. Therefore Gülen's meetings with heads of state, politicians, or other officials or authorities, local or foreign, have vexed them because they see this as stepping outside the 'meaning' that they have unilaterally assigned to him as a religious scholar and to civil society leaders in general.

However, the Movement's projects and institutions, in terms of both their nature and scale, constitute important *civic* initiatives, they are not narrowly 'religious' or 'Islamic' – the 'meaning' that the protectionist elite wish to impose upon them. The Movement's services are all integrative, inclusive and form part of a continual negotiation of meaning within the mainstream of society. The Gülen Movement has from the outset rejected exclusivist teaching based on the politics of 'identity' as potentially intolerant and a road to self-defeating fundamentalism. Independent polls have found that the majority of the public in Turkish and non-Turkish societies approve the works and values of the Movement. The Movement is nowhere viewed as a marginalized or 'fringe' actor. Indeed, its cultural action has served as mediator and helped to formulate, for real social needs, solutions at the level of individual autonomy, which can prepare the way for the development and integration of individuals into the contemporary world. It is a patient, educative process, working through consent and consensus, and helping to bring about gradual, durable transformation.

The vested interests in Turkey, however, oppose any modernizing transformation or the establishment of democratic norms in the country. They wish to retain the status quo, and seek to perpetuate the mechanisms of a closed society for as long as they can. Therefore, they continue to exert arbitrary controls, blocking or suspending democratic processes when it suits their interests to do so. A part of that has been their accusation that the Gülen Movement is unlawful, or has intentions that may prove unlawful. But the SMOs inspired by Gülen are institutionalized and legal in Turkey and abroad. It is true that the Movement's reflexivity has broken barriers between people from all segments of society and led many to reflect on the irrational polarization in Turkish society; it has restructured and revived collective energies through the development of new identities and new service-projects; and it has activated everyday communicative networks and raised new professionals and intellectuals. For all these reasons it is true to say that the Gülen Movement's worldview and services do indirectly affect the dominant political perspectives, but they do not infringe Turkey's (or any other country's) laws or institutions. In 2006, the Court declared that accusations of conspiracy against Gülen were unsubstantiated and so dropped the case. Gülen was acquitted.

6.1.3 The Gülen Movement as civil society actor

Chapter 4 explained how the Gülen Movement motivates people to take full advantage of their legal rights as citizens and act on their own authority so as to improve the quality of their own and others' lives. Association with the Movement is voluntary – individuals choose freely to join its associations and service-projects, and to enter and exit them without any cost. It engages their energies to implement their own development agendas. The SMOs are neither a part of governmental apparatus, acting for it, nor a conflictual agent acting against it. They emphasize social cohesion and collective organized altruism. They are not primarily commercial, aiming to serve the public and not simply to generate profits for those involved in them. They combine private structure and public purpose entitled by legal rights, and therefore provide society with private institutions serving public purposes. The Movement has proved itself as a third way, building 'social capital' in Turkey by boosting voluntary participation and competitiveness in civic services and non-political networks. Its voluntary organizations are supported by a moral sense and offer a space for citizens to educate themselves and help others. Therefore the origin, resources, target, field of action, and common features of the Gülen-inspired SMOs identify them as a civic initiative and a civil society movement.

The Movement has order-maintaining orientations, in that its activities remain within the social and structural limits, and that it does not identify a social adversary and contested resources or values. It did not come into being to react to the control and legitimacy of the System or its established norms, nor is it a vehicle for the expression by participants of inadequate assimilation of those norms. The types of service Gülen encourages – education, health, intercultural and interfaith dialogue, cooperation of civilizations – require action, and concern relationships in the everyday lives of all members of society. This action occurs at the lifeworld level and does not break the rules, so it remains always non-conflictual. However, it is also true that the Movement did not come into being through consensus over the procedures governing the control of resources – it is not out to defend the status quo governing the control of valued resources. It is, in short, not a claimant movement – it neither defends the advantages enjoyed by one group of people nor mobilizes on behalf of some other, underprivileged group (identifiable by ethnic, religious, social or political markers) to secure a better share for them of (state) resources. It altogether avoids formal politics and aims at precise, concrete, and unifying goals and services.

Those unifying goals could not be realized if the Gülen Movement promoted a special identity that isolates or insulates it from the wider society,

The Movement cannot be identified as a religious sect. It does not form a distinct entity within Islam or Turkey. It is not distinguished by having private sacred texts, or special refinements of belief or ritual practice; it has no formal leadership, no sheikh(s) or other sort of pseudo-priestly hierarchy; no ceremonies of initiation to mark affiliation, nor distinguishing costumes or emblems or other insignia of a closed group. It does not offer rewards or outcomes unattainable in real life by the ordinary means of individual and collective human effort. The authority of Gülen himself is not in even the least degree sacralized either by himself or Movement participants. He has never behaved or been accused of behaving unaccountably or arbitrarily: he has not instructed or induced anyone into deviations, violence or abuse of any sort. His teachings cover faith, religion, ethics, logic, psychological health, affective openness, and diverse philosophical reflections, especially on education: they contain no eccentric elements or coded meanings, unfamiliar to mainstream Muslims or outside observers of Islam. Movement participants are not recognized as a distinctive religious group either in Turkey or abroad.

The Movement cannot be identified as a group or faction aggregated around some idealized version (or myth) of the past. Gülen does not teach an understanding of the past that dreams of restoring sultanate or monarchy or other such model in the present. He has never seen the past as a strategy for reinforcement of the present political order, nor does he consider that a new model based upon the past can or should be reinstated. Instead, he offers models of self-improvement and social transformation: he looks for means and ends to go progressively beyond that which remains in the past. He emphatically rejects the idea of community or citizenship based on a homogenous racial, ethnic, cultural or religious identity that really existed or is fantasized to have existed in the past. Rather, he encourages the embrace of diversity as a resource, a richness in society. The Movement therefore does not invite to a flight into the myth of identity as an escapist illusion whereby the individual is magically freed from the responsibility of action in the complexities of social relationship. It reaffirms the meaning of social action as the capacity for a consciously produced human existence and relationships. This is an important and distinctive characteristic of the Gülen Movement. It means that there is no potential in this Movement for escape into a reductionism that ignores or cancels out the individual for the appropriated identity of community; it will not lapse into the pre-social, withdraw into a sect and dissolve into anachronism, utopian myth, or fantasies of magical rebirth.

The Movement has no central, dominant organization issuing or imposing a uniform doctrine. Its SMOs are in close informal contact but are institutionally and operationally independent. The volunteers who work in the Movement's highly dispersed and independent projects are secure, well-educated people, mostly graduates or post-graduates, giving freely their time and skills to provide services where they are needed. They do not as participants in the Movement draw back into themselves away from others, or break off links with social partners or sever relations with the outside world, or renounce alternative courses of action open to them. They operate in awareness of their commitment to the social field in which they belong and serve, and with which they interact. They share with the rest of the society a set of general issues, and common grounds and references. They hold that differences arising from ethnicity, beliefs, customs and traditions are richness, and should be, for the sake of the common good of all, accepted and appreciated in peaceful, respectful relationship.

The worldview of the Movement is opposed to isolationist withdrawal into an exclusivist community-based structure that would create in society ideological and ontological divisions that cannot be overcome. It does not demand a long novitiate, rigid discipline and intrusion into most or even all aspects of its participants' lives. It affirms the dilemmas of living a social life in complex systems and welcomes the responsibilities of working through those dilemmas. Its efforts in the field of education, interfaith and intercultural issues, and of transnational altruistic projects and institutions, prove it capable of processing information and emergent realities. It plays it part in peacefully addressing global concerns, and looks to identify common goals in collaboration with others while respecting indelible differences.

The Gülen Movement does not have a totalizing ideology with a claim to define and control the social field. It does not identify non-participants in negative terms. It does not designate internal or external scapegoats so as to turn aggressive energies onto itself or outwards to some 'other', individual or group. It does not conjure up a distant enemy, which would engender myth, ideology and rites. As its action is not directed towards a mythical adversary, the limits of the reference system of the Movement do not permit any aggressive and non-institutionalized mobilization to arise, or impractical demands incompatible with local realities, or any transgression of the System's compatibility limits (nationally or internationally) that may trigger conflict. Among its participants and volunteers, the ethic of responsibility combined with competitive spirit nurtures upward mobility. Such mobility is open to all and always possible since entry and exit from a project are always voluntary and carry no cost. Competitiveness for the sake of delivering better service is encouraged and predominates over primary solidarities – individuals are employed in the SMOs on the basis of professional competence rather than seniority in the Movement. This turnover in personnel not only brings fresh minds and energies into a project, it also prevents the rise of dogmatic or ideologically rigid leaders, and prevents the Movement from constructing an idealized self-image with exclusive values and from taking refuge in myth.

The proper definition of both general goals and particular objectives, the stress that is placed on ensuring the lawfulness and legitimacy of both means and ends, and the attainability and accountability of the projects that its volunteers take on, are other factors that clearly distinguish the Gülen Movement from cults and sects or other kinds of closed or exclusivist collective actors.

Far from seeking isolation or exclusivity, the Gülen Movement strives to become and act as a reconciling agent between diverse communities. Its efforts are actualized through legal, formalized and institutionalized means and goals. The Movement is thus properly identified and defined in terms of its social and multicultural relations, which underpin the projects, which in turn extend and reinforce those relations. The seeking of consensus among communities legitimates the transnational projects so that the Movement does not deviate into, or let others be led astray into, fundamentalism and sectarianism. The collective search and engagement for worldly and other-worldly well-being within the Movement has never assumed the character of militancy or sectarianism and indeed (notwithstanding the polemic of the protectionist elite in Turkey) it cannot ever do so.

That is because the social praxis of the Gülen Movement focuses on the role and needs of the *individual*, emphasizing self-reflexivity and self-realization. It addresses the individual dimension of social life; it may then be that, eventually, through the products it offers, it may affect the whole of society. Its space and the level where its new forms of social action originate are not political space or power, the space of government or regime. It educates and socializes individuals without individualizing and politicizing the social. It acknowledges that neither individuals nor a system ever undergo change at all levels at the same time and in the same way. Change requires time, sacrifice, commitment and patience, and can be achieved only through education, peace and co-operation of like-minded citizens and mutually tolerant civilizations.

Movement participants abide by the political system wherever they are, and display disinterest in gaining influence with the state apparatus. The Gülen Movement adopts forms of action and organization which are accountable and amenable to political mediation by the political system, without becoming identifiable with it. It cannot therefore be characterized as an oppositional actor.

The Gülen Movement represents its understanding through formal and institutionalized SMOs. As these institutions are mostly educational, they do not take sides with political parties or indulge in the same disputes and rhetoric. This conscious avoidance of political contention is reflected in Gülen's evaluation of Turkish history: he does not consider any action legitimate just because it would gain advantage for one's own side; neither does he accept that changing the party in power could change everything and save the country. Accordingly, the Movement does not form alliances with political parties. In contrast to political parties, its participation in social projects and social life demonstrates no interest in hierarchism or short-term gains. It sees that Islam does not need a state or political party to survive, but needs the educated, the financially well-off and a full democratic system. Also, Gülen's ideas differ from those of Islamists in that he emphasizes the entrance of Turkey and Turkish Muslims into mainstream global processes and a market economy, and in that he emphasizes intellectual development and mutual respect.

Gülen opposes the instrumentalization of religion in politics and has never advocated direct participation in party politics. He is against those who have reduced Islam to an ideology and so created a negative image of it. He distinguishes clearly between Islam, the religion, and Islam*ism*, an explicitly political ideology. Gülen says that politicizing religion does more damage, and does it more quickly, to religion than to the state. He believes religion deals above all with the immutable aspects of life and existence, whereas political, social, and economic systems or ideologies can only deal with some aspects of worldly life. Politicizing religion turns the mysterious relationship of humanity and the Divine into an ideology. This places a demand on religion to speak publicly on political issues that affect human dignity and welfare, stewardship of the environment, social justice and peace, within too narrow a framework of competing power groups, which divides communities instead of unifying them. Movement participants as citizens are actively and responsibly involved in their *polis* and are not single-issue voters or single-party loyalists.

Gülen not only directly criticizes the totalizing ideological character of Islamist political thought and activism but also argues consistently in favor of democracy and the modernization and consolidation of democratic processes, such as free elections and other principles at the core of liberal democracy today. He affirms that Islam commends government based on a social contract; it promotes the rule of law and rejects oppression against any segment of society; it promotes actions for the betterment of society in accordance with the consensus of the majority – all of this complements democracy rather than contradicting it. People elect the administrators and establish a council to debate common issues; also, society as a whole participates in auditing the administration's performance. This view of Islam could play an important role in the Muslim world by enriching local forms of democracy and extending it so that people are enabled to develop an understanding of the relationship between the spiritual and material worlds.

Gülen also points out that democracy needs to continue to develop. If human beings are considered as a whole, without ignoring the spiritual dimension of their existence, democracy could reach perfection and bring more happiness to humanity. Islamic principles of equality, tolerance, and justice can contribute to this. He argues that individual morality is pivotal to building and strengthening 'a just political order'. Thus, rather than leaving Turkey to remaining a closed society, Gülen supports initiatives for a democratic, pluralistic and free society.

As to morality and development, Gülen's forward-looking thought is a contemporary reformulation of the classical, mainstream teaching of Sufi masters like Rumi. It emphasizes the development of both heart and mind through education, engaging proactively and positively with the modern world and reaching out in dialog and a spirit of co-operation across the boundaries of religion, community, social class and nationality. Gülen has made efforts to establish dialogue among the various worldviews, cultures, religions and ethnic groups of Turkey and of the wider world. While Gülen and his thought are rooted in a faith-oriented vision of the world, his efforts for dialog extend beyond religious circles. He advocates peace, mutual respect, and dialog with ethno-religious minorities within Turkey and between nations as an integral part of Islam and of being a Turkish Muslim. That is the basis of his support for ties to the West and full membership and integration in the EU. He holds that Turkish society has much to gain from the achievements of rational knowledge in the West. By contrast, many from religious and secular protectionist circles have opposed rapprochement with the West. The Movement's work in Turkey has contributed a great deal to changing public attitudes on the value of such a rapprochement.

Gülen has also argued that combining the goals of industrialization and economic development with a form of non-dependent participation in the world system may be achieved through the democratization of Turkey. In his opinion democracy and development are interdependent and equally important, but democracy precedes development. He inspires Movement participants to strive for a society freed from hunger, poverty, gross inequalities in wealth and opportunity, and suppression of civil rights. He teaches that this can be reached only if, along with economic development, society guarantees improved forms of civic as well as political participation, equal rights, and respect for civil and cultural freedoms. He does not want change to lead to decreased participation in or isolation from the world system. The safe, reliable route to a transformation of institutions and settled mind-sets is through education, interaction, collaboration and consensus – not resort to violent or coercive means.

That is why Gülen urges people to respect the state and state organizations for the sake of what they are ideally supposed to stand for. He has criticized provocations that lead to societal tension and violence in Turkey or anywhere else. Even when speaking out against corrupted politicians, crooked party politics and dishonest dealing, people must be careful not to erode public respect for a state organization, its authority and true values. He holds that anarchic movements and actions, by destroy the atmosphere of peace, hinder free exchange of ideas, freedom of religion and conscience, and the supremacy of the rule of law and justice. He argues that 'even the worst state is better than the lack of it'. He does not sacralize the state but recognizes it as necessary, because the alternative is anarchy, chaos, and disorder. He therefore regards respect for the state and its institutions as a duty of citizenship. That is another pillar of his distancing the Movement from contentious political action.

He identifies lack of knowledge, and related problems concerning the production and control of knowledge, as the core problem in the world. It is a problem that cannot be solved through party politics but through education. Education is the key to becoming a better, productive and beneficial individual, whether one is Muslim or not. He believes that sciences, humanities and religion enhance and complement one another rather than compete and clash. His educational philosophy aims at personal enlightenment and lays equal stress on the inculcation of ethical values and a sound training in the secular sciences. The primary goal of the education in the Gülen-inspired schools is to ensure respect for objective and universal ethical values, values recognized and accepted in all cultural traditions. The schools, without exception, follow state defined curricula and are inspected by local authorities: they have never sought to teach a particular ideology or somehow prepare the ground for a seizure of power through political activism.

Before and after 9/11, Gülen condemned terrorism in clear and courageous public statements, and commented comprehensively and with considerable sophistication on the relevant issues. He explained that the fundamental principles of the religion are totally opposed to the political and ideological interpretations that underlie acts of terrorism; that these fundamental principles should be taught to Muslims and others through the education system. He urged administrators, intelligence services, scholars and community leaders to identify not only the originators but also the motivating factors behind terrorist acts. He has also averred that there are overt and covert multinational organizations who are bent on destruction and the aggravation of anxieties and fears in society.

Despite explicit statements, and despite some forty years of service-projects undertaken and carried out by the Gülen Movement, accusations are still made the Movement has a hidden agenda. Gülen has responded that he and all orthodox or Sunni Muslims reject subterfuge or dissembling in their faith and practice, and therefore do not condone it. The Gülen Movement is very explicit in its critique of conditions in countries where Islamist and subterfuge understandings prevail.

The development of political institutions in Turkey was lagging behind social and cultural change because of the system's backwardness, its bureaucratic, partisan and procedural stagnation, and its lack of qualified personnel. Realizing this, Gülen urged people to use their constitutional rights to serve society constructively and altruistically. The Gülen Movement revived the philanthropic dynamic, altruistic value and benevolence rooted in local tradition to fill the gaps left by government policies and discrimination. It mobilizes previous affiliations into a new system of relations in which they gain deeper meaning. It encourages transfer of dormant resources to the benefit of a new objective. Over time, it has transformed into a new transnational social movement capable of utilizing new resources for education and societal peace through altruistic action.

In the Gülen Movement voluntary action is justified by the belief that acting for the benefit of others is right and good and there is a moral duty to treat others fairly. This understanding is openly faith-inspired. The Movement views the world as a market where human beings can compete to win God's pleasure and approval: its maxims are 'serving people, serving God' or 'The best amongst you is the most beneficial to human beings'. Altruistic service of others is seen as an alternative and barrier to egoistic interests, and a remedy for societal discord, conflicts and violence. The Movement has been able to mobilize very large numbers of people both inside and outside Turkey: those who are not financially able give their time, thoughts, energy and moral support to collective services. The gratuitous and voluntary nature of participation and collectiveness in the action are distinguishing features of the services offered by the Movement. Projects are realized through informal, decentralized, permeable networks of friends, business associates and other like-minded people gathered round the particular objective. Projects, services, institutions and initiatives of the Gülen Movement are supported by a wide range of individual people, and also institutions and businesses. The voluntary action aims at producing benefits or advantages for subjects other than the volunteers – that is why the Gülen Movement is widely known as *hizmet*, or service for others.

An important feature of the Gülen Movement's form of altruistic action is its civic aspect. It provides many more opportunities for participation in collective action than political affiliation does. Altruistic action expresses membership in a far larger civil community than a political party. This feature is also visible in the transnational expansion of the Movement into different communities, and also in its development of services which bring participants into contact with people from ever more diverse segments of society. In interacting, participants and those with whom they come into contact in the collective action learn to negotiate, to present arguments, to be flexible and accommodate differences, to construct consensus.

The discourse and action of the Gülen Movement are shaping the consciousness that will contribute to the future development of democracy in Turkey. Gülen's call for democratization, freedom, equity, justice, and human rights, the redefinition of social and cultural objects, and the rule of law as the main basis for the regulation of the state–society relationship has symbolically confronted the vested interests in the country. He has brought about a shift towards civil society and culture, away from party politics, as new reference points in the mentality and attitudes of Turkish people. Rather than politics and confrontation, the Gülen Movement focuses on social renovations and inward transformation of individuals through science, education, dialog and democracy, and thus provides stability in times of turmoil.

6.1.4 Internal factors in the Gülen Movement

My broad conclusions from the discussion and analysis, in Chapter 5, of internal organizational and operational factors of the Gülen Movement were that its collective identity and action results from a combination of choices, values, goals, relations, services and representations, and is the outcome of conscious, laborious, intellectual and non-conflictual processes. The Movement interacts with the wider public, works within the known norms and limits, and constructs an identity. This interactive and communicative construction is cognitively framed. The Movement's ensuing identity and relationships in social life are dynamic and peaceful. Moreover, because it has been able to handle opposition to itself intellectually, to remain within the limits of the System, unaffected by environmental changes, its identity has gained a certain stability and permanence, so its collective actor is easily recognized by all. The identity of the Movement is thus the result of sequential but overlapping social and cultural factors, and has come to be recognized as non-contentious, constructive, pluralist, purposive, inclusive and peaceful. These features reveal the weaknesses of politically oriented readings of collective identity and action in current sociological approaches.

The active and social interactions in the Movement's service-networks value the views and efforts of every participant. They take part in collective reasoning on equal terms. They integrate into or contribute to relational service-networks voluntarily. They do not look to these networks as a quest for communal identity to replace or otherwise relocate primary associations based on gender, age, locality and ethnicity. Therefore, affiliation is not exclusive or alienating. Interpersonal contact is the primary vehicle of participation in the Movement. Just as there is no pressure to join, so also there is none to believe or conform: there have been no instances or accusations of coercive persuasion, manipulation of consciousness, forced self- or ego-destruction, brainwashing or psychological punishment or duress. None of these account for participation in the Movement: all participants are and remain involved as a result of free, conscious, voluntary choice. The service-networks give people resources to construct their own identity and make them responsible for that identity and their action. Through collective reasoning, they build direction and meaning for their existence. Identity in the Movement is not static – it results from an active effort and achieves continuity. Since participants willingly own and retain it, the identity is not something taken, given or imposed.

Through the relational networks, people orient themselves toward living at peace with others and become more able to reach out to other relations, goals and interests. In this way the collective, beneficial and altruistic services organized by the networks bring about the unified and homogeneous identity of the Gülen Movement.

The relationships in service networks are not hierarchical, mechanical or predetermined. One network does not impose on others a greater burden of limitations or liabilities. Relationships between as well as within networks are therefore marked by autonomy and interdependence.

While the Gülen Movement affirms its difference from all political and ideological movements and their actors, it does not cut itself off from society. On the contrary, it expresses its belonging to the shared culture of society and is recognized as a social actor for the common good and for a multicultural, diverse and pluralist society. This presupposes equality, a degree of reciprocity, and consolidation of democratic rights, practice and institutions in Turkey. The Movement's strategy is complete commitment rather than withdrawal. Participation in it leads to integration with and full commitment to the wider society. This is achieved through educational and cultural institutions and community work. The Movement co-operates with other legitimate and institutionalized organizations concerned with the same issues, developing and collaborating in joint initiatives based on compatible definitions. Therefore, the collective actor of the Movement is inclusive and integrative, and universalistic in its action and objectives.

The Gülen Movement produces new definitions and meanings by integrating the past and the emerging elements of the present into the unity and continuity of its collective actor. While the methods and means to accomplish services may change or develop, the core of the identity does not change over time and space: it holds steady. Especially during the period when Gülen was defamed there was strong support for the collective action of the Movement from a very diverse range of politicians, statesmen, civil society organizations, thinkers and journalists. This corroborates the idea that the identity of the Gülen Movement is expressive and integrative rather than alienated, alienating and temporal. It also confirms that its objectives and nature are not short-term, one-sided, partisan, conflictual and instrumental.

The Gülen Movement is a faith-inspired initiative, whose basic principles come from Islam's universal values. This does not make it radical, fundamentalist or sectarian, as it associates itself with purposive action, culture, education, communication, social relations and co-operation with others. The Movement recognizes specific levels and the plurality of levels in the construction of its action and identity. However, it does not offer to deny or annul differences, but gathers people around commonalities and mutually acknowledged references to serve humanity. This conscious collective construction of identity within a larger transnational environment and within reciprocal social relations makes the Movement increasingly self-reflexive, pluralist and integrative. So, the goals of the Movement are, once more, inclusive, universalistic, expressive and non-contentious.

There are no organizational features of the Movement that would accord to maintenance of the organization a higher priority than every other possible goal. It therefore has little to do with goal displacement. Each SMO is governed by its own internal rationale and constituted by specific relations, different societal ends, exchange and interaction between roles, and interpersonal and affective communication in lifeworlds. All SMOs are entirely located within the limits of compatibility of the System(s), and not oriented towards conflict. Individuals or service groups are connected by interdependent relationships. These relationships are negotiated, whereas the institutionalized relationships are formal and contractual.

The service-networks are manifold, variable in density, and there is division of labor in them. The Movement provides participants with access to control of resources and of the services pursued. This accounts for the strengths of the collective actor and nurtures social trust and honesty. Transparency, multiplicity, division of labor and diversity yield flexibility, adaptability, immediacy and efficacy. Furthermore, service-networks operate on their own, not from a single centre, although they maintain links to the collective actor through the circulation of information and professional personnel. Communication and exchange of experiences keep the managerially separate, autonomous networks in contact. Information, expertise, and patterns of behavior circulate, passing from one network to another, and bringing a degree of homogeneity to the whole. So, the service-networks are separate, diffused, decentralized, autonomous, homogeneous in terms of general goals, and permeable.

The Gülen Movement has participants or adherents; it does not have a system of formal membership. These participants are often more committed than those who hold membership in political organizations. In the service-networks, individuals replace one another but the projects continue. Individual needs and collective goals are not mutually exclusive. They coincide and interweave closely. The Movement becomes a means for people to transform latent potential into visible services. Continuity in the Movement is therefore not temporal, short-term, instrumental, particularistic or exclusive. The continuity between the individual or collective needs and goals is integrative, expressive, long-term, inclusive, universalistic, multiple and non-ideological.

Participation in services around a specific goal and the tangibility of the outcomes strengthen social cohesion, trust and solidarity. The external forms of mobilization, its rapidity, extension, and success reflect the inner cohesion or solidarity of the participants. The solidarity is cultural in character and located in the terrain of symbolic production in everyday life. To a certain degree, the solidarity of participants collectively is inseparable from their individual, personal quests and from their everyday affective and communicative needs. Solidarity in the Gülen Movement accompanies or naturally follows from action as a result of the accomplishment of service-projects: it is epiphenomenal. It is not the necessary condition of, nor the cause nor the goal of the formation and collective action of the Movement. It is a secondary or tertiary effect resulting from experiences and memories gained and retained from taking part in the collective action.

Movement participants do not belong only to a single network. They participate simultaneously in a number of areas of social life, in associations and networks of various kinds. These multiple belongings are a result of the complexity of human relationships. In each setting only a part of one's self, only certain dimensions of one's personality and experience, are activated. Participants are never asked when seeking integration into the multiple belongings to disrupt existing continuities. The nature of participation, commitment and personal fulfillment through multiple belongings in the Movement reveals the multiple layers of continuity – the continuity between individual and collective identity, between leisure and commitment, between self-fulfillment and participation, between calling or vocation and professionalism, between local and transnational, and between particular and general. All these continuities form the basis of material and non-material resources available in the Movement.

Participants often find inspiration in the ideas and tactics espoused and practiced by others. Multiple belongings integrate interests and facilitate diffusion. This brings openness, effectiveness, rapidity, and extension into organizational capacity, and both enables and ensures the multiple, decentralized, and diffused forms of organization and leadership that characterize this Movement. The practices of participants are also shaped by cultural representations diffused through media coverage. They learn about innovations, actions and successes in the Movement through mass media even when they have no direct connections with the networks concerned. With the help of such diffusion, the Gülen Movement has extended its action beyond Turkish national borders, developing contemporaneously and displaying significant similarities in different countries. Diffusion has also occurred in countries with no common strands of history and with few or no similarities in social and political structure. The Movement has facilitated diffusion through personal orientations, literature, conferences, the media and travel and visits. The cultural, educational, peaceful and collaborative understanding diffused through these channels has brought together different social, ethnic and religious entities around common meanings and values. Therefore, representation proves itself expressive, inclusive, multi-cultural, integrative, co-operative, productive, peaceful and efficient.

Participants are never required, or allowed, to challenge the constraints established by law or the general public. The history of the Movement has so far never shown any rupture or illegality.

The low or no cost of entry into and exit from project-networks explains the tendency of participation to become temporary, short-term and not totalizing. The plurality of goals and resources allows individuals to change networks with only minor consequences for the effectiveness of their contribution or network. Participation in the Movement is not isolationist or atomized because individuals do not join the service-networks on an individual basis, nor act or work in them out of self-interest. They always come to participate through relational channels, such as friends, neighbors, professional associates or associations. Within this Movement therefore belonging and relationship is heterogeneous and integrative.

The homogeneity of intention or goals and action coexisting with the heterogeneity of people and conditions gives greater specificity to the collective identity of the Gülen Movement. The relationship and direction is not towards radicalization and conflict; nor motivated by selective and solidaristic incentives. Rather, it is towards formalization and institutionalization of a civil, moderate, pluralistic, inclusive and progressive movement. As we have emphasized the Gülen Movement is nothing like a cult or sect or other forms of closed, exclusive grouping. Accordingly, it does not deploy ceremonial behavior, ritual, symbols, slogans, uniform dress, and other such devices to facilitate participation or to foster an identity or unity. Participation is based on information-sharing, exchange, interaction and taking an active role in the collective action, and takes the form of friendship-based circles. These relational networks tend towards informality – an aspect of their permeability and flexibility – people have simultaneously multiple interests and friendships, and have professionalized, altruistic and voluntary commitments.

At the time of joining the service-networks, individuals may well not have a profound personal involvement or commitment. Rather, their commitment and contribution grow as self-understanding and knowledge of the field in which they have come to contribute grow. This self-development progressively strengthens the participant's bond with a service-network, and may be construed as a cultural and symbolic investment. Relationships so formed and constructed tend as a result to be quieter, deeper, more binding and more enduring, than participation in short-term, single-issue mobilizations.

Coherence in the Movement comes from the self-reflexive capacity and the quality of direct participation in the collective action. This cultural, symbolic and plural form respects individual differences and needs. Sectarian solutions, marginalized ambitions or the actualization of interests formed outside the political system are not welcomed. This makes the Gülen Movement mainstream, inclusive, pluralistic, law-abiding, progressive and peaceful.

The Movement has an understanding of a permanent hierarchy of interests in society. Education, interfaith dialogue, and non-political, non-conflictual and non-violent community services and projects, improving oneself and developing social and cultural potential take priority in the movement. Within that, selection of projects looks to their practicability, legality, usefulness and effectiveness. They are never utilized or exploited by the actor of the Gülen Movement for 'a politics of signification'. The pattern of development, phase and specialization may change in secondary details from country to country. However, the central theme or goal of the Gülen Movement has been never to turn into a political, ideological, oppositional, conflictual or violent movement at any time or in any location. Participants are of course never required, but they are also not allowed, to challenge the constraints established by law or general public norms: the history of the Movement so far has never shown any departure from this principle.

The channels through which collective social power establishes and maintains itself in the Movement are the system of roles in the service-networks, consensual and adaptive exchanges among legitimate expectations and performances, progressive self-structuring according to local circumstances and ensuing mutable objectives, flexible formal structure with mechanisms open to negotiation and transaction. The service-projects are organized flexibly so as to accommodate and redefine their tasks and inner structures, in accordance with the feedback coming from the wider public and with suggestions from Gülen's counsel and his emergent interpretations of current events through the media, if such counsel is sought. Consensual decisions, societal feedback and the counsel and advice of Gülen and of other experts on specific fields and issues are each a permanent component in the Movement's growth and efficiency.

There is strong emphasis on the openness of the SMOs and their operating wholly within fields and limits defined and entitled by the System. The participants and SMOs are capable of absorbing change and producing collective and consensual decisions, attentive to feedback from inter-actor transactions. The degree of socialization or the immediate dependence on social relationships, and the will for services and modernization of SMOs indicate an integrative, adaptive, progressive, autonomous and complex social organization that, at the same time, does not ignore scholarly, consultative and conventional wisdom. The specificity of the organizational life of the Gülen Movement can thus be characterized as collective, consensual, flexible, adaptive, pluralist, participatory, democratic and progressive.

Autonomy is also an important defining feature of networks and SMOs. This is achieved through delegation, creation of a specialized body of representatives, and bureaucratic and non-bureaucratic boards based on equality. On a whole range of matters about particular projects, decision-making is not concentrated at the top, with certain individuals. There is a preference for continual turnover in network or project leadership. Representatives within networks are subject to recall at all times by those they represent. The right to take part in decision-making belongs to all who come to the network meetings. Free participation and self-willed contribution, openness and responsiveness to technical expertise and professional competence overcome the risk of oligarchies forming and charismatic leaders emerging. All these features or components are where the social power and authority generate. They require and utilize autonomous conscious decisions and the kind of participation which reflects strong beliefs about democracy, which is a lever for positive transformation.

The social composition of the service-networks includes a high percentage of people from a middle or high social position. Their high-level engagement, involvement and integration in initiatives related to education, culture, interfaith dialog, societal peace and civilizational co-operation, mean that they cannot be called or considered as socially marginal; rather, they are recognized as bearers of solid, universal ethical values or value-orientations. Individuals develop a certain vision of the world, become sensitive to local and global concerns and causes, and acquire the information and necessary skills and competence to participate effectively in service-projects. This socio-cultural background of the participants helps us to understand how and why the Movement has not become, nor shown any signs of becoming, radicalized, nor caused cleavages within itself or within Turkish society. The Movement values highly individual achievement in the private domain, and in the public domain expansion of freedom of expression, democratic participation, and self-government. The participants are educated and socially cognizant of the realities of modern life. They are not misguided, neither beguiled by a utopian vision, nor an authoritarian coercive leader. They do not defy authority to bring regime change in Turkey. In sum, they were not and they do not become marginal, underprivileged, alienated, contentious, conflictual or revolutionary.

The Movement is 'universalistic' in orientation and successful because, rather than seeking advantages only for its participants or benefiting only its constituents, it seeks to serve and benefit society as a whole. The associative, occupational, communitarian and institutional channels to handle demands are always open and help prevent segregation and conflict. This gives the Movement a fairly unified and coherent identity and reality. The sources of, and resources for, the Movement's frames of reference are education, cultural experience and awareness, religious consciousness through knowledge and study, participation in social and communitarian representative bodies, responsibility and altruism, societal accord, tolerance, peace, democracy, and co-operation of civilizations. It has proved itself able to facilitate and increase individuals' willingness to get involved in service-projects within these frames of reference, through relationship with like-minded people. As the Movement operates and focuses on education, health, media, publishing, finance and humanitarian aid and relief, the collective actor is complex, composed of many SMOs pursuing similar goals but different strategies – the like-minded people can nevertheless be and need to be as diverse as are the opportunities for action.

The interweaving of the service-project mentality with different integrative strategies makes the SMOs successful. Also, employment is based on specialized training and on formal certification organized and issued by the state(s). Employment and advancement is in accordance with knowledge, achievement, professional expertise and competence rather than seniority or preference given to friends and relatives. This makes the SMOs leading institutions in their field inside and outside of Turkey.

Some of the SMOs are formally linked institutions but not centralized. Unlike in centralized organizations, power does not reside in a single leader, or a central committee. SMOs in the Movement modify themselves in secondary details in response to local peculiarities, to opportunities and constraints deriving from local conditions. The openness, visibility and accountability of the SMOs in their local setting improves their effectiveness and enhances their legitimacy.

Team-work and competition along with co-operation and consultation between service-projects are encouraged but not competition between individuals. Competition is not for differentiation but is a motivational device to strive for the best and progress. Different initiatives may overlap and individuals may fulfill a number of functions contemporaneously due to multiple and inclusive networks. Division of labor in the institutionalized organizations is based on formal criteria, while in relational networks tasks are allocated in an informal manner, and mainly according to the skills that members are able and willing to contribute to the projects.

While the grassroots provide a flow of resources, and while the SMOs process and broadcast information and outcomes, some other networks perform a kind of intermediate representational function. This framework of complementary and collaborative effort results in diffusion of themes and experience, and circulation of volunteers and expertise. Therefore, while each SMO represents the collective purpose, no single service-network or SMO reflects or claims to represent the Gülen Movement's collective and entire interests. Nor yet does the Movement have a political wing, party or umbrella organization. It is not based on, influenced by, affiliated with, or supportive of the interests or policies of any political entity. It therefore does not and cannot generate sub-groupings, cliques or a radical flank. What sustains the SMOs is commitment to a rich and supportive culture. They are formalized and engage in institutionalized strategies, not disruptive direct-action tactics. The collective action of the Gülen Movement is not a temporary instrument but a vocation, dedication.

Gülen himself has never made, accepted or approved any claim to leadership, religious or otherwise, of the Movement. Neither he nor anyone from the Movement has claimed for him mysterious powers of insight or special access to the truth. It is self-evident that his contribution to the thought and action of the Movement has been immense; self-evident too are the breadth of his learning, his personal sincerity and piety, his profound wisdom, and the power of his personal appeal when he calls people to care for and serve others. Nevertheless, for participants in the Movement, relationship with it is not based upon intense admiration for Gülen in person, but upon the goals and meaning of the Movement's action. The relationship between Gülen and the SMOs is loose – one of inspiring and motivating, rather than organizing or controlling.

Different demands arising within local networks enter their own local decision-making process and these processes are open to the participation and control of the various components locally or regionally. The leaders in service-networks act as circulators of information, of different perspectives and experience, within the Movement. In the outside world, they act as representatives of the network(s) and usually project an image of the services with which participants can identify and from which participants draw affective gratification and motivation. However, all individuals contribute through their everyday lives to social discourses on identity, faith, and remedies for social problems. They can model disciplined and moral lives, be financially and intellectually successful, give time and money or resources to support projects nation-wide and world-wide, and raise ethical and well-rounded children. The symbolic and expressive function of a network leader is to gather and co-ordinate individuals, and to represent projects that the individuals then consensually and altruistically work for.

Resources are not allocated among the actors of the Movement. All SMOs are formally structured so that resources cannot go unaccounted for. There has been no evidence of loss or misallocation of resources, which are, in any case, under the control and supervision of the state and legal authorities. Therefore, the institutions and the workers in them continue to be perceived, inside and outside Turkey, as trustworthy and commendable in the eyes of ordinary people and the regulatory authorities.

No individual has the right to distribute power either. Absence of the allocation of resources and power by an individual does not mean that there is no authority structure within the organization. The forms assumed by the distribution of managerial power can vary within the SMOs. Leadership is decentralized: the degree of autonomy of the different components of the Movement is great and overlapping of influence can occur. However, it should be noted that while the Movement as a whole, in respect to its SMOs, is decentralized, each SMO distinguished functions and authorities in its departments or managerial organization.

Participants collectively undertake interchange and consensus on new projects. The efficiency of decision-taking is explained by the constant interaction of many volunteers, the richness of that interaction, their frequent contact and multi-scale connectivity across multiple affiliations. This results in adaptive, spontaneous, self-organizing networks with representative leaders generated from the grassroots.

With legal constitutions, SMOs have obvious internal differentiation – functional division of labor, limits to the area of influence, mechanisms of horizontal and vertical coordination, leadership and personnel selection criteria, and the conservation of written records. Beyond what is written down in text of an SMO's legal constitution, there are no written or unspoken, covert or overt system(s) of laws and regulations that govern procedure or behavior in particular circumstances.

The norms within the networks guarantee integration, and provide the critical point of reference for every process of action and transformation. The selected managerial committee and board together control, through collective reasoning, the transfer and redistribution of roles and resources. Those in a service-network can intervene in the relevant decision-making process. In addition to this participatory ethic, a commonly accepted practice of the Movement, directly derived from Islamic teachings, is that authority or power is not allocated to one who asks for it. Efficacy in the Gülen Movement comes from consensus, lack of competition for power and leadership, various forms of co-operation and exchange, reciprocal interaction, sacrifice, devotion, altruism, and working for and expecting reward only from God. Rather than a hierarchical order within SMOs, organizational or managerial order is found. Participants in service-networks have overlapping roles and functions which gives rise to an action-oriented or project-oriented structure accountable to all. These – rather than, as a reductionist outside observer might expect, authoritarian leadership by a single individual or elite group – are the variables by which the Movement achieves its objectives.

Incentives for individuals to engage in collective action include motives such as altruism, enlightened self-interest, compassion, religious conviction, or humanitarian commitment. The Gülen Movement is a call or vocation for many. Therefore, rather than self-interest and benefit calculation, or conflicts over the allocation of goods in the political market, individuals in the Movement refer to symbolic, normative and higher values and meaning. Participants can change their cultural coordinates and relational networks at any time and anywhere. This opportunity for inner and upward mobility is one of the incentives the Movement provides in equity for all participants. The urge for social mobility is strong in the Movement.

Fragmentation and schisms are less likely in the Gülen Movement for several reasons. Firstly, it does not have an ideology. What may be called the worldview or belief system of the Movement is not dogmatic, rigid or based on orthodoxy about abstract aims and ideals, whether located in an idealized or actual past. The Movement is occupied with values such as compromise, stability, protection of the life, honor and dignity of the human being, dialog and consultation, justice, equity, and human rights. Secondly, the Movement relies on social cohesion or unity of ideas, means and goals for continuous positive, constructive and non-confrontational activism rather than exclusive solidarity of its heterogeneous participants. What matters is not the number of participants but the quality of their inner commitment to voluntary, altruistic provision of services. Thirdly, the collective action does not aim by any means at ritual or sacral reaffirmation of any ideological principles or any individual(s). This prevents the radicalization of the image of action beyond its factual, practical meaning and contents. Furthermore, the project networks or the SMOs are not contentious subgroups which fail to respond to crucial needs in the political or social field, either inside or outside Turkey. Also, since there is no rigid ideology or orthodoxy to conform to, the SMOs are not looking to retrieve an original purity of the Movement or anything of that. Last but not least, there are no networks or SMOs which have broken off with any deviant or opportunist leaders or groups. For all of these reasons the Gülen Movement is prevented from decaying or breaking up into fundamentalist or regressive sects or politically oriented factions.

6.2 IMPLICATIONS FOR SOCIAL MOVEMENTS THEORY

The distinction between reality and its representation has blurred in contemporary societies. Societal processes increasingly take place at symbolic levels. Contemporary movements such as the Gülen Movement sideline the predominant forms of representation and codification; they struggle not for the institutions but against their imposition of codes and of their uniqueness in governing our relation with the world; they demonstrate the arbitrariness of the power and its domination; they strive to regain the right or capacity to redefine reality; they introduce social practices that are not solely an object of thought, an idea in the head, but actually can be lived on the ground; they recompose the various parts of the self; they orient their strategies towards the recovery of lost dimensions of humanity; they develop autonomous and gratuitous cultural models or forms of action that are not governed only by self-interested cost–benefit calculations; and they stress the spiritual dimension of human experience. All these make a contemporary analysis of the ideological dimensions of collective action more difficult.

The participation and contribution of the Gülen Movement in societal projects have different meanings for different people in Turkey. In the eyes of those who look on it favorably, the Movement recognizes that it belongs to the system and identifies itself with the general interest of Turkish society as a whole, and acts lawfully and legally within the confines granted by the System in the pursuit of collective shared objectives. However, for others, this participation and contribution are the covert claims of particular interests in a competitive context, an attempt to exert influence over the distribution of power to the benefit of 'the others' in Turkish society – notwithstanding the fact that collective cultural and altruistic services differ in nature from political participation.

The role of the political system in Turkey varies according to different cases, and differs especially from cases which have been studied in western Europe or North America. Conjunctural factors in Turkey are very different from those societies in which classical social movement theories arose and contemporary social movement theories have developed. For example, the development of liberal democracy in Turkey has been deliberately stalled several times by the actions of specific interest groups. Turkey's Islamic cultural history is another conjunctural factor which distinguishes the context of the Gülen Movement from the contexts of social movements so far examined by social movement theorists.

One of the implications of the Gülen Movement is that party politics in Turkey is unable to give adequate expression to collective demands because parties are structured to represent interests that are assumed to remain relatively stable, with a distinct geographical, occupational, social, or ideological base. Autonomy must be restored to civil society, not by collapsing it into the political dimension, but by taking the trouble to respect its distance. Yet the culture of special interest groups, as the events of February 28 1997 and the ensuing Process showed, has proved ill-prepared to undertake this task, as it has endeavored to reduce everything produced in civil society to politics, threat or manipulation. Another implication, significant for social movement theory, is that circumstances specific to Turkey over the last thirty years explain why the Gülen Movement does not map neatly onto general theoretical paradigms.

The repertoires of contention used by the radical and militant groups in Turkey, including the protectionist elite, can be persuasively explained using contemporary social movement theories. The ideology and applications of this protectionist group favors an authoritarian, tutelary attitude towards the public and an interventionist policy in respect of religion, participatory democracy and economic life. Domestic and international developments have not had much influence on their role and leadership. There is little recognition, on their part, that there may be a variety of models of social organization that could serve as a platform for Turkish identity, society, interests, in particular, and for global society and humanity in general. Because they draw on a materialistic and politicized set of values or framings shared by current social movement theories, their action can be successfully explained by those theories.

Like contemporary social movement theorists, these groups also do not acknowledge that internal motivations really influence people's action or behavior, nor do they recognize the range of such internal motivations. Instead they attribute all motivation for individuals and social movements to external factors – to the substructures of political or economic conditions.

In contrast to the protectionist elite and radical, militant groups, the Gülen Movement has proved itself successful in mobilizing inactive, dormant, but innovative energies present in Turkish and other societies. The participants have formed a large number of organizations operating across economic, political and cultural boundaries, and involved diverse people within a very short time over a large area to achieve joint projects. Unlike the protectionist elite, the Gülen Movement has shown that it can absorb pressures and ease tension within fragmented communities. It circulates and diffuses ideas, information, new patterns of action and cultures. It has transformed the potential for coercion within political systems into efforts to produce beneficial services. It has never shown any leaning toward violence, no matter what the provocation.

In spite of all the counter-mobilization by the vested interests in Turkey, the Gülen Movement has not developed any aspirations to evolve into a conflictual movement, a political party or to seek political power. On the contrary, Gülen remains determinedly in the mainstream Sufi tradition of dealing with the spiritual needs of the people, educating them, and providing stability in times of trouble. He has, as we have seen, been accused of covertly conspiring to get political power or undermine the status quo: but such accusations have been proven to be false and absurd fabrications. The overwhelming majority of the Turkish public continue to regard Gülen as a moderate Islamic scholar and do not consider him or the Movement he inspired to be subversive or conspiratorial in any way.

The Gülen Movement is not a struggle or mobilization for the production, appropriation, and allocation of a society's basic resources, nor is it engaged in conflict over imbalances of power and the means and orientation of social production; it is not materialistic, antagonistic or conflictual. Rather than referring to institutional change or to the modification of power relationships, it aims to bring interior change in persons, in their mindsets, attitudes and behavior. It teaches individuals to use their constitutionally given rights to contribute to and serve society positively. Therefore the Movement is a form of collective, purposive, non-conflictual, apolitical and organized social altruism that has arisen from civil society, which remains the boundary of its field of concern and action.

The Gülen Movement assumes a non-totalizing role as mediator of demands. It invites, and in a sense allows, society to take responsibility for its own actions within the legal boundaries. It helps to create common public spaces in which an agreement can be reached to share responsibility for a social field beyond party interests or positions. This generates openness in the system and innovative energies producing new SMOs; it develops new elites, bringing into the area of the decidable that which has been excluded, and it illuminates the problematic regions of complexity in a system. A collective actor of this character and quality is indispensable for the development of democracy and an open society in Turkey.

The participation and contribution of the Movement in societal projects affirms its belonging to and identifying with the general interest of the community. It acts lawfully and legally within the confines granted by the System in the pursuit of collective shared objectives. It does not attempt to exert influence over the distribution of power to the benefit of 'the others' in Turkish or other societies. This has two major outcomes at different levels of analysis. The first is the conclusion that it provides incentives for modernization of the political system, consolidation of civil society and pluralistic democracy, and institutional reform in Turkey. The second is that it renders previous conceptual frameworks in social movement studies inadequate and reveals the shortcomings of the categorical and biased approaches to faith-inspired communities, especially to peaceful, mainstream Muslims, and cultural Islam.

The Gülen Movement shows that other definitions and dimensions of human experience are possible and calls society to its responsibility. This is a symbolic challenge to the protectionist organization in Turkey. In the offer dimension, the Movement develops new models of social rationality. Its participants present society with cultural gifts through their actions. This concerns cultural codes, not confrontation and conflict. It allows a reappropriation of the multiformity of roles in service-work, for the very identity of the Movement depends on their success in providing services for the community. This social centrality of its collective actor, autonomous role in defining personal needs, constant mediatory relationship between welfare, health, education and the individual, family, and community, give everyday experience a function. Through its activity it visibly signals the societal and individual problems it addresses. Hence, its character arises as a symbolic challenge and the more prominent the prefiguration, the greater the symbolic challenge.

The Movement progressively modernizes its culture and organization. It has raised new qualified professionals to provide services. It employs sound rationality through the acceptable neutrality of technical expertise. It has successfully socialized and transmitted values and rules for the development of personal skills. By generalizing and accumulating the results of their actions, its service-networks and SMOs have produced interaction and mediation between institutions. The participants and the service-networks scrutinize their own limitations and this has made them reflective. All of these forms of training and work experience have yielded continuity. The Movement is successful because as a progenitor movement it has set original models and examples, and established successful institutions for other social actors to emulate.

As a contemporary movement, the modus operandi of the Gülen Movement is to fashion new meanings for social action and serve as a vital engine of innovation and peaceful transformation through education, interaction, and co-operation. To Movement participants, the contentious or political dimension stipulated by theorists of contemporary collective action and social movement theory often represents nothing more than a residue. Therefore, politically oriented (or motivated) reading of social movements should modify or broaden its perspectives if it is to be able to analyze movements such as the Gülen Movement effectively. Restricting analysis to the purely political dimensions of the observed phenomena (such as a clash with authority) means surrendering to reductionism. Such reductionism ignores the specifically socio-cultural dimensions of a collective action and focuses too heavily on the readily measurable features with high visibility.

As a faith-inspired civil-society initiative for altruistic educational projects and services, the source, origin, consequences and implications of the ideational and social praxis of the Gülen Movement are therefore also quite different from those in movements hitherto explored in social movement theory. In particular, altruistic service outweighs the other dimensions and thus gives a particular character to the Gülen Movement. This dimension of altruism in social movements is currently underplayed, denied or explained away in social movement theory. The importance of altruism as an internal factor in social movements needs to be recognized in future as a criterion or tool of analysis.

Social movement theories and theorists are relatively unfamiliar with peaceful faith-inspired movements that have arisen in Muslim societies or communities since the beginning of the twentieth century. Because the Gülen Movement originated and mobilized in a predominantly Muslim population, motivations for participation include values drawn from Islam, including altruism and other non-materialist values. The current social movement theories are unable to describe the Gülen Movement adequately because of their reductionism when dealing with faith-inspired movements generally and Islamic movements in particular – because they do not see or ignore the movement's framing and internal factors.

Furthermore, when analyzing social movements which meet counter-mobilization, it must be remembered that at any given time all the action of a social movement is not directed at the counter-mobilizing force and all the action of the counter-mobilizing force is not directed at one specific social movement. This is because the 'adversary' is also a social actor and may have multiple aims, some of them unconnected with the other social movement or actor. That is, neither is effectively limited by its opponent. This leads to the conclusion that where a social movement, such as the Gülen Movement encounters counter-mobilization as it has from the protectionist elite in Turkey – it may not be appropriate to analyze the action of both social actors in the encounter using the same criteria. For example, those who have counter-mobilized against the Gülen Movement are motivated in ways that are more 'predictable' for current social movement theories. Their action is contentious and materialistic, they are consciously engaged in a struggle to retain control of material resources and political power, and they draw on a set of values or framings which are more amenable to analysis by current social movement theories. If differences in internal factors of the mobilizing and counter-mobilizing force are not included in the analysis, then the recognition of the action of one party, for example the protectionist elite, may lead the researcher to a reductionist analysis of the other, here the Gülen Movement.

The identity or nature of the Gülen Movement is civic, social, interpersonal, consensual, affective, informal and integrative. It is not short-term, instrumental and particularistic. It is purposive and professionalized; organized, contractual and formal. It is cultural and vocational; self-reflective and altruistic. It is not contentious, political, marginalized, exclusivist and violent. It is project-based, educational, inclusive and universalistic. It is long-term, locational and transnational; pluralist, collaborative, democratic, mediating, civilizing and peaceful. The Gülen Movement is an apolitical, philanthropic, inter-civilizational civil society actor, whose efforts are most succinctly and aptly described as *collective social altruism*. In all times and places, Gülen and Movement participants have acted meaningfully to reduce aggression and discord, and proven that they are on the side of peace and co-operation.

APPENDICES

APPENDIX 1: WHAT IS DEEP STATE OR GANG?

(by Mehmet Ali Birand / *Turkish Daily News*, Saturday, June 3, 2006

We are facing a confusion of concepts. What is 'deep state?' Who are its members? And there are these 'gangs' people are talking about. The two should not be confused. I have prepared a dictionary for those who are interested. There are some often used concepts, the meanings of which the public knows very little about. We know what we are talking about, but these concepts create confusion among the public.

The questions are: 'What is the deep state?' and 'What is a gang?'

'Deep state' as a concept is understood by the public as representing elements of the military, police, National Intelligence Organization (MİT), the gendarmerie, the judiciary, some journalists and scientists and some youth wings of political parties. Deep state is a concept. It is not an organization or an association. However, it is believed that some people who think in the same way sympathize with some groups (gangs) that act in accordance with their beliefs.

A 'gang', on the other hand, can be divided into two categories.

According to public perception, one type of gang exploits the state's sympathies to commit public acts and flood the streets in the name of the state but in exchange is allowed to be involved in a range of crimes, including organized crime. These are just wannabe mafia groups. Among their members are well-known gangsters. They say they work for the state but are involved in drug trafficking and other illegal activities and are tolerated by the police. From time to time (especially in the 1990s) they were utilized by MİT, the police and the gendarmerie, some believe. They are known to have been involved in many assassinations and unsolved murders.

The second type of gang is one that solely seeks financial benefit for its members. Among their members are retired military and police officials and some civilians who call themselves 'patriots'. Generally, members have links to some of the security institutions of the state. They are secretly supported and are provided with guidance. However, the state is a strange entity. It uses others to get things done. But when things change it targets the same groups it used and sends them to jail. Our history is full of such occurrences.

Deep state members, beware!

APPENDIX 2: REASONED DECISION REVEALED: GÜLEN DOES NOT AIM AT CHANGING CONSTITUTIONAL SYSTEM

(Zaman, Saturday, 10 June 2006 at http://en.fgulen.com/content/view/2258/14/)

The Ankara 11th High Criminal Court has revealed the reasons promoting the acquittal of Fethullah Gülen.

The reasoned decision resolved that "There is no evidence proving that Gülen aimed at changing the Constitutional System or resorted to force and violence. On the contrary, he was threatened by fundamentalist terrorist organizations for his friendly attitudes towards the state."

The reasoned decision suggested the claims that Fethullah Gülen and associated institutions aimed at changing the constitutional system were not proven, and that Gülen never made a statement in relation to this issue, and that those claims were only comments and presumptions.

'No evidence was found to support the case; on the contrary, he was threatened by fundamentalist terrorist groups for his friendly attitudes towards the state. As it is stated in the law, at least two people are needed for the establishment of an organization, and as the file does not include another suspect; on the charges of organization and structure, the court was unable to prosecute. Fethullah Gülen and his associate can not be tried within law No. 3713 of the Counter Terrorism Act as charged in police reports, as the described crime and the elements of any crime do not exist in accordance with the 1st item of law No. 3713 of the Counter Terrorism Act.'

The court verdict noted that Gülen should be acquitted on the grounds of conscience and law, in accordance with the legal legislation and the evidence presented.

The court also awarded payment of expenses and court costs to the Turkish treasury.

APPENDIX 3

Questionnaire A was a closed questionnaire of 41 questions: the possible responses were Strongly Disagree (abbreviated as SD), Agree (A), Neutral (N), Agree (A) and Strongly Agree (SA).

Questionnaire A

A	Please put a cross (X) in one box only. Thank you for your cooperation.	SD	D	N	A	SA
1	I have material, personal and other expectations from the GM.	965	12	1		
2	There is a difference between my expectations before and after joining the GM.	756	18		204	
3	I feel and have developed a sense of ownership over objects in the GM.	895	83			
4	The GM devotes a considerable share of its resources to new projects, alternative openings and development.				39	939
5	The GM devotes a considerable share of its resources to the task of managing complexity, of consolidation of group solidarity, and of avoidance of disaggregation.	893	85			
6	We and the GM have an ideology.	971	7			
7	The GM will turn into a political and conflictual movement.	978				
8	The GM will turn into a sect or a cult.	978				
9	There is sacral celebration of Gülen and others in the GM.	970	8			
10	I have seen, heard of or experienced anachronistic and unrealistic things in the GM.	895	83			
11	The identity of the GM has isolated/alienated me from society.	978				
12	The GM reconciles and unites people on common grounds and references.				22	956
13	The GM has become a source of privilege for me in society.			4	145	829
14	There exists an overt and covert challenge to the System(s) by the GM.	959	19			
15	All the services given by the GM are a means to reach other motives, goals and ideologies.	978				
16	The GM calls for deeper integration of individual and/or collective practices.				33	945
17	The GM is reducible to a linear and easily recognizable form.	952	20	1	5	
18	There is unity of ideas, means and goals in the GM.	956	22			

A	Please put a cross (X) in one box only. Thank you for your cooperation.	SD	D	N	A	SA
19	There is a procedure and prerequisites to be admitted into the GM.	893	77		8	
20	I can know if a person is associated with the GM by checking his/her discourse and action.		1	3	23	951
21	Those who speak for and stand for the GM in public are fixed individuals.	870	103		5	
22	Identity changes over time and space in the GM.	901	76	1		.
23	Identity is something given and taken.	963	14	1		
24	Identity comes with intentions, services and action.		15		24	939
25	No matter what happens, I always stay in and stand by the GM.	968	10			
26	The GM has killed my speed and momentum in life.	951	27			
27	There are differences between the organizational apparatus and the general interest of the movement.	973	5			
28	I believe there exist different interests in the GM.	971	7			
29	I believe different interests compete for power in the GM.	965	19	1	3	
30	My concern is for the self preservation of the GM and solidarity.	863	77		38	
31	My concern is for the alternative projects, new openings and new relationships.		18		78	884
32	There are dissatisfied elements in the GM because of its management.	961	15	2		
33	Factions exist in the GM.	978				
34	There is a huge differentiation in the allocation of incentives, rewards and resources in the GM.	857	121			
35	Opinions, views and discourse are produced by and attributed to ideologues.	967	8		3	
36	The elites in the GM exploit opportunities and individuals to affirm themselves or to consolidate their positions.	971	7			
37	Control is applied to people's routines by the apparatuses of regulation which exact identification and consensus.	899	75		4	
38	The goals and objectives of the GM are clear.				9	969
39	There is respect in the GM for different views and diversity.		2	1	83	892
40	The GM is located at several different levels of the social system simultaneously.		3	1	79	895
41	The GM encourages the development of formal skills of action, decision-making and continuous learning.				19	959

APPENDIX 4

Questionnaire B comprised 13 questions with open-ended answers.

Questionnaire B

1 What comes into your mind first when someone mentions the GM?
(List your first five ideas only.)
- education and useful community services
- generosity–sacrifice
- altruism
- societal accord and peace
- world peace
2 What have you gained in the GM? (List first five gains only.)
- social, societal, professional and spiritual gains
- material and immaterial gains
- faith and peace
- hope
- friends-friendship, brotherhood/sisterhood
3 What are your short term goals in the GM? (List the first five only.)
- far better and higher quality educational services
- more educational institutions
- appealing and responding to many more people
- becoming more successful and more active
- getting more people to hear the community's message
4 What are your long term goals in the GM? (List the first five only.)
- to be useful/beneficial to all, to take services to many more
- to become the best, to do the best
- to earn God's approval and pleasure
- to be come more knowledgeable, successful and active
- to qualify to serve at better institutions
5 How did you join the GM? (List the first five only.)
- exemplary friends from the GM and their conduct and sincerity
- reading Gülen's works and listening to his lectures
- the overall meaning and the message of the altruistic services
- the worldview of the GM
- people at my immediate environment, neighbors, and relatives
6 What comes into your mind when Gülen is mentioned?
(List the first five ideas only.)
- sincerity, love of God and people and creation
- scholar, intellectual/science, knowledge and wisdom
- enthusiasm to serve (God and people)
- integrity, profound insight, foresight
- concern, pain and sacrifice for others

7   Have you found whatever you expected in the GM?

(Answer in not more than five words.)

- more than I expected
- everything I expected and more
- everything in the sense of intellectual, spiritual, vocational, social, professional

8   What would you do if you came back to life again?

(Answer in not more than 10 words.)

- would be the same and do the same job
- the same job-the same community/movement
- not different but almost something similar in the movement
- would wish to go to more poorer/undeveloped places to serve/to be useful
- not a director but a teacher at an educational institution

9   What is <u>not</u> permitted in the GM? (List five things only.)

- politics, violence and reactionary action/attitudes
- conflictual-oppositional action, violence
- personal and material gain by means of services
- any action/initiative without any collective reasoning, discussion and con-sultation
- extremism, immorality, bad habits

10   How do you make and take decisions in your unit?

(Answer in not more than 10 words.)

- with my friends/colleagues at my department/in my professional unit
- colleagues and administration all together
- all people at the committee/institution together

11   Where does your identity come from? (List five elements only.)

- deeds, action and intention
- deeds/work and its results
- community action, deeds and goals in the GM
- what the GM made me earn and gain in the services we give
- personal choice and character

12   What is your family background? (Answer in not more than five words.)

- urban-culture (78%)
- agricultural (22%)
- middle-class (44%)
- upper middle class, (20%)
- academic achievement (higher education) (18%)
- poor (18%)

13   How long have you been in the GM? (Number of years only)

- 2–3   (13)
- 4–5   (33)
- 6 –7   (79)
- 8–10   (50)
- 10+   (25)

APPENDIX 5: SPECIAL USAGES

I have not used any terms that are either unusual generally, or unusual in sociological discourse about social movements – any specialist terms will be easily understood in the contexts where they occur. However, a handful of words or expressions are used which, because of the specific (Turkish) context of this case study, have particular shades of meaning or resonance that may not be intelligible from the context. I list these words/expressions below in alphabetical order for ease of reference.

- *Atatürkism* or *Kemalism:* the official political system and 'ideology' of Turkey, named after Mustafa Kemal Atatürk, who laid down the ideology of his Republican People's Party in six 'fundamental and unchanging principles' – 'republican, nationalist, populist, etatist, laicist, and revolutionary' – later incorporated into the constitution to define the basic principles of the state.

- *The Chief of General Staff:* the Commander of the Armed Forces. In wartime, he acts as the Commander in Chief on behalf of the President. Commanding the Armed Forces and establishing the policies and programs related with the preparation for combat of personnel, intelligence, operations, organization, training and logistic services are the responsibilities of the Turkish General Staff. Furthermore, the Turkish General Staff coordinates the military relations of the Turkish Armed Forces with NATO and other friendly nations.

- *counter-mobilization:* used in this study to refer to the systematic efforts by the *protectionist elitists* to oppose the activities of all civil society movements in Turkey, and in particular the Gülen Movement.

- *dominant interests:* i.e. the interests of the *elitist-statist-secularist* group who wield power in Turkey, not always from behind the political stage.

- *elitists:* those who believe in their inherent superiority over others with an unquestionable right to preeminence, privilege and power. In Turkey, the *elitists* are the traditional Republican clique who define themselves as superior because of their 'Western' cultural preferences and practices, education, attitudes, etc. Their assumption is that these Western qualities give them a greater right to govern, if necessary by overturning the will of the people.

- *February 28 Process:* this refers to the sequence of measures and events that followed the *soft coup* of 1997: 'On the last day of February 1997, the regular monthly meeting of the military-dominated National Security Council [...] gave the Welfare-True Path coalition government a list of eighteen measures to be implemented without delay, including a clampdown on 'reactionary Islam'. [...] The military spent the next months waging a relentless public-relations campaign that turned society against the government and eventually forced the resignation on June 18 of Erbakan and his cabinet. The noose on civilian politics remained tight after that. Press freedom was severely curtailed, with many journalists and other public figures targeted by military-orchestrated smear campaigns. [...] What is called within Turkey 'the February 28 process' was not limited to the political wing of the Islamist movement. Islamic networks, sects, associations, and individuals were targeted for excoriation and sometimes prosecution or court-ordered bans on their activities.'*
- *hizmet:* word of Arabic origin (literally, 'service'), used in Turkish to mean disinterested voluntary beneficial service to others, especially provided by faith-inspired communities; the preferred term among participants in the Gülen Movement to describe their attitude and work.
- *Islamic:* adjectival form derived from Islam, referring to the traditional teachings of the religion, and expressly distinguished from *Islamist.*
- *Islamism, Islamist:* politically motivated understanding among Muslim activists, who believe in evolutionary or revolutionary transformation in society and political systems; Islam understood as ideology.
- *laicism:* a militant (Jacobin) form of *secularism* that demands the exclusion of religious belief and practice from public life, and expects to use state power to achieve that exclusion. In Turkey until now there has been little real distinction between *laicism* and *secularism.***
- *mobilization:* used in this study to refer to the efforts of the participants in the Gülen Movement to direct resources to achieve their goals in the form of service-projects.
- *multiple belongings:* simultaneous, purposive and voluntary participation in or affiliation to various social networks, projects and *SMOs.*
- *National Security Council (NSC):* a council of state consisting of the President, Prime Minister, a number of other ministers (as necessary and relevant to the issues being discussed), five top-ranking generals

from the Chief of Staff, plus other generals (the number of generals always exceeding the number of civilians on the council). The purpose of the *NSC* is to strongly advise the government on matters of national security, though its remit has gradually been extended to cover other aspects of Turkish public life, such as finance and culture.

- *protectionists:* those in the established leadership of Turkey with a strict nationalist, *secularist* and bureaucratic-authoritarian understanding who intend to perpetuate the status quo.

- *secularism:* legal and institutional separation of church and state, which, in the case of Turkey is understood to mean the separation/expulsion of religious authority from the state. In practice, *secularism* means regulation by the state, to a considerable extent, of the practice of religion through the Presidency of Religious Affairs (appointment of prayer-leaders to mosques, vetting content of sermons, religious education, etc.) The term *secularist* is widely used in Turkey to describe those who are actively opposed to religious practice in the public sphere – see *laicism* – and is so used in this study.

- *Social Movement Organization (SMO):* any formally established and institutionalized organization whose operations and goals coincide with the preferences of a social movement.

- *soft coup:* in February 1997, the newly elected government of Turkey was induced to resign by an open threat from a select group of generals at the Turkish Chief of Staff of a military coup. The government stood down and the military assumed control of the civil authority of the state. The *soft coup* has sometimes been referred to also as the 'postmodern coup'.

- *State-owned Economic Enterprises (SEEs):* Kamu Iktisadi Teskilatlari (KITs); monopolies, other state-sponsored and privileged businesses set up by the state.

- *statism, statists:* the doctrine that the state in Turkey should hold control of the major part of political and economic activity in the country and that this control should remain in the hands of the Republican *elitists.*

---

* Özel, 2003:87.

** "In fact, Turkish secularism derives from the radical Jacobin laicism that aims to transform society through the power of the state and eliminate religion from the public sphere." (Berkes 1998 in Yavuz & Esposito 2003)

- *symbolic challenge:* the production of new meanings, new social relations and services, which point up failures in state policy or inadequacies in the worldview of the *dominant interests*. (Different from physical or political challenge, which directly confronts the legitimacy of the authority of the state or its agents.)
- *vested interests:* the privileged group who currently enjoy financial and status benefits from the political and economic status quo in Turkey, and who are determined to hold on to their privileges by any means (including association with organized crime) and whatever the cost to the people or the society.

NOTES

0. INTRODUCTION

1   See §4.1.1, 4.1.3, 5.2.1. 5.2.6, 5.2.7, 5.3, and 6.1.3.
2   Turam, 2007:74–6.
3   See §3.2.10 and Appendix 2.
4   Turam, 2007:ix.

1. THEORETICAL BACKGROUND: COLLECTIVE ACTION AND SOCIAL MOVEMENTS THEORY

1   Garner, 1996:44.
2   Buechler, 2004:47.
3   Mamay, 1990.
4   Byrne, 1997:39–40; Aberle, 1982:315–16; Giddens *et al.*, 2004; Macionis, 1995:617.
5   Melucci, 1999:14.
6   Browning *et al.* 2000:59.
7   For more on the origins and identities of the 'classical' approaches, and differences about them, see Tilly, 1978:12–51; McAdam *et al.* 1988:696; Mayer, 1991:49; Jackall & Vidich, 1995:vii; Swatos, 1998; Neuman, 2006:79–109.
8   Snow, 2004:381; Williams, 2004:91–115, at 92–3; Melucci, 1999:287–9; Della Porta & Diani, 1999:2, 11.
9   Buechler, 2004:50.
10 Mayer, 1995:171; Scott, 1995:5–11, 45; Eyerman & Jamison, 1991:23.
11 Buechler, 2004:51.
12 Byrne, 1997:39, 40; Eyerman & Jamison, 1991:23–4; Melucci, 1999:288.
13 Zald & Ash, 1966:329.
14 McCarthy & Zald, 1977:1217–18.
15 Della Porta & Diani, 1999:16.
16 Snow *et al.*, 2004:6.
17 Melucci, 1999:29–30.
18 Cohen, 1985:664.
19 Gerlach & Hine, 1970:49–50.
20 Gamson & Wolfsfeld, 1993:115.
21 Tarrow, 1996a:874.
22 For more, see Chapter 1.2.

23   Melucci, 1999:84; Della Porta & Diani, 1999:1–2.

24   Snow *et al.* 2004:6.

25   Koopmans, 2004:40.

26   Lofland, 1996:177.

27   Göle (1997c) in Bozdogan & Kasaba, 81–99.

28   Melucci, 1999:31, 50, 99; Göle, 1997c (online text); Edwards & McCarthy, 2004:120.

29   Melucci, 1999:113.

30   Edwards & McCarthy, 2004:120.

31   Oberschall, 1993:337.

32   Earl (2004:513) lists the theorists: Cohen (1985), 'Strategy or Identity'; Melucci (1985), 'The Symbolic Challenge'; Offe, 1985:817–68; Pichardo, 1997:411–30. For more, see §3.2.1.

33   Koopmans, 2004:25.

34   Zunes, 1999:41–2.

35   For list of scholars involved see McAdam *et al.* 1996b:xi–xii.

2.   HISTORICAL BACKGROUND

1   UNESCO, 1963:98; Lewis, 1965:247–50.

2   Winter, 1984:185–8; Howard, 2001:193–4; Margulies & Yildizoglu, 1997:144–53; Ahmad, 1993:57; Metz, 1996:xxv.

3   Olson, 1989.

4   Aybars, 1975:228; Olson, 1989; Zurcher, 1994[1998]:180; Sluglett, 1976:116–25; McDowall, 1997:194–8; Kılıç, 1998:91–103; for all the verdicts of the ITs, see http://bucatarih.sitemynet.com/cum/ millimucadele/bthazirlik.html.

5   For more on Nursi, see *The Muslim World* (1999).

6   Mardin, 1989:90–102; Yavuz, 1999:584–605; Howard, 2001:95–6.

7   Ali, 1955:44; Howard, 2001:96.

8   Kongar, 1986:19.

9   *TIME*, 2003:A5; Kongar, 1986; Sakallioglu, 1996:234–5.

10   Arat, 1994:57–78.; Lewis, 1965:405; Kandiyoti, 1991:41; Lebor, 1997:222–3; Göle, 1991:57, 1997a:65; Eren, 1963:100–2; Metz, 1996:116–17.

11   Ahmad, 1993:80; Lebor, 1997:223; *Turkish Daily News*, 2001a; Howard, 2001:98–9; Lewis, 1965:419; Lewis, 1999:37–41.

12   Kamu Iktisadi Teskilatlari (KITs).

13   Özbudun, 1981a:228–40; Howard, 2001:99–102; Sönmez, 2003; *Cumhuriyet Ansiklopedisi, 1923–1940* (2002:182); Berkes, 1959:17; Özay, 1983:57; Metz, 1996:xxv, 124, 153.

14   Lewis, 1984:204; Hobsbawm, 1990:110; THC (Turkish History Committee) ([1930] 1996:466–7.

15   Toprak, 1981:42–3; Howard, 2001:103–4; Kasaba, 1997:29; www.ataturk.com/culture.htm.

16 Toprak, 1981:42.

17 Howard, 2001:105; *TIME*, 1933a:64; *TIME*, 1933b:18; Lewis, 1965:408.

18 Mardin, 1973:169–91; Sunar, 1998:141–54; Howard, 2001:106–7; Kongar, 1986:19–68; also <http://cgi.dostweb.com/pano/messages/ 25/2036.html?1047313781>.

19 *Turkish Daily News*, 2001a:no.464; see also <www.turkishnews.com/Ataturk/founder.htm>.

20 Özbudun, 1981a:91; Lebor, 1997:227; Howard, 2001:107–9; Metz, 1996:xxvi; Toprak, 1995:91.

21 Kongar, 1986:19.

22 Norton, 1995:153; Bozdogan & Kasaba, 1997:4–6; Göle, 1996b:60; Lebor, 1997:223; Kongar, 1986; Mardin, 1973:182.

23 Çandar, 1998a.

24 Howard, 2001:109–10; Metz, 1996:40.

25 The tax ended in late 1945.

26 Temkin, 1999:34–6; Metz, 1996:102; Howard, 2001:111–2; Cohen, 2001:R18; Ross, 1982:89–91.

27 International co-operation to 'promote and encourage respect for human rights and for fundamental freedoms for all.' For details, see <www.stradigma. com/english/july2003/documents/uncharter.doc>.

28 Howard, 2001:113, 116–7; Metz, 1996:40.

29 UNHCHR, 2001:5; Karaca, 1997; Ahmad, 1977:12; Howard, 2001:117; Bagci, 2000; Metz, 1996:40.

30 Howard, 2001:117–9; Metz, 1996:41.

31 Erdoğan, 2006: 17–45.

32 Ertürk, 1997; Howard, 2001:119–20; Metz, 1996:xxvii.

33 UNHCHR, 2001:5–6; Howard, 2001:120.

34 Such as the Sabanci and Koç groups.

35 Howard, 2001:120–3.

36 Howard, 2001:123; Kalaycioglu, 1997:123.

37 Shankland, 1999:38.

38 Criss & Bilgin, 1997; Hale, 1994:94–9; Howard, 2001:123–4, 127–31; Ahmad, 1977:147–76.

39 Howard, 2001:124–6; Metz, 1996:41–2.

40 Erdoğan, 2006:29–49.

41 Erdoğan, 2006:49–93.

42 Howard, 2001:134.

43 Metz, 1996:42; Howard, 2001:134–5.

44 Pugsley, 2007.

45 Howard, 2001:135–6; Çevik, 1997.

46 The number of soldiers has always been more than the civilians in the NSC.

47 Howard, 2001:136.

48 Bagci, 2000; Howard, 2001:136–7; Kongar, 2003.

49   Hale, 1994:94–9, 123–8, 138; Yenen, 2000; Metz, 1996:43.

50   The Justice Party (composed mostly of former Democrats) took 158 seats, the New
      Turkey Party (the breakaway Democrats) 65, and the Republican Peasants' Nation
      Party (rightist) 54.

51   Howard, 2001:137–9.

52   *Ibid.*, 139.

53   In 1969, the party changed its name to the Nationalist Action Party.

54   For more on Turkish nationalism, see Çağlar, 1990:79–101; Howard, 2001:139–40;
      Çevik, 1997; *Turkish Daily News*, 2001a.

55   *Turkish Daily News*, 2001a; Metz, 1996:46; Howard, 2001:140–1.

56   See <www.iso.com.tr>; Howard, 2001:141–2.

57   Metz, 1996:46–9, 164. For more on terror organizations in Turkey (1960–70), see
      <www.teror.gen.tr/english/turkey/leftist/1960.html>.

58   Howard, 2001:145–7; for more, see <www.cyprus-conflict.net/Ball%20-%2064.htm>.

59   UNHCHR, 2001:8; <www.teror.gen.tr/ english/turkey/leftist/1960.html>.

60   Howard, 2001:143–7.

61   Erdoğan, 2006:68–73.

62   *Ibid.*, 76–7.

63   *Ibid.*, 83–94.

64   *Ibid.*, 95–120.

65   *Ibid.*, 120–58.

66   Metz, 1996:49; Cornell, 2001:112; Howard, 2001:147; Dodd, 1983:12.

67   *Devlet Guvenlik Mahkemesi (DGM)*.

68   Cemal, 1998; Howard, 2001:147–8.

69   European Parliament (2000:9; <www.kibris.gen.tr/ english/index.html>; Metz,
      1996:318; Howard, 2001:148–51.

70   Howard, 2001:151–2.

71   *Ibid.*, 152–3; For more about its role and convictions, see on <www.tusiad.org> and
      'TUSIAD's By-law Article 2a'.

72   Ayata, 1997:67–9.

73   Howard, 2001:153; Metz, 1996:51–2; for details of the violent and terrorist groups
      and their killings by years, see CIPU-Ind.Homeoffice Country Information and Poli-
      cy Unit (Home Office) (2001:Annex C:1–2, Annex D:1–10.

74   Howard, 2001:153–4, 158–9; Metz, 1996:60–1; Kılıç, 1998:91–103.

75   Metz, 1996:153–4; Howard, 2001:155.

76   <http://en.fgulen.com/content/view/1055/12/>.

77   *Ibid.*

78   *Ibid.*

79   *Ibid.*

80   Howard, 2001:158; Metz, 1996:60–1.

81   Barkey, 2000:87–106; Howard, 2001:159.

82 For detailed discussion of internal and external enemies, see Özbudun, 1996:133–57; Howard, 2001:159–60.

83 *Ibid.*, 160–1; Metz, 1996:154–5.

84 Purvis, 2002:21; Greenwald, 1986; UNHCHR, 2001:18; *Turkish Daily News*, (1996d), (2001b).

85 Tutkun, 1998:109–29.

86 For details of the institutions, see Council of Higher Education (1996:38–97, and Tutkun, 1998; Howard, 2001:162–3.

87 Dorsey, 1997:44–58; Howard, 2001:163.

88 Hale, 1994:256–7; Howard, 2001:163–4; UNHCHR, 2001:8–9; Mater & Kurkcu, 2001; *Turkish Daily News*, 2000e.

89 Howard, 2001:164–5.

90 Hale, 1994:267–8; Metz, 1996:311; Howard, 2001:165.

91 <http://en.fgulen.com/content/view/1055/12/>.

92 Ficici, 2001:6–7, 10–13; Howard, 2001:165–6; Metz, 1996:154–6.

93 In the late 1980s, the state employed 30 percent of all non-agrarian workers.

94 For details, see Ficici, 2001; Howard, 2001:166–7.

95 Heper, 1990:460–71; Howard, 2001:164; *Turkish Daily News*, 2002.

96 Social Democrat Party.

97 Metz, 1996:68–9, 258–9; Howard, 2001:167–8.

98 Howard, 2001:169.

99 Shankland, 1999:27–8. About these schools, see above, p. 22, n.1.

100 Aktaş, 1990.

101 Özdalga, 1999:426; Ahmad, 1993:219–22; Howard, 2001: 169–70.

102 Göle, 1994:213; Metz, 1996:106.

103 Howard, 2001:170.

104 For all those discussions, see *Cumhuriyet*, on January 7, 8, 11, 17, 19, 1987; *Cumhuriyet* January 8, 1987, 'The Turban Cannot be worn for religious reasons'; 'The ban on the Turban is in the Constitution', *Sabah* February 2, 1997; and Göle, 2002:173–90.

105 See Göle, 1997b:46–58; *id.*, 2000:91–118; and Olson, 1985:161–70.

106 Metz, 1996:63–4.

107 Zurcher, 1998:365; Howard, 2001:172–3; Metz, 1996:64–8.

108 The Prime Minister in 1991.

109 For the relevant references see §2.2.16.

110 Founder and Secretary-General of the Patriotic Union of Kurdistan (PUK), President of Iraq since 2005.

111 McDowall, 1997:440; UNHCHR, 2001:11–12; Howard, 2001:173–4; Metz, 1996:xxxvi, 280–3, 306–7.

112 Howard, 2001:175–6; Metz, 1996:xxv–xxxviii, 282.

113 Howard, 2001:176; Metz, 1996:157–9.

114 This body answers to the office of the Prime Minister.

115 Howe, 2000:27–8, 211–3; Howard, 2001:176–7; Metz, 1996:xxxix.

116 Mason, 2000:66; Howard, 2001:177–8; Metz, 1996:267–9; Lebor, 1997:231–3.

117 *Turkish Daily News*, 1996b; Silvestri, 1999:178; Couturier, 1996:A3.

118 *Turkish Daily News*, 1997.

119 Aliriza & Baran, 1997; Howard, 2001:178–9; Dorsey, 1997:44–58; Howe, 2000:139–44.

120 Shankland, 1999:110, 204–8; Howard, 2001:179; Erdoğan, 1999:25–49.

121 Aras & Bacik, 2000:51.

122 *Turkish Daily News*, 1999d; Çevik, 2000d; Aliriza & Baran, 1997; Dorsey, 1997:44–58; *New Europe*, 1997; Karaman & Aras, 2000:58.

123 Kinzer, 1997.

124 Çevik, 1998; *Turkish Daily News*, 1998.

125 Aliriza & Baran, 1997.

126 *Zaman*, 2003a; *Turkish Daily News*, 1996d; UNHCHR, 2001:181.

127 UNHCHR, 2001:18; Howard, 2001:181; *Turkish Daily News*, 1996a.

128 Makovsky & Sayari, 2000:6.

129 Pope & Pope, 1999:352; Howard, 2001:181–2; Oruç, 1999; Çevik, 2000c; Komisar, 1997; Klose, 1997:4.

130 US Department of State, 2001:10; Howe, 2000:50; Howard, 2001:182–3; Komisar, 1997; Oruç, 1999; Barlas, 2006.

131 Howard, 2001:183; *Turkish Daily News*, 1999b.

132 US Department of State, 2001:10; Howard, 2001:183–4.

133 *Ibid.*, 184–5.

134 Belge, 2003.

135 Çevik, 1999c; Howard, 2001:185; Kinzer, 2001:41–8.

136 Howard, 2001:186.

137 Çevik, 2007.

138 Hobsbawm, 1990:20–3; Özbudun, 1981b:37.

139 Tapper & Tapper, 1987:1–78; Tapper, 1991:282–4.

140 Bozdogan & Kasaba, 1997:4.

141 Toprak, 1981:33.

142 Howard, 2001:102–3.

143 Gültaşlı, 1999.

144 Tapper & Tapper, 1987:7.

145 House of Commons, Foreign Affairs Committee, 2002:64–85.

146 Hale, 1994:119–20, 184–5, 251–2.

147 For more on the February 28 Process, see §3.2.8.

148 Reported in all Turkish newspapers during the banking crises in 2000.

149 Barlas, 2006.

150 Çarkoglu & Toprak, 2000:1–5; Turam, 2007:5

151 Eickelman, 1998:80–90; Dorronsoro & Massicard, 2005:2.

152 *Ibid.*.

153 Secor & O'Loughlin, 2004:50-66.

154 Ataman, 2002:122.

155 Özbudun & Tachau, 1975:473–9; Özbudun, 1981a:234, 237–8; Mardin, 1975:7–32; Kalaycioglu, 1997; Kalaycioglu, 1988:149–79; Çarkoğlu, 1998:544–53.

156 Bulaç, 2007:119.

157 Aliriza., 2000:1–5; *id.*, 2001:1–5; Kalaycioglu, 1997.

158 Kramer, 2000:91.

3. MOBILIZATION AND COUNTER-MOBILIZATION

1 Della Porta & Diani, 1999, 149, 173–4; Melucci, 1999:156; Williams, 2004:92; Earl, 2004:513; Edwards & McCarthy, 2004:120.

2 *Aksiyon*, 1998.

3 Gülen, 2004a:81; Gülen, 2005a:157.

4 Hunt, 2007:4, 6; Hendrick, 2007:31; Irvine, 2007:62–84; Stephenson, 2007:156–9; Bulaç, 2007:120; Weller, 2007:85–100.

5 Aslandoğan, 2007:vii.

6 Hendrick, 2007:12–13, 30–1.

7 *JWF*, 2004:7; Bulaç, 2007:118–9; Weller, 2007:86.

8 Önal, 1995; Ünal & Williams, 2000:210.

9 Öktem, 1996.

10 For more, see www.gyv.org.tr.

11 *JWF*, 2004. For more, see <www.abantplatform.com> or <www.kadip.com>.

12 Önal, 1995; Ünal & Williams, 2000:210.

13 Melucci, 1999:75.

14 Vergin, 1996.

15 *Ibid.*

16 Eickelman, 1998:80.

17 Ateş, 1996; Ünal & Williams, 2000:iii.

18 Agai, 2002:29.

19 Aslandoğan & Çetin, 2006:36–7.

20 Melucci, 1999:174–5.

21 *Ibid.*, 174.

22 *Ibid.*, 100, 357–60.

23 Bulaç, 2007:120.

24 For more, see Cizre-Sakallioglu, 1997:151–66.

25 Vergin, 1996; also cited in Ünal & Williams, 2000:154.

26 Yilmaz & Öztürk, 1997.

27 Gökçek, 2007:193.

28 Yavuz & Esposito, 2003:xiv; Bulaç, 2007:119.

29 Barton, 2005:43.

30 'STV and Kanal D [television] interviews with Gülen', cited in Ünal & Williams, 2000:186.

31 Barlas, 1995; Öktem, 1996; Ünal & Williams, 2000:210, 274–6.

32 *Zaman*, 2003b.

33 Murphy, 2004.

34 Çandar, 1998b.

35 Harvey, 1989:124.

36 Göle, 1996a; also cited in Ünal & Williams, 2000:372; and at <www.fethullahgulen.org/content/view/787/13/>.

37 Michel, 2005b:341–58.

38 Özdalga, 2005:443.

39 These themes will be dealt with as sub-sections in Chapter 5.

40 Özdalga, 2005:443; Ünal & Williams, 2000:313; Hendrick, 2007:31.

41 Weller, 2007:99.

42 Williams, 2004:104; Melucci, 1999:358.

43 *Ibid.*, 161, 182, 221, 225–8.

44 Ataman, 2002:126; Smith, 2001:17; Babahan, 2006.

45 For more, see *Turkish Daily News*, 2000c; Hekimoglu, 2000; Koru, 2000; Pope, 2000.

46 Gülen, 2004a:82.

47 The Fountain, 2002:7.

48 Gülen, 2004a:xiv.

49 Andrea, 2007:163. For more, see <http://en.fgulen.com/component/ option.com_weblinks/catid,298/Itemid,21/> and <www.pearls.org/>.

50 <www.zaman.com/?syf=about>

51 *Aksiyon, Sizinti, Yeni Ümit, Yağmur, Ekoloji, Fountain, Fontäne, Hira, Gonca, Ailem*

52 www.zaman.com, www.cihannews.com, www.stv.com.tr, www.thelight publishing.com/index.php.

53 Pope, 2005:372. English e-version Zaman Online became a daily print as *Today's Zaman* in 2007. See www.todayszaman.com/tz-web/.

54 Ten world language editions include Azerbaijan, Australia, Bulgaria, Romania, Macedonia, Kazakhstan, Kyrghizistan, Turkmenistan, Germany, and the US.

55 Özcan, 2003; for more, see <www.zaman.com/?bl=searchandsorgu=snd%20awards>.

56 Bonner, 2004:96–7.

57 Murphy, 2005:B01.

58 Melucci, 1999:227.

59 The Fountain, 2002:3–9.

60 Önis & Turem, 2001::24–5, 27. For more, see also *Turkish Daily News*, 1999c.

61 Ülsever, 2001a.

62 Bilici, 2006.

63 For more, see Cizre-Sakallioglu, 2003:309–32.

64 Özel, 2003:87; *Turkish Daily News*, 2000f; Koru, 2000; Pope, 2000; Birand, 2006a. For details, see §2.2.15 and §3.2.8.

65 Birand, 2006a

66 Kuru, 2005a:260; Kuru, 2005b:4–5.

67 Babahan, 2006.

68 *Zaman*, 2006a.

69 Frantz, 2000.

70 Personal interview with sociologist and author Ergene in 2005.

71 Bilici, 2006.

72 Deligöz, 2006; Birand, 2006a.

73 For more confessions, comment, and criticism by authorities and media members, see *Zaman*, 2006a), and national media in May 2006.

74 Reported in various Turkish media in the last week of February 2007.

75 Tarhan, 2004.

76 Taylor & Van Dyke, 2004:275; Melucci, 1999:114–15.

77 For more, see Sorokin (1959), and Brogan (1997), and <www.hewett. norfolk.sch. uk/CURRIC/soc/class/socmob.htm>).

78 For a different discussion of the services in terms of 'ethics of vocation' – as inner (religious) and outer (worldly) qualifications manifested at work, see Aslandogan & Çetin, 2007:40–61, and Agai, 2002:39–40, and Hendrick, 2007:13, 28, 31; for 'altruistic action', see below §4.1.5.

79 Taylor & Van Dyke, 2004:275.

80 Bulaç, 2007:115.

81 Karaman & Aras, 2000:47. For more on the SMOs established by the participants, see §5.2.4.

82 Kramer, 2000:221.

83 For more on such recognition and acknowledgement, see almost 130 articles from the Turkish and foreign media at <http://en.fgulen.com/content/ category/150/170/14/>.

84 Howe, 2000:39.

85 Mayer, 2004.

86 Melucci, 1999:108–9, 224, 381; Williams, 2004:97–8.

87 Özdalga, 2005:435.

88 Kebede *et al.* 2000:316.

89 Melucci, 1999:73.

90 Hendrick, 2007:26–31; Agai, 2002:47.

91 Hunt, 2007:4.

92 Özdalga, 2005:440.

93 See §2.2.15 and §3.2.8.

94 Özdalga, 2005:442.

95 Howard, 2001:141–7; Proyect, 2005.

96 Ergil, 2006.

97 Alpay, 1995a.

98 Alpay, 1995a.

99 Çevik, 2000a.

100 *Hürriyet*, 2000; *Mainichi Shimbun*, 2000; Bacık & Aras, 2002:397.

101 Oberschall (1973) cited in Melucci, 1996:291–2.

102 Dorsey, 2000; Pope, 1998.

103 Mengi, 1995; also cited in Ünal & Williams, 2000:166.

104 Birand, 2000a.

105 Yılmaz, 2005:400.

106 Özdalga, 2005:442.

107 Webb, 2000:20. Also available at <http://en.fgulen.com/content/ view/1214/14/>; for a similar conclusion, see also Frantz 2000.

108 BBC, 2000d; Stephenson, 2007:159; Benard, 2003:38; Aslandoğan & Çetin, 2007:53–4; Irvine, 2007:82–4; Hendrick, 2007:13, 29–31; Ateş *et al.* 2005:14.

109 *Fountain*, 2002:5.

110 For more on goals and SMOs, see chapter 5.

111 For more, see Ünal & Williams, 2000:305–31, and <http://en.fgulen.com/>, and also, Aslandoğan & Çetin, 2007:34–61; Yildirim, 2005:120.

112 Ünal & Williams, 2000:305–31.

113 Özdalga in Akman, 2003; Weller, 2007:94–9.

114 Gülen, 2004a:259.

115 The Light, Inc., 2006:4–5; Woodhall & Çetin, 2005:viii.

116 Ateş *et al.* 2005. For a specific website about these educational institutions, see www. turkokullari.net/.

117 Aslandoğan & Çetin, 2007:35.

118 Ünal & Williams, 2000:338–49; Agai, 2002:45–6; Ateş *et al.* 2005:9–15; Aslandoğan & Çetin, 2007:53–4.

119 Anadolu Agency, 1999.

120 Özgürel, 2000; also at <http://en.fgulen.com/a.page/press/columns/ 2000/ a700.html>.

121 Pope, 1998.

122 Özkök, 2004; Yilmaz & Öztürk, 1997; Ünal & Williams, 2000:226.

123 *Ibid.*, 333–4.

124 Koray, 1998.

125 *Turkish Daily News*, 2000a. Also at <http://en.fgulen.com/content/view/ 1062/14/>. The schools were also admired by local administrations, see <www. fethullahgulen. org/a.page/press/news/2004/a1866.html>; <www.fethullahgulen. org/ a.page/life/ commentaries/c167.html>.

126 Birand, 2000a.

127 For details of such people and their impressions, see Dinç, 1998, and <http:// en.fgulen.com/a.page/press/interview/a1216p5.html>, and also Ateş *et al.* 2005.

128 *Zaman*, 2004.

129 Gülerce, 2005.

130 Benard, 2003:38.

131 Bayekova in *Zaman*, 2004; Ünal & Williams, 2000:22.

132 Woodhall, 2005:2, 14.

133 Tekalan, 2005:3, 7–8.

134 Gülen, 2005a.

135 Short and full texts of the same article available at <http://en.fgulen.com/ content/ view/826/13/>; Ünal & Williams, 2000:162–5; Webb, 2000:78–89.

136 Ünal & Williams, 2000:22.

137 Melucci, 1999:359.

138 For more on altruistic action, see Melucci (1999:166–71) and §4.1.5.

139 Kramer, 2000:90.

140 *Ibid.*, xiii, 89.

141 Pope, 2005:26.

142 Benard, 2003:184; For more, see also §2.2.15.

143 Melucci, 1999:374.

144 Aliriza & Baran, 1997; Howard, 2001:178–9; Dorsey, 1997; Howe, 2000:139–44; Birand, 2001; *Zaman*, 2006a; *Zaman*, 2006c; Zaman, 2006d.

145 Aliriza & Baran, 1997; Howard, 2001:178–9; Howe, 2000:139–44.

146 Aras & Bacik, 2000:51.

147 Cizre-Sakallioglu, 2003:310.

148 Howe, 2000:243.

149 For details, see Hekimoglu, 2000; Koru, 2000; Pope, 2000; NTV-MSNBC, 2000b; *Zaman*, 2006a; *id.*, 2006d.

150 For more on what Eksi wrote about Birand, Çandar and Akin, see <www.cetim.ch/ en/interventions_details.php?iid=111 as of Oct 31, 2007.

151 Pope, 2000; *Zaman*, 2006a; *id.*, 2006d.

152 *Turkish Daily News*, 2000b; Ataman, 2002:126.
   Ibid., 126; Smith, 2001:17.

153 Önis & Turem, 2001:24–5, 27.

154 Howe, 2000:39.

155 Webb, 2000:21.

156 Birand, 2001; *id.*, 2006a; Çevik, 2000b.

157 Melucci, 375–7.

158 Kinzer was *The New York Times* journalist and *the Time* magazine correspondent for Turkey more than 20 years.

159 Kinzer, 2001.

160 Keneş, 2003.

161 Gülerce, 2004. For the results of other surveys conducted by Ntv-MSNBC and Ajan. net, see §3.2.11, and also Kaya, 2000.

162 For more on Susurluk, see *Turkish Daily News* (1996a), and *id.* (1996c); Berberoglu, 1996.

163 Ataman, 2002:122, 150.

164 Hale, 1999.

165   Eickelman, 2004:66–7.

166   Melucci, 1985:813.

167   *Ibid.*, 813. Also see Oberschall, 1993:337 and Earl, 2004:513.

168   Melucci, 1999:203, 215–16.

169   This will be further developed in §4.1.4.

170   In Ünal & Williams, 2000:174–5.

171   *Akşam*, 1995; <http://en.fgulen. com/a.page/life/relations/a767.html>; Ünal & Williams, 2000:175–6.

172   Akıncı, 1997; <http://en.fgulen.com/a.page/press/interview/ a1203.html>.

173   Melucci, 1999:219–21.

174   *Ibid.*, 303–5.

175   <http://en.fgulen.com/a.page/life/relations/a767p3.html>.

176   For more on Özgürel's (2000) article, see <http://en.fgulen.com/a.page/press/columns/2000/ a700.html>.

177   *Turkish Daily News*, 2000b.

178   Kramer, 2000:1, 8; Alpay, 2007.

179   Jung, 1999; Öniş, 2004:23; Yücel, 2002:3–4; 2004:2–6, 23–4; Dumanli, 2006; Alpay, 2007.

180   Ünal & Williams, 2000:147–9; Sykiainen, 2007:124–5.

181   Melucci, 1999:220–1.

182   Özdalga, 2000:89–90; *id.*, 2003:61–2; see also Akman, 2003.

183   Ünal & Williams, 2000:177.

184   Akıncı, 1997; also at <http://en.fgulen.com/a.page/ press/interview/a1203p4. html>; for a different answer to a similar question, see also <http://en.fgulen. com/a. page/life/relations/a767p5.html>.

185   İpekçi, 2007.

186   Hale, 1999; see quotation §3.2.8 on page 102.

187   Çevik, 2002.

188   Ülsever, 2001a.

189   Melucci, 1999:240–2.

190   BBC, 2000d; Rouleau, 2000.

191   Makovsky, 2000.

192   This will be further discussed as subsections in Chapters 4 and 5.

193   BBC's regional analyst, Pam O'Toole, 2000.

194   Morris, 2000.

195   *Turkish Daily News*, 2000e; NTV-MSNBC, 2000a; BBC, 2000a; *id.*, 2000b.

196   BBC, 2000c.

197   *Turkish Daily News*, 2002.

198   Melucci, 1999:354–5. Ideology is explored in §1.2.2.3, 4.1.4, 5.2.2 and 5.2.7.

199   As has been discussed in §2.2.14, 2.2.15, 2.2.16 and 3.2.8.

200   Çevik, 1999b.

201   Howe, 2000:38, 241.

202   *Turkish Daily News*, 2003. Also at <http://en.fgulen.com/content/view/1226/14/>.

203   For the reasoned decision of the Court, see Appendix 2.

204   Hendrick, 2007:13, 28; Özdalga, 2000; *id.*, 2003:62; Çetin, 2005:39; Çetin, 2006:1–21; Aslandoğan & Çetin, 2007:59; Tekalan, 2005:3.

205   Çetin, 2005:39.

206   Aslandoğan & Çetin, 2007:52–4, 58–9.

207   Çetin, 2006. This will be revisited in §4.1.5.

208   Aslandoğan & Çetin, 2007:33.

209   Özdalga, 2005:443. This will be revisited in §5.2.1 and 5.2.5.

210   This will be expanded on in §5.2.5.

211   This will be revisited in §5.2.1, 5.2.4 and 5.2.5.

212   Zald, 1996:269; Çetin, 2005:37; Aslandoğan & Çetin, 2007:46, 59.

213   Eickelman, 2004:66–7. This will be further dealt within 4.1.4, too.

214   Eickelman, 1998:90.

215   Kaya, 2000.

216   Melucci, 1999:177.

217   This will be further developed in §4.1.5.

218   Melucci, 1999:137, 328–9, 359.

219   This will be further developed in §5.2.2.

220   Zelyut, 1998; Ünal & Williams, 2000:292–3; Melucci, 1999:183; Barlas, 2000; NTV-MSNBC, 1998; http://tr.fgulen.com/content/category/29/69/15/; <http://tr.fgulen.com/content/section/29/15/>.

221   Bayramoglu, 1995; Ünal & Williams, 2000:160–1; <http://en.fgulen. com/ content/ view/822/13/>.

222   'Transnational Projects and Recognition' has already been discussed in §3.2.6.

223   Gülerce, 2004. For more, see <http://en.fgulen.com/a.page/life/education/a780p1. html> and <http://en.fgulen.com/content/view/780/16/>.

224   Barton, 2005:43.

225   Qur'an, 4:128.

226   Michel, 2005a.

227   Gülen, 2004a:250.

4.   CONJUNCTURAL FACTORS

1   Hefner (ed.), 2004.

2   Salamon *et al.* 2003:ii, 7–9.

3   Irvine, 2007:59, 67–72; Tekalan, 2005:3; Aslandoğan & Çetin, 2007:59. For more, see §5.2.3.

4   This topic will be further discussed in §4.1.5.

5   These issues will be further discussed in §5.2.1 and 5.2.4.

6   Szreter, 1999:2–3; Gülen in cited Ünal & Williams, 2000:21, 318; Çetin, 2006:1–21; Gülen, 2004a:210–14.

7   Putnam, 2000:19.

8   Weller, 2005b:272.
9   Stephenson, 2007:158–60; Gülen, 2005a:43–8; Irvine, 2007:65.
10 Sirianni & L. Friedland, 2006.
11 Kömeçoğlu, 1997:65, 78, 86.
12 This will be further studied in §4.1.4.
13 Ünal & Williams, 2000:iii, 326; Hermansen, 2005:4–5; H. Turgut, 1998; Fuller, 2004:53.
14 Michel, 2005b:351.
15 Ünal & Williams, 2000:313.
16 *Ibid.*, 156–7; Sykiainen, 2006:116; Altinoğlu, 1999:102; Yilmaz, 2005:397.
17 The cultural aspect, individual-oriented approach, public space and legality have already been discussed in §3.2.1, 3.2.2, 3.2.7, 3.2.11 and will be dealt with further in relevant sections in §5.2.1 and 5.2.2.
18 Gülen, 2004a:199.
19 Göle, 2002:173.
20 Gülen in Zeybek, 1997; Gülen in Ünal & Williams, 2000:36; Ashton, 2005:3–4.
21 Hendrick, 2007:30.
22 Melucci, 1999:22.
23 *Ibid.*
24 *Ibid.*, 22–3.
25 Webb, 2000:1; also at <http://en.fgulen.com/content/ view/1212/14/>. See also §2.2.4 to 2.2.10.
26 Bozdogan & Kasaba, 1997:4–6; Norton, 1997:153.
27 Interview with Aymaz in January 2005.
28 Yavuz & Esposito, 2003:xxv–xxvii; Yavuz, 2003a:1; Yavuz, 2003b:37–8; Hendrick, 2007:26.
29 Yavuz & Esposito, 2003:xxiv.
30 Yavuz, 2003a:1–2.
31 Jones, 2000:13.
32 *Ibid.*, 14.
33 *Ibid.*, 252.
34 Mellor, 2004.
35 Snow *et al.* 2004:8.
36 Koopmans, 2004:23, 24.
37 Della Porta & Diani, 1999:57.
38 Yavuz & Esposito, 2003:125.
39 *Ibid.*,126; Bal, 2004:138–40.
40 Edwards & McCarthy, 2004:116.
41 Yavuz & Esposito, 2003:xxvi.
42 Melucci, 1999:376; Kömeçoğlu, 1997:64.
43 *Ibid.*
44 Della Porta & Diani, 1999:57.

45 Webb, 2000:156–7; Ünal & Williams, 2000:21–2.
46 <http://en.fgulen.com/a.page/press/court.decisions/a1217p1.html>.
47 Hendrick, 2007:20.
48 Melucci, 1999:24.
49 Ünal & Williams, 2000:276.
50 The Light, Inc., 2006:5.
51 *Ibid.*, 200–1; Hermansen, 2005:, 4–5, Turgut, 1998; Ünal & Williams, 2000:276, 326.
52 Ünal & Williams, 2000:21–2; also: <http://en.fgulen.com/a.page/life/ biography/ a755.html>.
53 Melucci, 1999:34.
54 In Gündem, 2005:130.
55 Interview with Aymaz in January 2005.
56 Qur'an, 3:92, 2:48, 5:48, 23:61, 35:52. From the Hadith sources: Muslim, *Wasiyya* 14; Abu Dawud, *Wasaya* 14; Tirmidhi, *Ahkam* 36.
57 Melucci, 1999:25, 29, 31–2, 238.
58 Interview with Çapan in January 2005.
59 Director of International Security and Energy Programs at the Nixon Center, Washington.
60 Murphy, 2005.
61 Ünal & Williams, 2000:313; The Light, Inc., 2006:5; Gülen, 2004a:230.
62 Interview with Aymaz in January 2005.
63 Correspondence with Çapan in March 2005.
64 Snow *et al.* 2004:7.
65 Melucci, 1999:36–7.
66 Ashton, 2005:3–4.
67 Also cited in Ünal & Williams, 2000:159.
68 Bartholomew, 2004:4
69 Fuller, 2004:53.
70 As discussed in §2.2.1–3.
71 Yavuz & Esposito, 2003:*xxii.*
72 For more discussion and references, see §2.2 and 3.2.3.
73 Fuller, 2004:53; Cerrahoglu, 1995; Ünal & Williams, 2000:152.
74 Lofland, 1996:*229.*
75 Alpay, 1995a. Also Ünal & Williams, 2000:156–7; Sykiainen, 2006:121–2 ; Yilmaz, 2005:397.
76 As an example of considering the implications of religion in relation to the notion of 'social capital' generated and sustained among civic organizations, see Weller, 2005b:271–89.
77 For the recurrent theme of 'regime under threat' or 'national security syndrome', see §2.2.1, 2.2.12–14, 3.2.3–5, 3.2.8–9, 3.2.11 and 6.1.1. Yücel, 2002:23; Yavuz, 2003b:19–23; Yavuz & Esposito, 2003:xxvi.
78 For a similar discussion and more direct answers, see Gülen (2001b), 'Gülen's Testimony at the U.S. Attorney's Office' (Newark, NJ, 6.11.2001), and also Appendix 2.
79 Interview with Aymaz in January 2005.

80 Hermansen, 2005:9–10.

81 Barker, 2002.

82 Woodhall, 2005:4; Irvine, 2007:64–5; Aslandoğan & Çetin, 2007:48–9, 58–9. Also see §5.2.5.

83 This will be further discussed in §5.2.3 and 5.2.5.

84 This will be further discussed in §5.2.2 and 5.2.6.

85 Hermansen, 2005:4–11; Aslandoğan & Çetin, 2006:43.

86 Hermansen, 2005:4–5, 27; Turgut, 1998; Ünal & Williams, 2000:326; Gülen, 2004a:200–1.

87 This will be further discussed in §5.2.4 and 5.2.6.

88 Kuru, 2003:123.

89 Gündem, 2005:83–4.

90 Tekalan, 2005:7–8.

91 Gülen, 2004b:i, 19.

92 Gülen in Ünal & Williams, 2000:73. For more, see §5.2.1.

93 Gülen, 2004a:230.

94 *Ibid.*, 42.

95 *Ibid.*, 50.

96 *Ibid.*, 230.

97 Gülen in Ünal & Williams, 2000:73.

98 Kömeçoğlu, 1997:77–8.

99 Gülen, 1998b:19.

100 Gülen, 2005a:102.

101 Tekalan, 2005:8.

102 Hermansen, 2005:15.

103 Özdalga, 2005:440. Also see §3.2.4.

104 *Ibid.*, 435.

105 Aslandoğan & Çetin, 2006:50; Irvine, 2007:66–7.

106 Also see §5.2.6.

107 Barton, 2005:43.

108 Gülen in Ünal & Williams, 2000:84; Gülen, 2004a:199.

109 Gülen, 2005a:100.

110 *Ibid.*, 78–80.

111 Gülen in Ünal & Williams, 2000:21.

112 Gülen in Ünal & Williams, 2000:22–3; Woodhall & Çetin, 2005:viii.

113 Gülen, 1996:103; Michel, 2006:108–9.

114 Gülen, 2004a:199. See also Woodhall & Çetin, 2005:vii.

115 Michel, 2006:110.

116 Gülen, 1996:16; Gülen, 2000b:35, 44–5.

117 Michel, 2006:111.

118 Dinç, 1998; <http://en.fgulen. com/content/view/1216/14/>; Webb, 2000:95.

119 Melucci, 1999:104–5.

120 Bayat, 2005:894.

121 Woodhall & Çetin, 2005:xviii.

122 Michel, 2005b:349.

123 Gülen, 1996:90–3; Woodhall & Çetin, 2005:xviii.

124 Michel, 2006:107–8; see also the similar arguments and quotations in Webb, 2000:86.

125 Gülen, 1996:74; emphasis added.

126 Gülen cited in Sevindi, 1997a:July 20–29; *id.*, 1997b; Ünal & Williams, 2000:38.

127 Gülen, 1996:86.

128 *Ibid.*, 53.

129 Collectivity, affiliation and identity will be further discussed in §5.2.1.

130 This will be further developed in §4.1.5.

131 Gülen, 2005a:21.

132 Woodhall & Çetin, 2005:xv.

133 *Ibid.*, xiv–xv.

134 Melucci, 1999:189.

135 In Ünal & Williams, 2000:277; Michel, 2005b:344–6.

136 *Ibid.*

137 Melucci, 1999·189.

138 Barker, 2002; Della Porta & Diani, 1999:145.

139 Kömeçoğlu, 1997:77–8.

140 Gülen, 1996:86.

141 Sectarian understanding·will be studied further as a subsection in §5.2.7.

142 Interview with Aymaz in January 2006.

143 Also see §3.2.6.

144 Interview with Ergene in January 2006.

145 Interview with Çapan in January 2006.

146 Akman, 1995a; Ünal & Williams, 2000:i. Leadership will be discussed further in §5.2.5.

147 Gülen, 2005a:43–8.

148 Melucci, 1999:97.

149 Koopmans, 2004:24.

150 Williams, 2004:92.

151 Melucci, 1999:98–100; Williams, 2004:92–3.

152 Melucci, 1999:98, 102.

153 *Ibid.*,102.

154 Offe, 1985:24.

155 Della Porta & Diani, 1999:12.

156 Michel, 2006:107; Ünal & Williams, 2000:277–8; Yilmaz, 2005:397.

157 Ünal & Williams, 2000:277–8; also <http://en.fgulen. com/content/view/970/14/>.

158 Aslandoğan & Çetin, 2006:38; Hendrick, 2006:26; Sykiainen, 2006:113, 116; Michel, 2005b:351.

159 Çetin, 2005:39.

160 Barton, 2005:1.

161 Weller, 2005b:2–3.

162 For more see, Aslandoğan & Çetin, 2006:53, and Çetin, 2005:36–7.

163 Michel, 2006:107; Tekalan, 2005:3.

164 Gülen, 2005a:145.

165 *Ibid.*, 145–6.

166 Çevik (2000a) called the indictment that Gülen aims to turn Turkey into a religious state 'absurd'. For some history, see §3.2.3, 3.2.8, 3.2.10, and Appendix 2.

167 Frantz, 2000.

168 Melucci, 1999:233–4.

169 Ünal & Williams, 2000:277–8; Yilmaz, 2005:397. For non-party affiliation and success, also see §3.2.11.

170 Barton, 2005:2; Ünal & Williams, 2000:320.

171 Stephenson, 2005:13.

172 Gülen cited in Michel, 2005b:356; Gülen in Ünal & Williams, 2000:86; Çetin, 2005:5.

173 Gülen cited in Ünal & Williams, 2000:80.

174 For more, see Aslandoğan & Çetin, 2006.

175 Afsaruddin, 2005:22.

176 Tekalan, 2005:3.

177 Sevindi, 1997c; Ünal & Williams, 2000:38; Gülen, 2004a:223.

178 Hand, 2004:27.

179 Interviews with Gülen: by Akman for *Sabah*, 28.01.1995; by Sevindi for *Yeni Yüzyıl*, 22.07 (1997a); by Çalışlar for *Cumhuriyet*, 21.08.1995. Also Gülen in Ünal & Williams, 2000:187–92; Yilmaz, 2005:399.

180 Kuru, 2005a:265–8, 274; Yilmaz, 2005:405–6.

181 Balci *et al.* 2002:28. For more on relations with the West and the world, see <http://en.fgulen.com/a.page/life/relations/a771>.

182 Webb, 2000:iv; Aras, 1998.

183 Voll, 2005:245; Yilmaz, 2005:397; Ashton, 2005:3–4; Zeybek, 1997; Ünal & Williams, 2000:36.

184 Alpay, 1995a; also cited in Ünal & Williams, 2000:158.

185 For more similar arguments and quotations from Gülen, Sykiainen, 2006:110.

186 Gülen, 2004a:223.

187 Gündem, 2005:81.

188 *Ibid.*, 82. Also at <http://en.fgulen.com/content/view/1918/14/>.

189 Hunt, 2007:8–9.

190 Sykiainen, 2006:110. For more, see Chapter 3, esp. §3.2.1, 3.2.2 and 3.2.5.

191 Zeybek, 1997; Ünal & Williams, 2000:36.

192 Gülen, 2001a:138; *id.* 2004a:219.

193 Ashton, 2005:3–4.

194 Yilmaz, 2005:398.

195 Barton, 2005:9.

196 Gülen, 2004a:220.

197 *Ibid.*, 220–4.

198 This issue was looked at from a different perspective in §3.2.9.

199 Gülen, 2005b:452.

200 Eickelman, 2002:4.

201 Barton, 2005:17.

202 Gülen. 2005b:456.

203 Sykiainen, 2006:114, and Eickelman, 2002:4.

204 Gülen, 2004a:224.

205 Barton, 2005:17–18.

206 Webb, 2000:73–4; within the following media and press interviews: TRT (1995); *Zaman* (1995); NTV-MSNBC (1998); *Akşam* (1988); *Milliyet* (1988); STV News (1997); *Hürriyet* (1995); Also in Yılmaz (1997); *Zaman* (June 23); Yagiz (1997); Barış (1999); Gülen (2006); Dinc (1998); and all these preceding media and press interviews and more are available at <http://tr.fgulen.com/content/category/29/69/15/>, <http://tr.fgulen.com/content/section/29/15/>, <htp://en.fgulen.com/content/view/741/14/>.

207 Barton, 2005:39–41.

208 Gülen, 2005b:466–7.

209 Gülen in Yagiz (1997), in Ünal & Williams (2000:166, 167), in Zelyut (1998); Sykiainen, 2006:113.

210 Çetin, 2006:1–4; The Fountain, 2002:93; Frantz, 2000; Özdalga, 2005:433.

211 Lofland, 1996:146.

212 For social reductionism, see also §4.1.2 and 4.1.4.

213 Melucci, 1999:203.

214 Michel, 2005b:351.

215 Sykiainen, 2006:116.

216 Gülen in Ünal & Williams, 2000:99.

217 Cited in Cerrahoglu (1995), and Ünal & Williams, 2000:153.

218 Agai, 2004.

219 Karaman & Aras, 2000:56.

220 Michel, 2005b:354.

221 Gülen, 2004a:230–1; Gülen, 2000c:7–8.

222 Saritoprak & Griffith, 2005:336; The Light, Inc., 2006:5; Kuru, 2005a:254, 261, 264–5.

223 Gülen, 2004a:262.

224 Weller, 2007:92–9; Kurtz, 2005:373, 380; Michel, 2005b:369–70; Bulaç, 2007:120; Stephenson, 2007:158–9; Murphy, 2004.

225 Sykiainen, 2007:130–2.

226 Michel, 2003:70; Ergene, 2005:313; Aslandoğan & Çetin, 2007:55–60.

227 Aslandoğan & Çetin, 2006:44.

228 *Ibid.*, 49.

229 Michel, 2005a:51.

230 Melucci, 1999:31, 50, 99; see also Göle, 2002:174; Edwards & McCarthy, 2004:120.

231 Çetin, 2006:1. For more, see §2.2.3–10.

232 Gülen, 2004a:232, 240, 246, 249; Çetin, 2006:1.

233 Çetin, 2005:2; Gülen, 2004a:198. For more, see also *parallel narratives* in 2.2.4 –2.2.13.

234 Ünal & Williams, 2000:22–3; Sevindi, 1997c; Woodhall & Çetin, 2005:viii; Gülen, 2004a:199.

235 Woodhall & Çetin, 2005:viii.

236 Gülen, 2005a:94–5.

237 Gülen, 2004a:218; The Light, Inc., 2006:2–5.

238 Gülen, 2005a:50.

239 For more, see §5.2.4.

240 Po-Hi, 2002:45–7.

241 Sevindi, 1997a; also at <http://en.fgulen.com/ content/view/783/13/> and <www. nevvalsevindi.com/oku. php?id =347.

242 Gülen in Ünal & Williams, 2000:22, 328–31; Sevindi, 1997a.

243 The Fountain, 2002:2; BBC, 2000d; Stephenson, 2007:159; Benard, 2003:38; Aslandoğan & Çetin, 2007:46–59; Irvine, 2007:64–84; Hendrick, 2007:30–1; Tekalan, 2005:3, 7–8; also see §3.2.6.

244 Çetin, 2005:4.

245 Ünal & Williams, 2000:326.

246 Aslandoğan & Çetin, 2007:46–7.

247 Michel, 2005b:356.

248 Gülen, 2005a:50. Management and leadership will be discussed in §5.2.3–5.

249 Woodhall, 2005:9–10.

250 Aslandoğan & Çetin, 2006:43; Erdoğan, 2006:123.

251 Aslandoğan & Çetin, 2006:43; Gündem, 2005.

252 Ünal & Williams, 2000:29–45; Aslandoğan & Çetin, 2006:36–7; Gülen, 2004a:4, 148–51, 198–9, 218.

253 *Ibid.*, 201.

254 Genov, 1996; Ünal & Williams, 2000:330–1.

255 French, *altruisme*, from *autrui*, 'other people', from Latin *alter*, 'other'.

256 <http://en.wikipedia.org/wiki/Altruism>

257 Philosophers like Nietzsche and Ayn Rand have argued that altruism is predicated on false assumptions and is the reversal of morality and *not* virtuous. They assert that the assumption that others are more important than one's self is demeaning to the individual and that no moral obligation to help others actually exists. For a fuller ac-

count than is possible here of the Western philosophical and Islamic arguments, see Çetin, 2006:6, 12–13.

258 *Ibid.*

259 Bar-Tal, 1986:5; DiMaggio & Anheier, 1990:137, 153; Piliavin & Charng, 1990:55, 58.

260 Bar-Tal, 1986; also in Piliavin & Charng, 1990:30.

261 Interview with Çapan in January 2005.

262 A sponsor of the educational and interfaith dialogue efforts of the Gülen Movement, a chemicals wholesaler in Istanbul, interviewed in January 2005.

263 Another sponsor, a knitwear producer and exporter in Istanbul, interviewed in January 2005.

264 Gülen, 2004a:201. See also Sevindi (1997b) whose reports support the same argument: Gülen's understanding of service encompasses 'economic, cultural, and spiritual' dimensions.

265 Gülen, 2004a:214; Ergene in *ibid.*, viii–ix. Voluntary participation in a service-network will be expanded on in §5.2.1.

266 Melucci, 1999:167.

267 Interview with Tuzcu in January 2005.

268 Melucci, 1999:167.

269 Interview with Ergene in January 2005.

270 Aymaz, interviewed in January 2006.

271 Interview with Aymaz in January 2006.

272 DiMaggio & Anheier, 1990:151.

273 For more, see Weller, 2007:85–100, where he discusses how Toynbee's work can be illuminative today, with regard to the Gülen Movement and to Islam in Turkey and in the contemporary world.

274 Özdalga, 2005:429–30, 432–4.

275 *Ibid.*, 443; Frantz, 2000.

276 See §2.2.16.

277 Karaman & Aras, 2000:44.

278 Gülen, 2004a:246.

279 *Ibid.*, 82–3.

280 Yilmaz, 2005:406–7; Hunt, 2007:8–9.

281 This will be further analyzed in §5.2.4. See also, 3.2.3 and 3.2.4.

282 See §3.2.1–2 and 4.1.4.

283 Özdalga, 2005:443.

284 Aslandoğan & Çetin, 2006:43, 50–3.

285 Altinoğlu, 1999:102; Ünal & Williams, 2000:156–7; Sykiainen, 2006:116; Yilmaz, 2005:397.

286 These issues will be further explored in §5.2.1.

287 Kömeçoğlu, 1997:84–7; Bulaç, 2007:118–20; Eickelman, 1999:80–81; Yilmaz, 2005:397–8; Kurtz, 2005:377, 382; Weller, 2005b:2–3.

5.   INTERNAL ORGANIZATIONAL FACTORS AND COMPONENTS

[1]   For details, see §0.2.3.

[2]   This view is also expressed by Klandermans, 2004:361.

[3]   The individual view and collective reasoning will be expanded on in §5.2.3 and 5.2.5.

[4]   Like the youthful membership in the Communist Party in the 1930s.

[5]   This will be expanded on in §5.2.3.

[6]   Barker (1984) and Richardson (1993) cited in Lofland, 1996:234.

[7]   Melucci, 1999:74; See also §3.2.6 on acceptance, being a part of political and cultural diversity, and reciprocity.

[8]   The February 28 Process was explained in §2.2.15–16, and discussed in §3.2.3, §3.2.8.

[9]   See also §3.2.7 and 3.10.

[10]   See also §4.1.3 and 3.2.6.

[11]   See also §3.2.1, 3.2.5, 3.2.6, 3.2.8, 3.2.10, 4.1.5.

[12]   Michels, [1915] 1999) cited in Lofland, 1996:148.

[13]   McCarthy & Zald, 2003:135.

[14]   Zald & Ash (1966) cited in Della Porta & Diani, 1999:151.

[15]   Morris & Staggenborg, 2004:172.

[16]   Lofland, 1996:162.

[17]   Cook, 1971:774.

[18]   See also §3.2.1–2, 4.1.3–4.

[19]   <www.sociologyonline.co.uk/politics/michels.htm>.

[20]   Lofland, 1996:148–50.

[21]   Della Porta & Diani, 1999:147–51; Hyman, 1971.

[22]   This was dealt with in detail in chapters §3.2.8, 4.1.3–4.

[23]   Types of SMOs will be discussed in §5.2.4.

[24]   See also §3.2.1–2, 4.1.3–4.

[25]   Lofland, 1996:185.

[26]   Della Porta & Diani, 1999:11–12.

[27]   Hunt & Benford, 2004:438.

[28]   Lofland, 1996:195–7.

[29]   For 'social capital', see §4.1.1.

[30]   McCarthy, & Zald, 1987a:371, 375; Della Porta & Diani, 1999:145, 162.

[31]   See §3.23, 3.2.7, 3.2.11, and also, Hendrick, 2007:31.

[32]   Lofland (1996:221) gives the names and dates of the researches.

[33]   See also §4.1.3 on institutionalization even after the February 28 Process.

[34]   Lofland, 1996:195.

[35]   See §3.2.6, 3.2.11 and 5.2.4.

[36]   Della Porta & Diani, 1999:29; Melucci, 1999:308; McAdam & Rucht, 1993:58.

[37]   Gerlach & Hine, 1970:50.

38 For the continuity of the services and SMOs inside and outside Turkey, see §3.2.6 and 3.2.11.

39 Özdalga, 2005:434.

40 Melucci, 1999:176; see also §4.1.1, 4.1.2.

41 See also §4.1.4.

42 See §3.2.3, 3.2.4, 3.2.5 and 4.1.4.

43 For the continuity of the services and SMOs inside and outside Turkey, see §3.2.6, 3.2.11 and 4.1.1.

44 Melucci, 1999:116.

45 Lofland, 1996:201.

46 Byrne, 1997:15.

47 Della Porta & Diani, 1999:17; Melucci, 1999:308.

48 Diani (2004:348–9) uses 'overlapping affiliations' for this.

49 Melucci, 1999:124, 308.

50 Snow & Machaleck, 1984:180, and Kilbourne & Richardson, 1988:2, cited in Lofland, 1996:222, 223.

51 Snow & Oliver, 1995:574; Lofland, 1996:197, 228.

52 McAdam & Rucht, 1993:58.

53 See §4.1.3.

54 See §3.2.6 and 4.1.4.

55 Della Porta & Diani, 1999:246.

56 Whittier, 2004:547; see also §3.2.3.

57 Irvine, 2006:57–9, 66–7, 73.

58 This echoes Olson (1965) cited in Byrne (1997:41). For a definition of the term 'free-rider', see §1.2.2.1; also see Lofland, 1996:197; Melucci, 1999:63–7.

59 Lofland, 1996:197. Lofland, on pp. 224–5, explains how Turner & Killian ([1957] 1987:333) dismiss the free-rider problem as ultimately irrational.

60 Melucci, 1999:308–9.

61 See §4.1.2 on the non-contentious and non-conflictual nature of the Movement, and also Appendix 2.

62 Barglow, 1994:184.

63 Lofland, 1996:257–9.

64 See also *Zaman* (2006b), 'Unanimous Acquittal Ruled for Gülen' (June 5); and *Zaman* (2006h), 'Reasoned Decision Revealed: Gülen does not Aim at Changing Constitutional System' (June 10), National news.

65 Gülen, 2000c:7–8; Gülen, 2004a:199, 230–1; Ashton, 2005:3–4; Sevindi, 1997a; Alpay, 1995a; Kuru, 2003:123; Ünal & Williams, 2000:159; Gündem, 2005:83–4; Michel, 2006:108–9; Hermansen, 2005:27; Woodhall & Çetin, 2005:vii; Kömeçoğlu, 1997:84–7; Bulaç, 2007:101; Eickelman, 1999:3; Yilmaz, 2005:397–8; Kurtz, 2005:377, 382.

66 Melucci, 1999:131–2; Tilly (1990:93) refers to this as 'a hierarchy of advantage and opportunity'.

67   Snow & Oliver, 1995:587.

68   Gülen, 2000b:80.

69   Lofland, 1996:185.

70   Ateş *et al.* 2005.

71   Also, see §3.2.6 and 4.1.5.

72   See <www.kimseyokmu.com/> and www.gyv.org.tr/changelang. asp?lang=2>.

73   *DA*, 2004:66–76.

74   *Kadip*, 2004:12.

75   On continuity, see §3.2.6, 3.2.11, 4.1.1 and 5.2.1.

76   For more, see §4.1.4 and 4.1.5.

77   See §3.2.1 for public space, 3.2.4 for training people with new skills, 3.2.5 for gaining new elites to their thinking, support and projects.

78   For more, see §3.2.6.

79   Gülen, 2004a:44–5; Gülen in The Light, Inc., 2006:32.

80   Kurtz, 2005:373–84. See also §4.1.4.

81   Interview with Aymaz in January 2005.

82   *Zaman*, 2006e; *Zaman*, 2006f; *Zaman*, 2006g; Irvine, 2006:59.

83   Hendrick, 2006:21, 29.

84   Fuller, 2004:53; Turgut, 1998; Hermansen, 2005:, 4–5, Ünal & Williams, 2000:276, 326; Ashton, 2005:3–4; Irvine, 2006:55–6, 61, 63–4, 71, 74; Aslandoğan & Çetin, 2006:43–4; Baran in Murphy, 2005. For more, see §4.1.2 and 4.1.4.

85   Gamson (1974:35–41, *id.* (1975:93), cited in Lofland, 1996:292–3; Gamson in Lewis, 1975:516–17; Gamson in Kuriakose, 2006:PSC 129. For a detailed critique and suppositions for success, see Goldstone, 1980:1017–42.

86   Interview with Ergene in 2005.

87   Interview with Aymaz in 2005.

88   Irvine, 2006:59, 66–8.

89   Kuriakose, 2006:PSC, 129.

90   Aslandoğan & Çetin, 2006:46.

91   *Ibid.*, 36–7, 40–5; Irvine, 2006:59.

92   Özdalga, 2005:440.

93   These will be further discussed in §5.2.6 and 5.2.7.

94   Irvine, 2006:74.

95   Oberschall, 1973:135; Melucci, 1999:297; Della Porta & Diani, 1999:8–9; Stephenson, 2007:132.

96   Gülerce, 2004; Kaya, 2000. For more see §3.2.7 and 3.2.11.

97   Della Porta & Diani, 1999:32.

98   Ateş *et al.* 2005.

99   Lofland (1996:184–5, 195) agrees with McCarthy & Zald (1987a:341–58) that it is no accident that populations of affluent students are more frequently the sites of new SMOs than are more regimented populations.

100   Özdalga, 2005:440.

101 Tilly, 1978:52; Lofland, 1996:184–5; Della Porta & Diani, 1999:47–9; Edwards & McCarthy, 2004:119, 142–3; Diani, 2004:341; McCarthy & Zald, 1977:1224; Melucci, 1999:297–8.

102 Della Porta & Diani, 1999:63.

103 Diani, 2004:350–1.

104 Byrne, 1997:15; and see §4.1.5.

105 Aslandoğan & Çetin, 2006:47–8; see also Tekalan, 2005:6.

106 Irvine, 2007:66–7; Ünal & Williams, 2000:328, 338–47.

107 Gülen, 2005a:43–8, Gülen, 1998a:39–40; Irvine, 2007:66.

108 Gülen (2000b), *id.* (2004a), *id.* (2005a); Hunt, 2007:8–10; Hendrick, 2007:26–31; Stephenson, 2006:145–50; Michel, 2004a:i; Andrea, 2007:162–3; Gökçek, 2007:192–3.

109 Klandermans, 2006:364.

110 Melucci, 1999:292.

111 Della Porta & Diani, 1999:147.

112 McAdam *et al.* 1996a:4; Ferree & Mueller, 2004:576–607; Morris & Staggenborg, 2004:183; Lofland, 1996:1–3, 12.

113 Melucci, 1999:323.

114 Lofland, 1996:198.

115 *Ibid.*, 176–7.

116 McCarthy & Zald, 1977:1217–18.

117 Gupta, 2002:4.

118 Established political bodies support or initiate moderate competitors to more radical groups to prevent the radicals from eroding their constituency and to undermine radical ones. This mobilization is called the "radical-flank effect" (Haines 1984 cited in Koopmans, 2004:27). For more, see Gupta (2002).

119 Aslandoğan & Çetin, 2006:46.

120 Lofland, 1996:293.

121 Irvine, 2006:57–9.

122 For reaction to centralization, see Rucht, 1989:85, Della Porta & Diani, 1999:154, and Rucht, 1999:2–4.

123 Woodhall, 2005:4; Irvine, 2006:59.

124 Aslandoğan & Çetin, 2006:47.

125 Irvine, 2006:66.

126 Lofland, 1996:241; see also §3.2.8 for Movement responses to the February 28 Process.

127 See §4.1.2.

128 Özdalga, 2005:435–6.

129 As also indicated by Della Porta & Diani, 1999:17.

130 For more, see §3.2.3.

131 Taylor, 1989:761–70, and Lofland, 1996:199–200.

132 Kriesi, 1996:155–6.

133   Lofland, 1996:184-5.

134   See §4.1.2 for the non-contentious, non-conflictual character of the Gülen Movement.

135   Lofland, 1996:185.

136   See §2.2.6 to 2.2.12.

137   Gülen, 1999:4; Woodhall & Çetin, 2005:viii; Woodhall, 2005:4; Irvine, 2006:59; Aslandoğan & Çetin, 2006:42-4, 51-2. Also see chapters 3 and 4 and more specifically §4.1.1, 4.1.3 and 5.2.3.

138   Melucci, 1999:325-6.

139   Weller, 2007:99.

140   Della Porta & Diani, 1999:142-3, 181; Lofland, 1996:211-2; Morris & Staggenborg, 2004:171-3.

141   *Ibid.*, 171.

142   Melucci, 1999:313; Morris & Staggenborg, 2004:187.

143   Michels, [1915]1999:365; Melucci, 1999:313.

144   Cook, 1971:796; Melucci, 1999:313, 325; Tilly, 1978:41-50.

145   Chemers, 1997:1.

146   Weber, [1924]1947:358.

147   Gülen, 2005a:40.

148   Cited in Ünal & Williams, 2000:328.

149   Irvine, 2007:66.

150   *Ibid.*, 67.

151   See §3.2.6.

152   Lofland, 1996:159.

153   Della Porta & Diani, 1999:151.

154   Gülen cited in Gündem, 2005:83-4; see also <http://en.fgulen.com/content/view/1918/14/>.

155   Hadith (no. 4542) related on the authority of Abu Hurayrah, Islamic Scholar Software: *Sahih Muslim* cited in Beekun & Badawi (1999:1-3)

156   Greenleaf, 1970:7.

157   For ten principles/characteristics, see <www.butler.edu/studentlife/hampton/ principles.htm>. For more on Greenleaf, Spears and servant-leadership, see <www.greenleaf.org/leadership/servant-leadership/What-is-Servant-Leadership .html>; for a critique of servant leadership, see <www.leadersdirect.com/ critique.html>; in reply to objections in defence of servant leadership, see <www.leadersdirect.com/servant-reply.html>.

158   Irvine, 2006:59.

159   Interview with Ergene in January 2005.

160   Interview with Aymaz in January 2005.

161   Beekun & Badawi, 1999:3; *hadith* cited from *Sahih Muslim*, no. 1013.

162   Berger & Luckmann, 1966.

163   For articles and discussions, see <http://en.wikipedia.org/wiki/Social_con structionism>.

164 Berger & Luckmann (1996), Gamson & Meyer (1996), and McAdam *et al.* (1996b), are all cited in Della Porta & Diani, 1999:223–4.

165 McAdam *et al.* 1996a; Zald, 1996:261–74.

166 Edwards & McCarthy, 2004:120.

167 Lofland, 1996:197, 225.

168 Melucci, 1999:318, 327.

169 Snow & Oliver, 1995:584.

170 Also see §3.2.5, 3.2.6, 3.2.8 and 3.2.11.

171 See §3.1, 4.1.2 and 4.1.4.

172 Turner & Killian, [1957]1987:333, cited in Lofland, 1996:225.

173 See also Melucci, 1999:335.

174 Özdalga, 2005:440.

175 Stephenson, 2007:149.

176 Gülen, 2004a:200–1; Hermansen, 2005:4–5; Ünal & Williams, 2000:276, 326; Turgut, 1998. See also §4.1.2.

177 Aslandoğan & Çetin, 2006:36–7.

178 Melucci, 1999:315.

179 *Ibid.*, 295, 299–301; Finkel & Muller, 1998:37–8.

180 *Ibid.*, 37, 46–47.

181 Calhoun, 1991:69; McAdam, 1996:67. Also see 1.2.2.1.

182 Della Porta & Diani, 1999:9.

183 See also §4.1.1.

184 Klandermans, 2004:362–71.

185 *Ibid.*, 360, 404.

186 Della Porta & Diani, 1999:144, 161.

187 Melucci, 1999:255–7; Oberschall, 1993:17.

188 Lofland, 1996:210.

189 For more research on factionalism and schism, see Lofland, 1996:153–4.

190 McCarthy & Zald, [1987] 2003:134.

191 Fuchs, 2005:22–3; Fuchs, 2006:101–37.

192 Della Porta & Diani, 1999:26.

193 For more, see also §3.2.5 and 4.1.3.

194 Whittier *et al.* 2002:122.

195 Melucci, 1999:320–3.

196 See §4.1.3.

197 Sykiainen, 2007:124–6, 128–9.

198 See §4.1.3.

199 Williams, 2004:102.

200 Jung, 1999; Öniş, 2004:23; Yücel, 2002:3–4; Yücel, 2004:2–6, 23–4; Dumanli, 2006.

201 Özdalga, 2005:442.

202 *Ibid.*, 443.

BIBLIOGRAPHY

Aberle, D.F. (1982) *The Peyote Religion among the Navaho*, Chicago: University of Chicago Press. (2nd edition.)

Afsaruddin, A. (2005) The Philosophy of Islamic Education: Classical Views and M. Fethullah Gülen's Perspectives. Presented at the conference *Islam in the Contemporary World: The Fethullah Gülen Movement in Thought and Practice*, organized by the Boniuk Center for the Study and Advancement of Religious Tolerance at Rice University, Houston; the A. D. Bruce Religion Center University of Houston; and the Institute of Interfaith Dialog, Texas, and taking place at Rice University, Houston, Texas, November 12–13, 2005, pp.26.

Agai, B. (2002) Fethullah Gülen and his Movement's Islamic Ethic of Education. *Critique: Critical Middle Eastern Studies*, 11(1), 27–47.

———. (2004) Portrait of Fethullah Gülen: A Modern Turkish-Islamic Reformist. *Qantara.de*. Available from: <http://qantara.de/webcom/show_article.php/_c-478/_nr-216/i.html?PHP>.

———. (2005) The Followers of Fethullah Gülen and Their Activities in Albania and Germany: The Adaptation of a Turkish-Islamic Network and its Discourse to New Contexts. *Journal of Ethnic and Racial Studies*. forthcoming.

Ahmad, F. (1977) *The Turkish Experiment in Democracy, 1950–1975*. Boulder, CO: Westview Press.

———. (1993) *The Making of Modern Turkey*. London and New York, Routledge.

Akbal, O. (1987) Bu tutumla bu kafayla (trans: With this attitude and with this mentality'). *Cumhuriyet*, January 11.

Akıncı, U. (1997) Fethullah Gülen's Views on Turkey's Various Issues. *Turkish Daily News*, August 30. Also available from: <http://en.fgulen.com/a.page/press/interview/a1203.html>.

Akman, N. (1995b) Interview. *Nokta*, February 5–11, 16–18.

———. (1995a) Leadership. *Sabah*, January 23–30. Also available from: <http://en.fgulen.com/content/view/760/13>.

———. (2003) Gülen Suggests Non-violent Options to Young Activists. An Interview with Elisabeth Özdalga. *Zaman*, June 10. Available from: <www.zaman.com/default.php?kn=2656>.

Akşam (1988) Röportaj. Orhan Yurtsever's Interview. March 13.

Akşam (1995) Talk with Çetin, Head of the CHP. June 23.

Aktaş, C. (1990) *Kilik, Kiyafet ve Iktidar: 12 Marttan 12 Eylule.* Vol. 1. Istanbul, Nehir Yayınları.

Ali, K. (1955) *İstiklal Mahkemesi Hatıraları.* Istanbul: Sel Yayınları.

Aliriza, B. & Baran, Z. (1997) The Government Falters. *CSIS Report,* April 1997. Available from: <www.csis.org/turkey/TU9704.html>.

Aliriza, B. (2000) Turkey's Winter of Discontent. *CSIS Report,* December 5. Washington, DC, CSIS–Center for Strategic and International Studies, 1–5.

———. (2001) Turkey's Crisis: Corruption at the Core. *CSIS Report,* March 5. Washington, DC, CSIS–Center for Strategic and International Studies, 1–5.

Alpay, Ş. (1995a) Religion and Politics. *Milliyet,* February 18.

———. (1995b) Respect for Hodjaefendi. *Milliyet,* July 29.

———. (2007) Secularism without democracy is an illusion. *Today's Zaman,* April 30. Available from <www.todayszaman.com/tz-web/yazarDetay.do?haberno =109792>.

Altinoglu, E. (1999) Fethullah Gülen's Perception of State and Society, Istanbul: Bosphorus University. (unpublished thesis submitted to the Institute of Social Sciences in partial fulfilment of the requirements for the degree of Master of Arts in Political Science and International Relations, Boğaziçi University, pp.132)

Anadolu Agency (1999) News in English, 99-06-23 AA Daily, June 23: *Schools of Fethullah Gülen – Bostancioglu National Education Minister: There is No Problem in Our Schools. There are Problems at Home.* Available from: www.hri. org/news/turkey/anadolu/1999/99-06-23.anadolu.html#02 [October 4, 2005].

Andrea, B. (2007) Women and Their Rights: Fethullah Gülen's Gloss on Lady Montagu's "Embassy" to the Ottoman Empire, In: Hunt, R. A. & Aslandoğan, Y. A. (2007), 161–82.

Aras, B. & Bacik, G. (2000) The National Action Party and Turkish Politics. *Nationalism and Ethnic Politics* 6(4): 48–64.

Aras, B. (1998) Turkish Islam's Moderate Face. *Middle East Quarterly,* V(3). Available from: <www.meforum.org/article/404> [January 4, 2007].

Arat, Z. F. (1994) Turkish Women and the Republican Reconstruction of Tradition. In: Gocek, F. M. & Balagh, S. eds. *Reconstructing Gender in the Middle East: Tradition, Identity, and Power.* New York: Columbia University Press, 57–78.

Ashton, L. (2005) Defending Religious Diversity and Tolerance in America Today: Lessons from Fethullah Gülen. Presented at the conference *Islam in the Contemporary World: The Fethullah Gülen Movement in Thought and Practice,* organized by the Boniuk Center for the Study and Advancement of Religious Tolerance at Rice University, Houston; the A. D. Bruce Religion Center University of Houston; and the Institute of Interfaith Dialog, Texas, and taking place at Rice University, Houston, Texas, November 12–13, 2005, pp.9.

Aslandoğan, Y. A. & Çetin, M. (2007) Gülen's Educational Paradigm in Thought and Practice. In: Hunt, R. A. & Aslandoğan, Y. A. (2007), 35–61.

————. (2006) "The Educational Philosophy of Gülen in Thought and Practice", in Robert A. Hunt & Yüksel A. Aslandoğan (Eds) Muslim Citizens of the Globalized World: Contributions of the Gülen Movement (New Jersey, The Light, Inc.) 31-54.

Aslandoğan, Y. A. (2007) Preface. In: Hunt, R. A. & Aslandoğan, Y. A. (2007), vii-ix.

Ataman, M. (2002) Leadership Change: Özal Leadership and Restructuring in Turkish Foreign Policy. *Alternatives: Turkish Journal of International Relations*, 1(1), 120–53. Available from <www.alternativesjournal.net/volume1/number1/ ataman.pdf> [February 10, 2006].

Ateş, T. (1996) A Will That Can Solve Problems. In: Can, E. ed. (1996) *Ufuk Turu*. Istanbul, Milliyet Yayınları.

Ateş, T., Ortaylı, İ. & Karakaş, E. (2005) *Barış Köprüleri: Dünyaya Açılan Türk Okulları* (trans. Bridges of Peace: Turkish Schools Opening to the Whole World). Istanbul: Ufuk Kitapları.

Ayata, A. (1997) The Emergence of Identity Politics in Turkey. *New Perspectives on Turkey*, 17 (Fall).

Aybars, E. (1975) *İstiklal Mahkemeleri*. Ankara, Bilgi Yayınevi.

Aymaz, A. (2006) Onlarin 24 Saati Hizmet (trans: Their 24 Hours are service), *Zaman*, March 21. Available from: <www.zaman.com.tr/webapp-tr/haber.do?haberno=267583>.

Babahan, E. (2006) Andıç günü. *Sabah*, May 10.

Bacık, G. & Aras, B. (2002) Exile: A Keyword in Understanding Turkish Politics. *The Muslim World*, 92 (3–4), 387–418.

Bagci, H. (2000) Adnan Menderes and Turkish Politics. *Turkish Daily News*, May 26.

Bal, I. (2004) *Turkish Foreign Policy in the Post Cold War Era*. Boca Raton, Florida: Universal Publishers.

Balci, T., Burns, T. J., Tongun, L. (2002) Influence of Turkish Islamist Groups on Turkey's Candidacy to the European Union. Paper for presentation at the American Political Science Association annual meeting, Boston, August 29–September 1, 2002, pp.60.

Balim, C., Kalaycioglu, E., Karatas, C., Winrow, G., Yasamee F. eds. (1995) *Turkey: Political, Social, and Economic Challenges in the 1990s*, (Leiden, E.J. Brill.

Barglow, R. (1994) *The Crisis of Self in the Age of Information: Computers, Dolphins and Dreams*. London, Routledge.

Barış, F. (1999) Takiyye, Kitman ve Kripto Solcuları. *Zaman*, July 4. Available from: <http://tr.fgulen.com/content/category/785/208/76/> [May 5, 2007].

Barker, E. (1982) New Religious Movements: A Perspective for Understanding Society. Lampeter: Edwin Mellen Press.

————. (1984) *The Making of a Moonie: Choice or Brainwashing?* Oxford, Blackwell.

————. (1990) *New Religious Movements: A Practical Introduction*, London: Home Office.

————. (2002) *Introducing New Religious Movements.* Fathom Knowledge Network. Available from: www.fathom.com/feature/121938 [May 1, 2006].

Barkey, H. J. (2000) The Struggles of a Strong State. *Journal of International Affairs,* 54(1).

Barlas, M. (1995) Fethullah Gülen's Surprising Ramadan Dinner. *Sabah,* February 14. Available from <http://en.fgulen.com/a.page/tolerance.and.dialogue/ dialogue.and.tolerance.activities/a1314.html>.

————. (2000) Hocaefendi Sendromu. *Yeni Şafak,* September 29.

————. (2006) Denize Dusen Neye Sarilmalidir?' (trans. What Should a Person Who Falls into the Sea Seek Help From?] *Sabah,* May 6.

Bar-Tal, D. (1986) Altruistic motivation to help: Definition, utility and operationalization. *The Humboldt Journal of Social Relations,* 13, 3–14.

Bartholomew (2004) Islam, Secularism and Democracy: The Turkish Experience. From the "Message of His All Holiness Ecumenical Patriarch Bartholomew to the Abant Platform". Washington DC, April 19–20, 2004, pp. 4. Available from <www.sais-jhu.edu/mediastream/videoOndemand/PDF/Bartholomew. pdf>.

Barton, G. (2005) Progressive Islamic thought, civil society and the Gülen movement in the national context: parallels with Indonesia. Presented at the conference *Islam in the Contemporary World: The Fethullah Gülen Movement in Thought and Practice,* organized by the Boniuk Center for the Study and Advancement of Religious Tolerance at Rice University, Houston; the A. D. Bruce Religion Center University of Houston; and the Institute of Interfaith Dialog, Texas, and taking place at Rice University, Houston, Texas, November 12–13, 2005, pp.51.

Bayat, A. (2005) Islamism and Social Movement Theory. *Third World Quarterly,* 26(6), 891–908.

Bayramoglu, A. (1995) Fethullah Hodja and His Community. *Yeni Yüzyıl,* August 26.

BBC (2000a) Turkish Court Begins Trial of Islamic Sect Leader in Absentia. BBC Monitoring Service, UK, October 16.

BBC (2000b) Islamic Preacher Goes on Trial in Turkey. BBC Monitoring Service, UK, October 16. Source: Anatolia News Agency, Ankara, in English, October 16.

BBC (2000c) Islamist Party: Economic Crisis, Not Fundamentalism, Is Turkey's Chief Problem. BBC Monitoring Service: International Reports, UK, September 4. Source: Anatolia News Agency, Ankara, in Turkish, September 4, 2000.

BBC (2000d) Army Chief Demands Islamist Purge. August 31.

Beckford, J. (1989) *Religion and Advanced Industrial Society.* London: Unwin Hyman.

Beekun, R. & Badawi, J. (1999) Leadership: An Islamic Perspective. Herndon, VA: Amana publications. Available from: <www.islamists.org/images/ldrpro.pdf> [October 15, 2006].

Beinin, J. & Stork, J. eds. (1997) *Political Islam.* Berkeley, University of California Press.

Bekdil, B. (2006) A political autopsy report. *Turkish Daily News,* May 24.

Belge, M. (2003) Quotes from Dutch parliamentarian Arie Oostlander's Report on Turkey's Accession to European Union. *Radikal*, June 1.

Benard, C. (2003) *Civil Democratic Islam, Partners, Resources, and Strategies*. VA: RAND Corporation, pp. 88. Available from <www.rand.org/publications/ MR/ MR1716/MR1716.pdf> [October 4, 2005].

Benford, R. D. & Snow, D. A. (2000) Framing Processes and Social Movements: An Overview and Assessment. *Annual Review of Sociology* 26: 611–39.

Berberoglu, E. (1996) *Susurluk's* Missing Link Talks. *Radical*, April 29. Also available under *Turkish Daily News* (1996) *Susurluk's* Missing Link Talks. Turkish Press Scanner, April 30.

Berger, P. L. & Luckmann, T. (1966) *The Social Construction of Reality: A Treatise in the Sociology of Knowledge*. Garden City, NY: Anchor Books.

Berkes, N. (1959) *Turkish Nationalism and Western Civilization: Selected Essays of Ziya Gokalp*. New York: Columbia University Press.

———. (1998) *The Development of Secularism in Turkey*. New York: Routledge.

Bilici, A. (2006) How World Media Failed in the Court Attack. *Zaman*, May 6, 2006. Available from: <www.zaman.com/?bl=columnists& alt=&hn=334 24>.

Billig, M. (1995) Rhetorical Psychology, Ideological Thinking and Imagining Nationhood. In: Johnston and Klandermans eds. (1995), 64–81.

Birand, M. A. (2000a) Wasn't Gülen Supposed to Be a Saviour? Opinion. *Turkish Daily News*, September 2.

———. (2000b) Ecevit and the Military Differ in the Way They View Gülen. Opinion. *Turkish Daily News*, September 5.

———. (2001) February 28 Syndrome. Opinion. *Turkish Daily News*, January 16.

———. (2006a) Will ANDIÇ be repeated? Opinion. *Turkish Daily News*, May 11. Available from <www.turkishdailynews.com.tr/editorial.php?ed=mehmet_ ali_ birand>.

Birand, M. A. (2006b) What is deep state or gang? Opinion. *Turkish Daily News*, June 3. Available from:<www.turkishdailynews.com.tr/editorial.php?ed =mehmet_ali_birand>.

Blumer, H. (1953) Collective Behavior. In: Lee, A. M. ed. *Principles of Sociology*. New York: Barnes & Noble. Originally in: Park R. E. ed. (1939) *An Outline of the Principles of Sociology*. New York, Barnes & Noble (Revised 1951), 199–220.

———. (1957) Collective Behavior. In: Gittler, J. B. ed. *Review of Sociology: Analysis of a Decade*. New York: John Wiley & Sons.

Boggs, C. (1995) Rethinking the Sixties Legacy: From New Left to New Social Movements. In: Stanford, M. L. ed. *Social Movements: Critiques, Concepts, Case Studies*. Hampshire, MacMillan Press, 331–55.

Bonner, A. (2004) An Islamic Reformation in Turkey. *Middle East Policy*, XI(1), 84–97.

Bozdoğan, S. & Kasaba, R. (1997) Introduction. In: Bozdogan, S. & Kasaba, R. eds. (1997), 3–14.

————. eds. (1997) *Rethinking Modernity and National Identity in Turkey*. Seattle, University of Washington Press

Brogan, J. (1997) *Sociology at Hewett* [Internet]. Available from <www.hewett. norfolk.sch.uk/CURRIC/soc/class/socmob.htm>.

Bromley, D. G. & Hadden J. K. eds. (1993) *The Handbook of Cults and Sects in America*, Vol. B. Greenwich, Connecticut: JAI Press.

Browning, G. K., Halcli, A. & Webster, F. (2000) *Understanding Contemporary Society: Theories of the Present*, London: Sage Publications.

Buechler, S. M. (2004) The Strange Career of Strain and Breakdown Theories of Collective Action. In: Snow, D. A., Soule, S.A. & Kriesi, H. eds. (2004), 47–66.

Bulaç, A. (2005) Fethullah Gülen: An intellectual and religious profile. Presented at the conference *Islam in the Contemporary World: The Fethullah Gülen Movement in Thought and Practice*, organized by the Boniuk Center for the Study and Advancement of Religious Tolerance at Rice University, Houston; the A. D. Bruce Religion Center University of Houston; and the Institute of Interfaith Dialog, Texas, and taking place at Rice University, Houston, Texas, November 12–13, 2005, pp.13.

————. (2007) "The Most Recent Reviver in the 'Ulama Tradition: The Intellectual 'Alim, Fethullah Gülen". In: Hunt, R. A. & Aslandoğan, Y. A. (2007) 101-20.

Byrne, P. (1997) *Social Movements in Britain*. London, Routledge.

Çağlar, A. N. (1990) 'The Greywolves as Metaphor' in Finkel, A. & Sirman, N. *Turkish State, Turkish Society*, London: Routledge. 79–101.

Caldarola, C. ed. (1982) *Religions and Societies: Asia and the Middle East*. New York, Mouton Publishers.

Calhoun, C. (1991) 'The Problem of Identity in Collective Action' in Joan Huber (ed.) *Macro-Micro Linkages in Sociology* (Newbury Park, CA: Sage Publications), 51–75.

Çalışlar, O. (1995) Fethullah Gülen'den Cemalettin Kaplan'a, Interviews for *Cumhuriyet*, August 21.

Can, E. (1995) Ateş Böceklerinin Yanıp Sönen Işıklarına Aldanmayız. *Zaman*, September 13.

————. ed. (1996) *Fethullah Gülen Hocaefendi ile Ufuk Turu* (trans. *A Tour of the Horizon with Fethullah Gülen*). Istanbul, Milliyet Yayınları.

Çandar, C. (1998a) Continuation. *Sabah*, September 20.

————. (1998b) The Gülen-Pope Meeting. *Hürriyet*, February 14.

————. (2006) Early elections: A panacea for the plot and predicted tension? *The New Anatolian*, May 24.

Caplan, L. ed. (1987) *Studies in Religious Fundamentalism*. Albany, State University of New York Press.

Çarkoğlu, A. & Toprak, B. (2000) Religion, Society and Politics in Turkey. Summary report of survey research, 2000 [Internet], 1–5. Available from: <www.tesev. org.tr/eng/project/TESEV_search.pdf>.

Çarkoğlu, A. (1998) The Turkish Party System in Transition: Party Performance and Agenda Change. *Political Studies*, 46, 544–53.

Celani, C. (2004) Strategy of Tension: The Case of Italy. *Executive Intelligence Review* (Four-part series in the March 26, April 2, April 9, and April 30, 2004 issues of the EIR magazine). Available from <www.larouchepub.com/other/2004/ 3117tension_italy.html> and <http://en.wikipedia.org/wiki/Strategy_of_tens ion>.

Çelik, G. & Alan, Y. (2006) Fethullah Gülen as a Servant Leader. Presented at the conference *Islam in the Contemporary World: The Fethullah Gülen Movement in Thought and Practice*, organized by the Boniuk Center for the Study and Advancement of Religious Tolerance at Rice University, Houston; the A. D. Bruce Religion Center University of Houston; and the Institute of Interfaith Dialog, Texas, and taking place at Rice University, Houston, Texas, November 12–13, 2005, pp. 13; <www.fethullahgulenconference.org/dallas/ proceedings/ GCelikandYAlan.pdf>.

Cemal, H. (1998) Democratic patience instead of panic and hasty action. *Milliyet*, December 13.

Cerrahoglu, N. (1995) Differences Should Not Lead to Separation. Interview with Prof. Dr. Ali Yasar Saribay. *Milliyet*, August 10.

Çetin, M. (2005) Mobilization and countermobilization: The Gülen movement in Turkey. Presented at the conference *Islam in the Contemporary World: The Fethullah Gülen Movement in Thought and Practice*, organized by the Boniuk Center for the Study and Advancement of Religious Tolerance at Rice University, Houston; the A. D. Bruce Religion Center University of Houston; and the Institute of Interfaith Dialog, Texas, and taking place at Rice University, Houston, Texas, November 12–13, 2005, pp.33.

———. (2006) Voluntary Altruistic Action: Its Symbolic Challenge against Sinecures of Vested Interests. Presented at second *Annual Conference on Islam in the Contemporary World: The Fethullah Gülen Movement in Thought and Practice*, organized by the Department of Religious Studies at the University of Oklahoma, Norman, Oklahoma, the Institute of Interfaith Dialog, Texas, and Petree College of Art and Sciences at Oklahoma City University, November 3–5, 2006, at University of Oklahoma, Norman, Oklahoma, U.S.A, pp.21.

Çevik, I. (1997) Some People Have Discovered Aplarslan Turkes. Editorial. *Turkish Daily News*, April 7.

———. (1998) What shall we gain if MUSIAD is closed? Editorial. *Turkish Daily News*, May 26. Available from: <http://www.turkishdailynews.com.tr/archives. php?id=7283>.

————. (1999) Ciller should prepare for an honorable exit. Editorial. *Turkish Daily News*, November 6. Available from: <http://www.turkishdailynews.com.tr/ archives.php?id=12805>.

————. (1999a) 'The Voice of Reason from the Supreme Court'. Editorial. *Turkish Daily News*, April 28. Available from: <http://www.turkishdailynews.com. tr/ archives.php?id=12170>.

————. (1999b) All This Fight About Fethullah Gülen. Editorial. *Turkish Daily News*, June, 23. Available from: <http://msanews.mynet.net/Scholars/Cevik/; also at <http://en.fgulen.com/content/view/982/14/>.

————. (1999c) 'The USA: A Country Run by "We the People" '. Editorial. *Turkish Daily News*, September 29. Available from: <http://www.turkishdailynews. com.tr/archives.php?id=14287>.

————. (2000a) Is Gülen Really a Terrorist Leader? Editorial. *Turkish Daily News*, September 2. Available from: <hhttp://www.turkishdailynews.com.tr/ ar-chives.php?id=19302>.

————. (2000b) The 'Spokesmen' for the Military. Editorial. *Turkish Daily News*, May 25. Available from: http://www.turkishdailynews.com.tr/archives. php?id=17532>.

————. (2000c) Did They Tell Demirel the Truth about the Weapons? Editorial. *Turkish Daily News*, February 14. Available from: <http://www.turkishdaily news.com.tr/archives.php?id=16079>.

————. (2000d) Is this the role of a newspaper? Editorial. *Turkish Daily News*, June 30. Available from: <http://www.turkishdailynews.com.tr/archives.php?id= 18162>.

————. (2002) Corruption is Also a Top Threat. Editorial. *Turkish Daily News*, January 4. Available from: <http://www.turkishdailynews.com.tr/archives. php?id=26528>.

————. (2007) Welcome Pres. Gul, Goodbye Mr. Sezer, The New Anatolian, August 29. Available from http://www.thenewanatolian.com/opinion-28480.html

Chemers, M. M. (1997) *An Integrative Theory of Leadership*. Mahwah, New Jersey, Lawrence Erlbaum Associates.

Chong, D. (1991) *Collective Action and the Civil Rights Movement*. Chicago, University of Chicago Press.

CIPU-Ind.Homeoffice Country Information and Policy Unit (Homeoffice) (2001) *Country Assessment Turkey*, April, Annex C:1–2, Annex D:1–10. Available from <www.ind.homeoffice.gov.uk/default.asp?PageId=196>.

Cizre-Sakallioglu, U. (1997) The Anatomy of the Turkish Military's Political Autonomy. *Comparative Politics*, 29(2), 151–66.

————. (2003) Turkey 2002: Kemalism, Islamism, and Politics in the Light of the February 28 Process. *The South Atlantic Quarterly*, 102 (2/3), Duke University Press, 309–32.

Cohen, J. L. (1985) Strategy or Identity: New theoretical paradigms and contemporary social movements. *Social Research* 52(4), 663–716.

Cohen, S. (2001) Turkish Muslim Becomes Jewish. *The Sephardi Bulletin*, 55(4). Reprint 18.

Columbia Encyclopedia. 6th ed. (2002) New York, Columbia University Press. (The Columbia Electronic Encyclopedia available from <www.bartleby.com/65/la/LausanneTr.html>.

Cook, K. S., Fine, G. A. & House, J. S. eds. (1995) *Sociological Perspectives on Social Psychology*. Boston: Allyn & Bacon.

Cook, P. J. (1971) Robert Michels's *Political Parties* in Perspective. *The Journal of Politics*, 33(3), 773–96.

Cornell, E. (2001) *Turkey in the 21st Century: Opportunities, Challenges, Threats*. Surrey, Curzon.

Costain, A. N. (1992) *Inviting Women's Rebellion: A Political Process Interpretation of the Women's Movement*. Baltimore, Johns Hopkins University Press.

Council of Higher Education (1996) *Turkish Higher Education System and Institutions*. Ankara, Council of Higher Education.

Couturier, K. (1996) Erbakan Survives Criticism on Libya. *Financial Times*, October 17, p. A3.

Criss, B. & Bilgin, P. (1997) Turkish Foreign Policy towards the Middle East. *Meria Journal*, 1(1) [Online Journal]. Available from: <www.biu.ac.il/SOC/besa/meria/journal/1997/ issue1/jv1n1a3.html>.

Cumhuriyet Ansiklopedisi, 1923–1940, (2002). Ankara, Yapı Kredi Yayınları. (trans: *The Encyclopaedia of the Republic, 1923–1940*. Publications of the bank Yapı Kredi].

Cumhuriyet (1987), 'The Turban Cannot be worn for religious reasons' January 8; 'The ban on the Turban is in the Constitution'.

DA (2004) Dialog Eurasia Platform. Istanbul, Journalists and Writers Foundation.

Dalton, R. J. & Kuechler, M. eds. (1990) *Challenging the Political Order: New Social and Political Movements in Western Democracies*. New York, Oxford University Press.

Delaney, C. (1991) *The Seed and the Soil: Gender and Cosmology in Turkish Village Society. Comparative Studies on Muslim Societies*. Berkeley & Los Angeles, University of California Press.

Deligöz, Ö. (2006) JITEM Wanted to Kill Birand. *Zaman*, May 14. Available from: <www.zaman.com/?bl=national&alt=&trh=20060514&hn=33111>.

Della Porta, D. & Diani, M. (1999) *Social Movements: An Introduction*. Oxford, Blackwell.

Della Porta, D. (1995) *Social Movements, Political Violence, and the State*. Cambridge, Cambridge University Press.

Demirel T. (2004) Soldiers and civilians: the dilemma of Turkish democracy. *Middle Eastern Studies*, 40(1), 127–50. Available from: <http://dx.doi.org/10.1080/00263200412331301927>.

Diani, M. & Eyerman, R. (1992) The Study of Collective Action: Introductory Remarks. In: Diani, M. & Eyerman R. eds. *Studying Collective Action*. London: Sage, pp. 1–5.

Diani, M. (1996) 'Linking Mobilization Frames and Political Opportunities: Insights from Regional Populism in Italy'. *American Sociological Review*, 61/6, 1053–69.

———. (2004) Networks and Participation. In: Snow, D. A., Soule, S.A. & Kriesi, H. eds. (2004), 339–59.

DiMaggio, P. J. & Anheier, H. K. (1990) The Sociology of Nonprofit Organizations and Sectors. *Annual Review of Sociology*, 16, 137–59.

Dinç, A. (1998) Claims and Answers. *Aksiyon*, June 6, No. 183. Available from: <www.aksiyon.com.tr/detay.php?id=17027> English translation available from: <www.fethullahgulen.org/a.page/press/interview/a1216.html>.

Dodd, C. H. (1983) *The Crises of Turkish Democracy*. Beverly, England, The Eothen Press.

Donati, P. (1992) Political Discourse Analysis. In: Diani & Eyerman eds. (1992), 136–65.

Dorronsoro, G. & Massicard, E. (2005) Being a Member of Parliament in Contemporary Turkey. *European Journal of Turkish Studies*, Thematic Issue No. 3, p.30. Available from: <www.ejts.org/document502.html>.

Dorsey, J. M. (1997) Turkish Military "Advice" Reins in Islamist Erbakan Government. *Washington Report* [Internet], June/July, 44–58. Available from: <http://washington-report.org/backissues/0697/9706044.htm>.

———. (2000) Turkish Army Demands Mass Sacking of Islamists. *The Scotsman*, September 1, UK.

Dumanli, E. (2006) The Only Power that can Spoil the Insidious Plan in the Southeast. *Zaman*, March 31. Available from: <http://zaman.com/?bl= columnist-sandalt= andhn=31500>.

Earl, J. (2004) Cultural Consequences of social Movements. In: Snow, D. A., Soule, S.A. & Kriesi, H. eds. (2004), 508–30.

Edelman, M. J. (1971) *Politics as Symbolic Action*. Chicago: Markham.

Edwards, B. & McCarthy, J. D. (2004) Resources and Social Movement Mobilization. In: Snow, D. A., Soule, S.A. & Kriesi, H. eds. *The Blackwell Companion to Social Movements*. Malden, MA, Blackwell, 116–52.

Eickelman, D. F. (1998) Inside the Islamic Reformation. *Wilson Quarterly*, 22(1), 80–90. Also Available from: <www.l.u-tokyo.ac.jp/IAS/HP-e2/papers/ eickelman.html>.

———. (1999) The Coming Transformation of the Muslim World. *Middle East Review of International Affairs* 3(3), 78–81.

————. (2002) The Arab "Street" and the Middle East's Democracy deficit. *Naval War College Review*, LV(4), p.10. Available from: <http:// nwc.navy.mil/ press/Review/2002/autumn/pdfs/art3-a02.pdf> [October 9, 2006].

————. (2004) *Islam, Modernity, and Public Diplomacy in the Arab World: A Moroccan Snapshot.* Stanford, Hoover Press, 63–75.

Eisenger, P. K. (1973) The Conditions of Protest Behavior in American Cities. *American Political Science Review*, 67/1, 11–28.

Eksi, O. (2000) Character Assassination. *Hürriyet*, November 24.

Ercan, Ö. (1998) Gülen'in Verdiği Mülakat. (Question-Answer session with Gülen), April 5. *Milliyet*

Erdoğan, L. (2006) *Küçük Dünyam: Fethullah Gülen.* Istanbul, Ufuk Kitap.

Erdoğan, M. (1999) Islam in Turkish Politics: Turkey's Quest for Democracy without Islam. *Critique: Journal for Critical Studies of the Middle East*, Fall 1999, No.15, 25–49. Association For Liberal Thinking. Available from: www.liberal-dt.org.tr/dergiler/ldsayi14/1410.htm

Eren, N. (1963) *Turkey Today and Tomorrow: An Experiment in Westernization.* New York, Praeger.

Ergene, E. (2004) Introduction. In: Gülen (2004a), v-x.

————. (2005) *Geleneğin Modern Çağa Tanıklığı* (trans. The Witnessing of Tradition to the Modern Age). Akademi, Istanbul. Abridged version in article form titled, 'M. Fethullah Gülen and His Movement: A Common-Sense Approach to Religion and Modernity' available from: <http://en.fgulen.com/content/view/ 2278/14/>.

Ergil, D. (2006) The Problem of Opposition. *Turkish Daily News*, July 10. Available from: <www.turkishdailynews.com.tr/editorial.php?ed=dogu_ergil>.

Ertürk, A. (1997) What goes up must come down. Features section. *Turkish Daily News*, April 28. Available from: <www.turkishdailynews.com/old_editions/ 04_28_97/feature.htm>.

European Parliament (2000) *Briefing on Turkey and Relations with European Union*, Briefing No. 7, February 10, Luxembourg. Third update available from: <www.europarl.eu.int/enlargement/briefings/pdf/7a1_en.pdf>.

Evans, R. ed. (1969) *Readings in Collective Behaviour.* Chicago, Rand McNally.

Eyerman, R. & Jamison, A. (1991) *Social Movements: A Cognitive Approach*, Cambridge: Polity Press.

Ferree, M. M. & Mueller, C. M. (2004) Feminism and the Women's Movement: a Global Perspective. In: Snow, D. A., Soule, S. A. & Kriesi, H. eds. (2004), 576–607.

Ferree, M. M. (1987) Feminist Politics in the U.S. and West Germany. In: Katzenstein, M. & Mueller, C. M. eds. (1987), 64-88.

Ficici, A. (2001) *Political Economy of Turkish Privatization: A Critical Assessment.* Available at: <www.ksg.harvard.edu/kokkalis/GSW3/Aysun_Ficici.pdf>.

Finkel, S. E. & Muller, E. N. (1998) Rational Choice and the Dynamics of Collective Political Action: Evaluating Alternative Models with Panel Data. *American Political Science Review*, 92(1), 37–49.

Fireman, B. & Gamson, W. A. (1979) 'Utilitarian Logic in the Resource Mobilization Perspective' in Zald, M. & McCarthy, J. (eds.) *The Dynamics of Social Movements* (Cambridge, MA: Winthrop), 8–44.

Frank, A.W. (1996) Notes on Habermas: Lifeworld and System, the University of Calgary. Available from: <www.ucalgary.ca/~frank/habermas.html>.

Frantz, D. (2000) Turkey Assails a Revered Islamic Moderate. *New York Times*, August 25. Available from: <www.library.cornell.edu/colldev/mideast/ gulen. htm> [October 4, 2005].

Freud, S. (1922) *Group Psychology and the Analysis of the Ego*. Trans J. Strachey. London, The Hogarth Press.

Fuchs, C. (2005) The Self-Organization of Social Movements. [2006 version available from *Systemic Practice and Action Research*, 19(1), February, 101-37.] Available from: <http://igw.tuwien.ac.at/christian/SM1.pdf>.

Fuller, G. E. (2004) Turkey's Strategic Model: Myths and Realities. *The Washington Quarterly*, 27(3), 51–64.

Gamson, W. A. & Meyer, D. S. (1996) Framing Political Opportunity. In: McAdam, D., McCarthy, J. D., & Zald, M. eds. (1996a), 275–90.

Gamson, W. A. & Modigliani, A. (1989) Media Discourse and Public Opinion on Nuclear Power. *American Journal of Sociology* 95, 1–37.

Gamson, W. A. (1974) Violence and Political Power: The Meek Don't Make It. *Psychology Today*, 8, 35–41.

———. (1975) *The Strategy of Protest*. Homewood, Ill., Dorsey Press.

———. (1992) The Social Psychology of Collective Action. In: Morris & Mueller eds. (1992) 53–76.

Gamson, W. A. & Wolfsfeld, G. (1993) Movements and Media as Interacting Systems, *Annals of the American Academy of Political and Social Science* 528: 114-25.

Garner, R. (1996) *Contemporary Movements and Ideologies*. McGraw-Hill, New York.

Genov, I. (1996) Interview with "the teacher who builds hundreds of bridges". *Trud*, October 15. (Turkish version available from: <http://tr.fgulen.com /a.page/ asindan/roportajlar/gazeteler/bulgar.trudda.ivan.genov/a1933.html>.

Gerhardt, U. (2002) Worlds Come Apart: Systems Theory versus Critical Theory. Drama in the History of Sociology in the Twentieth Century, *The American Sociologist*, 33/2, 5–39.

Gerlach, L. P. & Hine, V. H. (1968) Five Factors Crucial to the Growth and Spread of a Modern Religious Movement. *Journal for the Scientific Study of Religion*, 7(1), 23–40.

————. (1970) *People, Power, Change: Movements of social transformation.* Indianapolis, Bobbs-Merrill.

Giddens A., Duneier, M. & Appelbaum, R. P. (2004) *Introduction to Sociology.* 5th ed. New York, W. W. Norton & Company. Also available from: <www.wwnorton.com/giddens4/chapters/chapter13/welcome.htm>.

Giddens, A. (1989) *Sociology.* Cambridge, Polity Press.

Giugni, M. & Passy, F. (1999) Models of Citizenship, Political Opportunities, and the Claim-Making of Immigrants and Ethnic Minorities: A Comparison of France and Switzerland. *American Sociological Association Section on Collective Behavior and Social Movements Working Paper Series*, 2(9), pp.1–26. Available from: <www.nd.edu/~dmyers/cbsm>.

————. (2000) Cleavages, Opportunities, and Citizenship: Political Claim-making by the Extreme Right in France and Switzerland. [Internet] Available from: <www.nd.edu/~dmyers/cbsm/vol3/yale.pdf >.

———— (2004) Migrant mobilization between political institutions and citizenship regimes: A comparison of France and Switzerland. *European Journal of Political Research* 43 (1), 51–82.

Giugni, M., McAdam, D. & Tilly, C. eds. (1999). *How Social Movements Matter.* Minneapolis, University of Minnesota Press.

Glock, C. (1959) The sociology of religion, in R. Merton, L. Broom, and L. Cottrell Jr. (eds.), *Sociology Today 1.* New York: Harper & Row. pp. 153-77.

Goffman, E. (1974) *Frame Analysis: An Essay on the Organization of Experience.* New York: Harper & Row.

————. (1981) A Reply to Denzin and Keller. *Contemporary Sociology*, 10, 60–8.

Gökçek, M. (2005) "Gülen and Sufism". Conference Proceedings, Islam in the contemporary world: The Fethullah Gülen Movement in Thought and Practice. Rice University Houston, Texas. pp.357-364.

Gökçek, M. (2007) Gülen and Sufism: A Historical Perspective. In: Hunt, R. A. & Aslandogan, Y. A. eds. (2007), 183–93.

Goldstone, J. A. (1980) The Weakness of Organization: A New Look at Gamson's *The Strategy of Social Protest. American Journal of Sociology*, 85(5), 1017–42.

Göle, N. (1991) *Modern Mahrem: Medeniyet ve Örtünme.* Istanbul, Metis Yayınları.

————. (1994) Towards an Autonomization of Politics and Civil Society in Turkey. In: Heper, M. & Evin, A. *Politics in the Third Turkish Republic.* Boulder, Westview Press, 213–22.

————. (1996a) Modernity Made Meaningful by Conservatism. In: Can, E. ed. (1996) *Ufuk Turu.* Istanbul, Milliyet Yayınları.

————. (1996b) *The Forbidden Modern: Civilization and Veiling. Critical Perspectives on Women and Gender.* Ann Arbor, The University of Michigan Press.

————. (1997a) The Gendered Nature of the Public Sphere. *Public Culture*, 10(1).

————. (1997b) Secularism and Islamism in Turkey: The Making of Elites and Coun-
ter-elites. *Middle East Journal*, 51 (1), 46–58.

————. (1997c) The Quest for the Islamic Self within the Context of Modernity. In:
Bozdogan, S. & Kasaba, R. eds. (1997), 81–99. Available from: <http://cia-
onet.org/book/bozdogan/bozdogan06.html>.

————. (2000) Snapshots of Islamic Modernity. *Daedalus*, 129 (1), 91–118.

————. (2002) Islam in Public: New Visibilities and New Imaginaries. *Public Culture*, 14(1), 173–90.

Greenleaf, R. (1970) *The Servant as Leader*. Indianapolis, IN., Greenleaf Center for
Servant-Leadership.

Greenwald, J. (1986) Italy a Thicket of Contradictions. *TIME*, April 7.

Gülen, F. (1996) *Towards the Lost Paradise*. London, UK, Truestar.

————. (1998a) Message to the President of the Angels' Movement. Available from:
<http://en.fgulen.com/content/view/970/14/>.

————. (1998b) *Criteria or Lights of the Way*. Izmir, Turkey: Kaynak.

————. (2000b) *Criteria or Lights of the Way*. London, UK, Truestar.

————. (2000c) At the Threshold of the New Millennium. *The Fountain*, No. 29,
4–9.

————. (2000d) *Pearls of Wisdom*. Vol.1. Fairfax, VA. The Fountain.

————. (2001a) A Comparative Approach to Islam and Democracy. *SAIS Review of
International Affairs*, XXI(2), 133–38.

————. (2001b) Gülen's Testimony at the U.S. Attorney's Office, Newark, NJ, on
6.11.2001. Available from: <http://en.fgulen.com/content/view/1050/ 14/>.

————. (2004a) *Toward a Global Civilization of Love and Tolerance*. Somerset, New
Jersey, The Light, Inc.

————. (2004b) *Key Concepts in the Practice of Sufism: Emerald Hills of the Heart*.
Vol.1. Somerset, New Jersey, The Light, Inc.

————. (2005a) *The Statue of Our Souls: Revival in Islamic Thought and Activism*.
Somerset, New Jersey, The Light, Inc.

————. (2005b) An interview with Gülen by Zeki Saritoprak & Ali Ünal. In: *The
Muslim World Special Issue*, 95(3), 447–67.

————. (2006) Bu Çağın En Sinsi Takıyyecileri. April 24. Available from: <www.
herkul.org> and <http://tr.fgulen.com/content/view/12133/9/>.

Gülerce, H. (2003a) Preface. In Koru, F. (2003) *Native and Peculiar: A Story for a
Nobel Prize*. Istanbul, Journalists and Writers Foundation.

————. (2003b) Mr Sezer unfortunately misled most of us. *Zaman*, July 7. Available
from:<www.zaman.com/default.php?kn=3045andbl=commentary>.

————. (2004) Gülen's Message to the European Union. *Zaman*, December 17.
Available from: <www.zaman.org/?bl=columnistsandtrh=20050301andhn=
14825> [October 1, 2005].

———. (2005) Gülen's warnings. *Zaman*, October 29. Available from: <www.za-man.com/?bl=columnists&alt=&trh=20051101&hn=25850>.

———. (2006) Siz de kaybedersiniz … . *Zaman*, May 12. Available from: <www.zaman.com.tr/?bl=yazarlar&alt=&hn=284386>.

Gültaşlı, S. (1999) Interview. *Turkish Daily News*, December 17.

Gündem, M. (2005) *11 Days with Fethullah Gülen: An analysis of a movement with question-and-answers*. 5th ed. Istanbul, Alfa. Available in English from: <http://en.fgulen.com/content/view/1918/14>.

Güney, A. & Karatekelioglu, P. (2005) Turkey's EU Candidacy and Civil-Military Relations: Challenges and Prospects. *Armed Forces and Society*, 31(3), 439–62.

Gupta, D. (2002) Radical Flank Effects: The Effect of Radical-Moderate Splits in Regional Nationalist Movements. Prepared for the *Conference of Europeanists*, Chicago, March 14–16, 2002, pp.46. Available from: <http://falcon.arts. cornell.edu/sgt2/PSCP/documents/RFEgupta.pdf> [February 10, 2007].

Haas, R. N. ed. (1999) *Transatlantic Tension: The United States, Europe, and Problem Countries*. Washington, DC, Brookings Institution Press.

Habermas, J. (1984) *The Theory of Communicative Action. Volume 1: Reason and the Rationalization of Society*. Trans. McCarthy, T. Boston, Massachusetts, Beacon Press.

Hale, W. (1994) *Turkish Politics and the Military*. London, Routledge.

———. (1999) Turkey's Domestic Political Landscape: A Glance at the Past and the Future. *The International Spectator*, XXXIV(1), 27–46. Available from: <www.ciaonet.org/olj/iai/iai_99haw01.html> [August 17, 2005].

Hallin, D. & Mancini, P. (1984) Speaking of the President: Political Structure and the Representational Form in US and Italian Television News. *Theory of Society* 13(6), 829–50.

Hand, N. (2004) *America and the 'Islamic Revival': Reconstituting US Foreign Policy in the Muslim World*. School of International Service, American University, pp.154. Available from: <www.drsoroush.com/PDF/E-CMO-20040412-America_ and_ the_Islamic_Revival-Natalie_Hand.pdf>.

Hannigan, J. A. (1991) Social Movement Theory and the Sociology of Religion: Toward a New Synthesis, *Sociological Analysis*, 52(4), 311-331.

Harvey, D. (1989) *"The Condition of Postmodernity," An Enquiry into the Origins of Cultural Change*. Oxford, Basil Blackwell.

Heberle, R. (1951) *Social Movements: An Introduction to Political Sociology*. New York, Appleton-Crofts.

Hefner, R. W. ed. (2004) *Democratic Civility: The History and Cross-Cultural Possibility of a Modern Political Ideal*. New Brunswick, Transaction Publishers. E-version available from Institute on Culture, Religion and World Affairs, Boston University, Brookline, MA at <www.bu.edu/cura/about/hefnermaterials/ hefnerdemocraticcivilityexc.htm>.

Hekimoglu, I. (2000) Journalist Çandar: "The media aristocracy resists change". *Turkish Daily News*, November 11.

Hendrick, J. D. (2006) Global Islam and the Secular Modern World: Transnational Muslim Social Movements and the Movement of Fethullah Gülen, A Comparative Approach. Presented at the second *International Conference on Islam in the Contemporary World: The Fethullah Gülen Movement in Thought and Practice*, organized by the Graduate Program in Religious Studies, Dedman College, Southern Methodist University, the Office of the Chaplain at Southern Methodist University, and the Institute of Interfaith Dialog, Texas, and taking place at Southern Methodist University, Dallas, Texas, March 4–5, 2006, pp.35.

———. (2007) The Regulated Potential of Kinetic Islam: Antithesis in Global Islamic Activism. In: Hunt, A. R. & Aslandogan, Y. A. eds. (2007), 12–33.

Heper, M. (1990) Motherland Party Governments and Bureaucracy in Turkey, 1983–1988. *Governance*, 2, 460–71. In *Turkish Daily News*, Feature Article, Heper, M. Turkey: Yesterday, today and tomorrow – Part Three. May 23, 2002.

Hermansen, M. (2005) Understandings of "Community" within the Gülen Movement. Presented at the conference *Islam in the Contemporary World: The Fethullah Gülen Movement in Thought and Practice*, organized by the Boniuk Center for the Study and Advancement of Religious Tolerance at Rice University, Houston; the A. D. Bruce Religion Center, University of Houston; and the Institute of Interfaith Dialog, Texas, and taking place at Rice University, Houston, Texas, November 12–13, 2005, pp.18.

Hirsch, E. L. (1986) The Creation of Political Solidarity in Social Movement Organizations. *Sociological Quarterly* 27, 373–87.

Hobsbawm, E. J. (1990) *Nations and Nationalism since 1780: Program, Myth, Reality*. Cambridge, Cambridge University Press.

House of Commons, Foreign Affairs Committee. (2002) Publication of Report Turkey. Press Notice No. 31 of Session 2001–02, dated April 29, 2002, 64–85. Available from: <www.parliament.the-stationery-office.co.uk/pa/cm200102/cmselect/cmfaff/606/60606.htm#note77>.

Howard, A. (2005) Impressions of Turkey: Learning About an Islamic Movement That Promotes Tolerance. *Jewish Herald-Voice*, September 1. Available from: <www.jhvonline.com>; also from <http://en.fgulen.com/content/view/1995/14/> [February 10, 2007].

Howard, D. A. (2001) *The History of Turkey*. Westport, CT, Greenwood Press.

Howe, M. (2000) *Turkey Today: A Nation Divided Over Islam's Revival*. Boulder, Colorado, Westview Press.

Hunt, R. (2007) Challenges in Understanding the Muslim Citizens of the Globalized World. In: Hunt, R. A. & Aslandogan, Y. A. eds. (2007), 1–10.

Hunt, R. A. & Aslandogan, Y. A. eds. (2007) *Muslim Citizens of the Globalized World: Contributions of the Gülen Movement.* Somerset, New Jersey, IID Press & The Light, Inc.

Hunt, S. A. & Benford, R. D. (2004) 'Collective Identity, Solidarity, and Commitment' in Snow, D. A., Soule, S. A. & Kriesi, H. eds. (2004), 433–58.

Hürriyet (1995) Özkök'le Röportaj, January 23–28.

Hürriyet (2000) NGO Fethullah. January 27. Available from: <http://arsiv. hurriyetim.com.tr/hur/turk/00/01/27/turkiye/10tur.htm> [October 5, 2005].

Hyman, R. (1971) *Marxism and the Sociology of Trade Unionism.* London, Pluto Press. E-version available from: <http://socserv2.mcmaster.ca/soc/courses/soc4s3/theory/hyman.htm#critiqueiron>.

Ilıcak, N. (2000) Çevik Bir'in Eylem Planı, *Yeni Şafak,* October 21, P.1

İpekçi, L. (2007) Türbandan korkanlara açık mektup, September 23, *Zaman.* Available from: <http://www.zaman.com.tr/wcbapp tr/haber.do?haberno= 591985>.

Irvine, J. (2006) The Gülen Movement and Turkish Integration in Germany. Presented at second *Annual Conference on Islam in the Contemporary World: The Fethullah Gülen Movement in Thought and Practice,* organized by the Department of Religious Studies at the University of Oklahoma, Norman, Oklahoma, the Institute of Interfaith Dialog, Texas, and Petree College of Art and Sciences at Oklahoma City University, November 3–5, 2006, at University of Oklahoma, Norman, Oklahoma, USA, pp. 55–74.

———. (2007) The Gülen Movement and Turkish Integration in Germany. In: Hunt, R. A. & Aslandogan, Y. A. eds. *Muslim Citizens of the Globalized World: Contributions of the Gülen Movement,* 62–84.

Jackall, R. & Vidich, A. J. (1995) Series Preface. In: Stanford, M. L. ed. *Social Movements: Critiques, Concepts, Case-Studies.* Hampshire, MacMillan Press, vii–xi.

Johnston, H. & Klandermans, B. eds. (1995) *Social Movements and Culture.* Minneapolis, University of Minnesota Press.

Johnston, H. (1995) A Methodology for Frame Analysis: From Discourse to Cognitive Schemata. In: Johnston, H. & Klandermans, B. eds. (1995), 217–46.

Jones, R. H. (2000) *Reductionism: Analysis and the Fullness of Reality.* Caranbury, New Jersey, Bucknell University Press.

Joppke, C. (1991) Social Movements during Cycles of Issue Attention. The Decline of the Anti-Nuclear Energy Movements in West Germany and the USA. *British Journal of Sociology* 42, pp 43–60.

Jung, D. (1999) Turkey at the Crossroads, March 1999, Copenhagen Peace Research Institute. Available from: <www.ciaonet.org/wps/jud01/> [September 9, 2005].

JWF (2004) *The Abant Platform.* Istanbul, Journalists and Writers Foundation.

Kadip (2004) *Intercultural Dialog Platform.* Istanbul, Journalist and Writers Foundation.

Kalaycioglu, E. (1977) The Logic of Contemporary Turkish Politics. *MERIA Journal,* September 1997. Available from: <http://biu.ac.il/SOC/besa/meria. html>.

———. (1988) Elite Political Culture and Regime Stability: the Case of Turkey. *Journal of Economics and Administrative Sciences,* Bogaziçi University, 2, 149–79.

———. (1997) The Logic of Contemporary Turkish Politics. *Meria Journal,* 1(3). Available from: <http://meria.idc.ac.il/journal/1997/issue3/ jv1n3a6.html>.

Kamış, M. (2006) Can Turkey Become North Korea? *Zaman,* June 7, 2006, <www. zaman.com/?bl=columnists&trh=20060629&hn=33799.

Kandiyoti, D. (1991) End of Empire: Islam, Nationalism and Women in Turkey. In: Kandiyoti, D. ed. *Women, Islam and the State.* Philadelphia, Temple University.

Karaman, M. L. & Aras, B. (2000) The Crisis of Civil Society in Turkey. *Journal of Economic and Social Research* 2(2), pp: 39–61. Available from: <http://jesr. journal.fatih.edu.tr/TheCrisisofCivilSocietyinTurkey.pdf>.

Kasaba, R. (1997) Kemalist Certainties and Modern ambiguities. In: Bozdogan, S. & Kasaba, R. eds. (1997), 15–36.

Katzenstein, M. & Mueller, C. M. eds. (1987) *The Women's Movements of the United States and Western Europe.* Philadelphia, Temple University Press.

Kaya, O. (2000) Gülen ılımlı din adamı (trans. Gülen is a moderate Islamic scholar). *Zaman,* September 15.

Kazancigil, A., & Özbudun, E. eds. (1981) *Atatürk: Founder of a Modern State.* London, Hurst.

Kebede A, Shriver, T. E. & Knottnerus, J. D. (2000) Social Movement Endurance: Collective Identity and the Rastafari. *Sociological Inquiry,* 70(3), 313–37.

Keneş, B. (2003) Velvet Revolution. Turkish Probe, Issue 544. *Turkish Daily News,* June 29.

Kilbourne, B. K. & Richardson, J. T. (1988) Paradigm conflict, types of conversion, and conversion theories. *Sociological Analysis,* 50(1), 1–21.

Kılıç, Ali (1955) *İstiklal Mahkemesi Hatıraları.* Istanbul, Sel Yayınları.

Kılıç, Ayla (1998) Democratization, Human Rights and Ethnic Policies in Turkey. *Journal of Muslim Minority Affairs,* 18(1), 91–103.

Kinzer, S. (1997) In Defense of Secularism, Turkish Army Warns Rulers. *New York Times,* March 2.

———. (2001) Turkey's Political Earthquake. *Middle East Quarterly,* Fall. 8(4), 41–48. Available from: <www.meforum.org/article/106>.

Kitschelt, H. (1985) New Social Movements in West Germany and the United States, *Political Power and Social Theory,* 5, 273–324.

———. (1986) Political Opportunity Structures and Political Protest: Anti-Nuclear Movements in Four Democracies. *British Journal of Political Science* 16, 57–85.

———. (1993) 'Citizens, Protest and Democracy', in Social Movements, Political Parties and Democratic Theory, Annals of the American Academy of Political and Social Science, July, 528/1, 13–29.

Klandermans, B. (2004) The Demand and Supply of Participation: Social-Psychological Correlates of Participation in social Movements. In: Snow, D. A., Soule, S.A. & Kriesi, H. eds. (2004), 360–79.

———. ed. (1989) *Organizing for Change: Social Movement Organizations Across Cultures.* Greenwich, Conn., JAI Press.

Klandermans, B., Kriesi, H. & Tarrow, S. eds. (1988) *From Structure to Action: Comparing Social Movement Research across Countries.* Greenwich, CT: JAI Press Inc.

Klose, B. (1997) A Sampling of this year's Hot but Hidden news stories. *Censored Alert: The Newsletter of Project Censored*, 1(3). CA, Sonoma State University, p. 4. Available from: <www.projectcensored.org/newsletter/vol1iss3.pdf> [October 14, 2004].

Kniss, F. & Burns, G. (2004) Religious Movements. In: Snow, D. A., Soule, S.A. & Kriesi, H. eds. (2004), 694– 717.

Koenig, T. (2004) 'On Frames and Framing, Anti-Semitism as Free Speech: A Case Study', Paper presented to Session PCR13 – Methods, Research, Concepts. IAMCR Annual Meeting, Porto Alegre, Brazil, July 25–30, 2004, pp.23. Available from: <www.lboro.ac.uk/research/mmethods/research/ case_ studies/hohmann/koenig_frames_hohmann_IAMCR_2004.pdf>.

Kömeçoğlu, U. (1997) *A Sociologically Interpretative Approach to the Fethullah Gülen Community Movement*, MA Thesis (unpublished), Sociology Department, Boğaziçi University, Istanbul.

Komisar, L. (1997) Turkey's Terrorists: A CIA Legacy Lives On. *The Progressive*, April. Available from: <www.totse.com/en/politics/terrorists_and_freedom_ fighters/ciaturkt.html>.

Kongar, E. (1986) Turkey's Cultural Transformation. In: Renda, G. & Kortepeter, C. M. ed. *The Transformation of Turkish Culture, The Ataturk Legacy*. Princeton, New Jersey, The Kingston Press Inc, 19 68.

———. (2003) Asker-Siyaset Iliskilerinde Unutulan Noktolar II. June 23. Available from: <www.kongar.org/aydinlanma/2003/368_Asker-Siyaset_ Iliskileri_II.php>.

———. (1986) Turkey's cultural transformation." In G. Renda and C. M. Kortepeter (eds) *The transformation of Turkish culture, the Atatürk legacy* (The Kingston Press. Inc: Princeton, New Jersey), 19–68, at 19. Available from <http://www.kongar.org /aen_tr.php>

Koopmans, R. & Statham, P. (1999) Ethnic and Civic Conceptions of Nationhood and the Differential Success of the Extreme Right in Germany and Italy. In: Giugni, M., McAdam, D. & Tilly, C. eds. (1999), 225–51.

Koopmans, R. (1995) *Democracy from Below*. Boulder, CO, Westview.

———. (2004) Protest in Time and Space: The Evolution of Waves of Contention. In: Snow, D. A., Soule, S.A. & Kriesi, H. eds. (2004), 19–46.

Koray, C. (1998) A Religious Scholar: Fethullah Gülen. *Aksam*, March 13.

Koru, F. (1997) The Pride of Turkey. *Zaman*, September 9.

————. (1997b) Nation Builds and Protects. *Zaman*, December 25.

————. (1998) When the Clouds Dispersed. *Zaman*, March 31.

————. (1998a) Not a Syndrome But a Story for a Nobel Prize. *Zaman*, March, 16.

————. (2000) A Simple Question. *Yeni Safak*, November 13.

Kramer, H. (2000) *A Changing Turkey: the Challenge to Europe and the United States*. Washington, DC, Brookings.

Kriesberg, L. ed. (1978) *Research in Social Movements, Conflict and Change 1*. Greenwich, Conn: JAI Press Inc.

Kriesi, H. (1989) New Social Movements and the New Class in the Netherlands. *American Journal of Sociology* 94, 1078–1116.

————. (1996) The Organizational Structure of the New Social Movements in A Political Context. In: McAdam, D., McCarthy, J. D., & Zald, M. eds. *Comparative Perspectives on Social Movements: Political Opportunities, Mobilizing Structures*. Cambridge, Cambridge University Press, 152–84.

————. (2004) Political Context and Opportunity. In: Snow, D. A., Soule, S.A. & Kriesi, H. eds. (2004), 67–90.

Kriesi, H., Koopmans, R., Duyvendak, J.W. & Giugni, M. (1995) *New Social Movements in Western Europe*. Minneapolis, University of Minnesota Press.

Kuriakose, S. (2006) Review of *The Strategy of Social Protest* by William Gamson. PSC 129. Available from: <http://web.syr.edu/~smkuriak/Gamson.html> [April 20, 2006].

Kurtz, L. (2005) Gülen's Paradox: Combining Commitment and Tolerance. *The Muslim World, Special Issue, Islam in Contemporary Turkey: the Contributions of Gülen*, 95(3), 373–84.

Kuru, A. T. (2003) Fethullah Gülen's Search for a Middle Way between Modernity and Muslim Tradition. In: Yavuz, M. H. & Esposito, J. L. eds. (2003), 115–30.

————. (2005a) Globalization and Diversification of Islamic Movements: Three Turkish Cases. *Political Science Quarterly*, 120(2), 253–74.

————. (2005b) Reinterpretation of Secularism in Turkey: The Case of the Justice and Development Party. Forthcoming in: Yavuz, M. H. ed. (2005) *Transformation of Turkish Politics*. Salt Lake City, University of Utah Press, pp.16.

Landau, J. M. ed. (1984) *Ataturk and the Modernization of Turkey*. Boulder, CO, Westview Press.

Le Bon, G. (1960) *The Crowd: A Study of Popular Mind*. New York, Viking.

Lebor, A. (1997) *A Heart Turned East: Among the Muslims of Europe and Africa*. London, Little, Brown and Company.

Lentin, A. (1999) Structure, Strategy, Sustainability: What Future for New Social Movement Theory? *Sociological Research Online*, 4(3). Available from: www.socresonline.org.uk/socresonline/4/3/lentin.html

Lewis, B. (1965) *The Emergence of Modern Turkey*. London, Oxford University Press. (First published 1961.)

———. (1968) *Emergence of Modern Turkey*, London: Oxford University Press. (2nd ed.)

Lewis, G. (1984) Ataturk's Language Reform as an Aspect of Modernization in the Republic of Turkey. In: Landau, J. M. ed. (1984), 195–214.

———. (1999) *The Turkish Language Reform: A Catastrophic Success*. Oxford, Oxford University Press, 37–41.

Lewis, J. M. (1975) Review of *The Strategy of Social Protest* by William Gamson. *Contemporary Sociology*, 4(5), 516–7.

Lipsky, M. (1968) Protest as a Political Resource. *American Political Science Review*, 62(4), 1144–58.

Lofland, J. (1996) *Social Movement Organizations: Guide to Research on Insurgent Realities*. New York: Aldine De Gruyter.

Lombardi, B. (1997) Turkey–Return of the Reluctant Generals? *Political Science Quarterly*, Summer 112(2), 191–215. Available from: <http://members.tripod. com/~Bregava/lombardi.htm>.

Lyman, S. M. (1995) *Social Movements: Critiques, Concepts, Case-Studies*. MacMillan, Basingstoke, Hampshire.

Macionis, J. J. (1995) *Sociology*. Englewood Cliffs, NJ, Prentice Hall Inc.

Mainichi Shimbun, (2000) Turkiye Modeli: Orta asya'ya cikis icin egitim ve isi birarada kullanmak. Tokyo, April 22, (trans. Turkey's Model: using education and business together while opening to Central Asia). Translated and published on 24/04/00 at <www.byegm.gov.tr/yayinlarimiz/disbasin/2000/04/25x04x00 . htm> [May 26, 2005].

Makovsky, A. & Sayari, S. eds. (2000) *Turkey's New World: Changing Dynamics in Turkish Foreign Policy*. Washington, Washington Institute for Near East Policy.

Makovsky, A. (2000) Turkey's Political Storm. Guest commentator, August 25, The International Institute for Strategic Studies. Available from: <www.iiss.org/> [January 21, 2005].

Mamay, S. (1990) Theories of social movements and their current development in Soviet Society. Working paper, presented at the Sociology Summer School for Soviet Sociologists at the University of Kent, Canterbury, July–September 1990. Available from: <http://lucy.ukc.ac.uk/csacpub/russian/mamay.html>.

Mardin, S. (1973) 'Center-Periphery Relations: A Key to Turkish Politics?' *Daedalus: Journal of the American Academy of Arts and Sciences* 102/1, 169–91.

———. (1975) Center-Periphery Relations: a Key to Turkish Politics? In: Akarli, E. D. & Ben-Dor, G. eds. (1975), 7–32.

———. (1982) Turkey: Islam and Westernization. In: Caldarola, C. ed. (1982), 170–98.

———. (1989) *Religion and Social Change in Modern Turkey: The Case of Bediuzzaman Said Nursi*. (Suny Series in Near Eastern Studies) New York, State University of New York.

———. (1996) An Exceptional Place of Integrating Intelligence. In: Can, E. ed. (1996). Available in English from: <http://en.fgulen.com/content/view/ 788/13/>.

Margulies, R. & Yildizoglu, E. (1997) 'The Resurgence of Islam and the Welfare Party in Turkey' in: Beinin, J. & Stork, J. eds. (1997), 144–53.

Mason, W. (2000) The Future of Political Islam in Turkey. *World Policy Journal,* XVII(2), 56–67.

Mastany, V. & Nation, R. C. eds. (1998) *Turkey between East and West: New Challenges for a rising Regional Power.* Boulder, CO, Westview

Mater, N. & Kurkcu, E. (2001) Army's role contested at the threshold. [Internet] Bianet, August 25. Available from: <www.bianet.org/2003/03/21_eng/news 4238.htm>.

Mayer, J. F. (2004) Gülen Movement: Modern Expression of Turkish Islam. Interview with Hakan Yavuz. First published July 2004 in *Religioscope.* Republished in *Journal of Turkish Weekly,* January 5, 2005. Available from: <www. turkishweekly.net/comments.php?id=106>.

Mayer, M. (1991) Social Movement Research on Social Movement Practice: The U.S. Pattern. In: Rucht, D. ed. (1991), 47–120.

———. (1995) Social Movement Research in the United States: A European Perspective. In: Stanford, M. L. ed. (1995), 168–95.

McAdam, D. & Rucht, D. (1993) Cross-National Diffusion of Movement Ideas. *Annals of the American Academy of Political and Social Sciences* 528, 56–74.

McAdam, D. (1982) *Political Process and the Development of Black Insurgency, 1930–1970.* Chicago, University of Chicago Press.

———. (1986) Recruiting to High-Risk Activism: The Case of Freedom Summer. *American Journal of Sociology* 92, 64–90.

———. (1996) Conceptual Origins, Current Problems, Future Directions. In: McAdam, D., McCarthy, J. D. & Zald, M. N. eds. (1996b), 23–40.

McAdam, D., McCarthy, J. D. & Zald, M. N. (1988), 'Social Movements' in: Smelser, N. J. ed. (1988), 695–739.

———. (1996a) 'Introduction: Opportunities, Mobilizing Structures and Framing Processes – Toward a Synthetic, Comparative Perspective on Social Movements' in McAdam, McCarthy, & Zald, eds. (1996b), 1–20.

———., eds. (1996b) *Comparative Perspectives on Social Movements: Political Opportunities, Mobilizing Structures and Cultural Framings.* Cambridge, Cambridge University Press.

McCarthy, J. D. & Zald, M. N. (1977) 'Resource Mobilization and Social Movements: A Partial Theory', *American Journal of Sociology* 82/6, 1212–41.

———. (1987a) The Trend of Social Movements in America: Professionalism and Resource Mobilization. In: McCarthy, J. D. & Zald, M. N. eds. (2003), 337–91. [Article originally published by General Learning Press, 1973.].

———. eds. ([1987] 2003) *Social Movements in an Organizational Society: Collected Essays.* New Brunswick, NJ, Transaction Publishers.

McDowall, D. (1997) *A Modern History of the Kurds*. Revised ed. London, I.B. Tauris.

Mellor, P. A. (2004) *Religion, Realism and Social Theory: Making Sense of Society*. London, Sage Publications Inc.

Melucci, A. (1985) The symbolic challenge of contemporary movements. *Social Research*, Vol. 52, No. 4, Winter, 789–815.

———. (1999) *Challenging Codes: Collective action in the information age*. Cambridge, Cambridge University Press. (Reprinted 1999; First edition 1996.)

Mengi, G. (1995) A New Phase. *Sabah*, February 16.

Metz, H. C. ed. (1996) *Turkey: A Country Study*. 5th ed. Washington, DC, Federal Research Division, Library of Congress.

Michel, T. (2003) Fethullah Gülen as Educator, In: Yavuz, H. and Esposito, J. (2003), 69–84.

———. (2004) Foreword, In: Gülen, F. (2004a), i–iii.

———. (2005a) Two Frontrunners for Peace: John Paul II and Fethullah Gülen. Presented at the *Frontrunners of Peace* symposia organized by the Cosmicus Foundation, Holland, at universities in Tilburg, Erasmus, and Amsterdam, March 16–18, 2005. Available from: <http://en.fgulen.com/content/view/1944/19/>.

———. (2005b) Sufism and Modernity in the Thought of Fethullah Gülen. *The Muslim World, Special Issue, Islam in Contemporary Turkey: the Contributions of Gülen*, 95(3), 341–58.

———. (2006) Gülen as Educator and Religious Leader. In: The Fountain (2006), 101–113. (A summary of the paper presented by Father Thomas Michel, in the *Fethullah Gülen Symposium* held at Georgetown University, April 2001.)

Michels, R. ([1915] 1999) *Political Parties: A Sociological Study of the Oligarchical Tendencies of Modern Democracy*. Trans. Eden & Cedar Paul. New Brunswick, NJ, Transaction Publishing. (First published 1915.)

Morris, A. & Mueller, C. M. eds. (1992) *Frontiers in Social Movement Theory*. New Haven, Conn., Yale University Press.

Morris, A. D., & Staggenborg, S. (2004) Leadership in Social Movements. In: Snow, D. A., Soule, S.A. & Kriesi, H. eds. (2004), 171–96.

Morris, C. (2000) Turkey Accuses Popular Islamist of Plot Against State. *Guardian*, September 1. Available from <www.guardianunlimited.co.uk/Archive/Article/ 0,4273,4057646,00.html>.

Moscovici, S. (1972 [1971]) 'Preface' in Moscovici, S. ed. *The Psychosociology of Language*. Chicago, Markham Publishing.

Murphy, B. (2004) 'A "Tense Cohabitation": Effort to Blend Islamic, Western Cultures in Turkey Prompts Suspicion'. Associated Press. Also available on different dates in American national dailies: *Houston Chronicle*, December 31, 2004, Available from: <www.chron.com/cs/CDA/ssistory.mpl/religion/2971903>.

Murphy, C. (2005) A Modern, Mystic Ramadan. *Washington Post*, October 4, 2005, B01. Available from: <www.washingtonpost.com/wp-dyn/content/ article/2005/10/ 03/ AR2005100301661.html>.

Neuman, W. L. (2006) *Social Research Methods: Qualitative and Quantitative Approaches*. 6th ed. Boston, MA, Pearson & Allyn and Bacon.

Norton, A. R. ed. (1997) *Civil Society in the Middle East*. Vol. 2. New York, E. J. Brill.

ntv-MSNBC (1998) Püf Noktası. Live TV Interview Program with Gülen, Taha Akyol and Cengiz Çandar. February 27.

ntv-MSNBC (2000a) Religious Leader Stands Trial in Absentia. October 17.

ntv-MSNBC (2000b) İsmet Berkan'ın 'Andıç' yorumu. November 04. Available from: <www.ntvmsnbc.com/news/41910.asp> [May 5, 2007].

Oberschall, A. (1973) *Social Conflict and Social Movements*. Englewood Cliffs, NJ, Prentice Hall.

———. (1978) The Decline of the 1960s Social Movements. In: Kriesberg, L. ed. (1978), 257–89.

———. (1993) *Social Movements: Ideologies, Interests and Identities*. New Brunswick, NJ, Transaction Publishers.

Offe, C. (1985) New Social Movements: Challenging the boundaries of institutional politics. *Social Research* 52(4), 817–68.

Öktem, N. (1996) Dialog. *Zaman*, October 7.

Oliver, P. E, Johnston, H., Snow D. A. & Benford, R. D. (2000) What a good Idea! Ideology and frames in social movement research. *Mobilization* 5(1), 37–54.

Olson, E. A. (1985) Muslim Identity and Secularisms in Contemporary Turkey: The Headscarf Dispute. *Anthropological Quarterly* 58(4), 161–70.

Olson, M. (1965) *The Logic of Collective Action*. Cambridge, MA, Harvard University Press.

———. (1993) Dictatorship, Democracy and Development. *American Political Science Review*, 87(3), 567–76.

Olson, R. (1989) *The Emergence of Kurdish Nationalism and the Sheikh Said Rebellion, 1880–1925*. Austin, University of Texas Press. Available from: www. xs4all.nl/~tank/kurdish/htdocs/his/said.html

Olzak, S. (2004) Ethnic and Nationalistic Social Movements. In: Snow, D. A., Soule, S.A. & Kriesi, H. eds. (2004), 666–93.

Önal, A. (1995) Valentine's Day and Fethullah Gülen. *Sabah*, 14 February.

O'Neill, M. J. (1999–2000) Media Power and the Dangers of Mass Information. Nieman Reports, The Nieman Foundation for Journalism at Harvard University. Double Issue, 53(4) and 54(1).

Önis, Z. & Turem, U. (2001) Entrepreneurs, Democracy and Citizenship in Turkey. RSCAS Working Papers, European University Institute, EUI RSC 2001/48, pp.39. Available from: <http://hdl.handle.net/1814/1757>.

Öniş, Z. (2004) Turkish Modernization and Challenges for the New Europe. Presented at the workshop *Beyond the Clash of Civilizations*, Trent University, Ontario, Canada, and at a seminar organized by the Department of Near Eastern Studies, Princeton University, USA (September 2004).

Oppenheimer, M. (1997) Social Scientists and War Criminals, *New Politics*, vol. 6, no. 3 (new series), whole no. 23, Summer 1997. Available from: <http://www. wpunj.edu/newpol/issue23/oppenh23.htm>.

Oruç, S. (1999) Police still seen as key to Susurluk probe. Domestic News Page. *Turkish Daily News*, January 12.

O'Toole, P. (2000) Gülen: The Face of Secular Islam. BBC News EUROPE, August 31, 2000, 20:43. Available from: <http;//news.bbc.co.uk/1/hi/ world/ europe/905262.stm>.

Özay, M. (1983) Turkey in Crisis: Some contradictions in the Kemalist Development Strategy. *International Journal of Middle Eastern Studies* 15, 47–66.

Özbudun, E. & Tachau, F. (1975) Social Change and Electoral Behavior in Turkey: Toward a 'Critical Realignment'? *International Journal of Middle East Studies* 6, 460–80.

Özbudun, E. (1981a) The Turkish Party System: Institutionalization, Polarization and Fragmentation. *Middle Eastern Studies* 17, 228–40.

———. (1981b) 'The Nature of the Kemalist Political Regime', in A. Kazancigil & E. Özbudun (eds), *Atatürk: Founder of a Modern State*, pp. 37-56.

———. (1996) The Ottoman Legacy and the Middle East State Tradition. In L. C. Brown (Ed.), *Imperial Legacy: The Ottoman Imprint on the Balkans and the Middle East*, New York: Columbia University Press, 133–57.

Özcan, Z. (2003) *Zaman* Wins Three International Awards in News Design. March 10, Available from: <www.zaman.com/?bl=national&alt=&hn=802>.

Özdalga, E. (1999) Education in the Name of 'Order and Progress': Reflections on the Recent Eight Year Obligatory school Reform in Turkey. *The Muslim World* 89(3–4), 414–38.

———. (2000) Worldly Asceticism in Islamic Casting: Fethullah Gülen's Inspired Piety and Activism. *Critique: Critical Middle Eastern Studies* 17, 84–104.

———. (2003) Secularizing Trends in Fethullah Gülen's Movement: Impasse or Opportunity for Further Renewal? *Critique: Critical Middle Eastern Studies* 12(1), 61–73.

———. (2005) Redeemer or Outsider? The Gülen Community in the Civilizing Process. *The Muslim World Special Issue, Islam in Contemporary Turkey: the Contributions of Gülen* 95(3). Blackwell Publishing, 429–76.

Özel, S. (2003) After the Tsunami. *Journal of Democracy* 14(2), 80–94.

Özgürel, A. (2000) Fethullah Gülen and the Threat of Subversion. *Turkish Daily News*, August 19.

Özkök, E. (2004) Fethullah Gülen'in Çevik Bir'e Teklifi (trans. Fethullah Gülen's proposal to Çevik Bir). *Hürriyet*, April 16.

Parsons, T. (1942) Some Sociological aspects of the fascists Movements. In: Parsons, T (1964) *Essays in Sociological Theory* (revised edition), New York: Free Press, 124–41.

Passy, F. & Giugni, M. (1999) Social Networks and Individual Preferences: Explaining Differential Participation in Social Movements. [Internet] Available from: www.nd.edu/~dmyers/cbsm/vol2/passy.pdf

Pichardo N. A. (1997) New Social Movements: A Critical Review, *Annual Review of Sociology*, 23, 411-30.

Piliavin, J. A. & Charng, H. W. (1990) Altruism: A Review of Recent Theory and Research. *Annual Review of Sociology*, 16, 27–65.

Poggi, G. (1990) *The State: Its Nature, Development and Prospects*. Cambridge, Polity Press.

Po-Hi, P. (2002) Social Enterprise: A Frontier for Alternative Entrepreneurship. Investment Promotion and Enterprise Development Bulletin for Asia and the Pacific, 45–52. Available from: <www.unescap.org/tid/publication/indpub 2322_chap3.pdf>.

Pope, H. (2005) *Sons of the Conquerors: the Rise of the Turkic World*. New York, Overlook Press.

Pope, N. & Pope, H. (1999) *Turkey Unveiled: A History of Modern Turkey*. New York, Overlook Press.

Pope, N. (1998) An Ottoman Empire of the Mind. *Turkey Update*. [March 19, 2002].

———. (1999) Parliament Opens amid Controversy. [Internet] *Turkey Update*. Available from: <www.TurkeyUpdate.com> [May 3, 1999].

———. (2000) Opposition Deputy Sues Retired General. *Turkey Update*, November 14. Available from: <www.turkeyupdate.com/andic.htm> [January 21, 2005].

Proyect, L. (2005) The Turkish Left. [Internet] February 10, 2005. Available from: <www.columbia.edu/~lnp3/mydocs/organization/turkish_left.htm> [October 1].

Pugsley, J. (2007) The Unique Strategy of Turkey's Oyak, *Global Pensions Magazine*, Jan 18. Available from <http://globalpensions.com/feature/feature_pdf_909.pdf>.

Purvis, A. (2002) Healing Old Wounds. *Time* (Europe), May 27. Vol. 159, p.21.

Putnam, R. D. (2000) *Bowling Alone. The collapse and revival of American community*. New York, Simon and Schuster.

Richardson, J. T. (1993) A Social Psychological Critique of 'Brainwashing' Claims About Recruitment to New Religions. In: Bromley, D. G. & Hadden, J. K. eds. (1993), 75–98. Available from: <www.cesnur.org/testi/Socpsy.htm>.

Ross, D. (1982) *Acts of Faith: A Journey to the Fringes of Jewish Identity*. New York, St. Martin's Press.

Rouleau, E. (2000) Military with Political Power: Turkey's modern pashas. *Le Monde diplomatique*, September 2000. Available from: <http://mondediplo. com/ 2000/ 09/10turkey>.

Rucht, D. (1989) Environmental movement organizations in West Germany and France – Structure and Interorganizational Relations. In: Klandermans, B. ed. (1989), 61–94.

———. (1990) The Strategies and Action Repertoires of New Social Movements. In: Dalton, R. J. & Kuechler, M. eds. (1990), 156–75.

———. (1999) The Profile of Recent Environmental Protest in Germany. Paper presented for the Workshop *Environmental Protest in Comparative Perspective* at the 27th Joint Session of ECPR Workshops in Mannheim, 26–31 March, 1999, pp.22. Available from: <www.essex.ac.uk/ECPR/events/jointsessions/ paperarchive/mannheim/w21/rucht.pdf>.

———. ed. (1991) *Research on Social Movements: The State of the Art in Western Europe and the USA.*, Frankfurt-am-Main: Campus Verlag & Boulder, CO: Westview Press.

Sahih Muslim, Volume 3. Islamic Scholar Software. Johannesburg, South Africa, Par Excellence Computers.

Sakallioglu, U. C. (1996) Parameters and Strategies of Islam-State Interaction in Republican Turkey. *International Journal of Middle Eastern Studies*, 28, 231–51.

Salamon, L. M., Sokolowski, W., & List, R. (2003) *The Johns Hopkins Comparative Nonprofit Sector Project*. Baltimore, Johns Hopkins Center for Civil Society Studies, pp.1–70.

Samanyolu TV (1999) Fethullah Gülen'e Göre Takiyye Nedir? June 21.

Saritoprak, Z. & Griffith, S. (2005) Fethullah Gülen and the 'People of the Book': A Voice from Turkey for Interfaith Dialogue. *The Muslim World Special Issue, Islam in Contemporary Turkey: the Contributions of Gülen* 95(3), 328–40.

Scott, A. (1995) *Ideology and the New Social Movements*. London, Routledge. (First printed 1990.)

Secor, A. J. & O'Loughlin, J. (2004) Social and Political Trust in Istanbul and Moscow: A Comparative Analysis of Individual and Neighbourhood Effects, pp.37. (In *Transactions* of the Institute of British Geographers, 30/1:50-66.)

Sevindi, N. (1997a) Twenty-first Century Utopia and the Dervish tradition. (From the series, 'The New York Interview with Fethullah Gülen', July 20–29) *Yeni Yüzyil*. English translation available from: <http://en.fgulen.com/a.page/ life/ commentaries/a783.html>.

———. (1997b) *Fethullah Gülen'le New York Sohbeti* (trans. The New York Interview with Fethullah Gülen). Istanbul, Sabah Kitaplari.

———. (1997c) Twenty-first Century Utopia and the Dervish Tradition. *Son Havadis*, April 21.

Shankland, D. (1999) *Islam and Society in Turkey*. Huntingdon, UK, The Eothen Press.

Silvestri, S. (1999) Libya and Transatlantic Relations: An Italian View. In: Haas, R. N. ed. *Transatlantic Tension: The United States, Europe, and Problem Countries.* Washington DC, Brookings Institution Press, 163–78.

Sirianni, C. & Friedland, L. (2006) Civil Society. The Civic Practices Network. [Internet] Available from: <www.cpn.org/tools/dictionary/civilsociety.html> [September 30, 2006].

Sluglett, P. (1976) *Britain in Iraq: 1914–1932.* London, Ithaca Press.

Smelser, N. J. (1962) *Theory of Collective Behavior.* New York, Free Press.

———. ed. (1988) *Handbook of Sociology.* Beverly Hills, CA, Sage Publications.

Smith, T. W. (2001) Constructing a Human Rights Regime in Turkey: Dilemmas of Civic Nationalism and Civil society. Presented at the American Political Science association annual conference in San Francisco, August 29–September 2, 2001. Panel 42–1–New Political science/Human Rights, Civil society, and Democratic Justice, pp.24.

Snow, D. & Machaleck, R. (1984) The Sociology of Conversion. *Annual Review of Sociology,* 10, 167–90.

Snow, D. & Oliver, P. (1995) Social Movements and Collective Behavior: Social Psychological Dimensions and Considerations. In: Cook, K. S., Fine, G. A. & House, J. S. eds. (1995), 571–99.

Snow, D. A. & Benford, R. D. (1988) Ideology, Frame Resonance, and Participant Mobilization. In: Klandermans, B., Kriesi, H. & Tarrow, S. eds. (1988), 197–218.

Snow, D. A. & Benford, R. D. (1992) Master Frames and Cycle of Protest. In: Morris, A. & Mueller, C. M. eds. (1992),133–55.

Snow, D. A. (2004) Framing Processes, Ideology, and Discursive Fields. In: Snow, D. A., Soule, S.A. & Kriesi, H. eds. (2004), 380–412.

Snow, D. A., Rochford, E. B., Worden, S. & Benford, R. (1986) Frame Alignment Processes, Micromobilization and Movement Participation. *American Sociological Review* 51, 464–81.

Snow, D. A., Soule, S.A. & Kriesi, H. eds. (2004) *The Blackwell Companion to Social Movements.* Malden, MA, Blackwell.

Sommerville, C. J. (1998) Secular Society/Religious Population: Our Tacit Rules for Using the Term Secularization. *Journal for the Scientific Study of Religion,* 37(2), 249–53.

Sönmez, M. (2003) Yoksullaşmanin 80 Yillik Öyküsü'. *Özgur Politika.* Research article. (trans: The story of an eighty-year-impoverishment.) April 15.

Sorokin, P. (1959) *Social and Cultural Mobility.* New York, The Free Press. Also available from: <www2.pfeiffer.edu/~lridener/DSS/Sorokin/SOCMOBLT. html>.

Soule, S. A. (2004) Diffusion Process within and across Movements. In: Snow, D. A., Soule, S. A. & Kriesi, H. eds. (2004), 294–310.

Stephenson, A. J. (2005) Making Modernity: A Gulen Community in Houston, Texas. Unpublished master's thesis, University of Houston.

———. (2006). Leaving Footprints in Houston: Answers to Questions on Women and the Gülen Movement. Presented at the second *International Conference on Islam in the Contemporary World: The Fethullah Gülen Movement in Thought and Practice*, organized by the Graduate Program in Religious Studies, Dedman College, Southern Methodist University; the Office of the Chaplain at Southern Methodist University; and the Institute of Interfaith Dialog, Texas, and taking place at Southern Methodist University, Dallas, Texas, March 4–5, 2006, pp.23.

———. (2007) Leaving Footprints in Houston: Some Women in the Gülen Movement. In: Hunt, R. A. & Aslandoğan, Y. A. (2007), 145–60.

Sunar, I. (1998) 'State, Society, and Democracy in Turkey'. In *Journal of Islamic Studies*, 9(1), January 1998, 103–06.

Swatos, Jr., W. H. ed. (1998) *Encyclopedia of Religion and Social Science*. AltaMira Press, A Division of Sage Publications, Inc. Content pages available from: <http://hirr.hartsem.edu/ency/Weber.htm> [June 14, 2006].

Swidler, A. (1986) 'Culture in Action: Symbols and Strategies'. *American Sociological Review* 51(2), 273–86.

———. (1995) Cultural Power and Social Movements. In: Johnston & Klandermans eds. (1995), 25–40.

Sykiainen, L. (2006) Democracy and the Dialogue between Western and Islamic Legal Cultures: Fethullah Gülen's Efforts for Tolerance. Presented at the second *International Conference on Islam in the Contemporary World: The Fethullah Gülen Movement in Thought and Practice*, organized by the Graduate Program in Religious Studies, Dedman College, Southern Methodist University, the Office of the Chaplain at Southern Methodist University, and the Institute of Interfaith Dialog, Texas, and taking place at Southern Methodist University, Dallas, Texas, March 4–5, 2006, (Conference Proceedings, pp.103–12).

———. (2007) Democracy and the Dialogue between Western and Islamic Legal Cultures: The Gülen Case. In: Hunt, R. A. & Aslandogan, Y. A. eds. (2007), 121–32.

Szreter, S. (1999) *Social Capital, the Economy and the Third Way.* (Draft Version) Available from: < http://www.netnexus.org/debates/3wayecon/library/docs/soccap.doc>.

Tapper, R. & Tapper, N. (1987) ' "Thank God We Are Secular!" Aspects of Fundamentalism in a Turkish Town'. In: Caplan, L. ed. (1987), 51–78.

———. (1991) Religion, Education and Continuity in a Provincial Town. In: Tapper, R. ed. (1991), 33–83.

Tapper, R. ed. (1991) *Islam in Modern Turkish Society: Religion, Politics, and Literature in a Secular State*. London, IB Tauris.

Tarcan, T. (1998) An Analysis of Ecevit's View on Gülen. Comment. *Zaman*, April 1.

Tarhan, N. (2004) 28 Şubat: Özeleştiriye hazır mıyız? (trans: February 28: Are we ready for self-criticism?) Open Letter–Comments. *Zaman*, February 28. Available from: <www.zaman.com.tr/?bl=yorumlar&alt=&hn=20813>.

Tarrow, S. (1989) *Democracy and Disorder: Protest and Politics in Italy, 1965–1975*. Oxford, Oxford University Press.

———. (1991) ' "Aiming at a Moving Target": Social Science and the Recent Rebellions in Eastern Europe', *Political Science and Politics*, 24/1, 12–20.

———. (1994) *Power in Movement: Social Movements, Collective Action and Mass Politics in the Modern State*. Cambridge, Cambridge University Press.

———. (1996a), 'Social Movements in Contentious Politics: A Review Article', *American Political Science Review* 90/4, 874–83.

———. (1996b), 'States and Opportunities: The Political Structuring of Social Movements' in McAdam et al. (eds.) (1996a), 41–61.

———. (1998) *Power in Movement: Social Movements and Contentious Politics*. Cambridge, Cambridge University Press, 2nd edn.

Taylor, C. (1994) *Multiculturalism*. Princeton, NJ, Princeton University Press.

Taylor, V. & Van Dyke, N. (2004) 'Get up, stand up': Tactical Repertoires of Social Movements. In: Snow, D. A., Soule, S.A. & Kriesi, H. eds. (2004), 262–93.

Taylor, V. (1989) Social Movement Continuity: The Women's Movement in Abeyance. *American Sociological Review* 54(5), 761–75.

Tekalan, S. (2005) A Movement of Volunteers. Presented at the conference *Islam in the Contemporary World: The Fethullah Gülen Movement in Thought and Practice*, organized by the Boniuk Center for the Study and Advancement of Religious Tolerance at Rice University, Houston; the A. D. Bruce Religion Center University of Houston; and the Institute of Interfaith Dialog, Texas, and taking place at Rice University, Houston, Texas, November 12–13, 2005, pp.9.

Temkin, M. (1999) Jewish World. *The Jerusalem Report*, May 24. Jerusalem. 34–6.

The Annals of the American Academy of Political and Social Science. (1993, July). Dalton, R. ed. The American 'New Left' and the European New Social Movements. Symposium on Citizens, Protest, and Democracy. Vol. 528: 56–74.

The Fountain (2002) *M. F. Gülen: Essays, Perspectives, Opinions*. Rutherford, NJ, The Light, Inc.

The Light, Inc. (2006) *M. Fethullah Gülen: Essays, Perspectives, Opinions*. Compiled by The Light, Inc. Rutherford, NJ, The Light, Inc. (First edition 2002. Revised edition by the Fountain 2004.)

The Muslim World (1999) *Special Issue: Said Nursi and the Turkish Experience* 89(3–4). CT, Hartford Seminary.

The Muslim World (2005) *Special Issue, Islam in Contemporary Turkey: the Contributions of Gülen*, 95(3). Hartford Seminary, Blackwell Publishing.

Tilly, C. (1978) *From Mobilization to Revolution*. Reading, Mass., Addison-Wesley.

———. (1985) Models and realities of popular collective action. *Social Research* 52(4), 717–49.

———. (1990) Transplanted Networks. In: Yans-McLaughlin, V. ed. *Immigration Reconsidered. History Sociology and Politics.* New York, Oxford, Oxford University Press.

TIME (1933a) 'Squinting Skyward Last Week'. January 9.

TIME (1933b) 'Word for God'. February 20.

TIME (2003) Special Section. 80 Days That Changed the World. March 31.

Toprak, B. (1981) *Islam and Political Development in Turkey.* Social, Economic, and Political Studies of the Middle East. Leiden, E. J. Brill.

———. (1995) Islam and the Secular State in Turkey. In: Balim, C. et al., 91–5.

Touraine, A. (1977) *The Self-Production of Society* (trans. Derek Coltman; Chicago: University of Chicago Press).

Toynbee, A. (1948) Islam, the West and the Future. In: Toynbee, A. Civilization of Trial. London, Oxford University Press, 184–212.

Transparency International (2001) Press Release: New Index Highlights Worldwide Corruption Crisis. Available from: <www.transparency.org>.

TRT (1995) Ateş Hattı Programı, Reha Muhtar'a Verdiği Cevaplar, July 3.

Turam, B. (2007) *Between Islam and the State: The Politics of Engagement,* Stanford, CA: Stanford University Press.

Turgut, H. (1998) Fethullah Gülen and the Schools: Excerpts from F. Gülen's Answers to Questions on Education and Turkish Educational Activities Abroad, 15 January–4 February. Yeni Yüzyil, January 27. *Available from: <http://en. fgulen.com/content/view/779/13/>.*

Turkish Daily News (1996a) 'Susurluk' [Turkish Press Scanner] (November 9 and 18).

Turkish Daily News (1996b) 'Turkish Press Scanner', October 10. Available from: <http://www.turkishdailynews.com.tr/archives.php?id=1190>.

Turkish Daily News (1996c) Susurluk's Missing Link Talks. Turkish Press Scanner, April 30.

Turkish Daily News (1996d) No one Can Cover up Susurluk. Domestic news Page. December 29.

Turkish Daily News (1997) Court Orders Arrest of Sincan Mayor. Domestic News Page. February 14.

Turkish Daily News (1998) 'Anti-Terror Branch after "Green Capital" '. Domestic news Page. April 22.

Turkish Daily News (1999) Retired commander seeks damages from Kutlular. Domestic News Page. November 6.

Turkish Daily News (1999b) After 20 Years, Ecevit Again Becomes Prime Minister. Domestic News Page. January 12.

Turkish Daily News (1999c) 'A Year of Ups and Downs For the Media Sector and 'Painful Shake-Up', Domestic News Page 2, Turkish Probe issue 113, January 10. Available from: <www.turkishdailynews.com.tr/archives.php?id=10563>.

Turkish Daily News (2000a) Ambassadors back Gülen schools in Asia. Domestic News Page. Also at TDN-Headlines Digest No. 451. Available from:<http://en.fgulen.com/content/view/1062/14/>.

Turkish Daily News (2000b) TGC: Media Conflicts of Interest Undermine Editorial Freedom. National News. August 11.

Turkish Daily News (2000c) Public Drive Against Corruption. National News. November 14.

Turkish Daily News (2000d) A Simple Question (by Fehmi Koru). The Turkish Press. November 14.

Turkish Daily News (2000e) 'Presidential Elections (Part 2): The Age of the "Soldier Presidents" '. Domestic news Page 2. April 5.

Turkish Daily News (2000f) Fethullah Gülen Trial Opens in Ankara. National News. October 17.

Turkish Daily News (2001a) 'CHP through the Time Tunnel. Turkish Probe', Issue 464. December 9.

Turkish Daily News (2001b) Ağca denies murdering Turkish newspaper editor. Domestic News Page. January 30. Available from: <www.turkishdaily news.com/old_editions/01_30_01/dom.htm>.

Turkish Daily News (2002) Court Postpones the Case to May 6. March 12. Available from: <http://en.fgulen.com/content/view/1056/14/> [January 12, 2007].

Turkish Daily News (2003) Court Postpones Trial against Gülen. March 11.

Turkish Daily News (2006) Net closing in on Council of State attack suspects. May 22.

THC (Turkish History Committee) ([1930] 1996) The Outline of Turkish History. Istanbul, Kaynak Yayınları. (Reprinted of the 1930 edition.)

Turner, R. H. & Killian, L. M. (1957) *Collective Behavior*. Englewood Cliffs, NJ, Prentice-Hall. (3rd ed., 1987)

Tutkun, O. F. (1998) An Historical Investigation on Birth of Turkish Higher Education. Pittsburgh. (Unpublished PhD thesis at the University of Pittsburgh.)

Ülsever, C. (2001a) Vural Savas vs Ahmet Necdet Sezer: End of a Prosecutor as a Closed System Ideologue. Opinion. *Turkish Daily News*, January 23.

Ülsever, C. (2001b) Will Turkey Demolish Her Fundamental Taboo? The Role of the Army. *Turkish Daily News*, August 14.

———. (2003) Status-quo Blocking Turkish Modernism. *Turkish Daily News*, February 4. Available from: <www.turkishdailynews.com/old_editions/ 02_04_03/ulsever.htm> [November 5, 2004].

Ünal, A. & Williams, A. (2000) Fethullah Gülen: Advocate of Dialogue. Fairfax, VA, The Fountain.

Ünal, M. (2000) Ekonominin 28 Şubat'ı. *Zaman*, December 1.

UNESCO (1963) Atatürk. Turkish National Commission for UNESCO.

UNHCHR (2001) Civil and Political Rights, Including the Question of Disappearances and Summary Executions: Extrajudicial, summary or arbitrary executions Report of the Special Rapporteur, Ms. Asma Jahangir, submitted pursuant to Commission on Human Rights, resolution 2001/45, Addendum, Mission to Turkey. pp.1–31.

US Department of State (2001) Patterns of Gobal Terrorism 2000. Annual Report. April. Department of State Publications. Available from: <www.usis.usemb.se/ terror/rpt2000/report2000.pdf>.

Vanneman, R. (2005) Sociology 432: Social Movements. Sociology 432 Home Page, Course Notes, University of Maryland. [Internet] Available from: <www.bsos.umd.edu/socy/vanneman/socy432/default.html>.

Varlik, B. (1981) Turkiye'de Radyo Yayınlarının Ilk Yillarina Iliskin Uc Belge. Iletisim 1981/1. Ankara, AITIA Gazetecilik ve Halkla Iliskiler Yuksek Okulu, 224–227.

Vergin, N. (1996) A Musical Composition, Not an Analysis. In: Can, E. ed. (1996). Available in English from: <http://en.fgulen.com/a.page/life/commentaries/a784.html>.

Voll, J. (2005) Fethullah Gülen Transcending Modernity in the New Islamic Discourse. The Muslim World Special Issue, Islam in Contemporary Turkey: the Contributions of Gülen, 95(3), July (2005), Hartford Seminary, Blackwell Publishing, 238–47.

Wang, S. (2005) State Effectiveness and Democracy: Asia Cases. [Internet] Available from: <www.cuhk.edu.hk/gpa/wang_files/State&Dem_Asia.doc>.

Webb, L. E. (2000) Fethullah Gülen: Is There More to Him Than Meets the Eye? Izmir, Mercury.

Weber, M. ([1922] 1968) Economy and Society. 3 vols. English translation. Roth, G. & Wittich, C. eds. New York, Bedminister Press.

———. ([1924] 1947) The Theory of Social and Economic Organization. Translators: A. M. Henderson and T. Parsons. Parsons, T. ed. New York, Free Press. (Original work published in 1924.)

Weller, P. G. (2005) Religions, Globalization and Dialogue in the 21st Century. Fethullah Gülen & Arnold J. Toynbee: A Comparative Conversation with Contemporary Realities. Presented at the conference Islam in the Contemporary World: The Fethullah Gülen Movement in Thought and Practice, organized by the Boniuk Center for the Study and Advancement of Religious Tolerance at Rice University, Houston; the A. D. Bruce Religion Center University of Houston; and the Institute of Interfaith Dialog, Texas, and taking place at Rice University, Houston, Texas, November 12–13, 2005, pp.20.

———. (2005b) Religions and Social Capital: Theses on Religion(s), State(s) and Society(ies) with Particular Reference to the United Kingdom and the European Union. The Journal of International Migration and Integration XI(2), 271–89.

———. (2007) Fethullah Gülen, Religions, Globalization and Dialog. In: Hunt, R. A. & Aslandoğan, Y. A. (2007) Muslim Citizens of the Globalized World: Contributions of the Gülen Movement, 85–100.

Whittier, N. (2004) The Consequences of Social Movements for Each Other. In: Snow, D. A., Soule, S.A. & Kriesi, H. eds. (2004), 531–52.

Whittier, N., Robnett, B. & Meyer, D. S. eds. (2002) *Social Movements: Identity, Culture, and the State.* New York, Oxford University Press, USA.

Wilde, J. (1998) Turkey on the brink. Unpublished interview with Fethullah Gülen for Time, January 12.

Williams, R. H. (2004) The Cultural Contexts of Collective Action: Constraints, Opportunities, and the Symbolic Life of Social Movements. In: Snow, D. A., Soule, S.A. & Kriesi, H. eds. (2004), 91–115.

Winter, M. (1984) 'The Modernization of Education in Kemalist Turkey' in J. M. Landau (ed.), *Ataturk and the Modernization of Turkey.* Boulder, CO, Westview Press, 183–194.

Woodhall, R. & Çetin, M. (2005) Preface. In: Gülen, M. F. (2005) *The Statue of Our Souls: Revival in Islamic Thought and Activism.* Somerset, New Jersey, The Light, Inc, xiii–xviii.

Woodhall, R. (2005) Organizing the organization, educating the educators: An examination of Fethullah Gülen's teaching and the membership of the movement. Presented at the conference Islam in the Contemporary World: The Fethullah Gülen Movement in Thought and Practice, organized by the Boniuk Center for the Study and Advancement of Religious Tolerance at Rice University, Houston; the A. D. Bruce Religion Center, University of Houston; and the Institute of Interfaith Dialog, Texas, and taking place at Rice University, Houston, Texas, November 12–13, 2005, pp.15. Available from: <www.fethullahgulenconference.org/houston/proceedings/RWoodhall.pdf>.

Yagiz, S. (1997) Gülen and Reconciliation. Takvim, April 18.

Yavuz, M. H. & Esposito, J. L. eds. (2003) *Turkish Islam and the Secular State: The Gülen Movement* Syracuse, Syracuse University Press.

Yavuz, M. H. (2004) Interview, in Mayer, J. F. (2004) Gülen Movement: Modern Expression of Turkish Islam. First published July 2004 in *Religioscope.* Republished in *Journal of Turkish Weekly*, January 5, 2005. Available from: <www.turkishweekly.net/comments.php?id=106>.

———. (1999) Towards an Islamic Liberalism? The Nurcu Movement and Fethullah Gülen in Turkey. *Middle East Journal* 53(4), 584–605.

———. (2003a) Islam in the Public Sphere. In: Yavuz, M. H. & Esposito, J. L. eds. (2003), 1–18.

———. (2003b) The Gülen Movement: The Turkish Puritans. In: Yavuz, M. H. & Esposito, J. L. eds. (2003), 19–47.

Yenen, S. (2000) Turkish Odyssey. Part 4. [Internet] Available from: <www. turkishodyssey.com/turkey/history/history4.htm#Republic>.

Yildirim, Y. (2005) Debating Moderate Islam. American Journal of Islamic Social Sciences, 22(3) (Book Reviews, review of M. F. Gülen, Toward a Global Civilization of Love and Tolerance), 118–20.

Yilmaz, I. & Öztürk, Ö. (1997) The Republic is Not a State. Milliyet, December 27.

Yilmaz, I. (2005) State, Law, Civil Society and Islam In Contemporary Turkey. The Muslim World Special Issue, Islam in Contemporary Turkey: the Contributions of Gülen, 95(3), 385–412.

Yılmaz, R. (1997) Hocaefendi'nin Takiyye Yaptığına İnanmıyorum. Interview with Atilla Dorsay. Zaman, June 23.

Yücel, G. (2002) New Dilemmas of Turkish National Security Politics: Old and New Security Concerns and National Development in the Post-1980 Era. Paper for presentation at the Fourth Kokkalis Graduate Student Workshop at JFK School of Government, Harvard University, Cambridge, Massachusetts, February 8–9, pp.24. Available from: <www.ksg.harvard.edu/kokkalis/ GSW4/ YucelPAPER.PDF>.

———. (2004) Turkish National Security Doctrine and Democratization in the New Security Environment. Paper prepared for presentation at the conference, Challenge and Change for the Military Institution: The Military Profession and Military Leadership in the 21st Century, Royal Military College, Kingston-Ontario, Canada, October 25–27, pp.24. Available from: <www.rmc.ca/ academic/conference/iuscanada/papers/yucel_turkish.pdf>.

Zald, M. N., & McCarthy, J. [eds.] (1979) *The Dynamics of Social Movements.* Cambridge, MA: Winthrop.

Zald, M. N. (1996) Culture, Ideology and Strategic Framing. In: McAdam, McCarthy, & Zald, eds. (1996a), 261–74.

Zald, M. N., & Ash, R. (1966) Social movement organizations: growth, decay and change. Social Forces 44, 327–40.

Zaman (1995) Eyüp Can'ın Ufuk Turu Röportajı. August 14.

Zaman (1998) An Analysis of Ecevit's View on Gülen. Comment. April 1.

Zaman (2003a) Sedat Bucak Acquitted of Guerilla Charges by Bulent Ceyhan & Nuri Imre. June 27. Available from: <www.zaman.com/default.php?kn= 2938>.

Zaman (2003b) Mutafian: We Follow the Path Opened by Gülen. National News. October 28.

Zaman (2004) Kyrghyz Grants Gülen "Contribution to Peace" Award. National News. March 11. Available from: <http://en.fgulen.com/content/view/ 1872/22/>.

Zaman (2006a) 'Dinç Bilgin: "Medya, 28 Şubat sürecinde haberleri emirle yapıyordu."' May 5. Available from: <www.zaman.com.tr/?bl=politika&alt=&hn=282493>

Zaman (2006b) Unanimous Acquittal Ruled for Gülen. June 5. Available from: <www.zaman.com/?bl=nationalandalt=andtrh=20060506andhn=32854>; also from <http://en.fgulen.com/content/view/2225/14/>.

Zaman (2006c), Andıç, Silahlı Kuvvetler'e de büyük zarar verdi. May 12. Available from: <www.zaman.com.tr/?bl=haberler&alt=&hn=284413>.

Zaman (2006d) Andıç mağdurları sordu: Savcılar neden harekete geçmiyor? May 13. Available from: <www.zaman.com.tr/?bl=haberler&alt=&hn=284649>.

Zaman (2006e) Turkish Schools, Model for Education in Romania. February 17. Available from: <http://en.fgulen.com/content/view/2184/14/>.

Zaman (2006f) Gul Proud of Turkish Schools Abroad. February 23. Available from: <http://en.fgulen.com/content/view/2190/14/>.

Zaman (2006g) Indonesian President Thanks Turks for Donations. June 1. Available from: <http://en.fgulen.com/content/view/2249/14/>.

Zaman (2006h) Reasoned Decision Revealed: Gülen does not Aim at Changing Constitutional System. National News. June 10. Available from: http://en.fgulen.com/content/view/2258/14/>.

Zdravomyslova, E. (1996) Opportunities and Framing in the Transition to Democracy: The Case of Russia. In: McAdam, McCarthy, & Zald, eds. (1996a), 122–40.

Zelyut, R. (1998) Papa'yla Kim Buluşsaydı? (trans: Who else should have met with the Pope?) Akşam, February 13. Available from: <http://tr.fgulen. com/a.page/basindan/kose.yazilari/1998/subat.1998/a3431.html> [January 16, 2007].

Zeybek, N. K. (1997) The Hodja Spoke. Son Havadis, April 21.

Zunes, S. (1999) Unarmed Resistance in the Middle East and North Africa. In: Zunes, S., Kurtz, L. R. & Asher, S. B. (1999), 41–51.

Zunes, S., Kurtz, L. R. & Asher, S. B. (1999) Nonviolent social movements: a geographical perspective. Malden, Mass, Blackwell.

Zurcher, E. J. (1998) Turkey: A Modern History. London/New York, IB Tauris.

INDEX